Chatbots and Beyond

Series Editor
Jean-Charles Pomerol

Chatbots and Beyond

Exploring the Future of Conversational Technology in Education

Edited by
Vikas Kumar
Manju Lata

iSTE

WILEY

First published 2025 in Great Britain and the United States by ISTE Ltd and John Wiley & Sons, Inc.

ISTE Ltd
27-37 St George's Road
London SW19 4EU
UK

www.iste.co.uk

John Wiley & Sons, Inc.
111 River Street
Hoboken, NJ 07030
USA

www.wiley.com

Library of Congress Control Number: 2025938716

British Library Cataloguing-in-Publication Data
A CIP record for this book is available from the British Library
ISBN 978-1-83669-010-8

The manufacturer's authorized representative according to the EU General Product Safety Regulation is Wiley-VCH GmbH, Boschstr. 12, 69469 Weinheim, Germany, e-mail: Product_Safety@wiley.com.

Contents

Foreword

The 4th Industrial Revolution has opened the digital era with rapid changes and developments, spread across economic and social life. Along with the continuous development of artificial intelligence (AI) and systems, diverse conversational models are reshaping the way people participate in learning, communicating, sharing and adding on to their knowledge. One of the remarkable progressive models for sharing and communicating is the continuous development of chatbots – intelligent virtual assistants capable of communicating and supporting users on AI platforms in many different areas of life, including in the field of education.

This book provides us with a rich, vivid approach, so that readers can deeply understand the role of chatbot technology in the modern education field. AI has emerged as a powerful tool to support research and learning activities, and has lead to flexible, creative and effective teaching in the context of digital technology and modern education. The book has raised general and specific issues about the application of chatbots in the field of education. In addition, the new discoveries and introductions in the book give readers interesting ideas to explore the unlimited potential of conversational technology (chatbot) in improving experiences.

Through a collections of scholarly chapters, readers will learn about the different experiences that chatbot technology applications can bring to help learners and teachers share, connect and support in the best way, to improve the effectiveness of teaching and learning activities. Lessons and ways to deploy and integrate chatbots in educational forms have been presented in detail in each chapter of the book, with content that not only stops at what is happening, but also points out the future trends of conversational technology in education that will have many major changes, with the ability to optimize technology in education.

Foreword written by Tuan Hung VU.

We are living in an era where technology and education are constantly intertwined to develop quickly and sustainably. Using a technology platform with a chatbot model and constantly advancing conversational technologies will not only be a matter of sharing knowledge, but more importantly, it will be a process of interacting and learning from each other. The book will be an important companion for those who want to understand, apply and promote the role of chatbots and conversational technology. This is also a source of inspiration for those who are passionate about finding breakthrough educational solutions and initiatives in the current digital age.

I respectfully invite readers to come together to build a learning society and develop a modern future education for everyone.

July 2025

Preface

The rapid advancements in artificial intelligence (AI) and machine learning have profoundly changed a number of sectors, including education. The emergence of conversational technologies and chatbots is one of the most significant advances that has created a significant impact on the education. Once considered innovations, these tools are now essential parts of educational environments. With the ability to facilitate personalized learning, immediate user support and streamlined administrative tasks, chatbots are reshaping the way we approach education. To identify the futuristic models and applications, this book presents the exciting possibilities of conversational technologies in the education domain.

As we look to the future, it is clear that chatbots are creating new learning opportunities in addition to improving the educational experiences of both teachers and students. By eliminating obstacles that frequently restrict opportunities, AI integration can democratize access to high-quality education. From providing real-time feedback on projects to responding to student inquiries, this book examines a number of use cases where chatbots have already had an impact. As these technologies grow increasingly prevalent in classrooms, campuses and other settings, it also looks at the opportunities, difficulties and ethical issues that come up. Policymakers and educators can better prepare for the upcoming revolutionary shifts by comprehending these dynamics.

However, chatbots are only one example of the conversational technology being explored in education. Voice assistants, AI-powered tutors and conversational agent-powered immersive learning environments are just the start of a much bigger development that will completely change the way we interact with information. This book acts as a manual for both comprehending the current uses of these technologies

---

Preface written by Vikas KUMAR and Manju LATA.

and projecting their future advancements. This book provides insightful information about the fascinating opportunities that await the field of education, regardless of whether you are a technologist, educator or student interested in the intersection of AI and learning.

The book covers the existing learning theories, why they have failed and what new theories have emerged. It also covers what new initiatives have emerged and how they have contributed to the AI-based teaching-learning processes. The book covers the experiences and thoughts of leading researchers from across the world and offers perspectives from the point of view of different stakeholders.

Chapter 1 by Ikbal Maulana discusses the nurturing of an inquisitive mind, with chatbots encouraging curiosity, critical thinking and a love of learning despite the ease of access to information. While the chatbots and AI can provide quick answers, it is essential to cultivate a mindset that goes beyond accepting surface-level responses. Questioning, analyzing and diving deeper into subjects is very much required to develop a thorough understanding. The chapter highlights that technological cognitive enhancement offers opportunities to boost mental capabilities; however, it also poses a risk of cognitive erosion due to constant digital distractions that reduce attention span. They should stimulate critical thinking by challenging users to question assumptions and engage in thoughtful dialogue.

In Chapter 2, Tiara Nur Anisah and Andika Andika present the integration of AI in education and its evolutionary effects on teaching and learning. This chapter critically examines the multifaceted impact of AI on the education system, exploring both its potential and its challenges. Starting with a review of the historical evolution of AI in education, this chapter explores important uses of AI applications such as adaptive learning systems, automated assessments and intelligent tutor systems. This chapter presents a comprehensive discussion of these issues, providing insight into the ongoing debate regarding the role of AI in education. The chapter also includes case studies of AI implementation in various educational institutions, highlighting the best practices and lessons learned.

In Chapter 3, Paruthi et al. shed light on the role of AI in higher education in the context of Industrial Revolution 4.0 and Education 4.0. Authors have argued that generative AI tools will help students by providing tailored tuition, real-time feedback, career guidance and a personal touch. The studies have also highlighted the ethical concerns associated with the AI integration. By using the TCCM (theory, context, characteristics, methodology) framework, this chapter has reviewed the major literature, and analyzed the findings and associated theories in this area. The chapter describes the theories like sociotechnical systems theory and paradox theory to understand the impact of AI on higher education, along with merits and demerits. The chapter proposes a balanced approach between using AI and the education system, which should be followed to reap the benefits and emphasizes the importance of critical thinking and curriculum frameworks for responsibly using AI in education.

Fotiadis et al. have dedicated their chapter toward using chatbot technologies for digital entrepreneurship education. Chapter 4 presents the development and implementation of chatbot technology for improving self-learning in digital entrepreneurship. It outlines the innovative methodologies and tools to effectively integrate AI in the educational frameworks. The research highlights the need for incorporating real-world simulations, adaptive learning paths, support mechanisms for teachers and learners, and student centric customization for successful education systems. By adopting these suggested enhancements, both user experience and engagement could be improved, thereby maximizing the effectiveness of educational initiatives.

Chapter 5 of the book explores the role of chatbots as virtual tutors in learning management systems (LMS). The chapter highlights the design principles that make chatbot tutors effective, including the use of natural language processing (NLP) and adaptive learning algorithms. Differences between traditional human based tutoring and chatbot tutors have also been outlined to effectively understand the changes led by technology centric education. Finally, the chapter considers future trends, including the potential for chatbots to evolve with advancements in AI and their role in shaping the future of digital education.

Chapter 6 addresses the integration of chatbots in key principles of the flipped classroom model, including the pre-class preparation and in-class active learning. The chapter highlights the importance of pre-class preparation, enabling students to acquire foundational knowledge independently before engaging in active in-class activities. However, ensuring effective pre-class preparation can be challenging, as it requires students to stay motivated, access relevant resources and address doubts in real time. Thus, the role of chatbots as a transformative tool for pre-class learning in flipped classrooms becomes very important. As educational technology continues to evolve, chatbots will play a crucial role in transforming flipped classrooms into more dynamic, effective and student-centered environments, preparing the learners for a digital future that values both independence and collaboration.

The integration of the chatbots with LMSs in flipped classroom settings is presented by Dalal and Bhattacharya in Chapter 7. Authors have considered the elements that may affect the integration of chatbots in management education institutions in India. Most important factors include the existing infrastructure of the institutions and their preparedness to integrate new technologies, and the updated pedagogical frameworks by incorporation of AI chatbots in the educational process. These factors greatly influence the incorporation of AI into institutions' LMS and flipped classroom models, leading to enhanced academic outcomes for students. This study employed the PLS-SEM tool to analyze the responses gathered from 162 educators across various business management institutions in India through an online questionnaire.

In Chapter 8, Faisol and Nurdiwaty investigate the relationships among perceived ease of use, technology integration quality, resource accessibility and academic performance, focusing on the mediating role of user engagement. Involving 120 university students, the research employed structural equation modeling-partial least squares (SEM-PLS) for data analysis. Findings reveal that perceived ease of use does not directly improve academic performance, indicating that ease of use alone is inadequate without active student engagement. Ultimately, user engagement mediates the relationship between technology integration quality and academic results, underscoring the need for educational institutions to prioritize student engagement alongside usability and technology quality to enhance educational outcomes, while integrating chatbots in education.

In Chapter 9, Paul and Rena examine the educational settings of the new era from the perspective of Fourth Industrial Revolution (4IR) technologies, including AI and data analytics. They have explored the AI-powered education and presented the effects of algorithms on the autonomy of instruction, teaching pedagogy and student experience at the faculty level. Ethical issues associated with the emerging technologies such as blockchain, virtual reality (VR) and augmented reality (AR) technologies have also been considered. This chapter scrutinizes successful universities to ascertain the different aspects, such as autonomy-based university strategies to encourage responsible innovation within existing regulation, appropriate regulation-based points to incentivize innovation and corporate responsibility, for one, and integrated approaches that work with Higher Education Institutions (HEIs), legislators and regulators to create flexible contexts that connect independence and responsibility. Authors have highlighted the importance of effective negotiation to leverage the 4IR technologies to build up resilience and augment societal engagement within the terrain of higher learning.

Chapter 10 presents a study on enhancing the educational experiences through data analytics with integration of chatbots. This chapter explores the data analytics approaches that can be used to make sense of data collected through chatbots. Basic statistical approaches have been presented in concert with more sophisticated approaches, such as NLP and machine learning algorithms. Authors have described how NLP can be used to determine user sentiment and intention, and how machine learning can predict future user needs and improve chatbot responses given the history of interactions. This chapter equips the readers with tools and knowledge that can help to transform the user interaction data with chatbots into valuable insights, giving a step-by-step guide. These insights can be very much helpful in driving better decision-making and user satisfaction.

Chapter 11 presents a specific case study on developmental aspects of chatbots with a specific purpose like rice leaf disease detection in the Mekong Delta Region of Vietnam. Authors have demonstrated how a chatbot-integrated deep learning approach can be followed to develop a chatbot-based solution in the academic environment. The proposed system comprises two primary components: a rice leaf disease detection model and an interactive chatbot, both of which work together to provide actionable insights to farmers. With a smartphone, farmers can capture images of rice leaves in the field, which are then analyzed by the system to detect common rice diseases. Upon diagnosis, the chatbot enables farmers to interact via text or voice to gain additional insights on treatment options, preventive strategies, disease forecasts and potential impacts on yield. This specific case study is an excellent example of how the chatbot modules developed in academic institutions can act as problem solvers.

And finally, Chapter 12 presents another case study on the development of chatbots in academic environments. It presents the opportunities, limitations and challenges associated with migration from traditional teaching methods to the latest AI-based tools. This chapter presents how traditional tools migrated to the web and expanded their teaching capability, enabling students and professionals to access advanced technologies. Authors have presented the interaction of EDA Playground and ChatGPT in the verification process. EDA Playground was able to expand access to verification tools and techniques, whereas with ChatGPT, the doubts and possible failures can be translated into steps that can be compiled. Thus, the union between these tools allowed this study to project challenges and opportunities for future generative AI tools.

Chapters in the book cover the different aspects of integrating chatbots in education. The models presented in the book have provided a comprehensive look into how conversational AI is reshaping the landscape of learning. As we move forward, the integration of chatbots and AI into educational environments promises to enhance accessibility, foster personalized learning experiences and reduce burdens on educators. However, it is crucial to approach these advancements with careful consideration of ethical implications, inclusivity and data privacy. With continued innovation and thoughtful implementation, conversational technology has the potential to democratize education, making it more adaptive and effective for learners around the globe. The journey of exploring this transformative technology is just beginning, and its possibilities for the future are both exciting and limitless.

July 2025

Acknowledgements

The creation of a work is made possible only through the support of remarkable individuals. The efforts and contributions of all individuals and groups toward this book are sincerely and deeply appreciated. We are thankful to Prof. Tankeshwar Kumar (Vice Chancellor, Central University of Haryana) and Prof. Manpreet Singh Manna (Vice Chancellor, Chandigarh University) for their constant encouragement and support to work on this project. Special thanks to Prof. Suneel Kumar (Registrar, Central University of Haryana) and Prof. Sandeep Singh Kang (Associate Director of CSE Department, Chandigarh University) for his overwhelming support and guidance.

The support from ISTE Ltd. and John Wiley and Sons is also appreciated. We are deeply grateful to the editorial and administrative staff for their guidance at every stage of compiling this volume. Our sincere thanks also go to the reviewers, whose detailed and constructive feedback greatly contributed to enhancing the quality of each chapter and the project as a whole. We are sincerely thankful to all the authors for their original contributions and working to the tight deadlines.

We would also like to thank our colleagues: Prof. Nguyen Tan Huynh (Dong Nai Technology University), Prof. Jakob Svensson (Malmö University), Prof. Subagyo (Nusantara PGRI University), Dr. Rachna Bansal (Sharda University), Dr. Deepshikha Chhabra (Chandigarh University, Dr. Christine Schrage (University of Northern Iowa), Prof. Siti Rochmah Ika and Dr. Gesty Ernestivita (Nusantara PGRI University), Dr. Gaurav Gupta (Amity University), Dr. Pawan Gupta (Chaudhary Bansi Lal University), Dr. G.K. Sethi (MLN College), Dr. Pooja Nanda (Amity University), Dr. Surender Kumar (Jaipuria Institute of Management), Dr. Anand Rai (G L Bajaj Institute of Management & Research) and other peers from academia, who have supported this project in different ways.

Acknowledgements written by Vikas KUMAR and Manju LATA.

We would like to express our heartfelt gratitude to our parents, family members and friends for their unwavering support and encouragement throughout the completion of this project.

1

Nurturing an Inquisitive Mind in the Era of All-Knowing Chatbots

The rise of artificial intelligence (AI) and chatbots capable of producing human-like text represents a technological revolution. As with any other revolution, people are not entirely certain of what they are experiencing. There is a mixture of excitement and concern. If these technologies are so intelligent and seem to be constantly improving, will they eventually replace humans in the workplace? Educators share similar worries. Students no longer need to slog through thick books – chatbots can summarize them in seconds. Writing, an essential skill in education, risks being neglected because chatbots make it easy to bypass the effort. This chapter argues that education, particularly in critical thinking, is now more important than ever for students. Regardless of how much data feeds chatbots, they cannot directly comprehend the ever-changing world of their users. Furthermore, chatbots can only process explicit, propositional knowledge – they lack the unspoken, intuitive knowledge that humans rely upon. This is why students with strong critical thinking skills continue to have the upper hand in using this technology effectively.

1.1. Introduction

Learning is endangered. The temptation to avoid learning has become almost irresistible, as modern information and communication technology (ICT) immerses students – many of whom have grown up as digital natives – in their devices, bombarding them with entertainment, emotionally charged content and endless interactions (Wilmer and Chein 2016; Hanin 2021). While students may struggle to resist digital distractions, they must still engage with learning to meet academic requirements. However, an even more concerning challenge now emerges from generative AI technology, which is beginning to erode the learning process by performing tasks that once required intellectual effort (Lata and Kumar 2022; Shum

Chapter written by Ikbal MAULANA.

2024). Essay writing, once one of the most challenging academic tasks for students, can now be completed by simply providing a chatbot such as ChatGPT with a basic prompt (Livingstone 2024; Lata and Sharma 2024a). As AI increasingly handles cognitively demanding tasks, a provocative and controversial question arises: Why endure the challenges of learning when technology provides readily available solutions, especially in an environment already saturated with digital distractions? This shift necessitates a critical re-evaluation of how educational systems can preserve the value of active learning in the AI age (Lata et al. 2024).

Humans have long sought ways to offload cognitive tasks when the mental load becomes too overwhelming (Risko and Gilbert 2016). Over time, they have developed tools to increase their cognitive capacity. Early technologies, such as pen and paper, were used to store memories, record knowledge and pass it on to future generations (Kumar and Lata 2022). Without such tools, managing complex calculations and preserving knowledge would have been nearly impossible. Devices such as the abacus enabled societies to carry out intricate calculations in daily commerce. Prior to the advent of digital technology, these tools primarily served as aids for cognitive tasks, with the core cognitive processes still taking place in the human mind (Carter 2018). Writing on paper, for example, served as an extension of memory, aiding in the organization of thoughts and fostering deeper reflection.

The initial digital technologies expanded human memory and simplified the retrieval of stored information. Organizing and calculating data became more manageable, but users still needed expertise to master both the technology and the subject matter they were analyzing. The emergence of large language model (LLM)-driven platforms such as ChatGPT has captivated the public with its extraordinary capabilities, offering direct answers to specific questions, which could render search engines obsolete (Lata and Kumar 2024). Although search engines have been criticized for promoting shallow thinking by making information easily accessible (Carr 2010), they still require users to engage with and interpret the results.

By early 2023, just 2 months after its release, ChatGPT passed law exams in four courses at the University of Minnesota and a business exam at Wharton School of Business, according to professors at both institutions (Kelly 2023). This impressive performance propelled ChatGPT to an astonishing milestone of 100 million users in a two-month period. Its remarkable abilities – such as generating articles, essays, emails, jokes, poetry and job applications – demonstrated the technology's potential to transform the way we approach cognitive tasks (Milmo 2023).

The seduction of digital content can lead students to temporarily neglect their academic responsibilities (Bhardwaj and Kumar 2024). When they eventually recall these obligations, they often feel guilty and recognize that they must complete their tasks to pass their classes. However, with the rise of advanced chatbots, many academic tasks could be taken over if schools do not implement proper safeguards. This may foster complacency and irresponsibility, as students might question the need to perform tasks that chatbots can do more efficiently – especially when similar tools are being utilized in the workplace (Nanda and Kumar 2024).

This chapter explores why learning remains essential in an era of all-knowing chatbots, where these tools are ubiquitous and ready to answer any question. It argues that having access to chatbots is akin to having expert assistance, much like the privilege enjoyed by CEOs or heads of state. However, access to expert advice does not automatically result in wise or sound decision-making (Lata et al. 2024). Ultimately, it is still our responsibility to identify the problems to be solved, determine what additional information should be provided to chatbots to guide their reasoning effectively and so on.

1.2. Technological cognitive enhancement

Humans often struggle to manage all cognitive processes internally, especially when tasks impose overwhelming demands. To alleviate this burden, they offload portions of their cognitive processes onto external tools, using these tools to store and organize representational information. This reduces the need for internal mental effort. For example, people take notes, type on computers or create sketches to externalize and manage their thoughts more effectively (Risko and Gilbert 2016). The use of such cognitive tools allows humans to realize that they can manage more complex cognitive processes and, in turn, accomplish more intricate tasks (Loh and Kanai 2016). This achievement also stimulates the development and utilization of various cognitive tools (Kumar and Nanda 2024).

Human civilization has progressed due to its ability to develop and utilize two types of technologies: those that enhance cognitive capacity and those that extend physical abilities, such as strengthening muscles or augmenting vision (McLuhan 1964). Tools that extend the body enable humans to lift objects they otherwise could not, travel distances in hours that once took days, and achieve what was once impossible, such as crossing oceans. Performing complex tasks requires engaging in complex cognitive processes, such as considering various factors, making decisions and bridging cognitive gaps when coordinating multiple personnel. Today, such complex cognitive processes can involve heavy use of ICT (Nayar and Kumar 2015).

Throughout history, human cognition has been supported by various technologies, ranging from spoken language and writing systems to modern ICT (Loh and Kanai 2016). Writing systems enabled humans to preserve both private and collective memory and communicate ideas across distances and time. Even relatively simple technologies, such as printed media, played a crucial role in shaping society by facilitating the spread of new ideas (Lata and Sharma 2024b). For instance, the rise of Protestantism in Europe was closely linked to the availability of printing technology, which allowed Protestantism to capitalize on the growing vernacular print market. This surge in printed materials fueled a significant propaganda effort that shook the foundations of the Catholic church (Anderson 2006). However, printed media did not always lead to a more enlightened society; it also enabled the spread of superstitions, which could lead to harmful practices like witch-hunting, just as it could be used to combat them (Warfield 2020).

The use of paper and writing to store memories and share ideas across space and time has driven significant progress in human civilization. What once required decades or even centuries to achieve, using these memory-expanding tools has been dramatically sped up by technologies that automate cognitive processes. The automation of calculations, for example, has become indispensable in the workplace. Calculators have eliminated the need for manual calculations, and spreadsheets have further streamlined tasks by enabling users to organize, analyze and manipulate data with greater speed, ease and significantly reduced cognitive effort compared to working without such technologies.

ICT has vastly expanded and made external memory more accessible, enabling rapid retrieval of extensive information. What used to be a laborious task of locating specific phrases or sections in physical books or large libraries is disappearing with the advent of digitized versions of books. Via the Internet, we can effortlessly access both our own external memory and the collective memory of people around the world. Search engines facilitate information retrieval from virtually anywhere, but the ever-growing volume of information on the Internet requires us to carefully select and evaluate the search results.

1.3. From endless distraction to cognitive erosion

ICT plays a crucial role in globalizing the world market by enhancing connectivity among individuals and unifying previously fragmented markets in terms of geography and time (Bhardwaj and Kumar 2022). This connectivity intensifies competition among corporations and individuals, leading to increased cognitive strain (Colantone et al. 2019). The resultant mental fatigue creates a demand for cognitive relief or relaxation, a need that ICT helps meet (Sanz-Blas et al. 2013). Consequently, people increasingly turn to entertainment and activities that provide temporary escapes from these pressures, thereby fueling a global entertainment market heavily influenced by ICT.

Social media platforms such as TikTok and YouTube have become crucial parts of the entertainment industry. They enable both professional entertainers and amateurs to compete for audience attention, intensifying the battle for dominance in the attention economy (Ciampaglia et al. 2015). Industries such as social media, online gaming and video streaming employ advanced technologies to captivate users and maximize the time spent on their platforms (Wibowo et al. 2024). This constant influx of content can overwhelm users cognitively. However, because much of the Internet is driven by entertainment, many find pleasure in distraction rather than experiencing mental fatigue. The digital ecosystem, as a result, has eroded one of humanity's most valuable yet underappreciated skills: the ability to focus attentively and calmly on a single task or idea for extended periods (Hanin 2021).

The competition among entertainment businesses and individuals to capture audience attention extends into all market segments, including students. The negative impact of distractions from smartphones and social media is increasingly evident, as digital natives develop habits of media multitasking (Dontre 2021). Constant exposure to digital distractions can diminish students' capacity for deep thinking (Loh and Kanai 2016). Constant notifications and endless entertainment choices are breaking students' focus, causing procrastination and a lack of engagement with their schoolwork. This overload of distractions leads to poor time management and lower grades, as students find it difficult to concentrate and complete assignments effectively. Some may feel guilty and return to their studies, but they often just do the bare minimum to pass, which diminishes the value of their education.

ICT has evolved beyond expanding memory storage and retrieval; it now also assists, augments and even simulates cognitive processes to achieve cognitive goals (Ienca 2019). The rise of generative AI may weaken students' motivation to learn by offering shortcuts for tasks that traditionally require effort and practice. Chatbots, such as Google's NotebookLM, can be asked to digest long and complex texts, identifying key concepts and topics, summarizing and uncovering underlying assumptions. Critical reading has been one of the major cognitive skills nurtured in educational institutions because of its importance for intellectual development. In the past, encouraging students to read was not a significant challenge, as reading could also be a source of enjoyment (Lucantoni 2019). Writing essays, an even more cognitively demanding task, can now be effortlessly completed using ChatGPT (Livingstone 2024). These academic challenges, once fundamental to learning, can now be bypassed, diminishing the conditions that push students to engage deeply and develop critical thinking skills.

While distracted by social media or entertainment, students still need to complete their academic tasks. Despite being criticized for encouraging shallow thinking and giving users an illusion of knowledge mastery (Carr 2010), search engines still demand that individuals read and process search results, which is why educators can tolerate such tools. However, the rise of chatbots such as ChatGPT presents new challenges, as these tools might cause students to undervalue the importance of independently writing essays (Sharples 2022; Livingstone 2024). Essay writing is crucial for developing clear communication and critical thinking skills. Although essays convey a writer's thoughts, they are not merely transcriptions of fully formed ideas (Hunt 2010). Rather, writing is an intellectual exercise involving exploration, reflection and refinement of ideas, making it essential to the learning process.

The temptation to use chatbots to complete tasks can be irresistible for students. They may not be overly concerned that relying too heavily on AI can erode the development of their critical writing and thinking skills. The danger of chatbots lies in giving the illusion of knowing everything because they can answer any question with ease, while users themselves have not developed their critical thinking skills. Additionally, these technologies can create automation bias, leading users to trust machines more than humans (Khamassi et al. 2024), including themselves, thereby weakening their intellectual autonomy.

Previous ICT tools supporting cognitive processes, such as calculation and information storage and retrieval, were not considered threats, as they were not deemed essential intellectual capabilities for humans. The ability to effectively harness these technologies to achieve cognitive goals was seen as a key determinant of one's success as a cognitive agent in an increasingly complex environment (Risko and Gilbert 2016). The development of such skills requires time and effort; mere access to technology is insufficient for becoming a proficient cognitive agent. The mastery of these technologies is considered a skill not everyone can possess, and those who do are not on the same level.

Exercise in education is not always aimed at mastering skills directly applicable to the workplace. The nature of work and how it will be done will inevitably evolve with technological advancements, making it difficult to predict the exact skills needed in the future. However, what is certainly needed to face future challenges is the ability to think critically and possess an inquisitive mind. Critical thinking helps to avoid oversimplification and biases, leading to a better understanding of complex realities. This, in turn, can enhance academic performance and reduce susceptibility to unfounded claims (Killian 2024). Similarly, an inquisitive mind fosters creativity, innovation and problem solving by encouraging a deeper, more rational approach to decision-making (Gino 2018). Additionally, curiosity promotes open communication, trust and collaboration in the workplace, resulting in improved team performance and reduced conflict.

1.4. Fundamental differences between chatbots and humans

Regardless of the debate over whether computers can truly think (strong AI) or merely simulate thinking (weak AI) (Wakefield 2003), what is evident is that computers, along with the algorithms they run, can effectively simulate thought. They can respond to human input in ways that often appear indistinguishable from human responses. In 2017, Yuval Noah Harari remarked, "If you have enough data, and enough computer power, then you can create an algorithm that understands humans better than they understand themselves" (Hoppen and Harari 2017). Harari's claim is evident in the operations of various e-commerce and social media platforms, whether they use conventional algorithms or AI, which can predict user behavior and target them with personalized marketing. These platforms continually monitor user activity in minute detail, generating vast amounts of data to be analyzed. By identifying behavioral patterns and preferences, they can predict and influence users' future actions, making their strategies more effective and personalized. As a result, they can pinpoint user preferences and exploit them commercially, tailoring products, services and advertisements to maximize profit based on these insights (Maulana 2019). The effectiveness of using big data, collected from users' digital activities, for personalized marketing led to the emergence of what is called surveillance capitalism (Zuboff, 2015; Maulana 2019; Wood and Monahan, 2019). However, this knowledge is narrow and highly specific, focusing on immediate commercial gains, such as the types of products that consumers buy or the content that users frequently view. It is more accurate to refer to this as data analytics technology rather than a truly intelligent system, as it lacks broader cognitive capabilities and a deeper understanding beyond pattern recognition and prediction.

In 2022, OpenAI introduced an algorithm powered by a LLM in the form of ChatGPT (OpenAI 2022), a chatbot capable of generating responses to almost any prompt, showcasing a breadth of knowledge that could appear to surpass that of any individual. However, it remains debatable whether AI – or any algorithm – can truly understand humans better than we understand ourselves, as not all aspects of human experience are captured within the digital data that can be analyzed by machines. While we can imagine AI embodied in robots interacting directly with humans in real-life environments, as seen in science fiction movies, let us limit the discussion to LLM-driven chatbots, which operate within computers and interact with users through a computer interface. Current chatbots can acquire vast knowledge that is much greater than the knowledge anyone possesses. All textual information available in the world can potentially be fed as training data, making them as knowledgeable in terms of factual and propositional knowledge as the entire human population.

Current LLM-driven chatbots differ significantly from the classic concept of AI, known as good old-fashioned AI (GOFAI), which relied on symbolic reasoning and explicit programming of rules, as noted by Hubert Dreyfus. GOFAI sought to emulate human intelligence by encoding formal logic and predefined knowledge, assuming that intelligent behavior could be achieved through the logical manipulation of symbols. After decades of effort, the research program built on the assumption that human intelligence arises from using facts and rules has reached an impasse, with no indication that it will ever achieve success (Dreyfus 1992). In contrast, LLM-driven chatbots, such as those based on neural networks, operate on a different principle: learning from vast datasets through pattern recognition rather than explicit rule-based programming. This enables them to generate responses that seem intelligent and contextually appropriate. Unlike GOFAI, which followed predefined logical rules, these models produce text based on statistical associations (Gubelmann 2024), making them more flexible but also more opaque and limited in terms of genuine comprehension. Thus, while GOFAI pursued intelligence through structured logic, LLM-driven chatbots reflect the shift in AI toward machine learning and deep learning paradigms.

In the past, GOFAI was regarded as close to human intelligence, as it operated on the premise that consciously thinking humans manipulate symbols according to certain logic or rules. However, humans often act unreflectively (Heidegger 1962; Dreyfus 1992), navigating much of their daily lives through habits – such as waking up, going to the bathroom or preparing a meal without much thought – which extends to many of their digital behaviors as well. For example, checking social media, giving “likes” to preferred posts, or reacting angrily to political opponents are often automatic actions. However, humans also have the capacity to be reflective, sometimes becoming anxious or dissatisfied with their current situation. This dissatisfaction can break habitual patterns, prompting them to seek change. This unpredictability stems from the ability of humans to envision alternative futures and consciously shape their lives. While not everyone aspires or dares to change, humans are not bound by their present circumstances. They can question their existence and reflect on their place in the world. As Heidegger might suggest, humans are Dasein – beings defined by self-awareness and the capacity to project themselves into the future, transcending their current patterns and behaviors (Heidegger 1962).

Machines, on the other hand, tend to be more deterministic, although their behavior can appear unpredictable owing to their complexity and interaction with external factors. Computers have long demonstrated superior abilities in certain cognitive tasks, such as memorization, retrieval and calculation. With the advent of LLM-based chatbots, machines can now also generate responses to complex questions and produce content such as articles – tasks that many humans find cognitively demanding. While technological progress continues, we might imagine that AI evolves to a point where it could theoretically solve nearly any human problem or question. However, its statistical mechanism limits its capacity for the existential depth and unpredictable self-reflection that define human experience.

The current development of AI has driven tech giants such as OpenAI, Google, Meta and Microsoft to pursue artificial general intelligence (AGI) – systems that are as broadly capable as humans and able to understand, learn, and apply information across a wide range of tasks (Associated Press 2024). However, there is no consensus on what AGI will look like or its potential impact on human life. Instead of speculating on an uncertain future, it is more productive to focus on the immediate challenges posed by today's technology, particularly chatbots built on LLMs. While these systems may appear "all-knowing", they are fundamentally statistical models trained on vast datasets to approximate functions that map one set of values to another (Gubelmann 2024). For example, in machine translation, LLMs map a source-language sentence onto a target-language sentence. LLMs have gained recognition for their impressive ability to generate human-quality text, comprehend language and perform tasks such as answering questions, summarizing documents and suggesting sentence completions. A key feature of LLMs is their capacity to learn and adapt autonomously during the training process, refining their performance without direct human programming. However, their "knowledge" is not experiential but rooted in patterns derived from their training data.

Unlike humans, whose understanding is shaped by "being-in-the-world" – through experiences, perception and engagement with the world – chatbots exist solely within the confines of a computer. They cannot experience the world independently; their "knowledge" is limited to the data they are trained on and their interactions with users, lacking the experiential depth that characterizes human understanding. In Heideggerian terms, humans engage with the world directly, making sense of it through lived experiences, emotions and social interactions. This direct engagement shapes their understanding and being. Chatbots, however, lack this direct engagement. They do not see, feel or interact with the world in the human sense. Instead, their "being" is defined by algorithms and data, making them tools rather than entities with a sense of existence.

A chatbot's ontology can be seen as a manifestation of Heidegger's (1977) concept of "technology" as enframing. For Heidegger, technology reveals the world in particular ways, transforming and often concealing other modes of being. Chatbots reveal information and patterns through language, but their revelation is limited by their programming and data. They provide insights and answers but do so without the depth of understanding or intentionality that characterizes human thought.

Moreover, while both chatbots and humans can be biased by their training data, the scale is vastly different. Chatbots are trained on massive datasets, far beyond what any human could process in a lifetime. This extensive dataset allows chatbots to provide a wealth of information but also introduces the potential for biases that are embedded in the data. However, unlike static entities, chatbots can be responsive to users' feedback about bias and adapt their responses accordingly.

Current chatbots can conduct conversations that surpass human capabilities, especially in terms of their vast knowledge. However, they remain fundamentally different from humans, existing as digital entities within virtual realms, separate from the physical world where humans interact directly. What appears as "reasoning" in chatbots is actually the result of pattern recognition and probabilities, rather than genuine thinking and emotions. From a Heideggerian philosophical perspective, chatbots differ from humans in that humans may contemplate or question their own existence, whereas chatbots never regard their existence as an issue.

While computer software can be programmed to mimic emotions, it does not seem useful to make them overly emotional. Emotions such as boredom or sadness can indeed reduce the productivity of both technological and biological systems. However, when software or chatbots are designed to interact with human users, agents who experience genuine emotions, it is important to design them to exhibit empathy – responding thoughtfully and supportively – without actually experiencing emotions. Humans often attach emotions to their experiences. They may feel happiness when receiving empathetic attention and anxiety when facing threats or uncertainty, making emotional responses an integral part of their identity.

According to Heidegger, humans (or Dasein) project their lives into the future, often filled with both expectations and anxiety. As they navigate challenges and opportunities, including those shaped by technological advancements, individuals adapt based on their personal expectations. However, not everyone responds to these changes in the same way. Each person interprets their existence, challenges and aspirations uniquely. We define our own problems and interpret challenges differently, requiring specific and contextual knowledge to address them. The general knowledge stored in chatbots is not immediately applicable to personal situations. We cannot fully delegate problem solving to chatbots because our problems are shaped by our unique relationships with the world and our individual expectations. This kind of knowledge is deeply personal and contextual and cannot be fully captured by Wikipedia or any LLM.

1.5. What we can know that chatbots cannot

Using Merleau-Ponty's (2005) *Philosophy of Perception*, a key distinction between LLMs and humans can be highlighted: LLMs lack lived experiences and embodiment (Magee et al. 2023). Merleau-Ponty argued that perception is an active engagement with the world, grounded in our bodily presence. While LLMs such as ChatGPT simulate human subjectivity through language, they do not possess bodies or sensory experiences to inform their understanding. Their apparent understanding is derived exclusively from datasets, lacking the advantages of physical interaction or personal experience.

The absence of physical embodiment limits LLMs' ability to fully comprehend concepts such as physical pain or the joy of a warm embrace, which are deeply connected to sensory and emotional experiences. Although LLMs can generate language that appears emotionally resonant, they lack the inherent understanding derived from experiencing these events. Consequently, while LLMs can imitate human communication, they cannot replicate the profound depth of human perception and understanding, as Merleau-Ponty highlighted the crucial role of embodiment in cognition.

According to Michael Polanyi (1966, 2005), much human knowledge is tacit, meaning that it is understood and applied without being explicitly articulated in propositional terms. He argues that explicit knowledge is fundamentally based on tacit knowledge, as the process of comprehending and applying explicit knowledge depends on an underlying, often unspoken, foundation of tacit understanding. This perspective emphasizes the importance of experiential learning and personal involvement in the acquisition and application of knowledge. However, chatbots, which lack direct access to the world, are limited to propositional knowledge – the informational knowledge provided to them as training data. They do not possess tacit knowledge, which cannot be fully articulated or expressed as propositional information. As a result, tasks that require learning by doing cannot be effectively assisted by chatbots.

General LLMs, such as ChatGPT or Gemini, are trained on vast amounts of data that cover numerous topics and situations, but they do not prioritize one piece of information over another. As a result, these models often lack the contextual knowledge needed to fully understand specific scenarios. While extensive data allow LLM-based chatbots to assist in a wide range of situations, solving particular problems typically requires additional context-specific information. This means that while chatbots can help address challenges, users must provide the relevant, situated knowledge needed for effective solutions – knowledge that is often too specific and context dependent to be fully captured by LLMs. To greatly benefit from chatbots, users must identify and provide relevant situated knowledge to them. Situated knowledge is not readily available but must be actively acquired through direct experience and understanding in particular situations. This acquisition requires intelligence and critical thinking that humans need to develop rather than relying solely on AI.

Assume that having access to chatbots is similar to having very intelligent assistance that can help humans solve any problem. However, they cannot accompany us in real-life situations because they are always confined to a computer or server and cannot observe or provide unsolicited advice such as an expert person. Therefore, to get help from chatbots, users still need to be able to formulate the problems they want to solve. Formulating problems and detailing the factors influencing them are intelligent skills that require time to nurture. It is similar to being a journalist: asking questions is an intelligent skill that differentiates the experienced from the inexperienced. The quality of the answers and the flow of the conversation depend on the skill of the questioning journalist.

While some problems are generic and can be resolved using lessons learned from datasets, such as technical issues with hardware similar to others, humans also encounter unique problems shaped by specific circumstances. Chatbots may provide solutions without considering all the relevant factors, often making different assumptions about the conditions underlying the user's problems. To ensure their suggestions are appropriate, it is crucial to understand the arguments or reasons they provide. Therefore, prompting chatbots to clarify their reasoning, assumptions and considerations they have taken into account is essential. Without this critical evaluation of chatbot arguments, users risk blindly accepting recommendations that may be misaligned with the unique nuances of their situation.

In this sense, human judgment remains indispensable – not only for refining chatbot outputs but also for safeguarding the integrity and applicability of the solutions provided. Critical thinking ensures that the recommendations we receive are not only accurate but also contextually relevant and ethically sound, reinforcing the essential role of human intelligence in the age of AI. In short, while we allow chatbots to aid our thinking, it is ultimately our responsibility to evaluate the quality of their recommendations. This is essential because chatbots lack direct access to the world where our problems emerge. They rely on us to supply contextual and accurate information as the situation develops.

1.6. Using chatbots to cultivate critical thinking

As discussed in the previous section, effectively utilizing all-knowing chatbots requires critical thinking abilities. The inability to assess chatbot-generated recommendations can lead to errors in decision-making and task performance (Zhai et al. 2024). Overreliance on chatbots, especially when their suggestions are accepted without scrutiny, can erode users' cognitive abilities, diminishing their capacity to think independently and evaluate information critically. Therefore, critical thinking must be even more strongly encouraged in education, as the temptation to bypass it is so great with the ubiquitous availability of chatbots.

As preventing students from using chatbots is hardly feasible, researchers are exploring ways to develop students' critical thinking abilities while they engage with technology. In a world where AI is widely used, it is increasingly important for individuals to maintain intellectual autonomy (Carter 2018) and succeed in workplaces where critical thinking remains crucial. Although the temptation to avoid deep thinking is heightened by the convenience of chatbots, Fabio et al. (2024) demonstrate that cautious, intentional use of tools such as ChatGPT, coupled with increased experience, can actually enhance critical thinking abilities. This highlights the potential of chatbots as a resource for improving students' cognitive skills. However, to achieve this goal, educational frameworks must be redesigned to incorporate the presence of chatbots. For example, chatbots can provide formative feedback, identify weak arguments and prompt students to think critically. The key is in thoughtful integration, using these tools as companions for intellectual growth rather than shortcuts for bypassing essential learning tasks (Shum 2024).

It is interesting to explore chatbots' perspectives on the necessity of education in the age of intelligent chatbots and their role in fostering critical thinking. Two questions were posed to Gemini, ChatGPT and CoPilot, and the results are presented in Tables 1.1 and 1.2.

Table 1.1 shows that Gemini, ChatGPT and Copilot assert that educating children remains essential despite the prevalence of chatbots. They emphasize that human interaction, critical thinking, creativity and social-emotional development are irreplaceable. While AI tools can enhance education by providing information and support, they cannot fully substitute the depth of learning and personal growth offered by traditional methods. Integrating AI into education underscores the importance of balancing technological advancements with core educational practices, ensuring children acquire the necessary skills to thrive in our complex, ever-evolving world. From the perspective of marketing or public relations for the companies that create these tools, they are unlikely to present a viewpoint contrary to this.

Prompt: With the ubiquity of chatbots like you, is educating children still necessary, and for what purpose? Provide a summarized response in one paragraph.		
Gemini	**ChatGPT**	**CoPilot**
Education remains essential even in a world dominated by chatbots. While these AI tools can provide information and assistance, they cannot fully replace the need for human interaction, critical thinking, creativity, lifelong learning and ethical development. These aspects of education are crucial for children's well-being and success in a complex and ever-changing world.	Yes, educating children remains essential, even with the ubiquity of chatbots. While chatbots can provide quick access to information and assist with various tasks, education goes beyond acquiring knowledge. It fosters critical thinking, creativity, problem-solving and emotional intelligence – skills that cannot be fully developed by simply interacting with AI. Additionally, education helps children understand how to navigate complex social and ethical issues, make informed decisions and cultivate intellectual autonomy. Chatbots are tools, but education empowers children to use them wisely, ensuring they remain active participants in their learning and future decision-making.	With chatbots becoming ubiquitous, educating children remains essential. Education fosters critical thinking, creativity, emotional intelligence and social skills – qualities that AI cannot replace. It prepares children to question, innovate and understand complex concepts beyond mere information retrieval. While chatbots can support learning, the human touch in education nurtures holistic development, ensuring children grow into well-rounded individuals capable of navigating a dynamic world. Balancing AI with traditional education methods creates a more enriched learning experience.

Table 1.1. *Necessity of education in the age of intelligent chatbots*

While many educators are concerned that chatbots may encourage laziness among students by making it easy to delegate the answering of difficult questions or writing essays, Table 1.2 shows that chatbots can also be designed to nurture critical thinking in students. One major challenge in current education, especially in developing countries, is that each teacher is responsible for too many students to provide sufficient attention and feedback to their individual pedagogical needs. Chatbots can be designed to facilitate thoughtful discussions with students and engage them in interactive problem-solving activities.

Prompt: How can chatbots like you be used to nurture critical thinking in students? Provide a paragraph-long response to this query.		
Gemini	**ChatGPT**	**CoPilot**
Chatbots can be used to nurture critical thinking in students by providing them with opportunities to engage in thoughtful discussions and problem-solving activities. They can ask probing questions, challenge assumptions and provide feedback on students' responses. Additionally, chatbots can be used to simulate real-world scenarios and help students practice applying critical thinking skills to complex problems. By interacting with chatbots, students can develop their ability to analyze information, evaluate arguments and draw informed conclusions.	Chatbots like me can nurture critical thinking in students by serving as interactive tools that encourage inquiry-based learning. Instead of simply providing direct answers, I can guide students to ask deeper, more reflective questions, prompting them to explore topics further and think critically about the information they receive. For example, when a student asks a question, I can present various perspectives or ask follow-up questions that challenge their assumptions, encouraging them to consider alternative viewpoints. Additionally, I can help students break down complex problems into smaller, manageable parts, guiding them through the process of analysis, synthesis and evaluation – key components of critical thinking. By fostering a dialogue rather than delivering final answers, I can help students develop the intellectual curiosity and reasoning skills necessary for independent thinking.	Chatbots like me can nurture critical thinking in students by engaging them in interactive learning experiences that prompt analytical thinking and problem-solving. For instance, I can pose challenging questions, offer diverse perspectives and encourage students to question assumptions and evaluate evidence critically. Through guided dialogue, I can help students develop their reasoning skills by asking them to justify their answers, consider alternative viewpoints and reflect on their thought processes. This interactive approach not only fosters a deeper understanding of the material but also cultivates essential critical thinking skills that are crucial for academic and real-world success.

Table 1.2. *Use of chatbots to nurture critical thinking*

What is proposed above by the three chatbots has been explored by a number of researchers. Stimulating critical thinking in students by engaging them in a series of questions and answers, pioneered in Ancient Greece by Socrates, takes too much time for teachers. Additionally, students may be reluctant to engage in Socratic dialogue because they risk feeling humiliated or ashamed (Boghossian 2011). The availability of chatbots capable of engaging in Socratic dialogue can help both teachers and students (Gregorcic et al. 2024; Ma et al. 2024). The risk of feeling humiliated by chatbots can easily be eliminated. Students can freely explore different viewpoints and question their own beliefs and assumptions – in short, chatbots can be designed to foster deep thinking and active learning (Ma et al. 2024). Teachers can observe the Socratic dialogue between students and chatbots, assess their interactions and intervene when needed (Kumar and Rewari 2022).

We can take a critical stance on the answers given in Tables 1.1 and 1.2. The above chatbots are commercial products. Even though they have attracted enthusiasm and curiosity about their potential, there are still many people who are skeptical or cautious about their potential harms, particularly in education. Hence, their developers might have taken steps to avoid their chatbots giving controversial answers or any responses that may increase people's opposition to chatbots.

Education by human teachers can never be fully replaced, but chatbots can serve as valuable complements to traditional teaching. In some instances, chatbots may even be preferred due to their constant availability and tireless ability to respond to inquiries. This benefits not only students but also teachers, who can use chatbots to practice the Socratic method by simulating interactions with them as though they were students, allowing for continuous refinement of their teaching strategies (Gregorcic et al. 2024; Rai and Lata 2024).

1.7. Conclusion

ICT was initially developed to ease cognitive tasks. The term "computer" itself reflects its role in offloading computation from human cognition. ICT has also replaced paper as a tool for memory expansion, offering vast storage and easy information retrieval, thereby enhancing productivity by augmenting human cognitive abilities. However, this rise in productivity has also increased competition. With ICT driving global connectivity, competition has intensified further, sometimes leaving people overwhelmed by the relentless pursuit of success and survival. The pressures of this competitive environment have, in turn, fostered a market for cognitive relaxation and temporary escapes from demanding work. Unfortunately, industries providing these services – such as music, movies, online games and social media – actively strive to keep users constantly engaged. For students, these industries pose a persistent challenge, diverting attention away from academic responsibilities.

Chatbots powered by LLMs such as ChatGPT can be a risk to education if not used wisely. They might hold students back from developing important intellectual skills. Since these chatbots can generate human-like text and handle tasks that are used to take real effort, students might become overly reliant on them. Instead of spending time on activities that build their minds, such as reading a book or writing an essay, they might just let the chatbots do the work for them, making it harder to stay focused and avoid constant digital distractions. Relying on technology for such important intellectual tasks could weaken their critical thinking, problem-solving skills and ability to develop a deeper, more personal understanding of the world.

Humans with critical and inquisitive minds will still be needed in the age of all-knowing chatbots. Even though chatbots are trained with all available information in the world and can answer any question, they are missing two important things. First, human knowledge is either tacit or rooted in tacit knowledge, which cannot be fully articulated and hence not stored in LLMs. Second, chatbots cannot access the world directly, only through the information given by humans. While they are very good at answering general questions, their ability to solve situated problems depends on additional contextual information provided by users and the users' ability to formulate questions through iterative interactions. Hence, to address real problems, chatbots still require human users with critical and inquisitive minds.

To prepare students for a work environment where AI plays a crucial role, they need to develop critical and inquisitive minds and be trained to use AI critically to solve real-world problems. Integrating chatbots into education can provide interactive experiences, challenge assumptions, encourage deeper inquiry and offer personalized feedback. By engaging students critically with information, chatbots can help cultivate intellectual curiosity and reasoning skills.

Teachers can monitor students' interactions with chatbots and provide necessary feedback, acknowledging that different students will interact in varied ways. To ensure that the use of chatbots does not undermine the development of critical thinking, teachers should also focus on fostering creativity, emotional intelligence and social skills, which chatbots cannot emulate. By blending AI's strengths with traditional teaching, educators can create a richer, more engaging learning experience that equips students to navigate an increasingly complex world.

1.8. References

Anderson, B. (2006). *Imagined Communities: Reflections on the Origin and Spread of Nationalism* (Revised Edition). Verso, London and New York.

Associated Press (2024). "Godfather of AI" says there isn't a consensus on what "artificial general intelligence" means. *Fast Company* [Online]. Available at: https://www.fastcompany.com/91086862/godfather-ai-geoffrey-hinton-artificial-general-intelligence.

Bhardwaj, A. and Kumar, V. (2022). Web and social media approach to marketing of engineering courses in India. *International Journal of Business Innovation and Research*, 27(4), 541–555.

Bhardwaj, A. and Kumar, V. (2024). Challenges in online collaboration to augment Industry 4.0. *International Journal of Technology, Policy and Management*, 24(1), 71–92.

Boghossian, P. (2011). Socratic pedagogy: Perplexity, humiliation, shame and a broken egg. *Educational Philosophy and Theory*, 44(7), 710–720. doi: 10.1111/j.1469-5812.2011.00773.x.

Carr, N. (2010). *The Shallows: What the Internet Is Doing to Our Brains.* W.W. Norton & Company, New York and London.

Carter, J.A. (2018). Autonomy, cognitive offloading, and education. *Educational Theory*, 68(6), 657–673. doi: 10.1111/edth.12338.

Ciampaglia, G.L., Flammini, A., Menczer, F. (2015). The production of information in the attention economy. *Scientific Reports*, 5(1), 9452. doi: 10.1038/srep09452.

Colantone, I., Crinò, R., Ogliari, L. (2019). Globalization and mental distress. *Journal of International Economics*, 119, 181–207. doi: 10.1016/j.jinteco.2019.04.008.

Dontre, A.J. (2021). The influence of technology on academic distraction: A review. *Human Behavior and Emerging Technologies*, 3(3), 379–390. doi: 10.1002/hbe2.229.

Dreyfus, H.L. (1992). *What Computers Still Can't Do: A Critique of Artificial Reason.* MIT Press, Cambridge, MA.

Fabio, R.A., Plebe, A., Suriano, R. (2024). AI-based chatbot interactions and critical thinking skills: An exploratory study. *Current Psychology*. doi: 10.1007/s12144-024-06795-8.

Gino, F. (2018). The business case for curiosity. *Harvard Business Review* [Online]. Available at: https://hbr.org/2018/09/the-business-case-for-curiosity.

Gregorcic, B., Polverini, G., Sarlah, A. (2024). ChatGPT as a tool for honing teachers' Socratic dialogue skills. *Physics Education*, 59(4), 045005. doi: 10.1088/1361-6552/ad3d21.

Gubelmann, R. (2024). Large language models, agency, and why speech acts are beyond them (for now) – A Kantian-Cum-Pragmatist case. *Philosophy & Technology*, 37(32), 1–24. doi: 10.1007/s13347-024-00696-1.

Hanin, M.L. (2021). Theorizing digital distraction. *Philosophy & Technology*, 34(2), 395–406. doi: 10.1007/s13347-020-00394-8.

Heidegger, M. (1962). *Being and Time.* Basil Blackwell, Oxford.

Heidegger, M. (1977). *The Question Concerning Technology.* Harper & Row, New York and London.

Hoppen, N. and Harari, Y.N. (2017). How humankind could become totally useless. *Time* [Online]. Available at: https://time.com/4672373/yuval-noah-harari-homo-deus-interview/.

Hunt, L. (2010). How writing leads to thinking. *Perpectives on History* [Online]. Available at: https://www.historians.org/perspectives-article/how-writing-leads-to-thinking-february-2010/.

Ienca, M. (2019). Democratizing cognitive technology: A proactive approach. *Ethics and Information Technology*, 21(4), 267–280. doi: 10.1007/s10676-018-9453-9.

Kelly, S.M. (2023). ChatGPT passes exams from law and business schools. *CNN* [Online]. Available at: https://edition.cnn.com/2023/01/26/tech/chatgpt-passes-exams/index.html.

Khamassi, M., Nahon, M., Chatila, R. (2024). Strong and weak alignment of large language models with human values. *Scientific Reports*, 14(1), 19399. doi: 10.1038/s41598-024-70031-3.

Killian, K.D. (2024). Critical thinking: What it is and why it matters. *Psychology Today* [Online]. Available at: https://www.psychologytoday.com/us/blog/intersections/202409/critical-thinking-what-it-is-and-why-it-matters?form=MG0AV3.

Kumar, V. and Lata, M. (eds) (2022). *The Future of E-Commerce*. Nova Science Publishers, New York. doi: 10.52305/KMUB3774.

Kumar, V. and Nanda, P. (2024). Social media and micro-lessons: A new paradigm of online learning. In *Optimizing Education Through Micro-Lessons: Engaging and Adaptive Learning Strategies*, Ilic, P. (ed.). IGI Global, New York.

Kumar, V. and Rewari, M. (2022). A responsible approach to higher education curriculum design. *International Journal of Educational Reform*, 31(4), 422–441.

Lata, M. and Kumar, V. (2022). Fog computing infrastructure for smart city applications. In *Recent Advancements in ICT Infrastructure and Applications*, Chaturvedi, M., Patel, P., Yadav, R. (eds). Springer, Singapore.

Lata, M. and Kumar, V. (2024). A framework for security of public cloud environment. *International Journal of Electronic Security and Digital Forensics*, 16(4), 486–502.

Lata, M. and Sharma, V. (2024a). Cloud computing based blended learning: Quality assurance challenges. In *2024 International Conference on Communication, Computer Sciences and Engineering (IC3SE)*. IEEE, New York.

Lata, M. and Sharma, V. (2024b). Smart city environment management: Challenges and opportunities. *Grenze International Journal of Engineering & Technology (GIJET)*, 10(2), 2159–2166.

Lata, M., Kumar, V., Sharma, V. (2024). Cloud computing applications in online learning. *Grenze International Journal of Engineering & Technology (GIJET)*, 10(2), 408–411.

Livingstone, V. (2024). I quit teaching because of ChatGPT. *Time* [Online]. Available at: https://time.com/7026050/chatgpt-quit-teaching-ai-essay/.

Loh, K.K. and Kanai, R. (2016). How has the Internet reshaped human cognition? *The Neuroscientist*, 22(5), 506–520. doi: 10.1177/1073858415595005.

Lucantoni, P. (2019). Reading empowers: The importance of reading for students. *Cambridge English* [Online]. Available at: https://www.cambridge.org/us/education/blog/2019/03/06/reading-empowers/?form=MG0AV3.

Ma, T., Chen, R., LI, A.T., Liu, H. (2024). Socratic ChatGPT: Theory, design, and empirical evaluations. In *PACIS 2024 Proceedings*, Ho Chi Minh City [Online]. Available at: https://aisel.aisnet.org/pacis2024/track14_educ/track14_educ/12/.

Magee, L., Arora, V., Munn, L. (2023). Structured like a language model: Analysing AI as an automated subject. *Big Data and Society*, 10(2), 1–15. doi: 10.1177/20539517231210273.

Maulana, I. (2019). Big brothers are seducing you: Consumerism, surveillance, and the agency of consumers. In *Handbook of Research on Consumption, Media, and Popular Culture in the Global Age*, Ozgen, O. (ed.). IGI Global, Hershey, PA.

McLuhan, M. (1964). *Understanding Media: The Extensions of Man*. McGraw-Hill, New York.

Merleau-Ponty, M. (2005). *Phenomenology of Perception* (C. Smith, Trans.). Routledge, London.

Milmo, D. (2023). ChatGPT reaches 100 million users two months after launch. *The Guardian* [Online]. Available at: https://www.theguardian.com/technology/2023/feb/02/chatgpt-100-million-users-open-ai-fastest-growing-app.

Nanda, P. and Kumar, V. (2024). New generation technologies: Development vs. ethical challenges. *International Journal of Business Information Systems*, 46(3), 411–434.

Nayar, K.B. and Kumar, V. (2015). Benefits of cloud computing in education during disaster. In *Proceedings of the International Conference on Transformations in Engineering Education: ICTIEE 2014*. Springer, India.

OpenAI (2022). ChatGPT: Optimizing language models for dialogue [Online]. Available at: https://openai.com/blog/chatgpt.

Polanyi, M. (1966). *The Tacit Dimension*. The University of Chicago Press, Chicago.

Polanyi, M. (2005). *Personal Knowledge: Towards a Post-critical Philosophy*. Routledge, London.

Rai, S., and Lata, M. (2024). Futuristic outlook of online learning: The post-pandemic era. In *Technology-mediated Learning During the Pandemic*, Singh, J. and Kumar, V. (eds). Routledge, India.

Risko, E.F., and Gilbert, S.J. (2016). Cognitive offloading. *Trends in Cognitive Sciences*, 20(9), 676–688. doi: 10.1016/j.tics.2016.07.002.

Sanz-Blas, S., Ruiz-Mafé, C., Martí-Parreño, J., Hernández-Fernández, A. (2013). Assessing the influence of motivations and attitude on mobile social networking use. *Global Business Perspectives*, 1(2), 164–179. doi: 10.1007/s40196-012-0008-x.

Sharples, M. (2022). Automated essay writing: An AIED opinion. *International Journal of Artificial Intelligence in Education*, 32(4), 1119–1126. doi: 10.1007/s40593-022-00300-7.

Shum, S.B. (2024). Generative AI for critical analysis: Practical tools, cognitive offloading and human agency. In *CEUR Workshop Proceedings*, 3667.

Wakefield, J.C. (2003). The Chinese room argument reconsidered: Essentialism, indeterminacy, and strong AI. *Minds and Machines*, 13, 285–319.

Warfield, A. (2020). Witchcraft and the early modern media. In *The Routledge History of Witchcraft*, Dillinger, J. (ed.). Routledge, Oxford.

Wibowo, A.P., Kusumawati, R.D., Kumar, V. (2024). Gamification as a strategic move: Redefining storytelling through a unique medium. In *Marketing and Gamification*, Gupta, S., Nagina, R., Paruthi, M., Gupta, G. (eds). Routledge, New York.

Wilmer, H.H. and Chein, J.M. (2016). Mobile technology habits: Patterns of association among device usage, intertemporal preference, impulse control, and reward sensitivity. *Psychonomic Bulletin & Review*, 23(5), 1607–1614. doi: 10.3758/s13423-016-1011-z.

Wood, D.M. and Monahan, T. (2019). Platform surveillance. *Surveillance & Society*, 17(1–2), 1–6.

Zhai, C., Wibowo, S., Li, L.D. (2024). The effects of over-reliance on AI dialogue systems on students' cognitive abilities: A systematic review. *Smart Learning Environments*, 11(1), 28. doi: 10.1186/s40561-024-00316-7.

Zuboff, S. (2015). Big other: Surveillance capitalism and the prospects of an information civilization. *Journal of Information Technology*, 30(1), 75–89.

2

Artificial Intelligence (AI) in Education

The integration of artificial intelligence (AI) in education has become a transformative force in the teaching and learning landscape. This chapter critically explores the multifaceted impact of AI on the education system, exploring both its potential and its challenges. Starting with a review of the historical evolution of AI in education, this chapter delves into key applications of AI, such as adaptive learning systems, automated assessments and intelligent tutor systems. These innovations are analyzed in the context of increasing the efficiency, personalization and accessibility of education. However, AI adoption also raises significant ethical and privacy concerns, as well as challenges related to the digital divide and accessibility. This chapter presents a comprehensive discussion of these issues, providing insight into the ongoing debate regarding the role of AI in education. The chapter also includes case studies of AI implementations in various educational institutions, highlighting best practices and lessons learned. This chapter aims to contribute to the academic discourse on AI in education by offering a balanced view that is essential for educators, policymakers and researchers in navigating the complexities of AI integration.

2.1. Introduction

Technological advances have changed the way humans interact with each other, work and learn (Bhardwaj and Kumar 2024). AI is one of the most innovative transformations in the field of digital technology (Zawacki-Richter et al. 2019). In the context of formal and non-formal education, AI has potential as a tool for changing the landscape of education. AI provides solutions to various problems that have been carried out with limited human capabilities (Dwivedi et al. 2021). AI also allows users to change learning systems to be more effective and efficient in a more systematic manner. AI in the world of education in the form of applications is widely used, starting from adaptive learning systems, so that the subject matter can be adjusted to the needs of students. The chatbot feature can be used by students to

---

Chapter written by Tiara Nur ANISAH and Andika ANDIKA.

answer questions even outside of class hours, thus creating a more satisfying student learning experience with fun learning methods. Administrative and time-consuming tasks such as scheduling, assessment and data processing can easily be completed with the help of AI. Thus, teachers can allocate their time to focus more on direct interaction with students (Kumar and Rewari 2022).

AI in the world of education seems to open up new horizons, making everything both more complicated and easier. The learning process can be carried out more precisely with personalized learning (Somasundaram et al. 2020). More informed and data-driven decision-making can also be easily performed with the help of AI-based systems (Nanda and Kumar 2023). However, even though the presence of AI offers a variety of conveniences, the use of AI also has several challenges, including in terms of data privacy and ethical issues (Alhitmi et al. 2024). Using AI in an unwise way can have a detrimental negative impact. In this chapter, we will learn the extent to which AI can be utilized in the world of education, what opportunities and challenges we face and see what the AI trends will be in the future (Kumar and Lata 2022). With this understanding of the discussion about AI in the world of education, it is hoped that it will add an insight for readers about how AI can be optimally integrated into the world of education without neglecting the ethics and values that must be maintained.

At the start, AI in education and its associated development were more due to luck and the developer's capacity than to their interest or opportunity (Luckin et al. 2022). At this point, building a better understanding of how AI can be applied and utilized effectively and efficiently becomes even more important to benefit as well as minimize negative risks along the road. Of course, these propositions require collaborative cooperation based on cooperation between technology developers, teachers, policymakers and the wider community. With this, we need to know that AI is not only a tool that supports the education system but is also helping build a more inclusive and equitable educational existence. Therefore, collaborative and wise cooperation in both fields will unlock the potential for the promotion of double access, personalization and relevance of learning by encouraging the achievement of greater targets.

2.2. Basic concepts of artificial intelligence in education

AI is a technology that allows computers to perform tasks that require human intelligence, and is not limited to language understanding, pattern recognition and decision-making. In the context of education, AI is implemented to vitalize learning with two mechanisms: personalization and automation. The implementation of AI in learning, such as adaptive learning, allows the system to design the right material for each student so that the material provided helps students achieve optimal results

(Chassignol et al. 2018). The application of AI in education will help automate administrative workloads so that they can be reduced (Zawacki-Richter et al. 2019).

2.2.1. *Definition of artificial intelligence in education*

AI is a simulation of the intelligence possessed by humans that is modeled in a machine and programmed to be able to think like humans. The Oxford Dictionary states that AI is the development of computer systems so that they can perform many tasks that require human intelligence. According to Chen et al. (2023), AI is the activity of providing a computer-like machine with the ability to display behavior that is considered to be intelligent if the ability is displayed by a human. Hwang et al. (2020) interpret AI as an effort to model human thought processes and design machines to imitate human behavior. In addition, there is also an opinion that AI is the intelligence shown by an artificial entity (Jiang et al. 2022). Intelligence is created and put into a machine (computer) to be able to do the work that humans can do. On the basis of some of the above understandings, AI is an intelligence that is programmed in such a way that it has extraordinary intelligence that resembles may even surpass human intelligence. In the context of education, although the concept of a self-aware AI is still in the theoretical stage, several AI applications are very advanced and have the potential to support education, namely, creating an adaptive learning system as a tutor for students that helps students in understanding lessons, automatically assessing students' work, including exams and assignments, developing students' social and emotional skills and analyzing learning data and making decisions (Pedro et al. 2019).

2.2.2. *History and evolution of AI in education*

The evolution of AI dates back several decades. The concept of AI was first introduced from the 1960s to the 1970s. Initially, AI in the world of education emerged through the development of computer-based systems, commonly known as computer-assisted instruction (CSI). The PLATO (Programmed Logic for Automated Teaching Operations) program was a computer-based program that integrated AI for the first time. The program was designed in the 1960s at the University of Illinois and was designed to adapt learning materials to students' abilities. From the 1980s to the 1990s, a system called the intelligent tutoring system (ITS) began to appear. The purpose of this system was to personalize learning by simulating interactions between teachers and students. The cognitive model at the ITS allowed students to better understand the material and provide feedback quickly so that the learning process was effective.

With the beginning of the 21st century, the evolution of AI began increasingly showing significant progress along with the development of information and communication technology. AI, which initially functioned only to personalize and analyze in real time, can now automate various administrative tasks to provide suggestions and recommendations for a more adaptive learning system according to the needs of each student (Luckin and Holmes 2016). In fact, in the world of higher education, AI has been widely used to help automate lecturer tasks in the preparation of scientific articles with various conveniences. The development of AI, which is accelerating from year to year, is expected to make a significant contribution to the transformation of education globally. The use of AI in the field of education is expected to further increase effectiveness and efficiency as well as accessibility to create innovative and sustainable learning models (Nayar and Kumar 2015).

2.2.3. *Categories and types of AI used in education*

In the world of education, many types of AI exist according to their respective functions. The presence of several AI applications will help the learning process and make students and teachers understand the material on a more personal basis (Nanda and Kumar 2024). The application of AI in the world of education allows the learning process in educational institutions to run effectively and efficiently. Some of the types of AI that can be used in learning are as follows:

1) Chatbot

This technology is commonly used by students to help them ask questions, provide study advice or provide explanations more conceptually. Chatbots built using AI, such as ChatGPT, are the most widely used by students because they can provide more natural and responsive interactions than simple chatbots.

2) Machine learning

Machine learning is commonly used by students to develop predictive models. This model serves to assist students in determining the most effective teaching method. This model can also process historical data from students so that it can produce models that can be used to estimate student performance in the future.

3) Adaptive learning

Adaptive learning technology is a learning method that allows students to learn at their own pace. AI-based adaptive learning technology can be used to analyze student data and determine their level of understanding so that it can tailor learning according to the needs of each student.

4) Virtual reality (VR) and augmented reality (AR)

VR and AR can be used in the world of education to create realistic and interactive student learning experiences. For example, students can learn various histories through the experience of walking in a virtual museum or studying molecular structures through VR simulations. With this AI tool, students can understand the material more easily and with more fun.

5) Natural language processing (NLP)

NLP is a type of AI that addresses the ability of computers to understand natural human language. For example, writing or voice is often used by humans in everyday conversations. NLP was created by combining computational linguistics with statistical models, machine learning and deep learning. All these elements are then used to help computers process human text and audio data, making it understand the data to get the full meaning, complete with intent and sentiment.

The combination of several types of increasingly sophisticated AI technologies can improve learning effectiveness, helping students to understand better and develop skills necessary for the future.

2.3. Implementation of AI in education

2.3.1. *AI in adaptive learning*

Using AI in adaptive learning is an innovative step for educational institutions (Gligorea et al. 2023). By using the system, everything can be done automatically, such as collecting and analyzing student data on the basis of interactions with the material that has been learned. The data collected consist of a set of information regarding students' speed in completing assignments, error patterns and the difficulties students face during the learning process (Bhardwaj and Kymar 2022). It is very possible to provide material according to the needs of each student. From these data, the AI system will automatically analyze and recommend subject matter according to students' level of difficulty and ability at a certain level and provide feedback quickly. Thus, students can learn according to their rhythm without feeling hampered by the uniform learning speed. Each student certainly has a different way of learning, so AI technology can be used to collect data and information about the learning habits of each student and then recommend the right way of learning for each student (Gligorea et al. 2023). This means that AI is crucial in adaptive learning, especially with respect to scale (Kumar and Nanda 2024). In Indonesia, a geographically diverse and populous nation, it is common for classrooms to accommodate over 20 students. While this number may seem moderate compared to global averages, it is important to recognize that the country's educational context often involves teachers managing multiple subjects within a single classroom. It would be difficult for an educator to understand his students individually without the help of AI technology. Several AI platforms can be used to apply adaptive learning. Starting from the simplest approach, which can be implemented daily, especially by schools, namely, Google Workspace for Education users. One feature in Google Classroom is practice sets, which are a series of features that help educators focus more on the uniqueness of each student. Practice sets help create a more private learning path between educators and students so that educators can better understand each student's unique needs and provide more personalized feedback. This feature enables educators to transform traditional learning content into interactive tasks, thereby enhancing the engagement and enjoyment of both teaching and learning activities.

In accordance with the Indonesian Ministry of Education, Culture, Research, and Technology (*Permendikbudristek*) Order No. 16 of 2022 on process standards for early childhood, primary, and secondary education, three key stages are identified for ensuring effective and efficient learning. These stages – planning, implementation and assessment – serve as fundamental components in the design of educational practices. While the reference to *Permendikbudristek* provides a regulatory framework, it is crucial to understand the broader implications these stages have on the structure of educational systems and their alignment with evolving pedagogical standards. Teachers can use AI when implementing process standards:

1) Planning, where we have to create a teaching module or syllabus. Examples of AI that can be used for this include, amongst others, ChatGPT, Schemely, Auto Classmate or AI Assistant.

2) Implementation, where we have to teach. Surely, we can use a video or presentation as a teaching tool, and to create that video or presentation, we can take advantage of Pictory, Canva or Runway.

3) Assessment, where we have to make formative assessments (quizzes) as well as check and correct long description questions and essays. For this purpose, the AI that we can use is ChatGPT or AI Assistant. To check for plagiarism, we can use Turnitin or Content Detector.

2.3.2. *AI in the writing of a scientific journal*

The presence of increasingly sophisticated AI technology today has a significant role in helping researchers write scientific articles. The use of this technology can help teachers and lecturers in compiling scientific papers more efficiently and effectively. One strategy that can be applied is the use of AI to assist in the writing process, such as data analysis, article structuring and checking the correctness of the information presented. AI can be used to provide recommendations for searching scientific journals by keywords, compiling abstracts, improving grammar and also performing plagiarism analysis automatically. Users can be more efficient in searching for references, analyzing the veracity of information and better compiling scientific articles. The integration of AI technology in scientific paper writing training can provide benefits in speeding up the writing process, improving accuracy and facilitating reference management. Several AI tools are widely used in the world of education to help prepare scientific articles. The following are some examples:

1) Research Rabbit (https://www.perplexity.ai/)

Research Rabbit is an amazing AI tool that can quickly track the entire literature review process. This AI can create a collection of reputable scientific article references that can be filtered based on user preferences so that users get similar things that are recommended. The way to use Research Rabbits is to upload research papers on a specific topic to create a collection of research papers, and then, on the basis of the uploaded topic, this AI will recommend more relevant research and even newer research papers in a more comprehensive and informative manner. With Research Rabbit, users can see which papers are the most cited. Users can also filter by author so that they can see which research papers they have published and choose them to read. In this way, it helps researchers conduct faster and more effective literature surveys, and the best part is that this tool is completely free, so researchers can make the most of this particular AI tool to conduct quality literature surveys.

2) Chat PDF (https://www.chatpdf.com/)

Chat PDF is an AI-based tool that makes it possible to chat with PDFs and get answers to questions. This system functions similarly to ChatGPT, where the AI model takes responsibility for generating answers. When a question is posed, the model searches relevant data across a wide array of sources and then provides a coherent response based on the gathered information. In the case of Chat PDF, if the user asks a question, the user must first upload the file to be asked; then, Chat PDF will try to answer it. This AI will be very useful for beginners who are new to a particular field of research. However, the shortcomings of Chat PDF, which has many technical terms for the language used and tends to be complex, may cause some users not to be able to fully understand the answers provided by Chat PDF. To support scientific writing, PDF chats can be very useful, as researchers can ask questions to understand what is written in the research paper.

3) Trinka (https://www.trinka.ai/)

Trinka, which is commonly used as a grammar correction tool, is a revolutionary site that functions to help write scientific articles and is designed specifically for writing articles in the academic field. The use of Trinka AI not only catches complex errors in terms of technical and scientific writing, but also corrects sentence structure, tone, language usage and language style. Currently, Trinka has other interesting features, such as plagiarism checks, citation checks, journal finders and so on. However, more people are using Trinka for grammar checks. The application of this AI tool has the potential to significantly enhance the quality and coherence of documents, with improvements of up to 5,000 words in length. This capability makes it a highly recommended tool for document refinement and optimization.

4) Perplexity AI (https://www.perplexity.ai/)

Perplexity AI is an AI-based information search engine that uses large language model (LLM) technology that can answer various forms of questions, including difficult questions. The way Perplexity AI works tends to be the same as ChatGPT or Google Gemini; users can enter a question, and then Perplexity will answer it accurately. The difference between Perplexity AI and other AI tools lies in the accuracy of the source. In Perplexity, this tool will list the source of accurate answers. It can be said that the Perplexity information search engine is a combination of ChatGPT and Google Search. Researchers who want to find source justification for searchable statements can easily find them with the help of Perplexity AI. This will make it easier for researchers to compile scientific articles efficiently.

2.3.3. *AI in assessment*

The use of AI in assessment and evaluation has been proven to increase effectiveness and efficiency by cutting down on processes that were previously performed manually. Manual assessment, in addition to being time-consuming, often also causes bias. AI tools can perform an automated grading system on several teacher tasks, including checking student work, grading multiple-choice questions, and automatically evaluating and providing feedback quickly (Hwang et al. 2020). AI tools can be used in educational measurement and assessment. The following are some specific ways AI can be applied in educational assessment (Owan et al. 2023):

1) *Personalized learning*: tools and systems based on AI have the potential to customize learning experiences, increase the productivity of teachers and heighten student engagement (Mena-Guacas 2023). AI can help create personalized learning plans for individual students based on their learning progress, strengths and weaknesses. This can help students learn at their own pace and focus on areas where they need more support. AI-powered adaptive learning software such as DreamBox and Knewton use data analysis to create personalized learning plans for students based on their strengths and weaknesses.

2) *Intelligent tutoring systems (ITS)*: AI-powered tutoring systems can provide personalized support and feedback to students. These systems can adapt to students' learning styles and provide tailored instruction and support, helping students to improve their learning outcomes. These systems can help students remain motivated and engaged with their learning by providing immediate feedback. The system adapts to each student's learning pace and provides interactive instruction and practice problems. Educators can use ITS to provide individualized instruction, monitor student progress and identify areas where students need additional support. Examples include ALEKS, Carnegie Learning and Knewton.

3) *Automated grading*: AI can help automate the grading process, saving time for teachers and providing students with immediate feedback on their assignments. AI can provide feedback on grammar, spelling and syntax by analyzing essays, reports and other written assignments. By using automated grading systems, teachers can focus more on essential tasks such as lesson planning and supporting students, resulting in significant time savings (Adiguzel 2023). This can help students improve their writing skills and reduce the workload for teachers. For example, Turnitin's AI-powered software uses NLP to analyze essays and provide grammar, spelling and syntax feedback. The software can also detect plagiarism, helping teachers grade assignments more efficiently and accurately.

4) *Natural language processing*: the application of NLP in spelling and grammar evaluation can help students to read and write better. Students who are learning to write essays will receive feedback from the NLP-based application, especially related to grammar, spelling and also recommendations, so that the essays written can be better. NLP can also grade essays on grammar, structure, semantics and reasoning, which is an enormous time saver for educators. NLP can improve the quality of teaching for students and help educators improve the quality of learning. Applying NLP in an educational setting is not only helpful in developing effective language processes but also essential for improving academic performance. Currently, NLP research in education is still ongoing, but developments so far show that NLP can have a very positive impact on learning. For example, Grammarly's NLP-powered software provides real-time feedback on writing, including suggestions for grammar, punctuation and sentence structure.

5) *VR and AR tools*: VR and AR tools use immersive technologies to provide students with interactive, experiential learning experiences. Educators can use VR and AR tools to engage students in hands-on learning activities, provide real-world experiences and enhance student learning outcomes. Examples include Google Expeditions, Merge Cube and Nearpod VR.

2.4. Opportunities and impact of AI in education

2.4.1. *Opportunities and benefits of AI to improve the quality of education*

The presence of AI in education has a significant impact on improving the quality of education through effectiveness and efficiency. AI systems offer a variety of conveniences ranging from administrative load efficiency and learning personalization to assessment automation. There are opportunities for the use of AI in education (Bhutoria 2022):

1) *Efficiency of administrative burden*: the presence of AI in education offers convenience in administrative matters. Examples of administrative tasks for teachers include data management, scheduling and evaluation of exam results. By utilizing an AI-based system, data can be processed quickly and accurately so that teachers can focus more on strategic things to improve the quality of education.

2) *Learning personalization*: the use of an AI-based system will create a fun learning experience that can be adjusted to meet the individual needs of students according to each student's abilities. By looking at machine learning algorithms, student performance analysis can be performed with the help of AI and can offer material that is more relevant to the student's level of understanding. Thus, the personalization of learning will allow for more adaptive learning so that students' interest in learning increases.

3) *Increased accessibility and inclusion*: with AI, the accessibility of education can be further increased because AI, in addition to being able to translate into various languages, is also able to provide a variety of educational content in a format that is easier for all groups to access, including those who have special needs or who have different physical requirements.

Scientific article writing: the presence of AI is not only used to make it easier for students and teachers but can also be used for lecturers/researchers to assist in writing scientific papers. Starting from searching for articles using AI, abstracts are compiled, and sentences are corrected to analyze the data processing results.

2.4.2. *Impact of AI in education*

The use of AI in education, in addition to bringing direct benefits to the learning process, can also bring long-term benefits (Lata and Sharma 2024b). The burden of administration and data analysis, which can be automated with the help of AI-based systems, will certainly allow teachers to focus more on direct interaction with students and continue to develop the most effective and innovative learning methods (Celik 2023). Furthermore, with a personalized AI-based learning system and adequate tools, students can explore their potential more massively because they obtain a satisfying learning experience (Owoc et al. 2021). Overall, AI can revolutionize every aspect of education, from the learning experience to the management of educational institutions. The implementation of this technology must be performed wisely to maximize the benefits obtained. However, AI also has negative impacts along with potential dangers that may arise from these negative impacts. One of the negative impacts is the dependence on AI by teachers and students, which can reduce their learning ability. In addition, AI also has the potential to control national education policies, increase plagiarism and weaken the potential of students and teachers. Some of the impacts we need to know include the following:

1) Data privacy and security

The use of AI in education faces various challenges, such as ethics and privacy. One of the main issues is the collection and processing of student data. AI requires large and diverse data to be able to provide accurate recommendations and feedback. However, this data collection raises concerns about how it is used and stored and who has access to it (Akgun and Greenhow 2022; Lata and Kumar 2024). The use of AI and data collection are inseparable. Therefore, we need to ensure that users' data are well protected from security breaches and misuse by AI providers (Alhitmi et al. 2024).

2) Technology gap

The use of AI, which has a positive impact on education, can strengthen the technology gap between educational institutions that have access and institutions that do not. Educational institutions in big cities certainly have wider access to technological advances such as AI when compared to educational institutions in small or underdeveloped cities. Especially in a country such as Indonesia, the penetration of technology and the internet is uneven. The use of AI can widen the technology gap between regions that have sufficient resources and those that do not.

3) Dependence on technology

Overreliance on AI technology can reduce students' ability to develop interpersonal skills and critical skills in problem solving. For example, when given questions in the form of descriptions, students instead use platforms such as ChatGPT or Perplexity to generate answers and simply copy them to complete their assignments. In addition, the use of AI also causes algorithm imperfections. This is due to the large amount of data that AI algorithms study, so it is likely to have unintentional biases that can affect fairness in assessing students.

4) Cheating

The use of AI by irresponsible individuals can be used to cheat on exams or the preparation of work. AI can be a good plagiarism engine and can be used to copy other people's work without being caught. The existence of AI technology can make teachers and students tend to have a dependence on AI. This will result in weak analytical and critical thinking skills possessed by teachers and students. Reliance on AI can also lead to a loss of essential skills as well as independence in solving problems.

AI has indeed transformed the lives of mankind in almost all fields. Like a double-edged sword, AI could be a boon as well as a danger and a worry for humanity. Therefore, all of us need to raise awareness of the wise use of AI, especially in the context of education. We should not be lulled by the convenience of using AI so that we become too dependent on it and forget that it can erode our ability as humans to think critically and use reason (Lata et al. 2024).

2.4.3. *Digital divide and accessibility*

The advancement of AI technology does offer various benefits that are felt in the world of education. However, behind the positive impact obtained, there are challenges in its implementation, one of which is the digital divide. The digital divide is related to equal access to technology in certain groups based on their geographical location. This is an obstacle as well as a challenge for the government to integrate AI into all education sectors equally, especially in developing countries (Lata and Kumar 2022). Notably, not everyone has adequate access to AI technology effectively. For example, in developing countries, especially in remote areas far from urban areas, the internet connection is not evenly distributed. Slow connections and hardware unavailability are also obstacles for the region to take advantage of AI technology. Data released by the International Telecommunication Union (ITU) state that approximately 33% of the world's population does not have adequate internet access. Therefore, it affects their opportunities to utilize AI in the world of education (Lombardi 2023).

In addition to the gap in accessibility, the digital skills gap has also become a challenge in optimizing the use of AI. Unfortunately, there are still many students who come from remote areas with low economic conditions and do not have the skills to access technology due to a lack of adequate training. This further adds to the inequality in the application of AI to help adjust adaptive learning methods based on AI (Lata and Sharma 2024a). For this gap to be overcome, it is necessary to cooperate with the government and educational institutions to build the necessary infrastructure and technology.

2.5. Case studies of AI implementation in various educational institutions

The implementation of AI tools in the world of education is increasing. This makes it possible for AI to rival the level of human intelligence in analytical ability, whereas humans outperform AI in problems with a greater level of uncertainty and complexity. The following case studies show how AI has been applied successfully.

1) *Case study*: AI in adaptive learning in high schools in the United States (BPAI 2024)

Adaptive learning systems have been successfully implemented in high schools in the United States. This DreamBox Learning applies the use of system-based AI with adaptive learning. The difference in the level of students' ability to grasp the material and the different learning speeds of students make adaptive learning based on the AI system necessary because it can adapt the material to each student's ability. The implementation of DreamBox Learning takes place on an AI-powered adaptive learning platform within Howard County Public Schools (HCPSS) in Maryland, as well as across the network of charter schools operated by Rocketship Education. Both institutions utilize the Dreambox as an adaptive learning system in mathematics. This personalized system can monitor student activity in real time to identify errors from students' psychological causes. By adapting the content to the appropriate lessons, this AI tool has proven successful in improving student achievement. One study reported a positive association between DreamBox use and increased math test scores, although evidence of its impact on student achievement was mixed.

2) *Case study*: use of AI chatbots in universities

Leiden University in the Netherlands and several universities in Malaysia have successfully integrated AI chatbots to improve academic and administrative support services. The flexibility of chatbots allows for a wide range of applications in education services (Chen et al. 2023). A study from Deng and Yu (2023) stated that the presence of chatbots not only serves to speed up administrative processes but also increases student satisfaction by reducing waiting times and providing more responsive support.

– Leiden University in the Netherlands has been exploring the integration of AI chatbots in improving their education services. Their initiative focuses on understanding the implications of AI in education and providing support for its effective implementation (Leiden University 2024). Using AI chatbots, Leiden University has streamlined processes, such as responding to student inquiries and managing routine administrative tasks. Thus, they can increase efficiency and reduce waiting times. This initiative underscores the university's commitment to improving student services and reflects a forward-thinking approach to leveraging AI. Such adoption becomes an ideal example for other institutions to explore innovative applications of AI in addressing challenges in higher education.

– Universiti Teknikal Malaysia Melaka has also proven the significant influence of AI chatbots on student services. They utilize chatbots to provide a 24/7 service with FAQs, course registration guides and access to academic resources. Thus, the university can improve the efficiency of its administrative processes and increase student satisfaction by up to 20%. Students do not need to wait for the admin to reply to their questions, especially if it is outside of working hours. The use of AI in chatbots certainly helps increase the effectiveness and efficiency of administrative processes. Additionally, the reduction in administrative workload highlights the dual benefits of improving operational efficiency while improving the overall student experience, making it a model for leveraging AI in higher education.

2.6. Recommendations for AI development in education

AI is one of the products resulting from technological advances worldwide that is currently massively used by students and teachers. The variety of existing AI technology features certainly provides many benefits. However, thus far, there is still a debate over whether AI can facilitate students' critical thinking skills or vice versa. The issue of ethics and privacy is still a debate in the academic world, so it is a challenge in the implementation of AI. The following are recommendations for the development of AI in the world of education.

1) *Regulations and policies*: policies and regulations from governments to comprehensively utilize AI in education are essential. Things that are potential threats, especially in the context of the issue of student privacy, must be protected against through a series of supportive regulations. This aims to ensure that user security and AI can be used optimally. The European government have created the General Data Protection Regulation (GDPR), which has been successfully implemented, which can be used as an example for other countries.

2) *Ethical aspects*: the application of AI in ethics-related education needs to be considered in depth. This ethical aspect is also related to transparency in decision-making and the development of non-discriminatory algorithms. Research, according to Adams et al. (2023), has shown that ethics in the use of AI is useful to prevent losses and injustices for students, so it must be prioritized.

3) *Educator training*: the use of AI in the world of education has not been carried out optimally. This can be seen from the fact that adequate training is needed to be more optimal, both for teachers and students. The training provided can be in the form of an introduction to the features of the AI used, the correct procedure for using AI and how to integrate the sophistication of AI tools with learning methods. With an effective training program, this will increase the mastery of AI technology

and improve skills in using AI tools ethically. This enables AI to enhance its own utilization (Rai and Lata 2024).

4) *Multidisciplinary collaboration*: for the optimal use of AI to be carried out, collaboration from different disciplines and areas of expertise, including stakeholders consisting of educators, education service providers, technology providers, AI researchers and developers, government policymakers and students, is needed. This collaboration will support the creation of smarter and responsible use of AI technology and ensure that the AI solutions developed truly meet the needs of education and can be implemented sustainably.

5) *Evaluation and monitoring*: the application of AI in education requires regular evaluation and monitoring. This aims to ensure that the use of AI is carried out effectively. This monitoring can be in the form of learning effectiveness, accessibility, improving teacher efficiency, data quality and privacy, student learning quality, user satisfaction, curriculum adaptation and infrastructure availability.

2.7. Conclusion

The use of AI from various aspects of the world of education and the analysis of its impact on the education system have been widely explored. AI technology can adapt learning approaches by utilizing data, thereby increasing the effectiveness of students involved in the learning process. In evaluation and assessment, AI offers efficient feedback that can be provided in real time to monitor student progress, thus helping teachers identify and address learning difficulties in a more timely manner. However, despite the various conveniences that can be obtained, the adoption of AI in educational practices also has challenges, especially with respect to ethical and privacy issues. Ethics and privacy in the use of AI are useful for protecting students' data so that students can use AI optimally with maintained privacy. Other challenges related to inequality in access to technology make the digital gap in accessibility an issue that can exacerbate educational inequality. In the future, AI is expected to continue to develop even more to have a positive impact on the world of education. The existence of predictions for future trends indicates that AI can synergize when integrated with the right curriculum and learning strategies so that it can open up opportunities for innovation and improve the overall quality of education. Therefore, stakeholders in the world of education must continue to monitor the development of AI and prepare policies that support the effective and ethical application of this technology.

2.8. References

Adams, C., Pente, P., Lemermeyer, G., Rockwell, G. (2023). Ethical principles for artificial intelligence in K-12 education. *Computers and Education: Artificial Intelligence*, 4, 100131. doi: 10.1016/j.caeai.2023.100131.

Adiguzel, T. (2023). Revolutionizing education with AI: Exploring the transformative potential of ChatGPT. *Contemporary Educational Technology*, 15(3), 1–13.

Akgun, S. and Greenhow, C. (2022). Artificial intelligence in education: Addressing ethical challenges in K-12 settings. *AI and Ethics*, 2(3), 431–440. doi: 10.1007/s43681-021-00096-7.

Alhitmi, H.K., Mardiah, A., Al-Sulaiti, K.I., Abbas, J. (2024). Data security and privacy concerns of AI-driven marketing in the context of economics and business field: An exploration into possible solutions. *Cogent Business & Management*, 11(1). doi: 10.1080/23311975.2024.2393743.

Bhardwaj, A. and Kumar, V. (2022). Web and social media approach to marketing of engineering courses in India. *International Journal of Business Innovation and Research*, 27(4), 541–555.

Bhardwaj, A. and Kumar, V. (2024). Challenges in online collaboration to augment Industry 4.0. *International Journal of Technology, Policy and Management*, 24(1), 71–92.

Bhutoria, A. (2022). Personalized education and artificial intelligence in the United States, China, and India: A systematic review using a human-in-the-loop model. *Computers and Education: Artificial Intelligence*, 3, 100068. doi: 10.1016/j.caeai.2022.100068.

Celik, I. (2023). Towards Intelligent-TPACK: An empirical study on teachers' professional knowledge to ethically integrate artificial intelligence (AI)-based tools into education. *Computers in Human Behavior*, 138, 107468. doi: 10.1016/j.chb.2022.107468.

Chassignol, M., Khoroshavin, A., Klimova, A., Bilyatdinova, A. (2018). Artificial intelligence trends in education: A narrative overview. *Procedia Computer Science*, 136, 16–24. doi: 10.1016/j.procs.2018.08.233.

Chen, Y., Jensen, S., Albert, L. J., Gupta, S., Lee, T. (2023). Artificial intelligence (AI) student assistants in the classroom: Designing chatbots to support student success. *Information Systems Frontiers*, 25(1), 161–182. doi: 10.1007/s10796-022-10291-4.

Deng, X. and Yu, Z. (2023). A meta-analysis and systematic review of the effect of chatbot technology use in sustainable education. *Sustainability*, 15(4). doi: 10.3390/su15042940.

Dwivedi, Y.K., Hughes, L., Ismagilova, E., Aarts, G., Coombs, C., Crick, T., Duan, Y., Dwivedi, R., Edwards, J., Eirug, A. et al. (2021). Artificial intelligence (AI): Multidisciplinary perspectives on emerging challenges, opportunities, and agenda for research, practice and policy. *International Journal of Information Management*, 57, 101994. doi: 10.1016/j.ijinfomgt.2019.08.002.

Gligorea, I., Cioca, M., Oancea, R., Gorski, A.T., Gorski, H., Tudorache, P. (2023). Adaptive learning using artificial intelligence in e-learning: A literature review. *Education Sciences*, 13(12). doi: 10.3390/educsci13121216.

Hwang, G.-J., Xie, H., Wah, B.W., Gašević, D. (2020). Vision, challenges, roles and research issues of artificial intelligence in education. *Computers and Education: Artificial Intelligence*, 1, 100001. doi: 10.1016/j.caeai.2020.100001.

Jiang, Y., Li, X., Luo, H., Yin, S., Kaynak, O. (2022). Quo vadis artificial intelligence? *Discover Artificial Intelligence*, 2(1), 4. doi: 10.1007/s44163-022-00022-8.

Kumar, V. and Lata, M. (eds) (2022). *The Future of E-Commerce*. Nova Science Publishers, New York. doi: 10.52305/KMUB3774.

Kumar, V. and Nanda, P. (2024). Social media and micro-lessons: A new paradigm of online learning. In *Optimizing Education Through Micro-Lessons: Engaging and Adaptive Learning Strategies*, Ilic, P. (ed.). IGI Global, New York.

Kumar, V. and Rewari, M. (2022). A responsible approach to higher education curriculum design. *International Journal of Educational Reform*, 31(4), 422–441.

Lata, M. and Kumar, V. (2022). Fog computing infrastructure for smart city applications. In *Recent Advancements in ICT Infrastructure and Applications*, Chaturvedi, M., Patel, P., Yadav, R. (eds). Springer, Singapore.

Lata, M. and Kumar, V. (2024). A framework for security of public cloud environment. *International Journal of Electronic Security and Digital Forensics*, 16(4), 486–502.

Lata, M. and Sharma, V. (2024a). Cloud computing based blended learning: Quality assurance challenges. In *2024 International Conference on Communication, Computer Sciences and Engineering (IC3SE)*. IEEE, New York.

Lata, M. and Sharma, V. (2024b). Smart city environment management: Challenges and opportunities. *Grenze International Journal of Engineering & Technology (GIJET)*, 10(2), 2159–2166.

Lata, M., Kumar, V., Sharma, V. (2024). Cloud computing applications in online learning. *Grenze International Journal of Engineering & Technology (GIJET)*, 10(2), 408–411.

Leiden University (2024). AI in education [Online]. Available at: https://www.staff.universiteitleiden.nl/education/it-and-education/ai-in-education?utm_source=chatgpt.com.

Lombardi, M. (2023). Digital economy and digital divide. In *Global Handbook of Inequality*, Jodhka, S.S. and Rehbein, B. (eds). Springer, Berlin. doi: 10.1007/978-3-030-97417-6_48-1.

Luckin, R. and Holmes, W. (2016). *Intelligence Unleashed: An Argument for AI in Education*. UCL Knowledge Lab, London [Online]. Available at: https://www.pearson.com/content/dam/corporate/global/pearson-dot-com/files/innovation/Intelligence-Unleashed-Publication.pdf.

Luckin, R., Cukurova, M., Kent, C., du Boulay, B. (2022). Empowering educators to be AI-ready. *Computers and Education: Artificial Intelligence*, 3, 100076. doi: 10.1016/j.caeai.2022.100076.

Mena-Guacas, A.F. (2023). Collaborative learning and skill development for educational growth of artificial intelligence: A systematic review. *Contemporary Educational Technology*, 15(3), 1–17.

Nanda, P. and Kumar, V. (2023). Decision analytics for competitive advantage: Cases on using social media analytics. *International Journal of Technology, Policy and Management*, 23(4), 372–386.

Nanda, P. and Kumar, V. (2024). New generation technologies: Development vs. ethical challenges. *International Journal of Business Information Systems*, 46(3), 411–434.

Nayar, K.B. and Kumar, V. (2015). Benefits of cloud computing in education during disaster. In *Proceedings of the International Conference on Transformations in Engineering Education: ICTIEE 2014*. Springer, Delhi.

Owan, V.J., Abang, K.B., Idika, D.O., Etta, E.O., Bassey, B.A. (2023). Exploring the potential of artificial intelligence tools in educational measurement and assessment. *Eurasia Journal of Mathematics, Science and Technology Education*, 19(8), 1–15.

Owoc, M. L., Sawicka, A., Weichbroth, P. (2021). Artificial intelligence technologies in education: Benefits, challenges and strategies of implementation. In *IFIP International Workshop on Artificial Intelligence for Knowledge Management*. Springer International Publishing, Cham, 37–58. doi: 10.1007/978-3-030-85001-2_4.

Pedro, F., Subosa, M., Rivas, A., Valverde, P. (2019). Artificial intelligence in education: Challenges and opportunities for sustainable development. Working Paper, United Nations Educational, Scientific and Cultural Organization, 7 [Online]. Available at: https://unesdoc.unesco.org/ark:/48223/pf0000366994.

Rai, S., and Lata, M. (2024). Futuristic outlook of online learning: The postpandemic era. In *Technology-mediated Learning During the Pandemic*, Singh, J. and Kumar, V. (eds). Routledge, Delhi.

Somasundaram, M., Junaid, K.A.M., Mangadu, S. (2020). Artificial intelligence (AI) enabled intelligent quality management system (IQMS) for personalized learning path. *Procedia Computer Science*, 172, 438–442. doi: 10.1016/j.procs.2020.05.096.

Zawacki-Richter, O., Marín, V.I., Bond, M., Gouverneur, F. (2019). Systematic review of research on artificial intelligence applications in higher education – Where are the educators? *International Journal of Educational Technology in Higher Education*, 16(1), 39. doi: 10.1186/s41239-019-0171-0.

3

AI and Higher Education

This chapter provides insight into the role of artificial intelligence (AI) in higher education in the context of Industrial Revolution 4.0 and Education 4.0. AI has a transformative role in the education industry and has the ability to create new innovative methodologies for teaching, which contribute to attaining SDG 4 (quality education). With the support of organizations such as UNESCO, the challenges we face in integrating AI can be met. This chapter will emphasize the role of AI in the education industry by means of personalized learning and making administrative tasks simpler. Using generative AI tools will help the education industry help students more by providing tailored tuition, real-time feedback, career guidance and a personal touch. In addition, this chapter will also highlight the ethical concerns related to this topic. The reliability of these tools can increase, which may cause students to become increasingly creative. By using the theory, context, characteristics and methodology (TCCM) framework, this chapter will organize and analyze findings from various kinds of studies, and describes theories such as sociotechnical systems theory and paradox theory, which have been used to understand the impact of AI on higher education, along with its merits and demerits. This chapter suggests that there should be a balanced approach between using AI and the education system. It will emphasize the importance of critical thinking, focusing on students' intelligence and setting ethical standards for responsibly using AI. There must be a balanced, collaborative strategy to maximize the advantages in the higher education industry.

3.1. Introduction

In the era of the 4th Industrial Revolution, the need to upgrade the quality of education was advocated (World Economic Forum 2022). In this era, AI emerged as a crucial technology. Thus, it is proposed to accelerate the embrace of Education 4.0 via this technology and ensure that learners are equipped to flourish with it (Kumar and Rewari 2022). AI is able to bring an innovative change in teaching and learning methods, thereby addressing challenges in education and addressing Sustainable

Chapter written by Mandakini PARUTHI, Sonam RANI, Sailaja BOHARA, Gaurav GUPTA and Amitabh BHARGAVA.

Development Goal 4, that is, quality education (Kumar and Nanda 2024). UNESCO is also supportive of its member states in mobilizing the potential of defining technology in an attempt to achieve the Education 2030 Agenda, that is, ensuring the main principle of inclusive and equitable quality education. This agenda in turn promotes lifelong learning prospects for all individuals[1].

As there are several inequalities concerning easy access to information and research and a wide variety of cultural terminologies, UNESCO mandates a human-focused approach to AI. AI must reduce the technological gap between (and within) countries. Every individual must take advantage of this technological disruption and attain knowledge and innovation. In one of the Forbes Advisor Surveys conducted in October 2023, more than 50% of educators from the United States believed that AI exercises a positive effect on teaching and learning procedures. A study by Bhutani and Wadhwani (2018) revealed that schools, colleges and universities have integrated various AI-enabled intellectual, adaptive and customized learning systems, which have created a market worth US$ 6 billion in 2024. Therefore, the placement of AI in education has reshaped the foundations of the teaching and learning process (Lata and Sharma 2024a).

AI-driven tools need to be used as assistants for teaching, administration and research, allowing teachers to concentrate more on engaging students. AI also provides personalized student support in tutoring, facilitating administrative tasks, providing career guidance, etc. Appropriately embracing AI technology in higher education paves the way for critical thinking amongst the youth. These critical thinkers comprehending and working together with AI will surely lead to drastic changes in labor markets. The education system needs to be transformed to train young people in the future's technology-impelled economies. A human-focused approach is needed to successfully implement these emerging technologies in the education system.

3.2. Defining AI

AI focuses on developing intelligent machines and systems that are capable of quickly performing tasks, which typically require human intelligence. Generative AI (GenAI) is a term used to define a specific class of AI models that give rise to seemingly innovative output in the form of text, images, video or any other form (Ivanov et al. 2024). GenAI has long been on the market, but the launch of ChatGPT ignited the discussion threads among academic communities (Lata and Kumar 2022). As a result, researchers have become increasingly interested in the usefulness of GenAI applications in terms of student learning, knowledge and the education system at large.

1 See: https://www.unesco.org/sdg4education2030/en/sdg4.

3.3. Need for AI in higher education

1) *To bridge the student teacher gap*: it has been projected that an additional 44 million teachers are projected to achieve targets set by Sustainable Development Goal (SDG) 4 by 2030. There exists an acute global student–teacher ratio gap between developing and developed countries (World Economic Forum 2024). Experts believe that the need for teachers will continue to increase for reskilling, upskilling and continuous education owing to disruptions faced by global labor markets.

2) *Automation of redundant administrative work*: moreover, nowadays teachers are devoting their productive time to doing repetitive administrative work. These non-teaching administrative tasks affect teachers' work–life balance (Nayar and Kumar 2015). Here, AI can be used productively to automate and streamline administrative tasks. This will help in saving teachers' time, which they can use in engaging students deeply.

3) *Data-driven insights*: educational institutions can integrate AI technologies into students' assessments to gain real-time insights into students' learning patterns. This can further help in recognizing areas of strength and weakness. AI can also be used to predict if a student is about to fail in a course or wants to drop a course. In this case, accurate measures can be devised to address the problem beforehand.

4) *Meeting digital skill shortage*: at global and local levels, there exists a persistent shortage of digital skills and AI talent (Bhardwaj and Kumar 2024). As a digital skill shortage exists, the risk of involuntary job loss is present. Organizations automate the majority of tasks. To avoid this situation, the workforce needs to reskill and upskill in a number of skills that must include working with AI. The next-generation workforce needs ethical and safe producers, users of AI technologies.

3.4. Research methodology

A systematic literature review was conducted to examine the interconnections between financial inclusion, financial literacy, individual well-being, financial independence and the role of banks. Using the Scopus and Web of Science databases, the primary emphasis was placed on Scopus because of its broader subject coverage. In this context, Scopus yielded six times more relevant articles than Web of Science based on specified keywords. The Scopus search included terms such as "AI", "Artificial Intelligence", "Virtual Reality", "Higher Education" and "Education", initially producing 5,680 articles. The selection was refined by limiting the articles to peer-reviewed journal articles, excluding conference papers, and filtering for English-language publications within the domain of business and management (Kumar and Lata 2022). This filtering reduced the number of articles to 508. A further focus on top journals narrowed this to 233 articles. After excluding those studies that were conducted before 2018 and focused on the most cited papers after 2018 until 2023, 32 articles that specifically address AI and higher education were selected. The criterion of selecting the top cited journal was to focus more on the "A" category from ABDC.

To organize and analyze the data, the theory development, context, characteristics, and methodology (TCCM) framework was used to synthesize insights from the selected articles. An Excel spreadsheet was used to systematically categorize each article by author(s), title, publication year, source title, key findings, applied theories, contextual applications of AI, characteristics of AI and higher education and employed methodologies. This approach enabled a structured synthesis of the findings, supporting theory development and providing insights into AI and higher education within various contexts (Lata and Sharma 2024b).

Sr. No.	Author	Theory	Context	Characteristics/findings	Methodology
01	Lin et al. (2018)	Economic theories	Improving online education efficacy using AI	Enhanced engagement in asynchronous learning with AI-based interactions	Use of AI-based robotic players
02	Wogu et al. (2019)	Marxian alienation theory	AI in education and its impacts on traditional education processes	AI impacts critical thinking and diminishes teacher roles in education	Ex post facto method, deconstructive analysis
03	Malhotra et al. (2019)	Technological Innovation Systems (TIS)	Intersectoral learning in solar, wind, and battery sectors	Highlights sector-specific learning patterns and policy needs	Embedded mixed-method design, interviews with industry actors
04	Leahy et al. (2019)	Critical futures studies	Future educational spaces shaped by emerging technologies	Emphasizes flexibility and diversity in educational futures	Conceptual framework with six pillars, thematic analysis
05	Nuseir et al. (2020)	Resource-based theory, contingency theory	AI tools as the future in education	Shows positive impact of AI tools if used in the education sector	SEM-PLS for data analysis
06	Goralski and Tan (2020)	Sustainable development and AI	AI's role in achieving sustainable development goals (SDGs)	AI could accelerate or hinder SDGs depending on regulatory frameworks and ethical integration	Case studies on AI in different sectors, analysis of public policy

07	Liu et al. (2020)	AI and technological innovation	Impact of AI on technological innovation in Chinese manufacturing sectors	AI promotes innovation through knowledge creation and spillover, with sector-specific impacts	Empirical analysis with panel data, fixed and random effects regression
08	Qasim and Kharbat (2020)	Curriculum redesign for AI	Modernizing accounting curriculum with technology integration	Blockchain, AI and data analytics integration enhance curriculum relevance	Theoretical framework, curriculum redesign
09	Brunetti et al. (2020)	Multistakeholder digital transformation	Challenges and strategies in the Tyrol-Veneto macroregion	Three pillars (culture and skills, infrastructure, ecosystems) essential for regional digital transformation	Qualitative research, text mining and content analysis using IRaMuTeQ and NVivo
10	Javaid and Haleem (2020)	Industry 5.0 Framework	Development of industrial revolutions	Emphasizes safety, quality and waste reduction in manufacturing	Literature review of Industry 5.0 applications
11	Dwivedi et al. (2021)	Integrated framework for AI	AI's transformative potential across industries, challenges, and digital transformation	Highlights AI potential to impact the future for industries and society	Mixed methods, combining positivist and interpretive paradigms; Big Data for construct proxies
12	Gansser and Reich (2021)	UTAUT2 model	Acceptance factors for AI products across segments	Safety and security have varying influences in mobility, household, and health segments	Survey, confirmatory factor analysis
13	Damerji and Salimi (2021)	Diffusion of innovation (DIT)	AI adoption in accounting education	Technology readiness influences AI adoption, with mediation by perceived usefulness	Quantitative correlation design, online questionnaire
14	Hendershott et al. (2021)	Decision theory and game theory	Issues in FinTech including mobile payments and blockchain	Identifies significant tech impacts and FinTech opportunities	Regularized linear regression, feature selection using LASSO
15	Kolade and Owoseni (2022)	Sociotechnical systems	Impact of digital transformation on work dynamics	Highlights reskilling and upskilling needs in digital transformation	Systematic literature review, thematic analysis

16	Iskender (2023)	No specific theory	ChatGPT's impact on higher education	ChatGPT provides utility but risks diminishing critical thinking skills	Analysis of responses, interviews with ChatGPT
17	Javaid et al. (2023)	AI in education	ChatGPT applications in education	ChatGPT aids personalized learning, automates grading and enhances efficiency	Discussion of AI applications
18	Ratten and Jones (2023)	No specific theory	ChatGPT's role in management education	Emphasizes integration of ChatGPT into management education for creativity	Case study analysis, conceptual exploration
19	George and Wooden (2023)	Literature review methodology	Higher education institutions, particularly universities transitioning to "smart universities" that leverage AI for academic purposes	AI-driven LMSs for personalized learning, NLP for automated feedback, computer vision for emotional assessment, and AI for administrative automation	Systematic review, meta-analysis
20	Khogali and Mekid (2023)	Social ontology, Latané's social impact theory	Societal impact of AI advancements	Highlights societal risks and job loss due to automation	Hybrid narrative and thematic analysis
21	Halaweh (2023)	No specific theory	Examines ChatGPT concerns in education	ChatGPT can enhance learning but poses risks for academic honesty	Reflection notes for feedback
22	Lim et al. (2023)	Paradox theory	Generative AI in education, balancing benefits with ethical issues	Generative AI offers benefits and risks in education, requiring careful adoption to balance outcomes	Critical analysis with paradox theory lens

Table 3.1. *TCCM table (theory, context, characteristics and methodology)*

Theory

In this theoretical framework, researchers explored numerous studies that focus on the diverse ways in which AI can transform higher education and the adjacent areas.

Dwivedi et al. (2021) presented an integrated conceptual framework that highlights the potential of AI, which has led to vast changes in the policies and practices used for education and enhanced efficiency and decision making based on data. The approach suggested by Dwivedi et al. (2021) also aligns with that of Goralski and Tan (2020), who explore how AI supports attaining the United Nations' SDGs, but they also explore how strategic AI simultaneously drives policy and innovation and the public. Dwivedi et al. (2021) also highlighted the transformative capabilities of AI across various sectors and its significant role in boosting digital transformation. This integrated framework digs into the potential of AI to transform various sectors, such as business operations and various industries, such as health, education, manufacturing, tourism, and cosmetics, and pinnacles its capacity to improve efficiency, accuracy, productivity and innovations. Nevertheless, as this AI system brings a lot of benefits to various areas, this framework highlights the cons which come along with the adoption of AI such as, most importantly, ethical concerns, technological limitations, breach of data privacy; and to control all of this, we need relevant regulatory policies (Lata and Kumar 2021). Notable attention is given to the significance of cultural and country-specific factors, which play pivotal roles in the adoption of AI and its impact on culture and societies. For example, in the case of developing countries, these highly techno-advanced AI solutions are not easily accepted or adopted, as infrastructure, political factors and regulatory policies and readiness at the social level are lacking (Nanda and Kumar 2024).

This study uses mixed methodology, as it considers positivist and descriptive paradigms. This framework is used to measure the adoption rate by quantitative data and sociocultural impact by AI by qualitative data. Additionally, for other constructs, such as market readiness, the rate of adoption of innovation and its impact on industry are measured by the help of Big Data analytics.

This framework serves as a guiding pathway for researchers, policymakers and business leaders to work on the implementation of innovation strategies involving AI for socioeconomic and cultural development. This framework considers all those factors that are important for AI adoption and for its effective implementation so that it minimizes the heedless negative repercussions. "Unlikeness", a theory explored by Lim et al. (2023), explores the challenges and dualities in adopting AI in the education sector. This theory is useful for understanding how to balance between risk and benefits by understanding the way organizations and systems manage competing demands.

In the context of generative AI, this theory shifts the focus to key areas such as how AI has revolutionized education by enabling instant content creation and strengthening accessibility as well as personalized learning experiences.

Despite the numerous benefits of implementing the AI in education and other sectors, this theory also highlights the challenges that accompany ethical concerns, such as high chances of data privacy breaching, over dependence on technology, and dangerous moves that are more likely to destroy critical thinking ability among students, as they become attracted to easier approaches (Lata and Kumar 2024).

Paradox theory suggests that we should follow the balanced approach between the adoption of AI in education and its readiness solution with short-term technological advancements and consequences for long-term implications. For example, as AI has no benefits and enhances learning outcomes, it is also important to pay attention to challenges such as misinformation and equitable access. With this methodology, a researcher can explore both sides of the coin with the help of paradox theory and identify the challenges and solutions in implementing AI in sectors. By considering all issues, paradox theory provides a blueprint for AI adoption with minimum challenges in education institutions, policy makers and technology developers. With respect to AI integration into various sectors, both theories make significant contributions. Paradox theory provides an in-depth analysis of how to manage competing demands, specifically in fields such as education. However, an integrated framework for AI pays attention to socioeconomic and cultural factors and the impact of AI adoption on them. Both studies highlight and make a significant contribution to AI adoption and its revolutionary capabilities. Lim et al. (2023) adopted paradox theory that emphasizes the dual role approach of AI, which benefits the sector by expanding access facilities and disrupting the critical thinking ability of students. Socio–technical system theory was explored by Kolade and Owoseni (2022) and addresses the issue of job challenges and how AI impacts jobs and workforce potential, and demands the new skill set in response to digital transformation. This theory incorporates two theories, social ontology and Latané social impact theory, to explore the impact of AI on societal implications. Social ontology theory pays attention to how structure and norms are influenced by advanced technological innovations, whereas Latané social impact theory examines how group and individual behavior can be influenced by the presence and actions of another person.

This chapter incorporates social ontology and Latané's social impact theory to analyze the social consequences of advancements in AI. Social ontology is concerned with the reality of the social world and how it works in conjunction with technological advancements. On the other hand, Latané's social impact theory looks at how individuals and groups behave and make decisions based on the presence of others. When used in relation to AI, these frameworks help in understanding how societies and individuals work in conjunction with AI. Note that there is the problem of increasing unemployment due to automation as a result of the integration of AI. For example, the manufacturing and customer service sectors are changing dramatically because people are being replaced by machines and software. This has several consequences for the economy, the social structure and the well-being of people. The current research applies a mixed method approach that includes a narrative and a thematic analysis. This approach incorporates storytelling into the research process along with a systematic analysis of themes to capture a rich understanding of the social response to AI (Rai and Lata 2024). The findings revealed that while AI results in increased efficiency and new products and services, it also exacerbates socioeconomic inequalities, raises ethical questions and requires new forms of regulation to address negative impacts. In other words, this research demonstrates that AI is a double-edged sword that offers opportunities as well as threats to society, hence highlighting the need for proactive management of the impacts it has on societies and individuals. Here, the diffusion of innovation theory by Damerji and Salimi (2021) is used to analyze the adoption of AI in accounting education to show how technological readiness and perceived ease of use affect adoption. Damerji and Salimi (2021) used diffusion of innovation theory (DIT) to determine the adoption of AI in accounting education with the help of technology readiness and perceived usefulness. In the work of Everett Rogers, DIT is a theory that seeks to explain how innovations are adopted and diffused within a particular system over a period of time with the help of five attributes: relative advantage, compatibility, complexity, trialability and observability. According to DIT, innovations are adopted by individuals or organizations in different stages, such as knowledge, persuasion, decision, implementation and confirmation. In the context of accounting education, DIT is used to determine how educators perceive AI tools and make decisions on whether to use them in their teaching practice. The work also reveals that technology readiness, which is the readiness of educators and institutions to accept new technologies, has a great impact on AI adoption. This readiness is mediated by the perceived usefulness of AI, which can be defined as educators' perceptions that AI tools have the potential to improve teaching and learning processes (Lata et al. 2024). For example, AI can take over monotonous task paths, such as those for students, thus grading and offering tailored benefits for learning in accounting programs. The current study employs a quantitative correlational design that uses technologically advanced online questionnaires and collects positive data perceptions to analyze these beneficial relationships. The AI results indicate that to adopt institutions, DIT concepts such as trialability or the ability to test drive AI tools before fully embracing them, and observability or the extent to which the effects of AI on learning outcomes can play a crucial role in the adoption process, are likely. This research can be useful to academic institutions and policy makers, as it reveals that there is a need to enhance the technological infrastructure, educate educators on the use of the system and prove how it will benefit the learners for it to be well embraced in accounting education. Adopting DIT, this work presents a systematic way of encouraging innovation in education. Nuseir et al. (2020) used resource-based contingency theories to analyze how AI technology can be useful in optimizing resources and addressing particular issues in global supply chains. In their work, Nuseir et al. (2020) applied resource-based theory (RBT) and contingency theory to analyze how global supply chains adopt and implement new technologies. Thus, the integrated approach enhances the understanding of the contextual factors that affect technology adoption and performance in volatile conditions and a competitive environment. According to the Resource-Based theory, an organization's capacity to utilize special resources and capabilities that are valuable, rare, inimitable, and non-substitutable (VRIN framework) determines its competitive advantage. According to the report, entrepreneurial skills like creativity, flexibility, and strategic decision-making are vital assets that support the uptake of cutting-edge technologies such as automation, blockchain, and AI-driven analytics in the context of global supply chains. Businesses that successfully use these competencies will be in a better position to improve supply chain resilience, cut expenses, and streamline processes. Companies can leverage their core competencies to optimize operations and enhance supply chain robustness while reducing costs. Contingency theory, which posits that there is no single best way to organize, provides a framework for understanding how organizational success depends on aligning technology adoption with the operating environment. This study highlights that global supply chains operate in diverse and volatile environments, requiring companies to adapt their strategies to accommodate differences in market dynamics, cultural factors, and legal standards. For instance, a technology that can successfully be applied in a developed market may need some adjustments to be implemented in the emerging market. The work also reveals that the adoption of technology in supply chains has a positive effect on an organization's performance, whereby efficiency, customer satisfaction and competitive advantage are enhanced. They claim that organizations need to nurture entrepreneurial competencies such as risk-taking and proactiveness to manage the difficulties of implementing technological advancements within the supply chain management process. Hendershott et al. (2021) used decision assessment theory and game theory challenges and prospects that exist in the FinTech and sector blockchain. With an emphasis on theories, mobile money is an analytical approach to how decisions are made, especially in organizations and individuals' choices in situations that are competitive, complex and uncertain, such as the FinTech environment.

Decision theory is used to analyze how business and consumer choices are made with respect to Fintech products and services, for example, the adoption of mobile money and the use of blockchain for secure transactions (Hendershott et al. 2021). This aids in understanding how contextual factors such as risk and convenience affect users' decision making and how such factors affect the uptake of FinTech solutions. Decision theory (Hendershott et al. 2021) is a game theory that is used to simulate competition between FinTechs, traditional financial institutions and other new players in the digital economy. It looks at how these entities are able to come up with market share, partnership or even react to changes in legislation. For example, FinTech companies set prices strategically and introduce new products to capture customers while banks can decide to partner with or introduce new technologies. Methodologically, the study applies various statistical analyses, including regularized linear regression and feature selection, such as least absolute shrinkage and selection operator (LASSO), to analyze the most important technological and market determinants of FinTechs. According to generational theory, people's values, behaviors and preferences are influenced by the time and society in which they were born and brought up. This theory can then be applied to AI-enabled service-resistant robots according to our age, allowing us to visualize the cultural patterns. An acceptance study employs the statistical analysis using t-test or ANOVA (Analysis of Variance) to compare the user perceptions. Businesses and legislators hoping to encourage the use of service robots will greatly benefit from the insights this study provides. It is possible to increase acceptability and promote a more seamless integration of robotics into daily life by developing tactics that are specifically tailored to the needs of various generational and cultural groups. Wogu et al. (2019) investigated the effects of artificial intelligence (AI) on conventional educational procedures by using Marxian alienation theory. The idea, which has its roots in Karl Marx's critique of capitalism, explains how people might become estranged from their jobs, their communities, and even their own identities when confronted with technical or industrial systems. This theory offers a critical lens through which to analyze how AI can upend conventional roles and procedures in the educational field. Artificial intelligence (AI) can be applied to transform various aspects of the education system, enhancing conventional teaching roles and the teacher–student relationship. The use of AI-enabled tools includes intelligent tutoring systems, automated grading resources, and personalized learning platforms. While these technologies offer the potential to improve performance and individualization, they also have the potential to drive educators and learners away from the humanistic values of learning. Key findings are critical, as researchers claim that the use of AI in education leads to a reduction in students' ability to think critically. Prepackaged solutions and automated learning pathways that the AI offers may lead to students disengaging with the content or not being able to work on their problem-solving skills. The role of teachers as teachers, counselors and the main source of information is gradually being invaded by AI systems. This shift has also affected the job security of educators as well as personal interactions and guidance, which are crucial to the learning process. The study uses Marxian alienation theory, and these developments are discussed in terms of alienation. It applies Marxian alienation theory to frame these developments as a form of alienation: 1) *alienation from the process*: the teachers may develop a feeling of isolation from the teaching process since most of the responsibilities, such as lesson plan development and assessment, are handled by AI systems; 2) *alienation from the product*: the students may thus feel isolated from their learning achievements that they are receiving from the AI-based education system because the latter focuses on achieving standard and standardized results rather than creative and individualized results; 3) *alienation from social interaction*: this is because AI can also lead to the reduced use of collaborative learning and peer interactions, thus worsening the social aspect of learning. This study applies Marxian alienation theory to frame these developments as a form of alienation. Thus, these frameworks depict the complex influences of AI as a tool that stimulates development, improves performance and solves problems in the fields of education and industry.

Context

AI applications are used in all sectors, including healthcare and education (Bhardwaj and Kumar 2022). AI has allowed personalized and efficient grading to students by using tools such as ChatGPT, indicating the growing trend of integrating AI in higher education (Javaid and Haleem 2020). In a regional setting, Brunetti et al. (2020) examined AI's role in the Tyrol-Veneto macroregion, a moderately innovative area spanning parts of Italy and Austria. The work found that those whose technological infrastructure is less, needed to collaborate with different stakeholders to obtain good technological infrastructure for advanced digital transformation.

Iskender (2023) and Halaweh (2023) have discussed the various roles in higher education, such as grading manually, and manual feedback can also be removed. They discussed academic integrity and student privacy. Other studies, such as Kolade and Owoseni (2022), focused on the changes that AI is creating in traditional employment, as it has impacted the workforce in organizations. Other studies also suggest the role of AI in changing education management systems and engagement strategies for businesses. All of the above concepts have demonstrated the versatility and capability of AI in reshaping these industries.

Characteristics

In their investigations, the properties of AI are examined, and they offer both distinctive benefits and threats, which means that AI is equally a solution and a problem in various fields. According to Dwivedi et al. (2021) and Liu et al. (2020), AI can replace human labor in repetitive jobs, optimize processes and create new ideas that show AI's importance in various sectors, including education and manufacturing. Lim et al. (2023) investigated the characteristics of generative AI, which operates as an enabler and a constraint in higher education, indicating that it increases the ability to access education, especially if it is self-taught and curriculum, but it also creates risks of becoming over-reliant on trained data and limits a person's analytical ability. Halaweh (2023) and Iskender (2023) tend to go a step further in explaining these challenges by focusing on the role of AI in diminishing students' inventiveness and dependence on automated methods of accomplishing tasks that would otherwise need human judgment. Kolade and Owoseni (2022) and Goralski and Tan (2020) are examples of research that incorporate AI into a socioeconomic framework, which considers the opportunities and threats that AI presents to the labor market.

In the context of digital transformation, AI has largely improved the process of ensuring efficiency but has also raised important ethical issues related to data privacy, the loss of jobs and increased automation.

Methods

There are diverse methods across various disciplines showing the adaptability of AI in various sectors. Dwivedi et al. (2021) used a mixed approach in which positivist paradigms and interpretive paradigms were used to analyze the social and policy challenges posed by AI, thus enabling the exploration of such issues in depth and breadth. Liu et al. (2020) gauged AI's influence on technological innovation in several sectors by applying econometric models, particularly fixed and random effects regressions. This quantitative approach is supplemented with qualitative analyses, as was done by Brunetti et al. (2020), wherein NVivo software was used for content and text mining to harvest insights from stakeholder interviews regarding digital transformation processes in the Tyrol-Veneto region. Lim et al. (2023) adopted the approach of critical analysis based on paradox theory, which emphasizes the theoretical tension between AI's capabilities and constraints in educational contexts. Damerji and Salimi (2021) applied hierarchical regression to data collected from online questionnaires to determine how technology is adopted in education, especially with respect to perceived ease of use and perceived usefulness. Ratten and Jones (2023) employed case study and thematic analysis approaches, respectively, to explore the role of AI in enhancing management education and increasing supply chain operational efficiency. The experimental approach was displayed by Lin et al. (2018), wherein applications of AI and robotics were simulated in economic gaming and energy system analyses, respectively, offering insight into how AI is adopted in interactive and predictive tasks. The choice of methodologies, thus, together hints at the importance of a blend of qualitative and quantitative analyses in determining the complicated roles that AI assumes and its contextual impact, as it pertains to higher education versus other industries.

3.5. Discussion

The integration of AI in higher education reflects a transformative evolution driven by technological advancements and educational demands, as highlighted by various studies. Damerji and Salimi (2021) adopted DIT to analyze the adoption of AI in accounting education, whereas technology readiness and perceived usefulness play a critical role in determining acceptance. Technology preparedness refers to educators' readiness to use AI tools, including adaptive learning systems and automated grading software, which eases administrative burdens and facilitates personalization. Perceived usefulness is the mediator, as educators make decisions concerning AI to the extent to which it helps them streamline their process. Lim et al. (2023) discussed the application of paradox theory, showing those cases where AI has increased efficiency and accessibility; in addition, it has created a new threat in which there is too much dependency on AI applications, resulting in a loss of creativity. Kolade and Owoseni (2022) applied sociotechnical systems theory by highlighting the socioeconomic impacts of AI, such as the skilling of workforces and increasing demand for digital competencies to counter the job.

According to Brunetti et al. (2020), to implement successful AI integration, help is required from all stakeholders, as more resources are needed. Through this approach, only AI integration can be aligned with local technology needs. To integrate AI, we must ensure that cultural factors, institutional capacities and infrastructure can be distributed fairly (Javaid and Haleem 2020). There are many ethical concerns related to the use of AI. AI integration comes with the risk of data security, which is a cause of concern, and there are many other risks. For example, there is huge data on AI, such as ChatGPT, and any question or information that we require is given by it. This has undermined people's mindset creatively and critically. Policymakers need to address the regulatory gap and ensure that AI integration in education aligns with educational goals (Dwivedi et al. 2021).

3.6. Implications

The effects of integrating AI into higher education are far reaching in educational policy, pedagogy and organizational practice. As pointed out by Halaweh (2023) and Iskender (2023), the formulation of well-defined ethical principles is crucial for maintaining academic integrity, data privacy and equity. Some of the areas in which these guidelines should generatively consider AI include tools and how ethical they are to use to avoid dependency on the tools and process. Ensuring that AI enhances the ability of policymakers, they should also traditionally embrace teaching to consider other education and other policies that fields cut (Dwivedi et al. 2021). Solutions for AI include scalable technology that may be used by institutions and businesses, as well as helping governments address issues that have been identified in certain studies and problems (Brunetti et al. 2020). Additionally, AI implementation is not only a technological issue but also requires cooperation between educators and technological people. Collaborations between educators and technology experts can drive the development of adaptive AI solutions, enabling educational systems and related fields to better respond to evolving learning needs and challenges. In student healthcare experience, education (Javaid and Haleem 2020) shows how AI cannot only increase productivity but also address inequalities in areas where services lack access to possible proper healthcare and higher education systems.

The findings also reveal that professional development programs are crucial for educators to be fully ready to incorporate AI tools effectively. Studies by Lim et al. (2023) and Damerji and Salimi (2021) revealed that equipping educators with digital skills will help in reducing the fear of AI adoption and also in creating a positive team environment for teaching. For example, training programs that focus on the application of AI in customized tests or predictive analysis can assist educators in improving student achievement while upholding ethical standards. Using AI in the learning process also provides the possibility of solving other problems, such as the problems of workforce development and digital literacy. As Kolade and Owoseni (2022) maintain, the new socioeconomic context of the AI age requires attention to upskilling programs because of the growing technological content of the labor market. Thus, by teaching students to critically engage with AI technologies, institutions prepare them to enter workplaces that are increasingly dependent on digital skills. Finally, the development of plans for the equitable use of technologies remains important. Brunetti et al. (2020) and Lim et al. (2023) demonstrated the existence of a digital divide by region and therefore called for policies that can ensure equity in the use of AI. Underserved communities should be encouraged to develop their digital capacity through investments in infrastructure and digital resources to close the digital divide and provide access to learning opportunities.

3.7. Conclusion

Teachers assist in teaching, while AI supports the delivery of higher education and its individualized function in colleges. AI is transforming higher education by enabling personalized learning, streamlining administrative tasks, and enhancing student engagement. Studies reveal that when AI is effectively integrated into educational institutions, it can significantly improve students' learning outcomes and participation. However, the adoption of AI, particularly generative AI, raises ethical concerns related to academic integrity, data privacy, and the potential reduction in students' critical thinking and creativity. By applying theoretical frameworks such as socio–technical systems theory and paradox theory, this chapter highlights the complexities and contradictions of AI integration in education, emphasizing the need for a balanced approach to address these challenges while advancing educational innovation.

The further success of AI integration in higher education will depend on the ability of higher education institutions to develop a collaborative environment that is based on both human and technological interaction. To develop an AI-enhanced approach to learning, it is important that educators, administrators and policy makers work together to foster learning that is inclusive of critical thinking and responsible use of technology, and to prepare students for a future that will demand technological literacy. Through the development of strong policies, the formation of strategic partnerships and the encouragement of ethical AI use, higher education can leverage the use of AI to enhance traditional learning to the benefit of students and faculty.

3.8. References

Bhardwaj, A. and Kumar, V. (2022). Web and social media approach to marketing of engineering courses in India. *International Journal of Business Innovation and Research*, 27(4), 541–555.

Bhardwaj, A. and Kumar, V. (2024). Challenges in online collaboration to augment Industry 4.0. *International Journal of Technology, Policy and Management*, 24(1), 71–92.

Bhutani, A. and Wadhwani, P. (2018). Artificial intelligence (AI) in education market size by model (Learner, Pedagogical, Domain). Report.

Brunetti, F., Matt, D.T., Bonfanti, A., De Longhi, A., Pedrini, G., Orzes, G. (2020). Digital transformation challenges: Strategies emerging from a multi-stakeholder approach. *The TQM Journal*, 32(4), 697–724.

Damerji, H. and Salimi, A. (2021). Mediating effect of use perceptions on technology readiness and adoption of artificial intelligence in accounting. *Accounting Education*, 30(2), 107–130.

Dwivedi, Y.K., Hughes, L., Ismagilova, E., Aarts, G., Coombs, C., Crick, T., Williams, M.D. (2021). Artificial Intelligence (AI): Multidisciplinary perspectives on emerging challenges, opportunities, and agenda for research, practice and policy. *International Journal of Information Management*, 57, 101994.

Gansser, O.A. and Reich, C.S. (2021). A new acceptance model for artificial intelligence with extensions to UTAUT2: An empirical study in three segments of application. *Technology in Society*, 65, 101535. doi: 10.1016/j.techsoc.2021.101535.

George, B. and Wooden, O. (2023). Managing the strategic transformation of higher education through artificial intelligence. *Administrative Sciences*, 13(9), 196.

Goralski, M.A. and Tan, T.K. (2020). Artificial intelligence and sustainable development. *The International Journal of Management Education*, 18(1), 100330. doi: 10.1016/j.ijme.2019.100330.

Halaweh, M. (2023). ChatGPT in education: Strategies for responsible implementation. *Contemporary Educational Technology*, 15(2), 421.

Hendershott, T., Zhang, X., Zhao, J.L., Zheng, Z. (2021). FinTech as a game changer: Overview of research frontiers. *Information Systems Research*, 32(1), 1–17. doi: 10.1287/isre.2021.0997.

Iskender, A. (2023). Holy or unholy? Interview with Open AI's ChatGPT. *European Journal of Tourism Research*, 34, 3414. doi: 10.54055/ejtr.v34i.3169.

Ivanov, D., Guo, Z., Shen, B., Chang, Q.C. (2024). Analysis, optimization, and collaboration in digital manufacturing and supply chain systems. *International Journal of Production Economics*, 269, 109130.

Javaid, M. and Haleem, A. (2020). Critical components of Industry 5.0 towards a successful adoption in the field of manufacturing. *Journal of Industrial Integration and Management*, 5(3), 327–348. doi: 10.1142/s2424862220500141.

Javaid, M., Haleem, A., Singh, R.P., Khan, S., Khan, I.H. (2023). Unlocking the opportunities through ChatGPT tool towards ameliorating the education system. *BenchCouncil Transactions on Benchmarks Standards and Evaluations*, 3(2), 100115. doi: 10.1016/j.tbench.2023.100115.

Khogali, H.O. and Mekid, S. (2023). The blended future of automation and AI: Examining some long-term societal and ethical impact features. *Technology in Society*, 73, 102232.

Kolade, O. and Owoseni, A. (2022). Employment 5.0: The work of the future and the future of work. *Technology in Society*, 71, 102086.

Kumar, V. and Lata, M. (eds) (2022). *The Future of E-Commerce*. Nova Science Publishers, New York. doi: 10.52305/KMUB3774.

Kumar, V. and Nanda, P. (2024). Social media and micro-lessons: A new paradigm of online learning. In *Optimizing Education Through Micro-Lessons: Engaging and Adaptive Learning Strategies*, Ilic, P. (ed.). IGI Global, New York.

Kumar, V. and Rewari, M. (2022). A responsible approach to higher education curriculum design. *International Journal of Educational Reform*, 31(4), 422–441.

Lata, M. and Kumar, V. (2021). Smart energy management in green cities. In *Handbook of Green Engineering Technologies for Sustainable Smart Cities*, Saravanan, K. and Sakthinathan, G. (eds). CRC Press, Boca Raton.

Lata, M. and Kumar, V. (2022). Fog computing infrastructure for smart city applications. In *Recent Advancements in ICT Infrastructure and Applications*, Chaturvedi, M., Patel, P., Yadav, R. (eds). Springer, Singapore.

Lata, M. and Kumar, V. (2024). A framework for security of public cloud environment. *International Journal of Electronic Security and Digital Forensics*, 16(4), 486–502.

Lata, M. and Sharma, V. (2024a). Cloud computing based blended learning: Quality assurance challenges. In *2024 International Conference on Communication, Computer Sciences and Engineering (IC3SE)*. IEEE, New York.

Lata, M. and Sharma, V. (2024b). Smart city environment management: Challenges and opportunities. *Grenze International Journal of Engineering & Technology (GIJET)*, 10(2), 2159–2166.

Lata, M., Kumar, V., Sharma, V. (2024). Cloud computing applications in online learning. *Grenze International Journal of Engineering & Technology (GIJET)*, 10(2), 408–411.

Leahy, S.M., Holland, C., Ward, F. (2019). The digital frontier: Envisioning future technologies' impact on the classroom. *Higher Education Research & Development*, 38(5), 1068–1082. doi: 10.1080/07294360.2019.1604161.

Lim, W.M., Gunasekara, A., Pallant, J.L., Pallant, J.I., Pechenkina, E. (2023). Generative AI and the future of education: Ragnarök or reformation? A paradoxical perspective from management educators. *The International Journal of Management Education*, 21(2), 100790.

Lin, P.-H., Wooders, A., Wang, J.T.-Y., Yuan, W.M. (2018). Artificial intelligence, the missing piece of online education? *IEEE Engineering Management Review*, 46(3), 25–28. doi: 10.1109/emr.2018.2868068.

Lin, P.-H., Wooders, A., Wang, J.T.-Y., Yuan, W.M. (2020). Integration of AI in online education platforms. *Computers & Education*, 21(1), 156.

Liu, J., Chang, H., Forrest, J.Y.-L., Yang, B. (2020). Influence of artificial intelligence on technological innovation: Evidence from the panel data of China's manufacturing sectors. *Technological Forecasting and Social Change*, 158, 120142. doi: 10.1016/j.techfore.2020.120142.

Malhotra, A., Schmidt, T.S., Huenteler, J. (2019). The role of inter-sectoral learning in knowledge development and diffusion: Case studies on three clean energy technologies. *Technological Forecasting & Social Change*, 146, 464–487.

Nanda, P. and Kumar, V. (2024). New generation technologies: Development vs. ethical challenges. *International Journal of Business Information Systems*, 46(3), 411–434.

Nayar, K.B. and Kumar, V. (2015). Benefits of cloud computing in education during disaster. In *Proceedings of the International Conference on Transformations in Engineering Education: ICTIEE 2014*, Hubli.

Nuseir, M.T. and Aljumah, A. (2020). The role of digital marketing in business performance with the moderating effect of environment factors among SMEs of UAE. *International Journal of Innovation, Creativity and Change*, 11, 310–324.

Qasim, A. and Kharbat, F.F. (2020). Blockchain technology, business data analytics, and artificial intelligence: Use in the accounting profession and ideas for inclusion into the accounting curriculum. *Journal of Emerging Technologies in Accounting*, 17(1), 107–117.

Rai, S. and Lata, M. (2024). Futuristic outlook of online learning: The post-pandemic era. In *Technology-mediated Learning During the Pandemic*, Singh, J. and Kumar, V. (eds). Routledge, Delhi, 173–187.

Ratten, V. and Jones, P. (2023). Generative artificial intelligence (AI): Implications for management educators. *The International Journal of Management Education*, 21(3), 100857.

Vincent-Lancrin, S. and van der Vlies, R. (2020). Trustworthy artificial intelligence (AI) in education: Promises and challenges. OECD Education Working Paper No. 218, Paris.

Wogu, N.I.a.P., Misra, S., Assibong, P.A., Olu-Owolabi, E.F., Maskeliūnas, R., Damasevicius, R. (2019). Artificial intelligence, smart classrooms and online education in the 21st century. *Journal of Cases on Information Technology*, 21(3), 66–79. doi: 10.4018/jcit.2019070105.

World Economic Forum (2022). Catalysing Education 4.0: Investing in the future of learning for a human-centric recovery [Online]. Available at: https://www3.weforum.org/docs/WEF_Catalysing_Education_4.0_2022.pdf.

World Economic Forum (2024). Shaping the future of learning: The role of AI in Education 4.0 [Online]. Available at: https://www3.weforum.org/docs/WEF_Shaping_the_Future_of_Learning_2024.pdf.

4

Chatbot Technologies in Digital Entrepreneurship Education for Adults

This chapter focuses on integrating technology-enhanced learning and chatbot technologies in adult education, addressing the teaching of digital entrepreneurship. The study was carried out under the framework of the Erasmus+ project "Chatbot Technologies for Digital Entrepreneurship Education of Adult Learners" (CHAT2LEARN), which has successfully concluded. The project aimed to raise awareness among adult educators, teachers, tutors and training professionals about teaching digital entrepreneurship using chatbot-based technologies to enrich the educational landscape. The chapter presents the development and implementation of chatbot technology, aiming to improve self-learning in digital entrepreneurship through interaction with chatbot technologies. It provides educators and trainers with innovative methodologies and tools to effectively integrate new technological environments into their educational frameworks.

4.1. Introduction

The contemporary era of digital technology has profoundly integrated into daily life, influencing both the personal and professional spheres (Nanda and Kumar 2024). From virtual assistants such as Siri and Alexa to immersive 3D and 4D experiences, technological advancements are reshaping how people, particularly younger generations and entrepreneurs, interact with information and learning tools. This shift underscores a growing reliance on computer programs, mobile applications and ICT tools in various domains, such as banking, hospitality and education. Despite varying levels of digital skills across Europe, the demand for digital knowledge professionals is increasing, driven by trends such as online commerce and platform-based labor (Kumar and Lata 2022). These dynamics pose new challenges

Chapter written by Thomas FOTIADIS, Ioanna THEOPHILOU, Evangelia VANEZI, Christos METTOURIS and George Angelos PAPADOPOULOS.

and opportunities for educators and training professionals, necessitating innovative approaches to adult learning and skills development (Agarwal and Wadhwa 2020; Teja 2020; Chen et al. 2021).

Entrepreneurship education is essential for equipping individuals with the skills and knowledge necessary to succeed in an increasingly digital and innovation-driven economy. For example, CHAT2LEARN advocates the use of innovative learning methods, including AI-driven chatbot technology, in adult education, which enhances digital entrepreneurship. This approach not only promotes opportunities for self-directed learning but also prepares adult learners, educators and small businesses to address modern challenges by utilizing technology and innovative solutions (Lata and Kumar 2022). Furthermore, it encourages economic growth, adaptability and the development of a skilled workforce capable of driving innovation across various industries.

The chatbot developed operates with a predefined set of questions and answers designed specifically for educational purposes (Kumar and Nanda 2024). Regardless of user interaction, the system ensures that the information presented is accurate and relevant to the user's input. As noted by Kalla et al. (2023), generative models may introduce bias because they are trained on large datasets to establish relationships between words or sentences. The current chatbot presents learning modules that consist of preestablished content. These modules and materials are created by professionals and academically recognized individuals, ensuring that the information remains unaltered (Lata and Sharma 2024a).

The current research sets the stage for exploring the intersection of technology-enhanced self-learning and digital entrepreneurship, introducing the integration of chatbot technology (Lata et al. 2024). It focuses on developing and implementing innovative chatbot technologies for educators and trainers to adapt effectively and utilize them to enhance their learning experiences in the field of digital entrepreneurship (Kalla et al. 2023).

4.2. Literature review

The term "chatbot" refers to a computer program designed to provide services through dialogue (Copulsky 2019; Teja 2020). The history of chatbots dates back to the 1960s, with the creation of the first technological assistant named ELIZA in 1966 by Joseph Weizenbaum. ELIZA could recognize certain keywords and respond accordingly, mimicking a conversation with a person.

Early chatbots relied primarily on keyword matching mechanisms (Atlas 2023) or natural language processing techniques (Hsieh 2011; Moriuchi et al. 2021; Kalla et al. 2023). They were simpler and relied on keywords or preset scenarios to mimic human speech. For example, if a client said, "I want to start a new job in sales", the bot would recognize keywords such as "job" and "sales", and suggest suitable positions (if it was a recruitment bot), available courses on sales (if it was a learning bot), or guide the conversation to gather more details about the client's goals. Since 2000, more advanced chatbots have been developed, utilizing natural language processing to "understand" human speech and respond accordingly. These modern chatbots possess their own personalities, can analyze complex requests and perform a variety of tasks, making them smarter and often indistinguishable from humans (Rai and Lata 2024). Owing to machine learning algorithms, these chatbots can interact with clients, learn their needs and preferences, and offer tailored solutions to their problems (Moriuchi et al. 2021).

Typically, chatbots:

– target specific use cases or provide services to end users;

– use natural language to perform tasks or provide services;

– focus on answering certain types of questions and engaging users in conversations;

– are easier and more intuitive than many mobile and desktop applications, which often require navigation through screens, menus and tabs.

When a chatbot reaches a point where it is unable to provide a suitable reply, it usually either redirects the interaction to a domain it can handle or hands it over to a human who can provide the necessary information or support. Chatbots serve various functions, including chatting, entertainment, data query, task execution, answering questions and dialogue exercises (Hsieh 2011). For example, chatbots can function as agents to gather information from conversations to complete form-filling tasks such as booking air tickets or purchasing goods (Copulsky 2019). Muniasamy and Alasiry (2020) analyzed quality attributes from 32 papers and 10 articles, categorizing chatbot technologies based on similarity. They observed that these attributes align with the ISO 9241 concept of usability, encompassing the following:

– *effectiveness*: accuracy and completeness with which users achieve their goals (e.g. performance);

– *efficiency*: optimal use of resources to achieve these goals, including functionality and user-friendliness;

– *satisfaction*: this includes affect, ethics, behavior and accessibility.

Scalability and usability are critical factors influencing the user experience with chatbot technologies. Scalability pertains to the chatbot's ability to manage increasing amounts of users, interactions and content, whereas usability concerns whether users can effectively perform desired tasks with the chatbot (Weizenbaum 1966). Chatbot developers must anticipate all possible inputs in advance. Limited capacity for generalization means that chatbots may fail to function properly if the user input deviates from predefined patterns (Teja 2020). However, once trained, chatbots can generalize from new messages, allowing users to send messages that do not precisely match those in the knowledge base. Chatbots understand the conversation context through flows in the knowledge base, determining actions based on probabilities tied to recorded intentions (Agarwal and Wadhwa 2020; Lai 2020).

Several reviews on chatbot-related research have been conducted (Bhardwaj and Kumar 2022). For example, Lai (2020) focused on the use of chatbots in mental health, healthcare, clinical psychology, psychotherapy and education. Particularly after the COVID-19 pandemic, the integration of chatbot technologies in education has become pronounced, contributing significantly to enhanced self-learning concepts (Weizenbaum 1966; Andrade-Arenas et al. 2024).

In educational contexts, chatbots have been employed in both formal and informal learning environments to analyze learner conversations and provide interactive learning content and feedback (Muniasamy and Alasiry 2020; Chen et al. 2021; Kumar and Rewari 2023). Research indicates that chatbot interactions increase students' learning interest, spurring the development of educational chatbots (Copulsky 2019; Muniasamy and Alasiry 2020; Melián-González et al. 2021). Examples include chatbots used to train university students in negotiation skills, promote academically productive talk in multimedia courses and act as virtual patients to train nursing students' communication skills. However, some studies note limitations, such as a reduced interest in chatbots compared with peer interactions over time (Weizenbaum 1966; Chen et al. 2021). Educational chatbots hold significant potential for enhancing entrepreneurship education by providing interactive, personalized learning experiences that foster practical skills essential for entrepreneurial success (Lata and Sharma 2024b). These tools simulate real-world business scenarios, offering opportunities for decision-making and problem-solving. By delivering tailored feedback and guidance, educational chatbots enhance self-learning and develop critical thinking and adaptability, bridging the gap between theoretical knowledge and practical application (Weizenbaum 1966; Bond et al. 2023).

Chatbots provide students with a personalized, interactive learning experience that fosters creativity, critical thinking and problem-solving skills. Furthermore, according to Chen et al. (2021), these technologies aid in the development of entrepreneurial skills in the following ways:

– *Visionary thinking/opportunity recognition*: chatbots can be trained to offer information and insights into new opportunities, emerging technologies and current trends. Students benefit from developing a forward-thinking mindset as a result.

– *Creativity and innovation*: chatbots inspire students to think creatively and develop new ideas by providing tailored challenges and prompts.

– *Leadership and team management*: students can improve their leadership and management abilities by using chatbots to mimic real-life situations that call for leadership and decision-making.

– *Financial management*: chatbots can provide advice on efficient resource management, such as time management plans, financial planning and team management methods.

– *Adaptability and resilience*: chatbots assist students in developing adaptability by simulating situations that call for flexibility. They can also set personalized challenges and goals that nurture resilience.

The development of networking skills can be facilitated by the use of chatbots to link students with educators and business professionals. Furthermore, they provide feedback on communication abilities, helping students articulate their ideas and thoughts effectively. Entrepreneurs engaging in entrepreneurship education and initiating ventures can reduce unemployment rates and spur economic growth through innovative ideas, products, services and technologies. Despite advancements in generative chatbot technologies, their current state has not yet reached the level of replacing tasks performed by experienced educators (Shepherd and Majchrzak 2022; Kalla et al. 2023). This is especially true in entrepreneurship education, where educators seldom incorporate educational technologies into teaching and administrative practices (Obschonka and Audretsch 2020).

While the integration of chatbots into entrepreneurship is evident, there is a significant lag in the development of comprehensive theoretical frameworks to guide future practices (Kumar and Rewari 2022). Scholars and practitioners are keen to explore the potential of chatbot technologies in entrepreneurship. Early-stage research on AI in entrepreneurship has appeared in entrepreneurial journals (Chen and Devina 2021; Bond et al. 2023), but reviews addressing chatbot technologies in entrepreneurship education remain scarce (Copulsky 2019).

This chapter focuses on integrating technology-enhanced learning and chatbot technologies in adult education, particularly in teaching digital entrepreneurship. Its goal is to develop and promote chatbot environments in digital entrepreneurship, equipping adult educators and training professionals with technologies to integrate learning environments into educational practices.

4.3. Development of a chatbot learning environment

The chatbot learning environment was created using state-of-the-art web technologies. The development was based on the open-source content management system (CMS) WordPress, supplemented by various freely available plugins, such as the Ultimate Member for user management, which were configured to meet the specific needs of the chatbot learning environment. In addition to the WordPress platform, custom plugins were developed to provide the necessary functionality for the chatbot learning environment, incorporating several features tailored for both teachers and learners.

The developed chatbot tool was made publicly accessible online, offering free and open usage to both educators and learners. It included a variety of precreated integrated learning modules, lessons and quizzes for learners while also allowing teachers to create, incorporate and manage their own modules, as well as monitor their progress. The precreated learning modules were designed and developed by educational experts from the project partners' teams. New modules were designed by teachers, who were considered reliable individuals, ensuring that the content remained relevant and appropriate for the educational environment (Lata and Kumar 2024). To attain teacher status, individuals were required to submit a request to the platform's administration team, which had the discretion to approve or deny such requests. All the modules were made universally accessible to students in six different languages: Greek, Bulgarian, Spanish, Dutch, Italian and English.

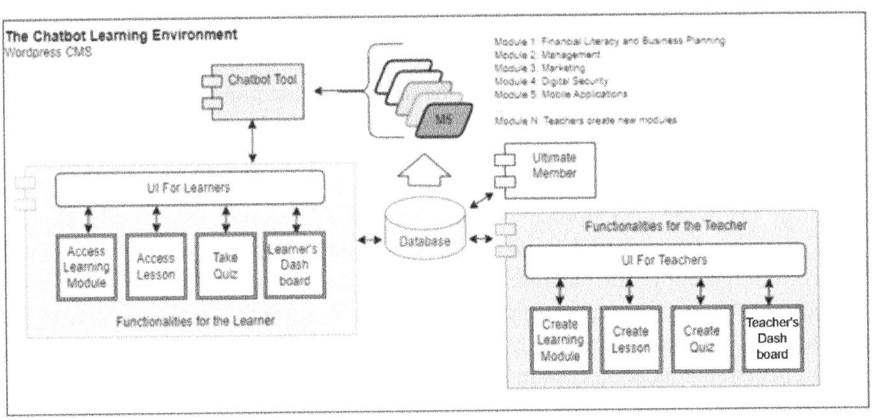

Figure 4.1. *The system architecture of the chatbot learning environment (figure created by the author). For a color version of this figure, see www.iste.co.uk/kumar/chatbots.zip*

Figure 4.1 illustrates the system architecture of the chatbot learning environment. The functionalities of the teacher plugin enabled the teachers to create learning modules, lessons and quizzes, which were stored in the database. Through the dashboard, teachers had access to these resources and could view or update them. The modules were then fed into the chatbot tool, which facilitated the learners' functionalities plugin. In the remainder of this section, all functionalities are presented in detail.

4.3.1. *Teachers*

Learning modules and lesson creation: teachers who wanted to prepare content for new learning modules initially completed a specific template, as outlined in the previous section. Once the learning module was set up in the template, it followed specific steps to add the module to the chatbot. Teachers first selected the "For teachers" menu option (Figure 4.2) and then chose "Add new module", where they provided a title for the new educational module.

To create lessons within the module, the teachers clicked on the "Add new lesson" option (Figure 4.2) and provided titles for each lesson. With the title set, they began crafting the lesson content, which consisted of a sequence of information blocks, as previously described. To add lesson information blocks, teachers selected the specific lesson and clicked "Add new". They then entered the text for all the information blocks and submitted it to proceed to the next step.

Upon submission, each question or information block received a unique code, which was essential for establishing connections between blocks within the chatbot. Teachers designated which information block would initially appear in the chatbot and linked each block to the subsequent one based on responses, following the template but utilizing the platform's unique codes.

Quiz creation: similar to content preparation, teachers first completed the template with their quizzes. To create a quiz in the chatbot environment, they navigated to a lesson and clicked on the "Quiz" option to create a quiz for that specific lesson. By selecting "Add new row", teachers were able to add quiz questions and complete the text areas with the corresponding questions. Possible responses to a question were added by clicking on "Edit", and feedback for each answer could also be provided. Additionally, teachers created overall quizzes for entire modules in the same manner (Figure 4.3).

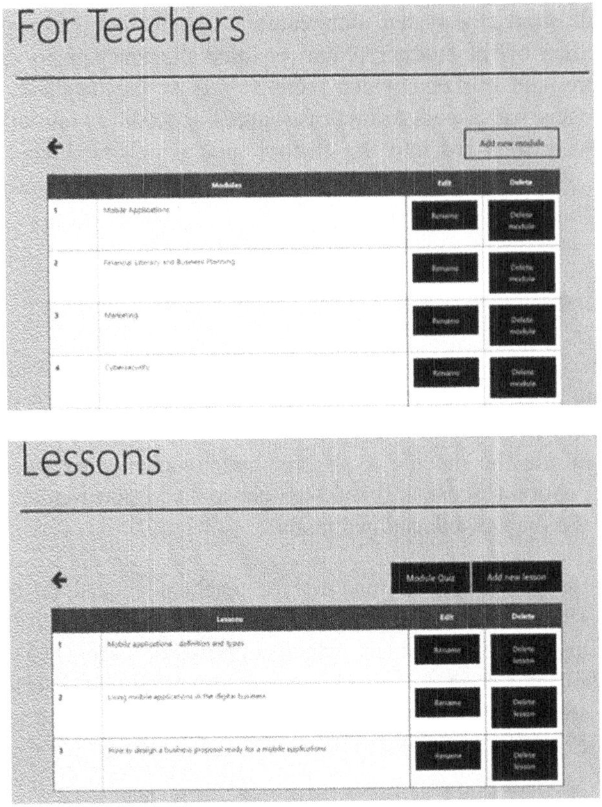

Figure 4.2. *"For teachers" – teachers can add or edit their modules*

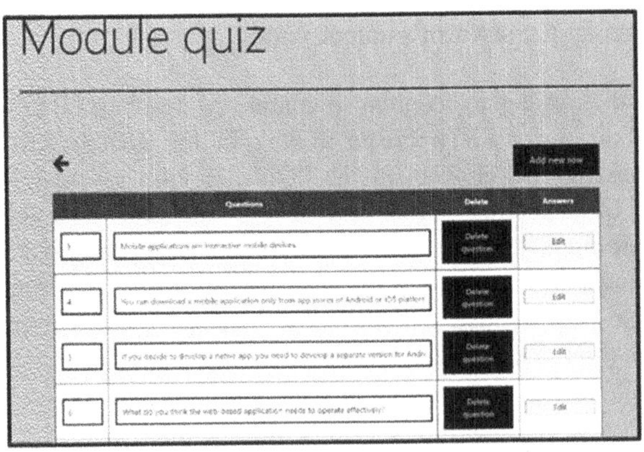

Figure 4.3. *Adding content to the module quiz*

Teacher's dashboard: teachers had access to a "Teacher's dashboard", where they were able to view and manage all of their added modules and module lessons. This dashboard provided detailed insights, including the number of learners who had taken each quiz, the number of learners who had passed each quiz and the specific question that had the most errors. Teachers could also edit their modules through the current interface.

4.3.2. *Learners*

The "For learners" menu option directed learners to the chatbot tool interface, as shown in Figure 4.3. In this interface, learners were able to access all available learning modules and lessons and take quizzes. The chatbot dynamically retrieved all the information from the "For teachers" database, presenting the information blocks in the sequence established by the teachers in the form of a dialogue between the chatbot and the learner. Learners can interact with four different types of information blocks within the chatbot:

a) *Multiple choice questions*: each question provided up to four possible answers, with each answer leading to a different path.

b) *Yes/no questions*: responses of "yes" or "no" directed learners to different subsequent information blocks.

c) *Informational blocks*: these blocks contained messages for learners to read without requiring a response.

d) *Continue blocks*: learners had to click "continue" to proceed with the lesson.

An example of such interactions is illustrated in Figure 4.4.

The chatbot also tracked learners' progress. Learners had to complete a lesson before they could access the lesson's quiz. Once a lesson was complete, the quiz became available for the learner to take at any time. Similarly, learners needed to finish all three lessons within a module before they could view and take the module's quiz. However, the learners had the flexibility to retake the lessons as many times as they wished.

Learner's dashboard: learners had access to a "Learner's dashboard", which displayed all the learning modules and module lessons, indicating whether each had been successfully completed by the learner. Upon completing a module, learners became eligible to receive a certificate.

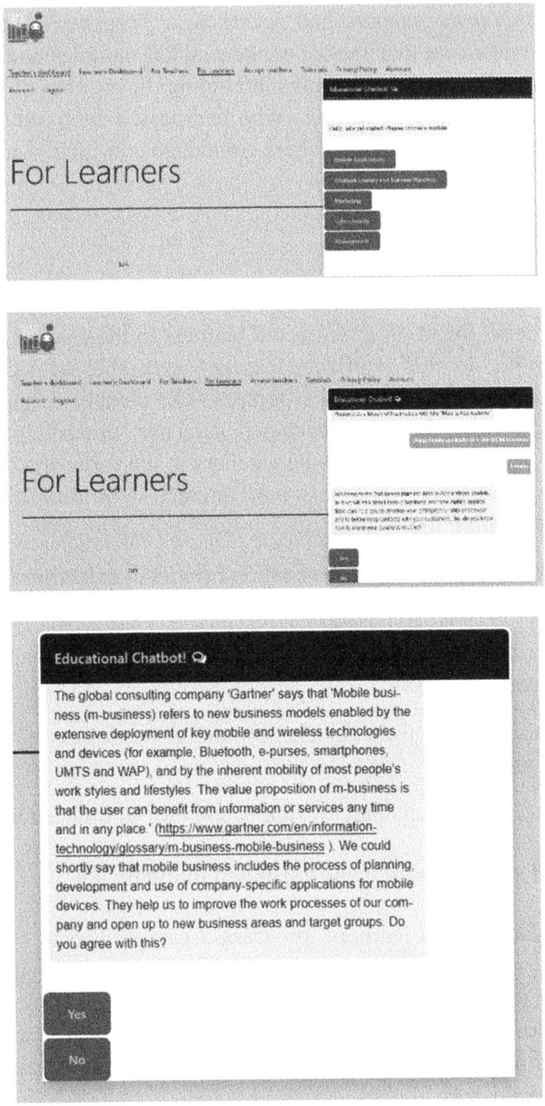

Figure 4.4. *Chatbot interaction with the learner*

4.3.3. *Multilingual*

Modules could be added in six different languages: Greek, Bulgarian, Spanish, Dutch, Italian and English. These languages were selected to accommodate the diverse linguistic backgrounds of the project's partners and target audience. Both the learners and the teachers were able to select their preferred language in their account settings. Once teachers selected a language, all their modules were created and linked to that language. Learners saw all available modules in their chosen language within the chatbot, enhancing accessibility and facilitating a better learning experience for users from various regions.

4.3.4. *Learning modules*

Modules	Lessons
Digital security	Managing digital security and privacy risk
	Digital security into business products and processes
	Cybersecurity for the digital transformation
Financial literacy and business planning	Personal financial management
	Principles of efficient budgeting, savings and investing
	Principles of effective business planning; CANVA model
Management	Leadership and motivation in small and medium enterprises
	Employment issues: overcoming gender bias in the workplace
	Conflict and stress management
Marketing	Customers: are they all the same? How to understand their needs and the "personas"
	Satisfy the customer? Good question! Think about suitable products and services and prices
	Where do I find customers? Market analysis, distribution channels and promotional tools
Mobile applications	Mobile applications – definition and types
	Using mobile applications in the digital business
	How to design a business proposal ready for a mobile application

Table 4.1. *Three lessons per module*

As mentioned above, the chatbot-based learning environment comprised five learning modules that covered various aspects of digital entrepreneurship. Each module included materials and learning scenarios specifically tailored for the chatbot environment. The topics encompassed the basic knowledge and skills necessary for individuals to effectively manage their digital entrepreneurship, which were as follows:

Module 1: Financial literacy and business planning.

Module 2: Management.

Module 3: Marketing.

Module 4: Digital security.

Module 5: Mobile applications.

Each module contained three lessons on the respective topic, a list of additional readings and self-assessment tests. Table 4.1 shows the chatbot lessons per module.

The modules, lessons and quizzes were specifically designed and developed for the chatbot learning environment within the context of the CHAT2LEARN project by educational experts from the project partners' teams. Four types of information blocks were defined to establish different forms of user interaction. These various blocks responded to distinct types of user interactions, as mentioned. Table 4.2 presents the four types of information blocks.

	Block type	**Description**
1	Yes/no question block	The Yes/No question block replicates "TRUE"/"FALSE" questions. The user has only two possible options to select from.
2	Multiple choice question block	The multiple choice question block has four possible choices at a maximum for the user.
3	Continue block	The continue block is an informational block that requires user interaction (pressing "CONTINUE") to confirm that they have understood and want to proceed forward.
4	Informative block	The informative block acts similarly to the "CONTINUE" block but requires no user interaction. The informative block just appears and the next question follows automatically.

Table 4.2. *Description of the information blocks*

4.3.5. *Courses content and quizzes*

In each module, pertinent bibliographic resources were reviewed to develop lesson content, information and quiz questions. General guidelines for content development were established and adhered to throughout the process.

Learning content: regarding the lesson content, Figure 4.4 illustrates the template that was created and utilized for developing the learning modules. Different information blocks were placed in separate rows within the template table, each linked to the others to comprise the module, which included a sequence of questions, continuations, and informative blocks forming the dialogue scenarios between the chatbot and the learners. In each row, or information block, the initial column of the table denoted the unique identifier (an increasing number) for each information block. The second column delineated the prompt that was presented by the chatbot to the learner at that point, whereas the subsequent four columns mapped to the choices (if any) provided by the chatbot along with each prompt. Each of these choices was linked to another information block via the unique identifiers corresponding to it. If the user selected a specific choice, they were redirected to the linked information block next. Depending on the type of information block, not all columns required completion. Multiple-choice questions could feature up to four potential answers, each directing a distinct information block. In contrast, the "YES/NO" questions necessitated only two responses, whereas the "continue" and "informative" types required only one option to be filled.

No.	Questions	Choice 1	Choice 2	Choice 3	Choice 4	Type
1	To start our topic of 'Digital Security as a Technical Problem', let's make sure that you know some basic principles. **Do you know what the CIA principles triad is?**	2 Yes	4 No			Yes/No
2	Great! Check your understanding by guessing which of the following statements is false: a) Confidentiality principle states that information is not made available or disclosed to unauthorized individuals, systems, or processes. b) Integrity principle states that data or information has not been changed, destroyed, destructed or in any way modified or lost in an unauthorized or accidental manner. c) Availability principle states that everything should be available for everyone.	3 Option: a	3 Option: b	5 Option: c		Multiple Choice

Figure 4.5. *The structure of the lessons*

Quizzes: the preparation of quizzes followed a consistent methodology that involved two distinct template tables for each quiz. The initial table, depicted in Figure 4.5, comprised three columns: the first for question numbering, the second for the actual questions and the third indicating the correct answer number, which served as a linkage to the subsequent table (Figure 4.5). The second table detailed the possible responses for each question. It consisted of three columns: the first for sequential numbering, the second listing each potential response option and the third providing feedback intended for presentation to the user upon selecting the correct answer.

Quiz

1	What is **NOT** an example of a web application attack? 1. Phishing 2. DoS 3. CIA Principles 4. Identity Theft 5. All the above	5
2	Is the following statement correct? Confidentiality principle states that information is not made available or disclosed to unauthorised individuals, systems, or processes.	6
3	What is a Worm in Digital Security? a) A type of virus that needs human initiation b) A type of virus that does not need human initiation c) A malicious software that gains access to unauthorised access to the computer system A large collection of compromised hosts that can be controlled by an attacker	9
4	Is Identity Theft a web attack? a) True b) False	11

1	1)	1	The correct answer is CIA principles.
2	2)	1	The correct answer is CIA principles.
3	3)	1	The correct answer is CIA principles.
4	4)	1	The correct answer is CIA principles.
5	5)	1	Very Good! All the CIA principles are NOT considered web application attacks.
6	True	2	True indeed. Confidentiality principle states that information is not made available or disclosed to unauthorised individuals, systems, or processes.
7	False	2	The statement is correct. Confidentiality principle states that information is not made available or disclosed to unauthorised individuals, systems, or processes.
8	A	3	The correct answer was b.
9	B	3	True, a worm is a type of virus but with the basic difference that it has the ability to spread automatically without human initiation
10	C	3	The correct answer was b.
11	True	4	Correct. Identity theft is a special case of data breach. It is an attack aiming to obtain confidential information that can be used to identify a person or even a computer system.

Figure 4.6. *Quiz template: tables 1 and 2*

4.4. Methodology

4.4.1. *Post-design phase and pilot implementation*

After developing the chatbot environment and learning modules, as well as incorporating feedback from project partners, several suggestions and adjustments were made. This preparatory phase was succeeded by the initiation of the pilot study, during which both quantitative and qualitative data were collected.

4.4.2. *Pilot study*

The methodology was implemented through a pilot study procedure to test and evaluate the interaction with the chatbot learning environment, including learning modules created by the five partners of the project: Cyprus, Bulgaria, the Netherlands, Italy and Spain. After the interaction with the chatbot environment, the participants from the five countries provided feedback answering an online evaluation form.

4.4.3. *Target group*

The target groups were adult educators interested in testing the chatbot for use in their classes; high school teachers who organize entrepreneurial training courses for their students, teachers and heads of vocational training bodies; business consultants; adult learners who want to improve their entrepreneurship skills and competences; small and microsized business entrepreneurs; social entrepreneurs; relevant public bodies; other stakeholders in the field of adult education; entrepreneurship; digital technologies; etc.

4.4.4. *Procedure*

Beginning the pilot study procedure, participants from the partner countries were contacted via email with all the appropriate information regarding the procedure, a detailed description of the pilot process, deadlines, links to tutorials and the evaluation form. Some participants were also contacted in person or via phone. The participants from each country were asked to test at least one assigned module. In total, 100 participants from five countries (20 participants per country) tested the chatbot, ensuring that each module was tested by at least 20 learners. The modules were translated into each partner's language.

Subsequently, the testing phase commenced with an online briefing session involving all participants, providing details regarding the pilot study's objectives and aims. Following the briefing session, the participants were introduced to the chatbot technology to familiarize themselves with its functionalities before independently interacting with it. After that meeting, the participants started working by themselves. The pilot study was conducted over a duration of 6 months.

4.5. Results

4.5.1. *Quantitative data*

The participants evaluated their interaction with the chatbot on a scale from 1 to 5, with 1 being the lowest and 5 being the highest, see Tables 4.3 and 4.4.

In summary, the chatbot environment received an above-average rating of 3.58 out of 5 points. The color choice was rated the lowest, whereas the clarity of the project results received the highest rating.

Chatbot Environment	Spain	Italy	Cyprus Bulgaria Netherlands	Average score for the five countries
Design (elements, layout, placement of objects, etc.)	3.35	2.65	4.568	3.52
Colors (of the background, fonts, images, logos, etc., and how they match together)	3.34	2.45	4.56	3.47
Ease to use/easy to navigate	3.2	2.85	4.68	3.58
Relevance of images to the concepts described	3.6	2.2	4.65	3.48
Clear project results	3.5	3.35	4.74	3.85

Table 4.3. *Evaluation of the chatbot interface*

Modules	Module 1	Module 2	Module 3	Module 4	Module 5
The module is relevant to my needs	3.83	3.74	3.83	4.29	3.98
The information of the module is sufficient	4.05	3.92	4.09	4.11	3.99
The information of the module is of high quality	3.82	4.03	4.14	4.16	4.08
The module is clear and concise	3.98	3.96	3.12	4.01	4.14
In my opinion this module could be easily transferred into practice	3.96	3.8	4.02	3.95	3.96

Table 4.4. *Evaluation of the chatbot content*

The pilot phase yielded a positive outcome, with participants providing constructive feedback. They mentioned that the chatbot environment and its modules performed above average, with an average rating of 3.58 out of 5 points. While the content of the modules received higher ratings than the chatbot environment itself, none of the components achieved an “excellent” rating.

4.5.2. *Qualitative data*

The outcomes of the qualitative research study revealed significant insights into interactions and learning experiences with chatbot technology. A recurring theme in the feedback was the relevance and quality of the educational content presented across various modules. The participants largely praised the high standard of the material, noting its strong applicability to real-world scenarios, which significantly enhanced their learning experiences.

The survey findings primarily highlighted the effectiveness of chatbot technologies as educational tools, the provision of essential informational resources and the overall improvement in the learning experience for users. However, educators emphasized the irreplaceable role they play as human instructors in the educational process, a role that cannot be replicated by chatbots.

Moreover, the participants expressed a strong need for greater flexibility and adaptability in the content. They advocated for the creation of personalized learning pathways that would allow them to navigate through different levels of complexity at their own pace, catering to their individual learning styles and needs. This approach recognizes the diverse abilities and preferences of each learner, promoting a more tailored educational experience.

The key recommendations that emerged from the analysis included the following:

– *Visual enrichment*: integrating a more diverse assortment of visual elements, such as images, graphs, and diagrams, into the content is essential. This multifaceted visual approach not only enhances the esthetic appeal of the material but also facilitates a deeper understanding of various topics, making the overall learning experience more engaging.

– *Simplification of content*: some users expressed concerns about the presentation of the content, noting that it was unappealing and did not encourage engagement or study. Suggestions for improvement included better segmentation, the use of bullet points and increasing the spacing between sections to create a more visually attractive learning environment.

– *Implementation of an autoscroll feature*: a frequently mentioned suggestion was the addition of an autoscroll option, which would enhance the flow of interactions with the chatbot and help learners focus more on the presented content.

– *Navigation*: navigation through the learning modules has also emerged as a significant concern. The participants reported frustration with having to return to the main menu when switching lessons and expressed a desire for a more seamless navigation system that would facilitate smooth transitions between topics, thereby helping them maintain momentum and focus.

From a technical perspective, several areas were noted for needed improvements, such as accelerating information delivery to enhance the overall user experience, ensuring a stable chatbot interface – especially when users encounter errors – and verifying the functionality of embedded links. Clearer guidelines were also highlighted as essential improvements to enrich the learning experience.

Despite the obstacles faced, the feedback collected from users was predominantly positive, with many praising the platform's intuitive and easy-to-navigate interface. Furthermore, users appreciated its educational value, noting how its features and content could significantly enhance the learning experience. This suggests that the platform holds considerable promise for achieving effective learning outcomes.

4.6. Discussion

The integration of chatbot technologies into adult education, especially in the realm of digital entrepreneurship, marks a considerable improvement in the development and provision of educational experiences. This chapter examines the technical components required to build an educational chatbot specifically designed for adult learners and summarizes the findings from a comprehensive pilot study carried out in five European countries. The goal of this research was to assess the effectiveness of the learning modules delivered through chatbots while also collecting valuable feedback from the participants.

The CHAT2LEARN project represents a significant transition toward incorporating technological advancements that cater to the varied and changing learning needs of students. The participants involved in the pilot study highlighted a key advantage of the program: the high standard and relevance of the material offered by the chatbot. The modules were thoughtfully crafted to encompass vital topics essential for those entering the realm of digital entrepreneurship, such as financial literacy, management techniques, marketing strategies, digital security protocols and mobile app development skills. The feedback revealed that adult learners perceived the content as engaging and directly applicable to the real-world challenges they encounter in their careers. This strong endorsement reinforces the effectiveness of the chatbot framework in providing substantial educational benefits that are both practical and pertinent.

The participants conveyed favorable opinions about the quality of the content, but they also offered recommendations for enhancing the chatbot interface.

Numerous users wanted a more attractive visual design, improved intuitiveness and greater flexibility in how they navigate their learning paths. These insights highlight the importance of aligning technological advancements with the principles of user-centered design. By achieving this alignment, educational institutions can improve learning results and foster a more engaging and fulfilling experience for adult learners.

Participants exhibited a nuanced and insightful perception of the relationship between chatbots and human educators within the educational realm. They recognized the important function of chatbots in enhancing learning and reinforcing key concepts; however, they also stressed that the richness and depth of human interaction cannot be replaced in regard to delivering a comprehensive and well-rounded educational experience. This understanding underscores the essential need to create blended learning models that carefully combine advanced technological tools, such as chatbots, with traditional teaching approaches.

These blended strategies hold the promise of addressing various learning preferences, promoting maximum learner engagement and ensuring that all students enjoy a deeply enriching educational experience. The insights gained from the CHAT2LEARN project illuminate both the thrilling prospects and the significant challenges tied to the incorporation of chatbot technology in adult education. By focusing on the relevance of content, addressing user experience challenges and acknowledging the critical importance of human educators, this initiative aims to pave the way for more effective and engaging educational methodologies, especially in the evolving arena of digital entrepreneurship.

4.7. Conclusion

The current research presents a groundbreaking initiative that effectively integrates chatbot technology with adult education, specifically within the field of digital entrepreneurship. The overwhelmingly positive feedback from participants underscores the chatbot's ability to greatly enhance learning experiences, although users have indicated that certain elements need refinement. Moving forward, continually refining this project by utilizing these insights to fully realize the potential of chatbots in educational environments is crucial. Given the swift advancement of digital technologies, research efforts such as this one provide a foundation for significant shifts in teaching practices, aligning them with the needs of the digital era.

The results of the study indicate that the chatbot-based learning environment created for digital entrepreneurship was generally well received by participants from five different countries. On average, attendees rated the initiative a solid 3.58 out of

5, reflecting their overall contentment. The modules focusing on essential aspects of digital entrepreneurship – such as financial literacy, management principles, marketing strategies, digital security issues and mobile app development – were especially praised for their high quality and relevance to current demands.

Nevertheless, while participants valued the content of the modules, they believed that the overall experience within the chatbot framework did not achieve an "excellent" rating. They acknowledged the engagement level and practical usefulness of the material but emphasized that chatbots cannot entirely substitute for the nuanced guidance provided by human instructors. Recommendations for enhancement included the incorporation of visual elements such as images and infographics to aid comprehension, enhancing the platform's usability for a more intuitive navigation experience and offering more flexible learning pathways along with varied certification options.

In summary, although the chatbot-driven learning environment demonstrates significant potential in promoting favorable learning outcomes in digital entrepreneurship, the research highlights areas that need improvement based on participant feedback. By adopting these suggested enhancements, both the user experience and engagement could lead to notable improvements, thereby maximizing the effectiveness of this educational initiative.

4.8. Future work

The future work aims to improve the chatbot-based learning environment tailored for digital entrepreneurship education by focusing on several key areas:

– *User interface and experience*: participants strongly recommend enhancing the visual appeal and overall usability of the chatbot environment. This can be achieved by incorporating various multimedia elements, such as vibrant images, detailed diagrams, informative infographics and engaging video content. These enhancements can make the learning experience more captivating and intuitive, attracting learners' interest and facilitating better understanding. Additionally, integrating features such as an autoscroll option, clear navigation paths and smooth transitions between lessons will streamline the learning process and increase user satisfaction and interaction.

– *Customization and adaptive learning paths*: there is a significant preference among participants for greater flexibility in their educational journeys, particularly the ability to navigate different levels of complexity. Future versions of the chatbot could utilize advanced adaptive learning algorithms to tailor the educational experience based on each learner's unique progress, interests and skill deficiencies. This personalized approach would cater to diverse learning styles and increase engagement and motivation by delivering customized content and appropriately challenging tasks.

– *Incorporating real-world simulations and case studies*: to enhance the practical relevance of the course materials, future modules could include a wider variety of real-world simulations and engaging case studies. These interactive components will allow learners to apply theoretical concepts to meaningful practical situations, promoting deeper understanding and essential skills acquisition in the field of digital entrepreneurship. By connecting theory with practice, learners can gain invaluable insights into the real-world applications of their studies.

– *Technical enhancements and stability*: feedback from participants highlights the need to improve the responsiveness, stability and functionality of embedded links within the chatbot environment. Prioritizing these technical enhancements is essential for ensuring a smooth and uninterrupted learning experience. Regular updates and comprehensive testing will help address technical challenges and maintain a high level of user satisfaction.

– *Support mechanisms for teachers and learners*: while chatbots are effective tools for self-directed learning, participants emphasized the importance of human interaction and mentorship. Future strategies should include strong support mechanisms that encourage engagement between learners and human instructors or mentors, especially when grappling with complex subjects or needing personalized feedback. This human element can significantly enrich the educational experience and provide learners with the guidance necessary for success.

– *Assessment and ongoing improvement*: establishing a dynamic feedback loop and a thorough evaluation system is crucial for the continuous enhancement of the chatbot-based learning environment. Regularly conducting surveys, focus groups and utilizing analytics can yield valuable insights into user satisfaction, learning outcomes and specific areas requiring further improvement. This data-driven approach ensures that updates and new features align with the genuine needs and preferences of users, fostering effective learning experiences.

– *Enhancing accessibility and localization*: given the diverse audience that spans various countries and languages, it is vital to prioritize initiatives that improve the accessibility and localization of content. This includes translating educational modules into multiple languages and adjusting the material to align with regional contexts and cultural nuances. Such efforts can significantly expand the reach and effectiveness of chatbot technology in adult education, ensuring that learners from different backgrounds can engage meaningfully (Bhardwaj and Kumar 2024).

4.9. Acknowledgments

The CHATBOT project (2020-1-CY01-KA204-065974) was funded by the European Union, and we would like to express our gratitude and appreciation to the consortium, Nikanor Ltd., Domspain Consulting SL, Lidi Smart Solutions, and Asset Basilicata, who contributed to the successful completion of the current project.

4.10. References

Agarwal, R. and Wadhwa, M. (2020). Review of state-of-the-art design techniques for chatbots. *SN Computer Science*, 1(5), 246.

Andrade-Arenas, L., Yactayo-Arias, C., Pucuhuayla-Revatta, F. (2024). Therapy and emotional support through a chatbot. *International Journal of Online & Biomedical Engineering*, 20(2), 114.

Atlas, S. (2023). *ChatGPT for Higher Education and Professional Development: A Guide to Conversational AI*. University of Rhode Island, Kingston, RI [Online]. Available at: https://digitalcommons.uri.edu/cba_facpubs/548. [Accessed 1 March 2023].

Bhardwaj, A. and Kumar, V. (2022). Web and social media approach to marketing of engineering courses in India. *International Journal of Business Innovation and Research*, 27(4), 541–555.

Bhardwaj, A. and Kumar, V. (2024). Challenges in online collaboration to augment Industry 4.0. *International Journal of Technology, Policy and Management*, 24(1), 71–92.

Bond, R.R., Mulvenna, M.D., Potts, C., O'Neill, S., Ennis, E., Torous, J. (2023). Digital transformation of mental health services. *npj Mental Health Research*, 2(1), 13. doi: 10.1038/s44184-023-00013-y.

Chen, J.S. and Devina, F. (2021). Usability and responsiveness of artificial intelligence chatbot on online customer experience in e-retailing. *International Journal of Retail & Distribution Management*, 49(11), 1512–1531. doi: 10.1108/IJRDM-08-2020-0312.

Chen, J.-S., Le, T.-T., Florence, D. (2021). Usability and responsiveness of artificial intelligence chatbot on online customer experience in e-retailing. *International Journal of Retail & Distribution Management*, 49(11), 1512–1531. doi: 10.1108/IJRDM-08-2020-0312.

Copulsky, J. (2019). Do conversational platforms represent the next big digital marketing opportunity? *Applied Marketing Analytics*, 4(4), 311–316.

Hsieh, S.-W. (2011). Effects of cognitive styles on an MSN virtual learning companion system as an adjunct to classroom instructions. *Journal of Educational Technology & Society*, 14(2), 161–174.

Kalla, D., Smith, N., Samaah, F., Kuraku, S. (2023). Study and analysis of ChatGPT and its impact on different fields of study. *International Journal of Innovative Science and Research Technology*, 8(3), 827–833.

Kumar, V., and Lata, M. (eds) (2022). *The Future of E-Commerce*. Nova Science Publishers, New York. doi: 10.52305/KMUB3774.

Kumar, V. and Nanda, P. (2024). Social media and micro-lessons: A new paradigm of online learning. In *Optimizing Education Through Micro-Lessons: Engaging and Adaptive Learning Strategies*, Ilic, P. (ed.). IGI Global, New York.

Kumar, V. and Rewari, M. (2022). A responsible approach to higher education curriculum design. *International Journal of Educational Reform*, 31(4), 422–441.

Kumar, V. and Rewari, M. (eds) (2023). *Pandemics in the Age of Social Media: Information and Misinformation in Developing Nations*, 1st edition. Routledge, New York. doi: 10. 4324/9781003315278.

Lai, C.-L. (2020). Trends of mobile learning: A review of the top 100 highly cited papers. *British Journal of Educational Technology*, 51(3), 721–742.

Lata, M. and Kumar, V. (2022). Fog computing infrastructure for smart city applications. In *Recent Advancements in ICT Infrastructure and Applications*, Chaturvedi, M., Patel, P., Yadav, R. (eds). Springer, Singapore.

Lata, M. and Kumar, V. (2024). A framework for security of public cloud environment. *International Journal of Electronic Security and Digital Forensics*, 16(4), 486–502.

Lata, M. and Sharma, V. (2024a). Cloud computing based blended learning: Quality assurance challenges. In *2024 International Conference on Communication, Computer Sciences and Engineering (IC3SE)*. IEEE, New York.

Lata, M. and Sharma, V. (2024b). Smart city environment management: Challenges and opportunities. *Grenze International Journal of Engineering & Technology (GIJET)*, 10(2), 2159–2166.

Lata, M., Kumar, V., Sharma, V. (2024). Cloud computing applications in online learning. *Grenze International Journal of Engineering & Technology (GIJET)*, 10(2), 408–411.

Melián-González, S., Gutiérrez-Taño, D., Bulchand-Gidumal, J. (2021). Predicting the intentions to use chatbots for travel and tourism. *Current Issues in Tourism*, 24(2), 192–210.

Moriuchi, E., Landers, V.M., Colton, D., Hair, N. (2021). Engagement with chatbots versus augmented reality interactive technology in e-commerce. *Journal of Strategic Marketing*, 29(5), 375–389.

Muniasamy, A. and Alasiry, A. (2020). Deep learning: The impact on future eLearning. *International Journal of Emerging Technologies in Learning*, 15(1), 188.

Nanda, P. and Kumar, V. (2024). New generation technologies: Development vs. ethical challenges. *International Journal of Business Information Systems*, 46(3), 411–434.

Obschonka, M. and Audretsch, D.B. (2020). Artificial intelligence and big data in entrepreneurship: A new era has begun. *Small Business Economics*, 55(3), 529–539. doi: 10.1007/s11187-019-00202-4.

Rai, S. and Lata, M. (2024). Futuristic outlook of online learning: The postpandemic era. In *Technology-mediated Learning During the Pandemic*, Singh, J. and Kumar, V. (eds). Routledge, Delhi.

Shepherd, D.A. and Majchrzak, A. (2022). Machines augmenting entrepreneurs: Opportunities (and threats) at the nexus of artificial intelligence and entrepreneurship. *Journal of Business Venturing*, 37(4), 106227.

Teja, S.V. (2020). Chatbot using deep learning. *Academic Leadership-Online Journal*, 21(6), 428–438.

Weizenbaum, J. (1966). ELIZA—A computer program for the study of natural language communication between man and machine. *Communications of the ACM*, 9(1), 36–45.

5

Role of Chatbots as Virtual Tutors in LMS

Online education is strongly influenced by artificial intelligence (AI) through various aspects, one of which is the learning management system (LMS) and the integration of AI on the platform. With respect to this integration, chatbots have become a great tool that highlights the potential to revolutionize the educational landscape. As AI-driven tools, chatbot tutors offer personalized, on-demand support, enhancing student engagement and learning outcomes.

This chapter delves into understanding chatbots as virtual tutors and further explores the design principles that make chatbot tutors effective, including the use of natural language processing (NLP) and adaptive learning algorithms. This chapter also explores the difference between traditional or human tutoring and chatbots as virtual tutors. Finally, we will consider future trends, including the potential for chatbots to evolve with advancements in AI and their role in shaping the future of digital education.

5.1. Introduction

In the era where the integration of chatbots as virtual tutors in the field of LMSs has led to a transformative shift in the sphere of modern education, it has also caused everyone to highlight how our educational needs are perfectly met (Kumar and Nanda 2024). The world is witnessing the dawn of an era where technological advancements seamlessly blend with pedagogy, transforming and enriching learning experiences (Nanda and Kumar 2024). With the expanding trend of educational institutions increasingly running to adopt digital platforms to facilitate learning, chatbots have become crucial tools for supporting both students and educators. These intelligent virtual assistants work together with AI and NLP to connect with learners in terms of meaningful interactions while providing immediate responses to

Chapter written by Shilpi CHAKRAVARTY, Mahesh Chandra JOSHI and Iti GAUR.

queries, personalized feedback and tailored learning pathways during their learning journeys (Aron 2011). By working as a 24/7 support system, chatbot tutors are ready to redefine traditional educational boundaries, enabling learners to seek assistance whenever and wherever they are in need of it.

Case study: IBM Watson and the revolution of AI in education

IBM Watson, a leader in AI, has been instrumental in integrating chatbots into educational platforms to redefine online learning. One prominent example is the implementation of Watson-powered virtual tutors within Pearson's learning management system (LMS). These AI-driven chatbots provide real-time assistance, personalized recommendations and detailed feedback to students, significantly enhancing their learning experience.

The chatbots use *natural language processing (NLP)* to understand and respond to students' queries conversationally, simulating human interaction. For example, students can ask complex questions about course material, and Watson provides accurate, context-aware responses. These interactions are further enriched by *adaptive learning algorithms*, which analyze individual performance and tailor recommendations to bridge knowledge gaps.

Unlike traditional tutors, Watson-powered chatbots are available 24/7, ensuring that learners can access support whenever needed. The scalability of such AI solutions allows educational institutions to support a massive number of students simultaneously, overcoming geographical and resource limitations.

IBM's collaboration with educational platforms demonstrates how AI-driven chatbots can complement human tutors by automating routine tasks and enabling personalized learning.

With ongoing advancements in AI, Watson continues to evolve, highlighting the potential for chatbots to play a pivotal role in shaping the future of digital education.

Box 5.1. *IBM Watson and the revolution of AI in education. Source: https://www.ibm.com/products/watsonx-assistant/case-studies*

The role of chatbots extends beyond merely providing answers to questions; they even serve as interactive learning companions that encourage and motivate learners to gain better experiences. While standing tall with the ability to judge the individual level of performance and adapt to their individual responses accordingly, chatbots can provide personalization that traditional educational methods sometimes lack. The focal point of chatbots is personalization, which allows learners to progress at their own speed or pace, receiving guidance and resources that are in complete sync with their unique and subjective learning styles and preferences (Lata and Sharma 2024a). Moreover, the chatbot tutors can also facilitate an educational environment, which is more inclusive, by serving diverse populations, which further includes non-native speakers and students with varying degrees of proficiency in their individual subject matters. Although it is also evident that some educational institutions are turning their way toward AI, others are still hesitating in moving toward accepting this side of technological innovation.

With the increasing demand for greater flexibility and accessibility in the field of education, chatbot tutors reflect a broader trend toward making use of technology to meet the needs of a dynamic learner population (Lata et al. 2024). Through the channel of focusing more on enhancing interactivity and offering immediate support, chatbot tutors are capable of not only improving the educational experience but also alleviating the administrative burdens faced by educators (Kumar and Rewari 2022).

This chapter takes a deeper dive into the multifaceted roles of chatbots as virtual tutors and explores their benefits, challenges and future potential, taking into account the evolving landscape of education and the connected areas (Lata and Kumar 2022). With these insights, we will gain an understanding of how chatbot technology is reshaping the way students learn and interact with educational content.

5.1.1. *Virtual tutors*

With advancements in technology, every aspect of human life has been affected by this rise in technology. There are now online-based software and platforms that provide personalized teaching and learning experiences through digital means, and this side of the education industry encompasses virtual tutoring. This side of the education industry has multiple facets and is also gaining popularity because of the flexible, accessible and often cost-effective alternatives to traditional face-to-face tutoring (Kumar and Lata 2022). It ranges from providing live one-on-one sessions with human educators to AI-powered systems that use algorithms to measure and assess students' performance.

Moreover, there are many added advantages that accompany virtual tutoring. It offers the greatest advantage of having personalized learning, which is also at the convenience and ease of the learner. Understanding an individual student's strengths, weaknesses and learning styles are what counts under personalized learning (Al Ka'bi 2023); hence, these virtual tutors, if they could be tailored, would surely be something worth counting upon. Students have access to lessons and resources, can hold discussions with other students and receive feedback from tutors as well as colearners while eliminating geographical barriers (Lata and Kumar 2024). These platforms have multimedia elements such as videos, interactive exercises and real-time quizzes to enhance engagement and retention.

Through their focus on enhancing interactivity and providing immediate support, chatbot tutors improve their educational experience while alleviating the administrative burdens faced by educators. For example, *Microsoft*, through its AI-powered chatbot integration into educational platforms such as Teams, offers a virtual assistant that handles routine queries about assignments, schedules and course materials. This not only streamlines administrative tasks for educators but also ensures that students receive real-time assistance, allowing teachers to focus more on core teaching activities and personalized student engagement.

Virtual tutors, which are AI powered, such as those used in platforms such as Duolingo or Coursera, adapt to individual styles and paces, which further offers customized support for progress. They also provide instant feedback, which helps in better understanding the concepts and increases the level of efficiency. With the rise in educational demand, virtual tutors are becoming an integral part of the modern education system. They are not in contradiction but rather complement the traditional pattern of teaching and open new avenues for personalized, self-paced learning, making education more accessible and dynamic.

5.2. Definition and role of virtual tutors in modern education

To provide learners with the best teaching experience, on the basis of their personal learning pace, designed as per the understanding of different sets of learners, today's world has virtual tutors, which are AI-powered or online-based educational systems. These tutors can handle the students' queries, provide feedback, answer questions and simulate the support typically offered by a human tutor. Unlike human tutors, these tutors are available in various forms (Rai and Lata 2024); sometimes in the form of chatbots, interactive platforms and sometimes software programs are integrated with educational technologies (Browne 2023).

Various forms of virtual tutors in modern education

1) Intelligent tutoring systems.

Intelligent tutoring systems (ITSs) are AI-powered platforms that adapt to individual student needs, providing personalized content and real-time feedback.

These systems are highly effective for subjects that require step-by-step guidance, such as mathematics or language learning.

EXAMPLE.–

– *Cognitive tutor by Carnegie learning*: this math-focused tutoring system adapts to students' progress and offers targeted support based on their learning gaps.

2) Virtual classrooms with AI-powered tutors.

These platforms simulate traditional classroom environments but integrate AI tutors to assist students during live lessons, providing real-time support and engagement. They help students answer questions, clarify doubts and offer explanations during lessons (Schiff 2021).

EXAMPLE.–

– *Google Classroom with integrated AI tutoring solutions*: the Google Classroom helps teachers manage classes and integrates AI-powered features that assist in grading and answering students' questions.

– *Microsoft Teams with AI education bots*: Microsoft Teams includes bots such as *TeachBot* to answer queries and guide students through lessons in real time.

3) Voice-assisted tutors.

These virtual tutors use voice recognition to provide hands-free, real-time verbal assistance. They are ideal for students who prefer oral communication or need assistance without having to type questions.

EXAMPLE.–

– *Google Assistant for education*: Google Assistant provides personalized educational support, from answering questions to helping students with homework.

– *Alexa-enabled educational skills*: Amazon's Alexa helps students with learning tasks, such as solving math problems or studying for exams, via voice-based interactions.

4) Gamified tutors and educational games.

These virtual tutors use gamification elements, such as challenges, quizzes and interactive problem-solving, to engage students in learning. They are especially useful for younger students or subjects who benefit from interactive learning.

EXAMPLE–

– *Duolingo*: an app that turns language learning into a fun, game-like experience with levels, rewards and challenges.

– *Prodigy*: a math-based game that helps students practice their skills through fun challenges and quests.

5) Virtual reality (VR) tutors.

VR tutors immerse students in an interactive virtual environment, allowing for hands-on, experiential learning. These tutors are often used in subjects that benefit from visual or experiential learning, such as science, engineering or history.

EXAMPLE.–

– *Labster*: a VR platform that offers interactive science labs where students can conduct virtual experiments, enhancing their learning experience.

– *Engage VR*: a platform that enables virtual classrooms and immersive learning, where students can participate in 3D experiences and engage with tutors and peers in real time.

6) Chatbot tutors.

AI-powered chatbots are often used as virtual tutors to provide instant support, answer queries and guide students through learning processes. They are available 24/7 and can assist with a variety of subjects.

EXAMPLE.–

– *Siri-based educational bots*: Siri can be used as a basic virtual tutor to provide answers, define terms or assist with problem solving.

– *ChatGPT (OpenAI)*: this AI-powered chatbot can help students with homework, explain concepts and provide detailed feedback.

5.3. Virtual tutors and learning management systems

Within LMSs, chatbots act as virtual tutors, guiding, supporting and providing answers to the questions posed by learners. They do so by leveraging AI and NLP. Their existence in the LMS enhances the user experience by automating responses, guiding users and offering personalized learning interactions. Moving further into this chapter, the following section provides an overview of how chatbots operate as virtual tutors within LMS:

1) *Automating routine queries*: before the incorporation of computers and other technologies in education, students and instructors use the pure application of human efforts for learning (Chen et al. 2020). To lessen the burden of administrative staff or faculty, chatbots are able to easily handle frequently asked questions and, if needed, other functions of the instructors. These questions are generally related to course logistics, deadlines, grading policies or navigation within the LMS. For example, if the student wishes to ask the deadline for the assignment, they may ask "what is the due date for the assignment?", and the chatbots would reply instantly with the date.

2) *Guiding through course materials*: it is often complex, especially for the learners who are enrolled in the online course for the first time, to navigate through the course material. Chatbots provide a rescue to them and help them find the right resources or navigate through complex LMS platforms. It can also be of great help to learners in finding the right module, supplementary materials or instructions. A student may raise a query: "Where can I find the recorded version of the live lecture on the LMS?", and the chatbot would direct them with the path to find the answer.

3) *Personalized learning and progress tracking*: Chatbots track the progress of learners and, if needed, offer personalized feedback or recommendations on performance. If a learner is facing difficulty in understanding a concept, it would recommend that the student go for additional practice exercises. For example, when a student faces challenges in clearing a particular quiz, the chatbots would instantly suggest specific chapters or learning materials to revisit.

4) *Providing real-time feedback*: while the student is attempting any quiz or model questions, the chatbots would reflect immediate feedback; along with this, it would also quote the reasons why these answers are incorrect (Lata and Sharma 2024b). Such practices make the learning journey even more detailed and efficient. Suppose, a student ticked the wrong answer in question 5 of the quiz; then, the chatbot would reflect a message, "You missed question 5. Here is a link to review the topic on photosynthesis".

5) *Engaging in interactive learning*: Chatbots are designed such that they can easily reinforce learning by engaging students in active learning through conversation. It may pose quizzes or challenges that require the learner to brainstorm or revisit a particular quadrant on the LMS toward a specific topic. The chatbot here would itself suggest to the learner: "Let us review yesterday's lesson on chemical reactions".

6) *Encouraging motivation and engagement*: setting goals, sending reminders and more by chatbots often encourage participation and learners' engagement. They

can act as accountability partners by reminding students to complete tasks and celebrate milestones, such as finishing a course module.

7) *Facilitating peer interaction and collaboration*: holding group discussions and encouraging interactions with participants constitute another feature of chatbots, which further encourages collaborative learning by connecting students to their peers for group discussions or projects. Chatbots can prompt learners to join discussion forums or group assignments within the LMS.

8) *Assisting teachers and admins*: another side of chatbots involves helping the instructors grade, tracking student participation and answering repetitive student questions. This leaves instructors with more time to focus on more complex educational tasks and interactions with students. A chatbot can easily help instructors automatically check if students have completed the required reading and can generate a report with this information.

9) *Data collection and analysis*: LMS gathers data regarding student interactions, performance and engagement, and chatbots handle these pieces of information. An up side to this is that the instructors can easily analyze which topics students are struggling with, and they may come up with the solutions to these problems. For example, chatbots might reflect that "36% students are struggling with the algebra portion of the chapter".

If we look at the summarized version of chatbots under the LMS, then the chatbots can act as virtual tutors by automating responses, guiding learners through content, offering personalized learning experiences, and reducing the workload for educators.

5.4. Designing an effective chatbot tutor

Designing a chatbot tutor is not a simple task and hence requires a blend of advanced technology, a user-centric design and educational insight. Chatbots make simple use of NLP, which further enables seamless interaction with students, providing human-like support and allowing learners to ask different questions. Furthermore, personalization is another important feature that chatbots hold, making them a tailor-made experience for learners in their journey of virtual learning. This helps in creating an engaging and effective learning experience that caters to individual needs (Elsen-Rooney 2023).

The capability of chatbots to provide feedback and follow-up on assessments is important because it enables the chatbot to grade quizzes, lay constructive feedback and develop some relevant learning materials. Another limitation is that the chatbots created must be able to provide positive reinforcement, which would in turn encourage students and motivate them for making learning progress. In addition, to maintain engagement, a user-friendly interface is an additional benefit that incorporates clear visuals, intuitive navigation and quickly responsive designs to grasp the connections and attention of learners. The chatbots must be designed with a clear focus on educational objectives while ensuring that they support specific learning goals or courses. Eventually, an effective chatbot tutor is required to be like an intelligent guide – which is available 24/7 to support, assess and adapt to students' requirements – that would in turn enhance both the learning experience and the outcomes.

5.4.1. *Key features and capabilities of a chatbot tutor*

A chatbot tutor is an amalgamation of multiple facets of a tutor. In addition, it also has the ability to be available 24/7 to learners, be flexible, provide real-time support, and help them navigate the LMS, etc. Apparently, chatbots are a saviour to learners, who need guidance over the platform of virtual learning. The learning journey of everyone may differ from each other, but there are still some underlying features that remain the same for the entire pool of learners (Labadze 2023).

1) *Natural language processing*: NLP makes it easier for chatbots to understand and interpret natural language-based questions from students, even when they are posed differently. This, in turn, enables a smooth, conversational interface that ensures the interaction of the chatbot, and the learner feels is human-like and really intuitive.

2) *Personalized learning*: individual student progress can be tracked, and learning content, questions, and feedback can be adapted on the basis of performance. Chatbots must also offer personalized study plans, recommendations and exercises that could be tailored to each student's learning requirements and pace.

3) *Real-time feedback and assessment*: a great chatbot provides instant grading for quizzes and assignments while providing constructive feedback and explanations. It must also suggest resources such as videos, articles or further exercises that are based on errors (or areas) where the student requires improvement.

4) *24/7 availability*: the chatbot developed must offer round-the-clock support, which would allow the students to access help whenever they are in need of it, beyond the regular operating hours. It must also answer queries, assist with assignments, and guide learners through course material at any point in time.

5) *Interactive learning*: the chatbot must be capable of engaging the students in active learning through quizzes, interactive questions and some real-time challenges, reinforcing the concepts they have learned. Gamified elements, such as rewards or

badges, must also be used to keep the students motivated and engaged throughout the course of learning.

6) *Content navigation and guidance*: Chatbots also help students find specific resources, assignments or modules within the LMS by following the guidance of the chatbots. The students are directed toward the supplementary material when they require any further explanations or in-depth understanding of a subject.

7) *Multilingual support*: Chatbots provide aid in multiple languages, cater to students who come from different linguistic backgrounds and support diverse pools of learners.

8) *Adaptability to learning styles*: Chatbots also adapt to different learning preferences and requirements of the learners, offering varied forms of content such as text explanations, videos, or, for that matter, even interactive exercises. This enables visual, auditory and kinesthetic learners to derive benefits from tailor-made interactions.

9) *Data collection and analysis*: this gathers data on the basis of learner interactions, performance trends and engagement to offer insights to instructors or, in addition, provide more personalized learning experiences. It tracks the pattern of learning and the flagged areas where the students might need extra help (Bhardwaj and Kumar 2022).

10) *Seamless LMS integration*: Chatbots integrate with LMSs for seamless and easy access to course materials and assignments and to track student progress. In addition, it automates administrative tasks such as assignment reminders, grading and progress tracking, which, in turn, help the admins.

The abovementioned features enable chatbot tutors to provide more personalized, interactive and even more accessible learning support while ensuring that an engaging and effective educational experience is provided.

5.5. Chatbot tutors versus human tutors

In the world of education, both chatbot tutors and human tutors play valuable roles, but they also differ in their capabilities in terms of their interaction styles and impact on learning. Here, we present a detailed comparison of both:

1) *Availability*: the chatbot tutors are available 24/7, which offers immediate assistance at any time. This flexibility of chatbots allows learners to receive help whenever needed, even outside regular operating or tutor hours (Masters 2023). However, human tutors are typically limited to scheduled sessions and working hours, which might not be in alignment with a student's requirements in the case of real-time help.

2) *Personalization*: on the one hand, chatbot tutors offer automated, data-driven personalization, which is based on a student's performance. This phenomenon can instantly adapt to questions, provide feedback and suggest resources tailored to individual needs. On the other hand, human tutors offer deep, nuanced understanding and real-time adaptability, which is completely based on a student's behavior, their emotions and feedback. The human tutors can respond to complex, subjective needs in ways through which an AI can never respond.

3) *Emotional and social support*: the chatbot tutors are limited in regard to providing empathy or emotional understanding. Although they can provide motivational phrases, they still lack the ability of human touch to provide encouragement, empathy and moral support, as machines are generated. In contrast, human tutors can connect emotionally, offer encouragement, address frustration and build a personal rapport with learners, which is crucial when students need emotional or motivational support.

4) *Consistency and scalability*: Chatbot tutors can easily handle large numbers of students at one glance while providing consistent responses, making them highly scalable. Chatbots can answer repetitive questions simultaneously and provide consistent feedback across all groups of students. On the other hand, human tutors offer personalized and more dynamic responses but are also limited in terms of the number of students they can help at a single time. The effectiveness of human tutors can vary on the basis of their workload or other factors.

5) *Cost and accessibility*: Chatbot tutors are comparatively more cost-effective and accessible to students worldwide, especially in regions where hiring human tutors can turn out to be expensive or sometimes even impractical. Human tutors are generally more expensive and less accessible than chabot tutors are, especially for students in remote areas or those with financial limitations (Nayar and Kumar 2015).

6) *Content expertise*: Chatbot tutors can easily be programmed with exhaustive knowledge across various subjects, which provides fact-based, consistent answers. However, chatbots might struggle with nuanced, complex queries or areas where judgment and interpretation are needed. On the other hand, human tutors can provide experience, real-world insights and experiences, and a deep understanding of subjects, enabling them to listen to the complex problems of learners.

7) *Interaction style*: Chatbot tutors provide comprehensively structured and automated interactions that can be more efficient for providing answers to factual questions and guiding through predesigned paths of learning. In contrast, human tutors offer sessions that are dynamic and interactive and that can evolve on the basis of a student's immediate response, which in turn provides a more personalized learning experience with complex problem-solving and discussion.

8) *Creativity and critical thinking*: although chatbot tutors are guided through factual or structured content, they do not have the ability to foster critical thinking,

creativity or problem-solving skills that require proper understanding. However, human tutors are capable of engaging students in discussions that also foster creativity, critical thinking and problem solving, encouraging students to know about ideas more deeply.

9) *Adaptability to learning styles*: the learning patterns can easily be adapted by chatbot tutors on the basis of data but may struggle to fully accommodate diverse, complex learning styles beyond what has been put into the system. On the other hand, human tutors can intuitively adapt to teaching methods, materials and styles on the basis of real-time feedback, allowing them to address specific learning challenges in diverse ways.

10) *Long-term learning relationships*: a transactional relationship is offered by chatbot tutors, who are focused on tasks and feedback but can never build long-term mentor–mentee connections. However, in the case of human tutors, they can easily develop strong, trusting relationships with students, becoming mentors and role models, which can have a long-term, deeper impact on a student's long-term learning journey.

On the one hand, chatbot tutors excel in offering immediate, cost-effective and scalable support for repetitive tasks, providing even more personalized feedback on the basis of data and handling simple questions very efficiently. On the other hand, human tutors are capable of offering greater emotional support and adaptability, and they hold deeper subject matter expertise, particularly for complex topics or students needing personalized, empathetic guidance. In a nutshell, if we talk about both of them, then an effective approach could involve having both – let us say for using chatbots for routine, immediate tasks and human tutors for personalized and connected, real in-depth learning.

5.6. Challenges in implementing chatbots as virtual tutors

The implementation of chatbots as virtual tutors presents a real set of challenges that can affect their effectiveness and overall integration into the education system. Next, we address these challenges while implementing chatbots as virtual tutors:

1) *Limited understanding of complex queries*: Chatbots excel in answering straightforward, factual questions such as "What is the capital of France?". However, when a student asks a complex question such as "How can cultural differences impact global marketing strategies?", the chatbot might struggle to provide a detailed, nuanced response. This can lead to students receiving unsatisfactory or irrelevant answers, limiting their learning experience.

2) *Lack of emotional intelligence*: a student may approach a chatbot feeling frustrated about a challenging topic, asking, "I do not understand this concept at all,

can you help?". The chatbot can provide factual explanations, but it cannot recognize the student's frustration or offer emotional support, such as saying, "I understand this is tough, but don't give up!". This lack of emotional intelligence can make students feel unsupported, negatively impacting their motivation.

3) *Inflexibility with unstructured learning*: a student in a philosophy class explores abstract concepts such as existentialism or ethics and asks, "What is the meaning of life according to Sartre?". The chatbot may struggle to engage in a deep, philosophical discussion because it is designed to follow predefined paths. This limitation restricts the ability to engage in open-ended, creative problem solving or discussions that require critical thinking and subjective exploration.

4) *Data privacy and security concerns*: when a student interacts with a chatbot, personal and academic data, such as assignments and grades, are collected and stored. If the platform does not ensure proper data protection measures, this sensitive information could be exposed, leading to concerns about breaches of privacy. Students in regions with strict data protection regulations, such as the EU (GDPR), may be reluctant to use such platforms because of these risks.

5) *Lack of human-like interaction*: while AI-powered chatbots such as those based on NLP can answer questions, they often struggle to replicate the warmth and conversational tone of human tutors. For example, a student might ask a chatbot, "I am feeling really stressed about my exams, do you have any tips?". The response might be a generic, mechanical suggestion such as "study hard," rather than empathetic advice from a human tutor who understands the student's emotional state.

6) *Integration with LMS*: a student trying to access chatbot assistance through their school's LMS might face issues if the chatbot is not integrated properly with the system. For example, a student could click on a chatbot icon but experience slow loading times, glitches, or the inability to access help. This poor technical integration would frustrate students and educators alike, making it difficult to leverage the benefits of AI tutoring effectively.

5.7. The future of chatbot tutors in LMSs

The future of chatbot tutors in LMSs holds exciting potential, as advancements in AI and NLP continue to evolve. Here is an outlook on how chatbot tutors may transform education in the coming years:

1) *Increased personalization and adaptive learning.*

– *Future trend*: as AI and machine learning models advance, chatbot tutors will become better at analyzing student data to offer highly personalized learning experiences. They will be able to detect individual learning patterns, strengths and weaknesses in real time, adapting content dynamically to match each student's unique pace and learning style.

– *Impact*: students will receive custom-tailored resources, quizzes and assignments that are closely aligned with their progress, making learning more efficient and engaging.

2) *Enhanced emotional intelligence and human-like interaction.*

– *Future trend*: developments in emotional AI (affective computing) will allow chatbot tutors to better understand students' emotional states, such as frustration or confusion, through voice, text or facial recognition technologies.

– *Impact*: chatbots will be able to provide emotionally supportive responses, offer encouragement or adjust the difficulty of content on the basis of the student's emotional and cognitive needs. This will make chatbot interactions feel more human and empathetic.

3) *Multimodal learning and immersive experiences.*

– *Future Trend*: chatbots will integrate with emerging technologies such as augmented reality (AR) and VR, enabling them to offer immersive, multimodal learning experiences. Students interact with both text and 3D simulations or visualized learning environments guided by a chatbot tutor.

– *Impact*: this can enhance learning in subjects such as science, history or engineering by allowing students to explore complex concepts in a more engaging and hands-on way, improving comprehension and retention.

4) *Greater integration with advanced LMS platforms.*

– *Future trend*: chatbot tutors will become more seamlessly integrated into advanced LMS platforms, with improved compatibility and functionality. They will be able to manage a wider range of administrative tasks, such as scheduling study sessions, monitoring group projects, and tracking overall class progress.

– *Impact*: this integration will make LMS platforms smarter and more autonomous, reducing the workload for both educators and students while streamlining educational management.

5) *Collaboration with human tutors for hybrid learning.*

– *Future trend*: the future will likely see a hybrid tutoring model, where chatbot tutors collaborate with human tutors, each addressing different needs (Bhardwaj and Kumar 2024). While chatbots handle routine tasks, assessments and quick queries, human tutors will focus on complex discussions, mentorship and emotional support.

– *Impact*: this hybrid approach will provide students with the best of both worlds – efficiency from chatbots and in-depth learning from human tutors – resulting in a more comprehensive educational experience.

6) *NLP advancements*.

– *Future trend*: as NLP technology continues to improve, chatbots will become more adept at understanding and responding to a broader range of questions and contexts, including complex, open-ended queries. They will engage in deeper, more meaningful conversations with students.

– *Impact*: chatbots will be able to handle higher order thinking tasks, such as reasoning, explaining abstract concepts or debating ideas, making them more effective for subjects who require critical thinking and creativity.

5.8. Conclusion

By providing personalized, scalable and accessible learning experiences, chatbots play a significant role in the evolving educational landscape. As the fields of AI and NLP continue to marvel and grow, these virtual tutors, in the near future, will surely become more adept at understanding student needs, offering even more customized feedback, and adapting to the learning paths in real time. The fact that they are available all of the time, makes it easier for the students to obtain access to immediate support, making learning even more flexible and, consequently, surely independent of time constraints. Administrative burdens can also be reduced for educators by automating routine tasks, such as grading, progress tracking and a special task – assignment reminders. However, if we look at the darker side of this, then this advancement in technology will not always have a good impact; rather, it could kill the creative skills of the students (Shidiq 2023). In fact, in the words of Cooper (2023), for some subjects, such as science, teachers make use of different strategies to differentiate instructions.

Chatbots definitely excel; in regard to laying the factual content and handling repetitive queries, chatbot tutors will never be able to replace them, but they will complement human educators. The amalgamation of human emotional intelligence and AI-powered efficiency is surely capable of creating a hybrid learning environment where both of the tutors are coming together to address what the student fully needs. Chatbot tutors surely integrate immersive technologies, namely, AR and VR, and are definitely able to offer more engaging, multimodal learning experiences. Chatbot tutors will help democratize education in this evolving landscape by making personalized learning support even more widely and flexibly available, driving forward a more inclusive and efficient model of education in the coming years.

5.9. References

Al Ka'bi, A. (2023). Proposed artificial intelligence algorithm and deep learning techniques for development of higher education. *International Journal of Intelligent Networks*, 4, 68–73.

Aron, J. (2011). How innovative is Apple's new voice assistant, Siri? *NewScientist*, 212(2836), 24.

Bhardwaj, A. and Kumar, V. (2022). Web and social media approach to marketing of engineering courses in India. *International Journal of Business Innovation and Research*, 27(4), 541–555.

Bhardwaj, A. and Kumar, V. (2024). Challenges in online collaboration to augment Industry 4.0. *International Journal of Technology, Policy and Management*, 24(1), 71–92.

Browne, R. (2023). Italy became the first western country to ban ChatGPT. Here's what other countries are doing. *CNBC*, New Jersey.

Chen, L., Chen, P., Lin, Z. (2020). Artificial intelligence in education: A review. *IEEE Access*, 8, 75264–75278.

Cooper, G. (2023). Examining science education in ChatGPT: An exploratory study of generative artificial intelligence. *Journal of Science Education and Technology*, 32(3), 444–452.

Elsen-Rooney, M. (2023). NYC education department blocks ChatGPT on school devices, networks. *Chalkbeat*, New York.

Kumar, V. and Lata, M. (eds) (2022). *The Future of E-Commerce*. Nova Science Publishers, New York. doi: 10.52305/KMUB3774.

Kumar, V. and Nanda, P. (2024). Social media and micro-lessons: A new paradigm of online learning. In *Optimizing Education Through Micro-Lessons: Engaging and Adaptive Learning Strategies*, Ilic, P. (ed.). IGI Global, New York.

Kumar, V. and Rewari, M. (2022). A responsible approach to higher education curriculum design. *International Journal of Educational Reform*, 31(4), 422–441.

Labadze, L., Grigolia, M., Machaidze, L. (2023). Role of AI chatbots in education: Systematic literature review. *Int. J. Educ. Technol. High. Educ.*, 20, 56.

Lata, M. and Kumar, V. (2022). Fog computing infrastructure for smart city applications. In *Recent Advancements in ICT Infrastructure and Applications*, Chaturvedi, M., Patel, P., Yadav, R. (eds). Springer, Singapore.

Lata, M. and Kumar, V. (2024). A framework for security of public cloud environment. *International Journal of Electronic Security and Digital Forensics*, 16(4), 486–502.

Lata, M. and Sharma, V. (2024a). Cloud computing based blended learning: Quality assurance challenges. In *2024 International Conference on Communication, Computer Sciences and Engineering (IC3SE)*. IEEE, New York.

Lata, M. and Sharma, V. (2024b). Smart city environment management: Challenges and opportunities. *Grenze International Journal of Engineering & Technology (GIJET)*, 10(2), 2159–2166.

Lata, M., Kumar, V., Sharma, V. (2024). Cloud computing applications in online learning. *Grenze International Journal of Engineering & Technology (GIJET)*, 10(2), 408–411.

Masters, K. (2023). Ethical use of artificial intelligence in health professions education: AMEE Guide No. 158. *Medical Teacher*, 45(6), 574–584.

Nanda, P. and Kumar, V. (2024). New generation technologies: Development vs. ethical challenges. *International Journal of Business Information Systems*, 46(3), 411–434.

Nayar, K.B. and Kumar, V. (2015). Benefits of cloud computing in education during disaster. In *Proceedings of the International Conference on Transformations in Engineering Education: ICTIEE 2014*, Hubli.

Rai, S. and Lata, M. (2024). Futuristic outlook of online learning: The post-pandemic era. In *Technology-mediated Learning During the Pandemic*, Singh, J. and Kumar, V. (eds). Routledge, New Delhi.

Schiff, D. (2021). Out of the laboratory and into the classroom: The future of artificial intelligence in education. *AI & Society*, 36(1), 331–348.

Shidiq, M. (2023). The use of artificial intelligence-based ChatGPT and its challenges for the world of education; from the viewpoint of the development of creative writing skills. In *Proceedings of International Conference on Education, Society and Humanity*, Probolinggo, 353–357.

6

Pre-Class Learning in a Flipped Classroom and the Role of Chatbot

There are two key principles around which the whole concept of the flipped classroom model revolves: pre-class preparation and in-class active learning. The pre-class preparation enables students to acquire foundational knowledge independently before engaging in active in-class activities. However, ensuring effective pre-class preparation can be challenging, as it requires students to stay motivated, access relevant resources and address doubts in real time. Chatbots, powered by artificial intelligence, offer innovative solutions to these challenges by providing personalized, interactive and accessible support for pre-class learning. This chapter aims to understand the potential of the chatbot as a transformative tool for pre-class learning in flipped classroom.

6.1. Introduction

The 21st century presents a dynamic and rapidly changing world where technology has become an indispensable part of life (Nanda and Kumar 2024). The easy availability of a large amount of information has made things more complex, as students, at times, are not able to decide what to consume and what to discard, and teachers face the challenges of keeping students motivated and engaged in the classroom (Lata and Sharma 2024a). To thrive in this kind of environment, there is a need for an educational approach that goes beyond the traditional classroom teaching style and equips students with the required skills to succeed (Kumar and Rewari 2022). The traditional teaching style puts the teachers at the center of the teaching process and they are the primary source of knowledge. The students are merely the recipients of the information; this leads to insufficient students' engagement in the classroom and a loss of interest. The digital age demands a shift

Chapter written by Sandhya RAI and Vy Ngoc LE HO.

away from rote memorization and passive learning toward an approach that cultivates creativity, problem-solving skills, adaptability and collaborative abilities (Nanda and Kumar 2024). Although traditional classroom teaching methods have many merits, the major challenges include the inability to match the individual learning styles of the students and engage them effectively in the classroom (Nayar and Kumar 2015). The flipped classroom approach provides a pedagogical shift that redefines the conventional teaching style and supports a more comprehensive teaching learning environment (Kumar and Nanda 2024). The flipped classroom is a student-centered instructional approach where the traditional learning structure is reversed. Instead of receiving lectures and learning concepts in class and then doing homework, the students are encouraged to review the study material, usually in the form of videos and reading at home, and then, the classroom hours are utilized for activities such as discussions, problem solving and hands-on projects that reinforce the concepts mentioned in the study materials. It is an innovative teaching approach that has gained significant attention in recent years across various educational disciplines (Nayan and Rawian 2022).

In this method, students are encouraged to review instructional materials such as reading materials, online videos and pre-recorded lectures or online modules outside the class. The class time is then dedicated to active learning where the students participate in discussions, interactive activities, collaborative projects, hands-on activities and problem-solving exercises (Fung et al. 2021). There are many definitions (Sams and Bergmann 2013) of the flipped classroom in the literature, but all these definitions agree with one common approach in which there are two phases: pre-class preparation and in-class collaboration. Pre-class preparation usually takes place through pre-readings, online or recorded lectures, videos and learning management system (LMS)-based study materials. Digital technologies such as video streaming and podcasts can also be used to achieve effective integration of pre-class and instructor-led learning activities (Sams and Bergmann 2013; Bhardwaj and Kumar 2024). This pre-class exposure to content encourages independent learning and allows individuals to progress at their own pace. Thus, by shifting traditional lectures outside the classroom, students arrive prepared and ready to participate actively in collaborative and interactive activities. They also provide teachers with increased opportunities to provide individualized support, guidance and feedback, addressing specific areas of difficulty and nurturing students' strengths. The class time is transformed into a dynamic arena for interactive and hands-on activities, facilitating discussions and collaborative problem-solving and promoting peer-to-peer learning, which in turn fosters teamwork skills and communication abilities in the students (Lata and Sharma 2024b). Transitioning from a teacher-centered sphere to a student-centered one, the flipped classroom permits learners to take ownership of their educational journey. The flipped classroom model shifts the focus from passive learning to active engagement and encourages students to prepare before class, allowing for more interactive and participatory learning sessions led by teachers.

Many studies have investigated the impact of the flipped classroom on improved learning and student engagement. For example, a study conducted in nursing education revealed that students taught using the flipped classroom method achieved significantly higher final exam scores than those in traditional classrooms. Research has also revealed that the flipped classroom group demonstrated improved learning attitudes, autonomous learning abilities and critical thinking skills (Deng 2016). Many studies have suggested a positive impact of the flipped classroom model on overall teaching effectiveness. Studies on vocational music, engineering and humanities suggest that the flipped classroom enhances students' interest in independent learning (Dou 2023), improves final test scores by 15% (Lin 2019), and has a positive effect on students' psychological needs and class perceptions. A study on 90 neurology residents divided into an observation and a control group – the control group following traditional learning method and observational group taught using flipped classroom approach – indicates that the independent learning ability and critical thinking ability of the observation group were better than those of the control group (Zhang et al. 2024). Similarly, in a study of dental anatomy students, the flipped classroom model not only improved students' examination scores and practical skills but also improved their comprehensive abilities, including critical thinking and teamwork (Wang et al. 2019). In academic writing classes, students reported positive perceptions of flipped learning, indicating improvements in their writing skills (Junio and Bandala 2019). The flipped classroom model contributed not only to academic development but also to the development of essential skills for the modern workforce. Studies indicate that the flipped classroom approach significantly improves information literacy levels, including information consciousness ability and morality (Zhang 2018), and promotes skills such as application, analysis and evaluation (Kim et al. 2014); these skills are considered higher order thinking skills and are very helpful in students developing independent thinking skills.

6.1.1. *Pre-class learning*

The flipped classroom consists of four key features: pre-class learning, active in-class learning, the teacher as a facilitator and the student-centered approach. Pre-class learning consists of a foundational knowledge acquisition phase that takes place prior to in-class activities. In this phase, students gain a theoretical understanding of the concept by reading instructional materials, watching instructional videos or finishing online modules. This prepares the students for in-class discussions and applications (Lata et al. 2024). Pre-class learning plays a crucial role in the success of flipped classroom models and overall student achievement. It serves as the foundation for in-class activities and enables students to engage in more active learning experiences during face-to-face sessions. Effective pre-class learning is important for the success of the flipped classroom. Pre-class learning ensures that the students are able to acquire basic content knowledge that has been removed from the traditional classroom setting (Larson and Linnell 2023) and allows the instructors to focus learner-centered experiences during face-to-face sessions (Lee and Choi 2019). The pre-learning helps in achieving the following:

– Students can refer to multiple materials at their own pace and gain a deeper understanding of the concepts. Active engagement with material promotes better understanding, reinforces knowledge and improves long-term retention. Studies have shown that students who actively participate in pre-class learning tend to perform better on assessments.

– It provides instructors with the flexibility to design in-class activities on the basis of students' strengths and weaknesses, queries asked and learning outcomes desired from the course, making learning a more personalized learning experience. It also provides more scope for in-depth discussions of problem-solving activities, simulations and case studies during class hours.

– Pre-class learning acts as a foundation for future classes; it provides the confidence and motivation required for students to remain active in class and contribute in a meaningful way. It also helps students develop essential skills such as time management, self-directed learning and critical thinking.

Various studies have been conducted to understand the significance of pre-class learning. Research conducted by Lee and Choi (2019) indicates that pre-class learning influences the overall success of flipped classroom learning. Students who engage effectively with pre-class activities tend to perform better in subsequent in-class sessions. It also plays a significant role in developing students' self-directed learning skills, improving student engagement, enhancing learning outcomes and providing flexibility and accessibility (Lata and Kumar 2024).

6.2. Pre-class learning: importance, roles and methods

The importance of pre-class learning lies in its ability to free up valuable classroom time for higher order activities and discussions. The kind of material available to the students as a part of pre-learning plays a very important role in this phase. Research indicates better performance in the week where the instructional materials were in the form of videos than in the week where the materials were in the form of reading materials (Lee and Choi 2019). It is not only the type of material but also the modality of the pre-class learning material that affects the student's performance; small video bites have been found to be more effective than conventional video lectures or interactive reading materials (Che et al. 2020). In the case of video-based materials, videos with pop-up questions or discussion-board activities have been found to result in significantly greater learning achievement and self-efficacy than traditional video lectures (Long et al. 2019). In regard to assignments, those with clear objectives, guidance and hands-on practice are preferred by students (Han and Klein 2019). Another pre-class material that generates interest, improves students' understanding of concepts and keeps interest alive is simulations; simulations have been found to have a significant effect on student understanding and participation in class discussions.

There is not one format of pre-class materials that suits all, each different type has its own share of benefits and limitations; where the written materials require minimum technological intervention, the videos and simulations require an active device and internet availability. However, videos and simulations are more interactive than readings (Bhardwaj and Kumar 2022). The impact of different kinds of pre-class material suggests that educators should consider incorporating a variety of formats to cater to different learning styles and course preferences. The material provided should also be such that it caters to students of various learning styles and linguistic backgrounds and helps them bridge the knowledge gap (Kumar and Lata 2022). Comprehensive pre-class materials ensure that all the students obtain the required functional knowledge before class. There are three major types of pre-class learning profiles: lecture-focused, quiz-focused and balanced approaches, each associated with varying levels of performance (Sun and Xie 2020). On the basis of the nature of the course and the expected learning outcome, a particular profile of pre-class material can be followed. The quality and design of pre-class activities are crucial for ensuring student engagement and learning outcomes (Rai and Lata 2024). The following are the popular pre-class learning strategies followed in the flipped classroom:

Video-based learning material: one of the most common materials provided as a part of pre-class learning is video-based study material. However, it is crucial to consider the design of these videos. Interactive videos based on knowledge integration theory have been found to be more effective than ordinary videos in improving learning achievement, self-efficacy and cognitive skills (Long et al. 2019).

Reading assignments: traditional textbook reading assignments remain a valuable pre-class learning method. When combined with carefully designed reading quizzes, they can effectively prepare students for in-class discussions. In language courses, the reading material could also contain vocabulary building materials. Strategies such as checking word meanings, reviewing newly learned words and self-encouragement to use new vocabulary in conversations have been identified as preferred methods among students (Hoa et al. 2024).

Problem-based learning tasks: assigning small problem-solving tasks related to the upcoming class topic can stimulate students' curiosity and prepare them for more in-depth discussions during class time.

Reflective journaling: asking students to write brief reflective journals on pre-class materials can enhance their critical thinking skills and help them connect new information with their existing knowledge.

Online quizzes: implementing online quizzes that students complete before class can help assess their understanding of pre-class materials and identify areas that need further explanation during the in-class session. The implementation of pre- and post-reading techniques in reading comprehension classes has yielded positive results. Students have demonstrated favorable attitudes toward these methods, recognizing their advantages in enhancing reading comprehension skills.

Collaborative online discussions: encouraging students to participate in online discussions or forums before class promotes peer learning and helps students articulate their thoughts on the subject matter. On these forums, students can put their questions, opinions and feedback and provide support to other students.

Each of these formats can help students gain a better pre-class learning experience. The following broad outline can be followed for designing the pre-class learning material:

Selection of format: there are multiple formats that can be adopted for pre-class activities, such as watching videos, listening to podcasts, reading articles and cases, and participating in quizzes, games and simulations; however, the final choice depends upon the type and level of content complexity, the learning objectives to be achieved and the preferences of the students. While the right format needs to be selected, the quality, accessibility and length of the material should also be considered. The focus should be on engaging students in active learning and not bombarding them with too much information. Reading materials, a textbook-style reading, remains a traditional yet effective method for pre-class learning (Han and Klein 2019). However, to enhance their effectiveness, these readings are often accompanied by reading quizzes or other assessment tools to ensure comprehension and engagement. While videos are great for explaining complex concepts, reading materials are useful when one is looking for references or background information; the quizzes are helpful to understand the prior knowledge and podcasts are good to listen to stories and interviews; games are helpful in learning and practicing skills, and simulations develop problem-solving skills.

Nature of pre-class activity: the more interactive the pre-class activity, the better it is. There should be enough scope for curiosity, to simulate interest and encourage participation. The reading material can be made attractive and engaging via the addition of annotations, poll, quizzes, audio video elements and comments. The quizzes can be made more engaging by adding elements of gamification, such as leader boards, badges and points; similarly, simulations can involve animations. The implementation of gamification in pre-class learning activities has shown promise in enhancing student engagement in terms of behavior, emotion and cognition (Yin and Chen 2020). Another approach involves student participation in video production, which has been found to positively impact students' satisfaction with the pre-class learning experience (Liu et al. 2024). Having a platform to collaborate and communicate with peers or with faculty encourages students to share their thoughts, questions and feedback and integrate learning. In language learning contexts, various strategies have been employed for pre-class vocabulary acquisition, including context drills, word-on-board games, flash-card games, mini-presentations, role-playing, dictionary use and blended learning approaches (Alghamdi and Al Ahmed 2018). Compared with traditional teaching methods, these methods have proven effective in improving students' vocabulary acquisition.

Materials aligned with the learning outcomes and the in-class activities: the pre-class activities should be such that they are relevant and are aligned with the learning outcomes and the in-class activities. There should be a clear goal and purpose for which they are designed. They should be helpful in creating a logical sequence and should serve as a basis for discussion, exploration and application.

Provision for feedback and support: there should be enough provision for timely support and feedback in pre-class activities. Answering questions via chat or e-mail, providing hints and links for further readings are a few methods that can be adopted to provide support. Students should also be encouraged to provide support to each other, especially by creating learning communities or peer review platforms.

6.3. Pre-class learning chatbots

6.3.1. *Types of chatbots*

Recent advancements in artificial intelligence and machine learning have led to the development of chatbots capable of engaging in conversation with human users. The basic definition of chatbots is that they are computer programs that simulate and process human conversation (either written or spoken), allowing humans to interact with digital devices as if they were communicating with a real person. They are designed to simulate human conversation through natural language processing to understand and respond to user queries in a human-like manner. The types of chatbots can range from simple rudimentary programs that respond to specific keywords to sophisticated AI-powered assistants that can understand and respond to complex queries and deliver personalized answers. In the education sector, Wollny et al. (2021) classified AI chatbots into three major categories: mentoring chatbots, assisting chatbots and learning chatbots.

Mentoring chatbots: these are chatbots that are designed to provide support similar to that provided by human mentors. They provide personalized guidance and support by helping users with self-awareness, skill development and careers advice. They also provide suggestions regarding relevant training materials and track progress. They help the user develop an understanding of themselves, their strengths and weaknesses and help them identify any gaps in their knowledge. The same information can also be used to offer suggestions on specific skills to be acquired and the source of relevant course or course material and practice exercise. They help users set realistic and achievable goals, break them down into smaller steps and map progress. It is a digital mentor with 24/7 availability.

Assisting chatbots: these chatbots are designed to interact with the user through voice or text and provide information or help in completing a task or answering a question in a conversational manner. Students can use these chatbots for information retrieval, task management, course assistance and problem solving. These chatbots can process information from multiple sources to provide relevant answers to the student's queries. This helps students develop a better understanding of the pre-class materials. When embedded in an institution's LMS, they can help students answer questions about deadlines and assignments and track progress. Students can also set reminders and take their help in organizing tasks.

Learning chatbots: these chatbots are designed to facilitate learning and knowledge acquisition. They act as virtual tutors and provide explanations of the topics, guide students through the learning material and provide personalized learning experiences. These chatbots are designed such that they can adapt to the learner's pace and style and can create a more engaging and effective learning experience. They also provide access to expert knowledge and offer interactive exercises and quizzes. On the basis of the user's performance in the exercises and quizzes, they can provide immediate feedback that can be used for planning further topics to be learned and help learners strengthen their understanding. These chatbots are designed such that they can help learners practice and apply their knowledge in a safe and controlled environment and can connect with subject experts and receive personalized advice.

6.3.2. *Role of the chatbot in pre-class learning*

Multiple studies have suggested that the flipped classroom facilitates improvement across subject disciplines (Cheng et al. 2019); however, its practices are not without challenges. Many students face challenges with the pre-class component, which is the basis of the flipped classroom. Major challenges include a lack of guidance and help at home during pre-class learning (Akçayır and Akçayır 2018). In addition, there are other challenges, such as monitoring pre-class preparations, access to resources on the basis of students' interest and constant support. For all such conditions, AI chatbots can be used to provide assistance in the following manner.

Real-time assistance: AI chatbots can facilitate real-time communication between students, offer suggestions, solve questions, provide answers, guide students through course materials and promote effective collaboration even outside the physical classroom. The flipped classroom approach, which involves students engaging with course material at home and participating in active learning during class, can be significantly augmented by integrating chatbot technology (Varnavsky 2022). Chatbots can serve as virtual assistants, providing 24/7 support to students as they work through pre-class materials. They can help students prepare well for in-class activities by answering questions, clarifying concepts and providing additional resources. They can also help students set reminders to review content, display relevant content and links, access learning through tests and control questions (Varnavsky 2022). This type of continuous support keeps the student motivated to learn and provides continuous engagement with the course content outside the class hours.

Customized content: providing customized content is another area where chatbots can be very effective in flipped classrooms. Traditional one-size-fits-all teaching methods often fail to address the diverse learning styles, paces and preferences of students. Chatbots bridge this gap by delivering customized content designed to enhance engagement and improve learning outcomes. As students interact with chatbots, leveraging natural language processing and machine learning techniques can adapt to their learning style and provide customized exercises, targeted explanations and tailored content to suit the needs of individual students. It also offers feedback and guides students on the basis of their proficiency level and learning pace (Li et al. 2023). These personalization approaches allow students to engage with course material at their own speed, reinforcing concepts they find challenging and glancing through the familiar content. Chatbots that are designed to cater to multiple learning styles and preferences and that are aligned with different learning pedagogies also exist. Different kinds of multimedia elements, such as text, images, videos and audio, can be incorporated into these chatbots to cater to diverse learning needs and help retain student attention (Almada et al. 2022).

Facilitate self-paced learning: self-paced learning has become an essential component of modern education, allowing learners to progress at a speed that suits their individual needs and schedules. In this context, chatbots are emerging as powerful tools that enable and enhance self-paced learning by offering interactive, personalized and readily accessible educational support. As chatbots are available 24/7, they allow students to access information and assistance regardless of time zones, classroom hours or fixed schedules. They can also adapt to individual learning styles and preferences and help in delivering content in a format that best suits each learner. As they can track the learner's progress, chatbots can adjust to the difficulty level and pace of learning on the basis of the learner's strengths and weaknesses. They can also provide immediate answers to learner questions, reducing frustration and preventing learning disruption. Complex topics can be broken down into smaller, more manageable subtopics on the basis of individual needs.

Virtual teaching assistance: chatbots can also serve as virtual tutors, providing instant answers to students' questions and clarifying complex topics before class. This immediate feedback helps students build confidence and reduces anxiety about upcoming lessons. As virtual teaching assistants, they help students by providing explanations, answering questions and clarifying confusion (Tam et al. 2023). Research indicates that in higher education, chatbots have shown promising results as virtual teaching assistants (Essel et al. 2022). Those who interacted with a chatbot performed academically better than those who interacted solely with the course instructor. In mathematics education, AI chatbots such as ChatGPT, Gemini and Perplexity have shown a very high level of impact on factors such as effectiveness, engagement, accessibility and personalization (Luzano 2024). There are many examples of the application of AI chatbots as virtual teaching assistants. For example, the use of chatbots in tourism courses has a positive effect on the development of intercultural communication and conversation through conversation practices and problem-solving tasks. Similarly, in mathematics education, chatbots can guide students through problem-solving processes and help them develop mathematical thinking skills before class sessions.

Progress monitoring and support: chatbots can analyze and assess student learning and help teachers identify a student's level of understanding of a topic (Okonkwo and Ade-Ibijola 2021). Individualized learning materials can be provided to topics where a student is facing challenges, and the collected data can also be used to profile the student and plan his future journey in the course by identifying the students at risk of failure and offering appropriate guidance (Zawacki-Richter et al. 2019). The data collected from the chatbot about students' interactions, test results and frequently asked questions can also be used to customize classroom activities to address specific learning needs.

Immediate feedback: when working on pre-class materials, there are instances in which students feel a need for feedback and support, and any delay can decrease their motivation for learning. Timely feedback also helps in reinforcing learning and enabling students to identify mistakes. With their ability to analyze responses in real time, AI-powered chatbots can provide instant feedback, effectively bridging the gap between independent study and classroom instruction and helping students identify areas that require further attention (Hew et al. 2021). Timely feedback allows students to correct their errors in time, thus preventing them from working in the dark and repeating mistakes. The feedback also allows students to identify the knowledge gap and work on the same, thus making them better prepared for in-class discussions and activities. Owing to their all-time availability, accessing information from chatbots is faster than interacting with teachers (Murad et al. 2019). Chatbots are capable of replying to emails to provide students with instant answers (Merelo et al. 2022). Students no longer need to wait for a response from their teacher, and the teacher does not need to spend time writing emails. Sandoval (2018) noted that teachers used FAQ-type chatbots to answer common administrative questions related to the course syllabus. Chatbots can provide students with immediate feedback, assisting in the metacognitive processes of learning (Chang et al. 2022).

6.3.3. *Examples of merger of chatbot and flipped classroom*

With the popularity and enhanced capability of AI and machine learning models backed by large language models, chatbots are increasingly being integrated into educational settings. They help institutions by offering innovative ways to enhance learning, provide personalized instruction and support students and educators in various subjects. The major benefit of using these AI-powered tools is their ability to provide clock services, thus enabling instant feedback and interactive learning experiences (Ghayoomi 2023).

There are numerous chatbots currently available that are changing education; in language education, chatbots have shown promising results. Studies have shown that AI chatbot-based instruction can reduce students' anxiety about learning English writing by offering immediate feedback and allowing students to learn at their own pace (Hawanti and Zubaydulloevna 2023). The AsasaraBot, designed to teach high school students' cultural content in English or French, has proven effective in combining language learning with cultural education. Similarly, the chatbot Mission Fluent has shown notable improvements in English pronunciation among vocational students in Hanoi (Hoang et al. 2023). A chatbot called Replika was explored by Lin and Mubarok (2021) in language learning, where it allowed the students to interact and practice English speaking. It is not only readymade chatbots or applications that were used by the researchers; there were instances where customized chatbots and applications were built; for example, Varnavsky (2022) developed an application based on Python programming and incorporated the same Telegram (a messaging application) for outside-classroom learning and built an application for assessing students' performance where they detailed the variable and system parameters to understand the time taken to complete the pre-class quiz and the fraction of correctly answered pre-class quizzes. They also integrated the application of Facebook and Telegram for easy access. Researchers have also used platforms such as Google Dialogflow and IBM Watson Assistant (Huang et al. 2019) to develop chatbots for pre-class learning. However, these were customized for intent, entity and dialogues; the intent included the possible question the user may ask, the entity included the keywords to be used for answering questions and the dialogues were content or flow of content relevant to the course.

Some examples of readily available chatbots include Koanly's chat tutor and Streebo's Smart Bots. While Koanly's chat tutor is designed to answer questions and provide study support and review, students can access instant and personalized help adapted to their individual needs and schedules, eliminating temporary barriers to learning. The Streebo chatbot contributes to pre-class learning not only by answering questions but also by providing review and support and offering detailed explanations, suggesting additional materials and adapting its approach according to the student's progress. Both of these applications offer review and support in real time, facilitating continuous learning.

The integration of deep learning techniques in chatbot development has further enhanced its capabilities in educational settings. Models using long short-term memory (LSTM) networks and attention mechanisms can process complex, multi-sentence queries, allowing for more natural and context-aware interactions with students (Joshi et al. 2023). This advanced natural language processing enables chatbots to provide more accurate and relevant responses to student inquiries, effectively simulating a one-on-one tutoring experience.

6.4. Challenges of integrating AI chatbots into flipped learning

Although chatbots have the potential to significantly enhance pre-class learning by providing personalized support, increased engagement and data-driven insights for instructors, reducing anxiety, promoting self-study skills and offering flexible learning opportunities, the implementation of chatbots in flipped classrooms is not without challenges. The major roadblocks include limited technical functionality, lack of authenticity in interactions and insufficient student motivation (Lo and Hew 2023). The other challenges include ethical considerations, technical limitations and pedagogical challenges (Lata and Kumar 2023).

Chatbots collect and process large amounts of student data to provide personalized learning to students; however, the way these data are stored, shared and protected is also a question (Baskara 2023). To maintain trust in the learning environment, ensuring that a student's personal information remains confidential and is not misused is highly important. There can also be situations where chatbots may end up providing biased answers due to the kind of data they are trained with, which can lead to biased answers or a reinforcement of stereotypes, impacting the development of inclusive, secure and equitable learning.

Integrating chatbots in flipped learning represents a transformative step toward modernization; however, there are challenges in terms of reliability and scalability. The successful integration of chatbots is possible only when diverse queries can be handled simultaneously without providing inaccurate responses or crashes. Past studies have indicated that, at times, chatbots may not be successful in solving unstructured problems and queries raised by students (Huang et al. 2019), and they also face challenges in terms of speech recognition accuracy and response accuracy (Timpe-Laughlin et al. 2022). There is a need to develop algorithms that are capable of understanding complex and varied student inputs, particularly in a multilingual or culturally diverse setup. One should remember that technical glitches such as misunderstanding user queries or providing irrelevant answers can undermine trust in the technology. There are cases where students depend on chatbots for limited questions and upon human support for the rest (Timpe-Laughlin et al. 2022). To maximize the potential of chatbots in flipped classrooms, factors such as content design, ease of usage, content presentation, user engagement, security, flexibility and alternative learning approaches and formats need to be considered (Wiboolyasarin et al. 2024).

6.5. Conclusion

Although the use of chatbots in flipped classrooms is still in its early stages, it presents a promising avenue for enhancing student engagement, supporting personalized learning and improving overall educational outcomes. With the constant refinement of chatbots and embedded technology, we can expect to have more tailormade chatbots for education, especially in the context of pre-learning. Chatbots have great potential to become an integral part of the flipped classroom experience. By providing round-the-clock access to personalized content and feedback and facilitating active learning, chatbots have empowered learners to take charge of their pre-class learning needs. However, they should not be taken as a replacement for human interaction; rather, they should be considered as a part of a large support system. There is a need to strike a balance between leveraging chatbot capabilities and preserving the human elements of empathy and mentorship. While designing and implementing AI-driven chatbots, it is important to ensure that they align with pedagogical goals and support learning (Uzunboylu and Karagozlu 2015;

Almada et al. 2022). Successful integration should also address challenges such as data privacy, bias and accessibility. With the growing adoption of AI chatbots in education, there is a need to explore ways to optimize their usage and understand their impact on learning outcomes. Future chatbots should be capable of understanding complex queries and providing unbiased correct answers. By leveraging the power of both human instruction and AI-powered assistance, more dynamic and effective learning environments that cater to the diverse needs of modern students can be created. When implemented thoughtfully, they can serve as powerful allies in the flipped classroom model, bridging the gap between independent study and classroom learning. As educational technology continues to evolve, chatbots will play a crucial role in transforming flipped classrooms into more dynamic, effective and student-centered environments, preparing learners for a future that values both independence and collaboration.

6.6. References

Akçayır, G. and Akçayır, M. (2018). The flipped classroom: A review of its advantages and challenges. *Comput. Educ.*, 126, 334–345. doi: 10.1016/j.compedu.2018.07.021.

Alghamdi, A.K. and Al Ahmed, S. (2018). Effective methods for teaching English vocabulary to Saudi female students. *Journal of Education and Learning (EduLearn)*, 12(1), 118–125.

Almada, A., Yu, Q., Patel, P. (2022). Proactive chatbot framework based on the PS2CLH model: An AI-deep learning chatbot assistant for students. In *Proceedings of SAI Intelligent Systems Conference*. Springer, Cham.

Baskara, F.R. (2023). Chatbots and flipped learning: Enhancing student engagement and learning outcomes through personalised support and collaboration. *IJORER: International Journal of Recent Educational Research*, 4(2), 223–238.

Bhardwaj, A. and Kumar, V. (2022). Web and social media approach to marketing of engineering courses in India. *International Journal of Business Innovation and Research*, 27(4), 541–555.

Bhardwaj, A. and Kumar, V. (2024). Challenges in online collaboration to augment Industry 4.0. *International Journal of Technology, Policy and Management*, 24(1), 71–92.

Chang, C.-Y., Kuo, S.-Y., Hwang, G.-H. (2022). Chatbot-facilitated nursing education: Incorporating a knowledge-based chatbot system into a nursing training program. *Educational Technology & Society*, 25(1), 15–27 [Online]. Available at: https://www.j-ets.net/collection/published-issues/25_1.

Che, Z., Hew, K.F., Lo, C.K. (2020). Pre-class learning strategies of a flipped lesson: A randomized comparative study of student achievement and cognitive load. In *Learning Environment and Design: Current and Future Impacts*, Ma, W.W.K., Tong, K.-w., Tso, W.B.A. (eds). Springer, Singapore.

Cheng, L., Ritzhaupt, A.D., Antonenko, P. (2019). Effects of the flipped classroom instructional strategy on students' learning outcomes: A meta-analysis. *Educational Technology Research and Development*, 67, 793–824.

Deng, W. (2016). Application of flipped classroom teaching mode based on constructive theory in the course of introduction to nursing. *Chinese Journal of Practical Nursing*, 1429–1433.

Dou, Y. (2023). Innovation of flipped classroom teaching mode in college vocal music teaching. *Frontiers in Art Research*, 5(2), 76–79, doi: 10.25236/FAR.2023.050215.

Essel, H.B., Vlachopoulos, D., Tachie-Menson, A., Johnson, E.E., Baah, P.K. (2022). The impact of a virtual teaching assistant (chatbot) on students' learning in Ghanaian higher education. *International Journal of Educational Technology in Higher Education*, 19(1), 57.

Fung, C.H., Besser, M., Poon, K.K. (2021). Systematic literature review of flipped classroom in mathematics. *Eurasia Journal of Mathematics, Science and Technology Education*, 17(6), 1–17.

Ghayoomi, M. (2023). Applications of chatbots in education. In *Trends, Applications, and Challenges of Chatbot Technology*, Kuhail, M.A., Shawar, B.A., Hammad, R. (eds). IGI Global, Hershey, PA.

Han, E. and Klein, K.C. (2019). Pre-class learning methods for flipped classrooms. *American Journal of Pharmaceutical Education*, 83(1), 6922.

Hawanti, S. and Zubaydulloevna, K.M. (2023). AI chatbot-based learning: Alleviating students' anxiety in English writing classroom. *Bulletin of Social Informatics Theory and Application*, 7(2), 182–192.

Hew, K.F., Huang, W., Du, J., Jia, C. (2021). Using chatbots in flipped learning online sessions: Perceived usefulness and ease of use. In *Blended Learning: Re-thinking and Re-defining the Learning Process*, Li, R., Cheung, S.K.S., Iwasaki, C., Kwok, L.F., Kageto, M. (eds). Springer, Cham. doi: 10.1007/978-3-030-80504-3_14.

Hoa, H.T., Le Thi Thanh Nga, N.T., Hanh, B. (2024). A study on some strategies to improve vocabulary for first-year English major students at Hung Yen University of Technology and Education. *Journal of Science Hanoi Open University*. doi: 10.59266/houjs.2024.368.

Hoang, N.T., Han, D.N., Le, D.H. (2023). Exploring chatbot AI in improving vocational students' English pronunciation. *AsiaCALL Online Journal*, 14(2), 140–155.

Huang, W., Hew, K.F., Gonda, D.E. (2019). Designing and evaluating three chatbot-enhanced activities for a flipped graduate course. *Int. J. Mech. Eng. Rob. Res.*, 8(5), 813–818. doi: 10.18178/ijmerr.8.5.813-818.

Joshi, S., Shinde, S., Shinde, P., Sagar, N., Rathod, S. (2023). Chatbot using deep learning. *International Journal of Scientific Research in Computer Science, Engineering and Information Technology*, 9(1), 228–232.

Junio, D.A. and Bandala, A.A. (2019). Innovating academic writing through flipped classroom instruction. In *2019 IEEE 11th International Conference on Humanoid, Nanotechnology, Information Technology, Communication and Control, Environment, and Management (HNICEM)*.

Kim, M.K., Kim, S.M., Khera, O., Getman, J. (2014). The experience of three flipped classrooms in an urban university: An exploration of design principles. *The Internet and Higher Education*, 22, 37–50.

Kumar, V. and Lata, M. (eds) (2022). *The Future of E-Commerce*. Nova Science Publishers, New York. doi: 10.52305/KMUB3774.

Kumar, V. and Nanda, P. (2024). Social media and micro-lessons: A new paradigm of online learning. In *Optimizing Education Through Micro-Lessons: Engaging and Adaptive Learning Strategies*, Ilic, P. (ed.). IGI Global, New York.

Kumar, V. and Rewari, M. (2022). A responsible approach to higher education curriculum design. *International Journal of Educational Reform*, 31(4), 422–441.

Larson, M.P. and Linnell, J. (2023). Are students coming to class prepared? The importance of pre-class learning in a flipped classroom. *Issues in Accounting Education*, 38(3), 183–205.

Lata, M. and Kumar, V. (2023). Challenges to IoT security: Industry perspective. *Grenze International Journal of Engineering and Technology (GIJET)*, 9(1–2), 61–67.

Lata, M. and Kumar, V. (2024). A framework for security of public cloud environment. *International Journal of Electronic Security and Digital Forensics*, 16(4), 486–502.

Lata, M. and Sharma, V. (2024a). Cloud computing based blended learning: Quality assurance challenges. In *2024 International Conference on Communication, Computer Sciences and Engineering (IC3SE)*. IEEE, New York, 1731–1736.

Lata, M. and Sharma, V. (2024b). Smart city environment management: Challenges and opportunities. *Grenze International Journal of Engineering & Technology (GIJET)*, 10(2), 2159–2166.

Lata, M., Kumar, V., Sharma, V. (2024). Cloud computing applications in online learning. *Grenze International Journal of Engineering & Technology (GIJET)*, 10(2), 408–411.

Lee, J. and Choi, H. (2019). Rethinking the flipped learning pre-class: Its influence on the success of flipped learning and related factors. *British Journal of Educational Technology*, 50(2), 934–945.

Li, Y., Qu, S., Shen, J., Min, S., Yu, Z. (2023). Curriculum-driven Edubot: A framework for developing language learning chatbots through synthesizing conversational data. *arXiv*. doi: 10.48550/arXiv.2309.16804.

Lin, Y. T. (2019). Impacts of a flipped classroom with a smart learning diagnosis system on students' learning performance, perception, and problem solving ability in a software engineering course. *Computers in Human Behavior*, 95, 187–196.

Lin, C.J. and Mubarok, H. (2021). Learning analytics for investigating the mind map-guided AI chatbot approach in an EFL flipped speaking classroom. *Educ. Technol. Soc.*, 24, 16–35. doi: 10.30191/ETS.202110_24(4).0002.

Liu, J., Cao, S., Liu, X., Ye, C., Siano, P. (2024). Pre-class mode "flipped" again: Making videos instead of just watching them. *Heliyon*, 10(6), e28105.

Lo, C.K. and Hew, K.F. (2023). A review of integrating AI-based chatbots into flipped learning: New possibilities and challenges. *Frontiers in Education*, 8, 1175715.

Long, T., Zhiyan, W., Yang, X., Chen, L. (2019). Investigating the impact of interactive pre-class learning videos on pre-service teachers' learning performance in flipped classroom. In *2019 International Symposium on Educational Technology (ISET)*. IEEE, 155–159.

Luzano, J.F.P. (2024). Reshaping mathematics instruction via impact of AI chatbots on secondary education pre-service teachers. *International Journal of Studies in Education and Science*, 5(3), 233–245.

Merelo, J.J., Castillo, P.A., Mora, A.M., Barranco, F., Abbas, N., Guillén, A., Tsivitanidou, O. (2022). Exploring the role of chatbots and messaging applications in higher education: A teacher's perspective. In *Learning and Collaboration Technologies: Novel Technological Environments*, Zaphiris, P. and Ioannou, A. (eds). Springer, Cham, 205–223. doi: 10.1007/978-3-031-05675-8_16.

Murad, D.F., Irsan, M., Akhirianto, P.M., Fernando, E., Murad, S.A., Wijaya, M.H. (2019). Learning support system using chatbot in "Kejar C Package" homeschooling program. In *2019 International Conference on Information and Communications Technology (ICOIACT)*. IEEE, 32–37. doi: 10.1109/ICOIACT46704.2019.8938479.

Nanda, P. and Kumar, V. (2024). New generation technologies: Development vs. ethical challenges. *International Journal of Business Information Systems*, 46(3), 411–434.

Nayan, S. and Rawian, R.M. (2022). A preliminary study on learners' perception on out of class autonomous vocabulary learning strategies. *Malaysian Journal of Social Sciences and Humanities (MJSSH)*, 7(5), e001487.

Nayar, K.B. and Kumar, V. (2015). Benefits of cloud computing in education during disaster. In *Proceedings of the International Conference on Transformations in Engineering Education: ICTIEE 2014*. Springer, Delhi, 191–201.

Okonkwo, C.W. and Ade-Ibijola, A. (2021). Chatbots applications in education: A systematic review. *Computers and Education: Artificial Intelligence*, 2, 100033. doi: 10.1016/j.caeai.2021.100033.

Rai, S. and Lata, M. (2024). Futuristic outlook of online learning: The post-pandemic era. In *Technology-mediated Learning During the Pandemic*, Singh, J. and Kumar, V. (eds). Routledge, Delhi.

Sams, A. and Bergmann, J. (2013). Flip your students' learning. *Educational Leadership*, 70(6), 16–20.

Sandoval, Z.V. (2018). Design and implementation of a chatbot in online higher education settings. *Issues in Information Systems*, 19(4) [Online]. Available at: https://www.researchgate.net/publication/328245964_Designing_Chatbots_for_Higher_Education_Practice.

Sun, Z. and Xie, K. (2020). How do students prepare in the pre-class setting of a flipped undergraduate math course? A latent profile analysis of learning behavior and the impact of achievement goals. *The Internet and Higher Education*, 46, 100731.

Tam, W., Huynh, T., Tang, A., Luong, S., Khatri, Y., Zhou, W. (2023). Nursing education in the age of artificial intelligence powered Chatbots (AI-Chatbots): Are we ready yet?. *Nurse Education Today*, 129, 105917.

Timpe-Laughlin, V., Sydorenko, T., Daurio, P. (2022). Using spoken dialogue technology for L2 speaking practice: What do teachers think? *Comput. Assist. Lang. Learn.*, 35, 1194–1217. doi: 10.1080/09588221.2020.1774904.

Uzunboylu, H. and Karagozlu, D. (2015). Flipped classroom: A review of recent literature. *World Journal on Educational Technology*, 7(2), 142–147.

Varnavsky, A.N. (2022). Chatbot to increase the effectiveness of the "flipped classrooms" technology. In *Proceedings of 2022 2nd International Conference on Technology Enhanced Learning in Higher Education*. IEEE, Lipetsk. doi: 10.1109/TELE55498.2022.9801001.

Wang, W., Wang, Q., Luo, X. (2019). Evaluation of the effect of flipping classroom in the teaching of marketing. In *2019 International Conference on Advanced Education, Management and Humanities (AEMH 2019)*. Atlantis Press, Dordrecht.

Wiboolyasarin, W., Wiboolyasarin, K., Tiranant, P., Boonyakitanont, P., Jinowat, N. (2024). Designing chatbots in language classrooms: an empirical investigation from user learning experience. *Smart Learning Environments*, 11(1), 32.

Wollny, S., Schneider, J., Di Mitri, D., Weidlich, J., Rittberger, M., Drachsler, H. (2021). Are we there yet? – A systematic literature review on chatbots in education. *Frontiers in Artificial Intelligence*, 4. doi: 10.3389/frai.2021.654924.

Yin, H. and Chen, Y. (2020). How gamification affects students' engagement and language learning beliefs in pre-class learning of flipped EFL courses: A theoretical analysis. In *Proceedings of the 2nd World Symposium on Software Engineering*, 211–215.

Zawacki-Richter, O., Marín, V. I., Bond, M., Gouverneur, F. (2019). Systematic review of research on artificial intelligence applications in higher education – Where are the educators? *International Journal of Educational Technology in Higher Education*, 16(1), 1–27. doi: 10.1186/s41239-019-0171-0.

Zhang, S. (2018). The effect of teaching mode of flipped classroom on medical students' information literacy. *Chinese Journal of Medical Education Research*, 260–264.

Zhang, J., Chen, H., Wang, X., Huang, X., Xie, D. (2024). Application of flipped classroom teaching method based on ADDIE concept in clinical teaching for neurology residents. *BMC Med Educ*, 24, 366. doi: 10.1186/s12909-024-05343-z.

7

Leveraging Chatbots in Management Education: Enhancing LMS Integration and Flipped Classroom Models

The swift progress in artificial intelligence (AI) has sparked interest in the integration of AI chatbots into the teaching and learning processes of higher education institutions. This research examines the many elements that might affect the integration of chatbots into learning management systems (LMSs) and flipped classroom (FC) models of management institutions in India. Three primary factors have been identified, namely, educational institutions' existing infrastructure and preparedness to integrate new technologies and pedagogical frameworks due to the incorporation of AI chatbots in the educational process, as well as students' attitudes toward embracing and utilizing these technologies throughout their academic experience. These factors strongly influence the incorporation of AI into institutions' LMS and FC models, leading to enhanced academic outcomes (AOs) for students. The study employed PLS–SEM to analyze the responses of 162 educators across various business management institutions in India through an online questionnaire. A five-point Likert scale was used to capture the responses. This research offers direction for educators and business management institutions in incorporating emerging AI technology into their instructional methods to improve student learning by capitalizing on the benefits of this technology and addressing potential drawbacks, especially in the context of business management education.

7.1. Introduction

The advent of technology is changing the way things are being executed in different fields, including education (Kumar and Bhardwaj 2020). New approaches to teaching are being implemented in higher education institutions, including flipped learning and enhancing the working of learning management systems (LMSs) by

Chapter written by Arunava DALAL and Subhajit BHATTACHARYA.

integrating AI and chatbots. For example, AI can help in social learning through integrated group sessions by enabling online community engagement (Zawacki-Richter et al. 2019; Ernestivita et al. 2024). These new technologies are expected to improve student engagement and learning outcomes through personalized support (Tangkittipon et al. 2020; Lin and Mubarok 2021). The FC inverts the traditional classroom setting where students engage in direct learning outside of the class and utilize class time for problem solving and higher order thinking (Yusuf and Taiye 2021), which leads to higher students engagement and motivation (Almodaires et al. 2019). Chatbots can simulate human interactions, providing students with personalized support through feedback and assessments (Kumar and Silva 2020; Chen et al. 2021), leading to an engaging and interactive learning experience for them (Suhel et al. 2020). Thus, teachers are increasingly using FCs and chatbots to enhance student learning outcomes, and these technologies are considered to be part of higher education institutions' LMSs for better outcomes (Aldahwan and Alsaeed 2020).

A study by Qazi et al. (2024) on the developments and challenges of AI-driven LMSs proposed enhancements in the LMS in the application layer and presentation layer in the form of FC models for effective learning environments and suitable user interface designs for better utilization of LMS facilities and resources, including AI-based chatbots (Lata and Kumar 2023). Other studies have examined the use of chatbots in the context of FCs (Baskara 2023; Khlaisang and Teo 2024) and integrated chatbots with existing LMSs (Aldahwan and Alsaeed 2020; Qazi et al. 2024) to improve student engagement and AOs. However, the use of chatbots in the learning context for higher education institutions is in the early stage, and as suggested by Baskara (2023), more research needs to be conducted in this field, which the present study intends to pursue. Few studies have investigated the key antecedents connected to student characteristics, pedagogical designs (PDs) and the preparedness of higher education institutions to embrace and integrate chatbots within their educational frameworks and FC methodologies for enhancing academic performance, especially in the realm of management education in developing countries such as India (Rai and Lata 2024).

This study aims to address the above research gap by conceptualizing a framework that leverages chatbots in management education by integrating them into the LMS and flipped learning models of institutions to improve the AOs of students. The current study has the potential to enhance faculty members' comprehension of the advantages associated with chatbot utilization, as these tools can significantly increase their productivity by allowing more time for high-value tasks and improved preparation for classroom activities. All of these factors ultimately lead to an enhanced reputation of the business school. The study analyzed the responses collected from 162 educators teaching in different business management institutions and management departments at universities across India, who are important stakeholders for any education institution, to develop the framework (Lata and Kumar 2022). The next section is related to the literature review and hypothesis development, followed by the methodology and results sections, where the outcome of the analysis is presented. The following section discusses the outcomes of the study, and finally, the conclusion section includes implications and limitations of the present study.

7.2. Literature review and hypothesis development

7.2.1. *Flipped classrooms*

An FC is a pedagogical approach that, as the name suggests, inverts the traditional classroom model by the use of technology. Here, the students watch online resources outside of the classroom, and the classroom is utilized to expand their knowledge through various activities, such as discussions and problem-solving (Brewer and Movahedazarhouligh 2018) using technologies suitable for interactive learning. FCs have been shown to improve high-order thinking and soft skills by allowing students to study at their own speed and utilizing technology both within and outside the classroom setting (Khlaisang et al. 2021; Ferguson 2023). According to some research, chatbots can complement key flipped learning concepts such as active learning and student-centered education (Diwanji et al. 2018), as chatbots can help students even after their class hours and stimulate group conversations and interactions.

7.2.2. *Learning management system*

An LMS, as defined by Oakes (2002), is both learner and organization focused, as it oversees the students' learning process within the competency of the organization. The LMS is expected to evaluate learners' existing knowledge and skills, collaborate with teachers and learners to set suitable learning goals, organize instruction, assess performance outcomes and facilitate enhancement of the overall learning environment (Watson and Watson 2007; Kadir and Aziz 2016). Therefore, an LMS can be a tool for advancing learner-centered education through collaborative learning (McConnell 2005; Migadadi 2009), interactive learning (Salajan et al. 2009) and adaptive learning (Brusilovsky and Peylo 2002) with the help of the successful integration of new technologies (Yang 2008), such as chatbots. AI can be used in adaptive education systems, for example, to create automated and reliable training-learning modules (Colchester et al. 2017) by evaluating student attributes to generate student profiles with the purpose of assessing their overall stage of knowledge (Aldahwan and Alsaeed 2020).

7.2.3. *Institute readiness*

Concerns related to the application of AI in the education sector, as discussed in the literature, are related to content flexibility, adoptability, reusability and the sharing and collaborative development of learning objects and structures (Aroyo and Mizoguchi 2003). The other challenges are related to the compatibility and integration of AI-related infrastructure (hardware and software systems) with existing facilities of institutions and organizations and the collection, control, storage and usage of data (Owoc et al. 2019). Having an adequate amount of data is a prerequisite to producing automated analytics that will improve the learning experiences of users, but technologies for capturing data are improving along with increases in costs, which can act as a deterrent for institutions, particularly those from low- and middle-income countries (Pedro et al. 2019). Data privacy, data security and student anonymity are other ethical and privacy concerns related to using chatbots in education (Bahja et al. 2020).

Educators are another type of stakeholder whose cooperation is critical for the institution's ability to benefit from AI and chatbots. The usefulness of the learning analytics provided by these new technologies is dependent on how instructors use them to integrate new abilities (Luckin et al. 2016; Lata and Kumar 2021). Education institutes must equip their faculty to effectively manage human and AI resources, interpret data provided by AI-enabled systems and enable teachers to incorporate digital skills as well as more interpersonal skills such as mentoring and emotional support, as they will have more time to engage in these activities with their students with AI taking over repetitive tasks (Pedro et al. 2019). As self-efficacy (SE), in the context of information technology, influences users' perceived usefulness of the technology and affects their attitudes toward adoption of the technology, the same thing holds for educators' adoption of AI technology (Motaghian et al. 2013; Teo and Zhou 2014; Yeşilyurt et al. 2016). Researchers have reported that teachers with greater SE are more likely to successfully incorporate technology-enabled teaching into their classroom (Kumar and Lata 2022).

As the benefits that an institute may achieve by implementing AI and chatbots in their classrooms and throughout their students' academic journeys are dependent on their willingness to do so and their ability to address technology- and content-related factors, the following hypotheses are proposed:

– *H1*: institute readiness (IR) plays a significant role in the process of integrating chatbots into the FC model of management institutions.

– *H2*: IR plays a significant role in the process of integrating chatbots into management institutions' LMSs.

7.2.4. *Students' attitudes*

Students are the prime stakeholders for any educational institution, and one of the main reasons for incorporating technological advancements in the workings of the institutions is to achieve better AOs for the students (Kumar and Rewari 2023; Mittal and Kumar 2024). However, students' attitudes (SAs) also play an important role in their ability to benefit from these developments, such as AI and chatbots. Learners in the digital era seek more interactive and advanced technology than the conventional classroom approach, which typically focuses on lectures and discussions (Khlaisang and Teo 2024). Chatbots have acquired significance among recent AI advancements with the debut of OpenAI's ChatGPT in November 2022 (OpenAI 2022) and their possible disruptive influence in academia is now being explored (Lo 2023). Li et al. (2023) identified concerns related to learning outcomes for students due to their academic integrity. A study by Stöhr et al. (2024) examined SA toward chatbots and reported that almost half of the respondents were concerned about the potential influence of chatbots. The same study, while evaluating the effect of chatbots on their learning, revealed that almost half of the respondents believed that chatbots made them more effective learners. Therefore, SA toward new technologies, as well as how they will embrace them and use them during their academic journeys while enrolled in courses at higher education institutions, are influenced by their attitudes. Thus, the following hypotheses are given:

– *H3*: SA significantly influence the process of integrating chatbots into the FC model of management institutions.

– *H4*: SA significantly influence the process of integrating chatbots into the management institutions' LMS.

7.2.5. *Pedagogical design*

A recent study by Stöhr et al. (2024) clearly highlighted that the majority of students are aware of the potential of chatbots for their learning process. This highlights the importance of modifying PD in higher education to harness the benefits of technological advancements (Singh et al. 2022). AI-based chatbots can deliver real-time individualized replies, creating a dynamic learning experience, but they may not provide a rigorous and standardized educational framework that is favorable for organized learning (Ateeq et al. 2024; Lata et al. 2024). The inherent interactive qualities of chatbots have been ascribed to increased involvement and enhanced retention among students through their active participation (Almusaed et al. 2023; Mogavi et al. 2024). Additionally, overreliance on technology may hamper the critical thinking ability of students (Dai et al. 2023). These factors may be considered while redesigning the pedagogical framework.

Given that PD will play an important role in integrating chatbots into higher education institutions' FC models and LMS to create superior learning experiences for their students, the following hypotheses are articulated:

– *H5*: PD plays a significant role in developing FC models in management institutions that integrate chatbots.

– *H6*: PD plays a significant role in integrating chatbots into the management institutions' LMS.

7.2.6. *Academic outcomes*

Chatbots have been shown to improve students' active learning by providing individualized support outside of class, clarifying topics, assisting them in answering questions and providing feedback on their work (Baskara 2023). The same study revealed that chatbots might increase students' academic achievements in a FC setting, but certain ethical and integrity problems must be addressed when chatbots and AI are employed in higher education. Similarly, integrating AI into LMSs has the potential to improve learning flexibility, resulting in greater academic achievements for students (Dżega and Pietruszkiewicz 2013). This technology's assets include autonomy and intelligence, which contribute to the increased effectiveness of the educational benefits it offers to students (Aldahwan and Alsaeed 2020) and better utilization of faculty resources, as AI will replace their repetitive work (Pedro et al. 2019). However, LMSs must overcome ethical challenges due to the AI-based content generation tools that students use to complete their assignments (Qazi et al. 2024; Sharma and Kumar 2017); therefore, educators' knowledge and skills are vital for developing assignments to improve students' AOs (Mollick and Mollick 2023). Considering these factors, the following hypotheses are proposed:

– *H7*: the chatbot-integrated FC model significantly influences students' AOs in management institutions.

– *H8*: chatbot integrated LMSs in business institutions significantly influence students' AOs.

7.3. Theoretical framework

On the basis of the literature review and the hypotheses that have been framed, a theoretical framework has been developed, as shown in Figure 7.1. The first-order constructs are IR, SA and PD. These factors influence the AI and chatbot integrated FC and LMS of business management institutions to provide superior AOs for students.

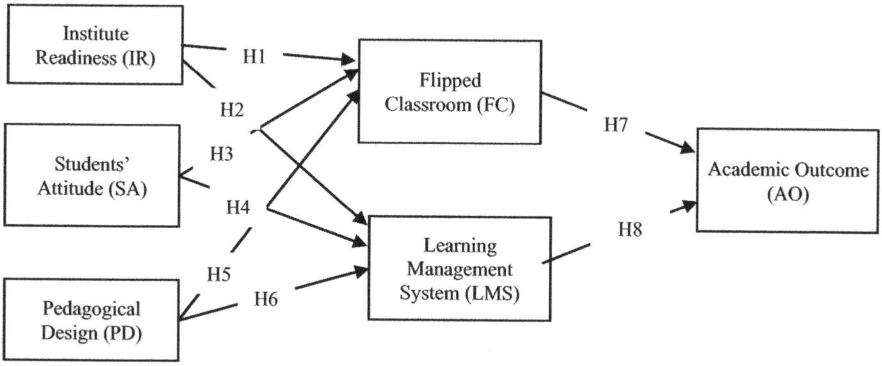

Figure 7.1. *Theoretical framework*

7.4. Methodology

Parameter	Definition	Frequency
Gender	Male	87
	Female	75
Age (years)	30–40 years	51
	41–50 years	79
	50 years and above	32
Teaching level	Graduate level	84
	Postgraduate level	78
Specialization	Marketing	53
	Finance	31
	Human resource	37
	Business analytics	15
	Supply chain	13
	Others	13
Experience	5–10 years	94
	10–20 years	55
	20 years and above	13
Location	North India	39
	South India	29
	East India	53
	West India	41

Table 7.1. *Demographic break-up of the respondents*

Data were collected from 162 faculty members at different business schools and universities in India offering graduate and postgraduate management programs across India. The minimum criteria for these responders were that they had been in the teaching profession for at least five years and had or intended to employ emerging technologies such as AI in their teaching methods. An online questionnaire with a five-point Likert scale, with 1 denoting strongly disagree and 5 denoting strongly agree, was prepared and shared among the target respondents. The literature guided the development of the questionnaire. The authors employed a convenience sample strategy for this study, distributing the questionnaire to their personal connections and relevant groups. Among the approximately 400 professors to whom the questionnaire was shared, 162 had complete responses. The responses were validated and analyzed via SmartPLS 3.0 software. Table 7.1 provides the demographic details of the respondents.

7.5. Findings

Table 7.2 shows the parameter estimation for the measurement model. As all of the item loadings exceed 0.70, the model's convergent validity is established (Byrne 2010). The reliability of the current model is apparent, as Cronbach's alpha coefficient values are greater than 0.70 for all of the reflective constructs (Fornell and Larcker 1981; Hair et al. 2012). CR values are above 0.7, indicating the internal consistency of the research model (Hair et al. 2012). Dijkstra–Henseler's rho (rA) values greater than 0.70 suggest that the model has stronger internal consistency reliability (Dijkstra 1983). The AVE for all of the parameters is greater than 0.5, demonstrating convergent validity (Hair et al. 2012).

Table 7.3 provides the adjusted R^2 values, which are above 0.5, suggesting that the model's observed variables are adequately explained by the input variables (Hair et al. 2012).

The model fit indices given in Table 7.4 indicate the acceptability of the model (Hair et al. 2012).

The Fornell–Larcker criterion is a widely used method for assessing the discriminant validity of measurement models (Fornell and Larcker 1981). Based on this criterion, the square root of the average variance extracted by a construct should exceed the correlation between that construct and any other construct. A discriminant test was conducted using the Fornell–Lacker criterion, as outlined in Table 7.5, and the results support that the variables are discriminant from each other.

Factors	Items	Item loadings	Cronbach's alpha	rho_A	Composite Reliability (CR)	Average Variance extracted (AVE)
Institute readiness (IR)			0.718	0.724	0.852	0.591
	Institutional IT infrastructure (IR1)	0.722				
	Digital policy (IR2)	0.803				
	Faculty's digital skills (IR3)	0.766				
	Faculty's self-efficacy (IR4)	0.782				
Flipped classroom (FC)			0.803	0.809	0.871	0.629
	Chatbot integration (FC1)	0.780				
	Interactive learning (FC2)	0.814				
	Active learning (FC3)	0.829				
	Student-centered education (FC4)	0.745				
Learning management system (LMS)			0.745	0.755	0.854	0.661
	Usage of chatbots (LMS1)	0.798				
	Student engagement (LMS2)	0.806				
	Adaptive education (LMS3)	0.834				
Pedagogical design (PD)			0.815	0.815	0.890	0.730
	Alignment with AI integration (PD1)	0.827				
	Learning outcomes (PD2)	0.881				
	Students' critical thinking (PD3)	0.853				
Students' attitude (SA)			0.784	0.790	0.874	0.699
	Academic integrity (SA1)	0.847				
	Students' motives (SA2)	0.864				
	Learning preferences (SA3)	0.795				
Academic outcome (AO)			0.868	0.868	0.910	0.717
	Academic performance (AO1)	0.839				
	Learning flexibility (AO2)	0.863				
	Better faculty resource utilization (AO3)	0.842				
	Sense of digital ethics (AO4)	0.841				

Table 7.2. *Measurement model parameter estimation*

Latent variables	R square	R square adjusted
Academic outcome (AO)	0.677	0.673
Flipped classroom (FC)	0.639	0.632
Learning management system (LMS)	0.603	0.596

Table 7.3. *Outcomes of R-square and adjusted R-square*

	Saturated model	Estimated model
SRMR	0.077	0.081
d_ULS	1.38	1.502
d_G	0.597	0.634
Chi-square	541.471	558.386
NFI	0.725	0.717
RMS_Theta	0.175032	

Table 7.4. *PLS–SEM model fit indices*

Latent constructs	AVE	CR	AO	FC	LMS	PD	SA	IR
Academic outcome (AO)	0.717	0.91	**0.847**					
Flipped classroom (FC)	0.629	0.871	0.706	**0.793**				
Learning management system (LMS)	0.661	0.854	0.789	0.678	**0.813**			
Pedagogical design (PD)	0.73	0.89	0.626	0.718	0.704	**0.854**		
Students' attitude (SA)	0.699	0.874	0.486	0.566	0.583	0.543	**0.836**	
Institute readiness (IR)	0.591	0.852	0.73	0.687	0.642	0.579	0.525	**0.7687**

Table 7.5. *Discriminant validity: Fornell–Larcker criterion: composite reliability (CR), the square root of the average variance extracted (AVE) (in bold) and correlations between constructs (off-diagonal)*

Table 7.6 displays the results of hypothesis testing after bootstrapping was performed with 2,000 subsamples to ensure optimum finding stability (Hair et al. 2012) using SmartPLS 3.0. There is no collinearity between the formative indicators since the VIF values are less than 3 (Hair et al. 2011). All of the hypotheses exhibit a significant correlation with the path model, as shown in Figure 7.2.

Hypotheses	Relationship	Original sample (O)	Sample mean (M)	Standard deviation (STDEV)	T statistics (|O/STDEV|)	*p* values	VIF	Decision
H1	Institute readiness (IR) -> Flipped classroom (FC)	0.363	0.368	0.081	4.466	0	1.67	Supported
H2	Institute readiness (IR) -> Learning management system (LMS)	0.289	0.295	0.068	4.227	0	1.62	Supported
H3	Students' attitude (SA) -> Flipped classroom (FC)	0.141	0.144	0.064	2.194	0.029	1.56	Supported
H4	Students' attitude (SA) -> Learning management system (LMS)	0.198	0.191	0.087	2.267	0.024	1.52	Supported
H5	Pedagogical design (PD) -> Flipped classroom (FC)	0.431	0.422	0.076	5.678	0	1.706	Supported
H6	Pedagogical design (PD) -> Learning management system (LMS)	0.429	0.431	0.073	5.847	0	1.700	Supported
H7	Flipped classroom (FC) -> Academic outcome (AO)	0.316	0.317	0.075	4.238	0	1.84	Supported
H8	Learning management system (LMS) -> Academic outcome (AO)	0.575	0.577	0.069	8.354	0	1.85	Supported

Table 7.6. *Results of the structural model (standardized regression outcomes)*

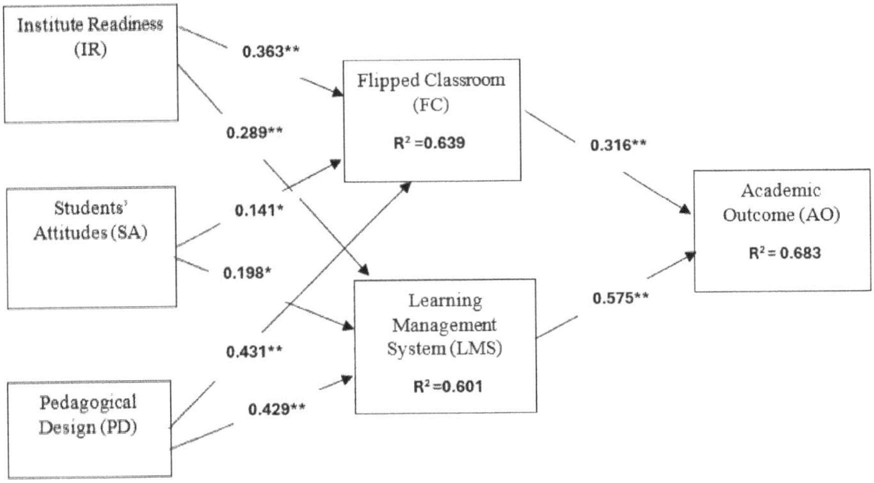

Figure 7.2. *Tested model. ** denotes a p value significant at the 1% level, whereas * signifies a p value significant at the 5% level*

7.6. Discussion

The present study was intended to identify the different factors that influence the successful integration of chatbots into institutions' existing LMS and FC models for better AOs, specifically in the context of business management institutions in developing countries such as India. To address this research gap, the study analyzed the responses of 162 educators who are teaching at different B-schools and management departments in universities across India for graduate and postgraduate courses via the PLS–SEM method. The study revealed that IR and PD significantly influenced chatbot integrated FCs and LMS at the 1% level, whereas SAs influenced FCs and LMS at the 5% level. AO was significantly influenced by FC and LMS at the 1% level.

An institute's ability to adapt to new technologies and incorporate them into its teaching methods via a chatbot-integrated LMS and FC model is determined by its data infrastructure, content and faculty members' ability to adopt new teaching methods for better learning experiences for their students. In the suggested model, all of these aspects are accounted for under "institute readiness". The element "digital policy" has greater item loading than the other components in this construct. This illustrates the respondents' concerns about data security, privacy and other ethical issues linked to data collection and use in the AI-integrated education paradigm (Lata and Kumar 2024). The institute's willingness to train its faculty members to use new technologies effectively, as well as the faculty's self-efficacy in embracing AI and chatbot-related LMS and FC teaching methods, will play a significant role, according to model analysis (Nanda and Kumar 2024).

According to the literature, the use of chatbots in the education process can increase student engagement (Almodaires et al. 2019; Tangkittipon et al. 2020; Lin and Mubarok 2021), improve students' problem-solving skills (Yusuf and Taiye 2021) and provide interactive (Suhel et al. 2020) and adaptive learning experiences (Brusilovsky and Peylo 2002). However, this can occur if pedagogy is matched to extract the best from these technologies while incorporating them into the institute's teaching process via the LMS and FC. The construct "pedagogical design" in the model adds to its relevance. According to the responses to the online survey, two variables in this construct, "learning outcomes" and "students' critical thinking" abilities, had relatively high item loadings. This underscores the fact that integrating chatbots with FC models and LMS will improve students' learning experiences regardless of class time, but overreliance on technology can potentially impair students' critical thinking ability. As a result, it is crucial to develop pedagogies that capitalize on the benefits of technology while overcoming the problems it presents in students' learning journeys.

The existence of educational institutions depends on their students, and processes are designed with this vital stakeholder in mind. As a result, the theoretical model takes into account "students' attitude" as well. The effectiveness of adding chatbots to FC models and LMSs is dependent on students' attitudes toward the use of these technologies. In the suggested model, the indicators "students' motives" and "academic integrity" have considerably higher item loadings. Earlier studies on students' motivation for using AI tools such as ChatGPT revealed a positive inclination among the majority of respondents (Ajlouni et al. 2023; Stöhr et al. 2024), but a number of studies (Sharma and Yadav 2022; Farhi et al. 2023; Li et al. 2023) have raised concerns about its use by students, claiming that it can have a negative impact on their learning processes due to their academic integrity. The current study underlines the same beliefs, and the high item loadings indicate their considerable effect, according to the responses of faculty members who agreed to participate in the survey.

An educational institution will seek to provide improved AOs for students through the integration of chatbots utilizing AI, and the conceptual model provided in this chapter is an attempt in that direction. The high item loadings for all indicators of the construct "academic outcome" show the significance given by respondents. The high point of this education process with the integration of chatbots is the students' learning flexibility, which may help them improve their academic performance if worries about digital ethics are addressed. This will also provide faculty members with more time to engage in more productive work, since repetitive tasks may be handled by AI (Pedro et al. 2019).

7.7. Conclusion

Recent studies have examined the various opportunities and concerns associated with incorporating AI into the higher education process (e.g. Tangkittipon et al. 2020; Lin and Mubarok 2021; Sharma and Yadav 2022; Ajlouni et al. 2023; Farhi et al. 2023; Li et al. 2023; Stöhr et al. 2024); however, Baskara (2023) suggested that more research is needed in this field to better understand its implications. This chapter aims to fill this research gap by identifying the important characteristics that might lead to improved student academic performance by including chatbots in institutions' LMS and FC models. The study identified three key elements, namely, institution readiness, PD and students' attitudes, as important when higher education institutions implement or improve their LMSs and flipped class models through chatbot integration to improve their academic performance.

Institutional readiness emerged as a significant factor, suggesting that if business schools intend to implement AI and chatbots in their educational methodologies, their current digital infrastructure and content must be sufficiently ready to harness the advantages of the new technology while also ensuring that faculty members are prepared to embrace the pedagogical shift. The research highlighted the significance of modifying PD to facilitate a dynamic learning experience for students through the integration of AI chatbots. Students' attitudes significantly influence the advantages derived from AI and chatbot-integrated LMSs and FC models, as students recognize chatbots' potential to enhance their learning efficacy, contingent upon overcoming the ethical challenges associated with the use of chatbots for answering quizzes and assignments, which may hinder their analytical skills.

7.7.1. *Implications*

Studies have focused on the implementation process of AI in education institutes (Khlaisang and Teo 2024; Qazi et al. 2024), understanding teachers' perspectives of adoption of AI in higher education institutes (Wang et al. 2021) and students' perceptions and usage of AI chatbots during their higher education (Ajlouni et al. 2023; Stöhr et al. 2024); however, few studies have attempted to incorporate all of these elements together in one study. The current study attempts to take a comprehensive approach by incorporating each important factor that might influence the process and empirically testing them. To the best of our knowledge, none of the previous studies have specifically considered the aspect of AI integration in business management institutions. This study analyzed the perspectives of educators involved in business management education for at least five years, highlighting the important factors influencing AI integration in these educational institutions. Different fields of study require different pedagogical approaches; therefore, performing domain-specific research, which is the other theoretical contribution, might be beneficial.

The findings of this study highlight critical aspects that business management institutions must consider when implementing AI in their LMS and FC formats. The first step is to evaluate their current LMS and select the best AI-based solution that can be integrated with it. The second is to evaluate and train their faculty so that they can provide their best while employing AI-integrated education technologies such as LMS and the FC method of teaching. Ateeq et al. (2024) highlighted the basic disparities in teaching techniques between traditional classroom methods and AI-supported FC models, as well as their incorporation into the institute's LMS. This emphasizes the importance of having a new pedagogical method, which the current study has emphasized – this is the third contribution. AI-integrated education systems can have drawbacks, such as affecting students' critical thinking abilities (Dai et al. 2023) as they grow overly reliant on technology, and academic integrity (Qazi et al. 2024) can be a source of concern. Therefore, the fourth implication is how professors should create assignments and quizzes so that students may continue to apply their critical thinking abilities, even after using AI chatbots such as ChatGPT. The assessment and grading procedure of students must also be reconsidered with the inclusion of AI in the education process.

7.7.2. *Limitations and future research directions*

The current investigation took place in India, analyzing a total of 162 responses. An increased sample size can enhance the comprehension of the factors affecting students' AOs as a result of the integration of AI in the educational delivery process of institutions. Similar studies can be expanded to various disciplines, such as humanities, engineering and law, to comprehend and examine the unique factors pertinent to each domain, as every field presents its own distinct academic outcomes for students. The findings may be extended to other developing nations, enhancing the broader relevance of this research.

7.8. References

Ajlouni, A.O., Wahba, F.A.A., Almahaireh, A.S. (2023). Students' attitudes towards using ChatGPT as a learning tool: The case of the University of Jordan. *International Journal of Interactive Mobile Technologies*, 17(18), 99. doi: 10.3991/ijim.v17i18.41753.

Aldahwan, N. and Alsaeed, N. (2020). Use of artificial intelligent in learning management system (LMS): A systematic literature review. *International Journal of Computer Applications*, 175(13), 16–26.

Almodaires, A.A., Alayyar, G.M., Almsaud, T.O., Almutairi, F.M. (2019). The effectiveness of flipped learning: A quasi-experimental study of the perceptions of Kuwaiti pre-service teachers. *International Education Studies*, 12(1), 10–23.

Almusaed, A., Almssad, A., Yitmen, I., Homod, R.Z. (2023). Enhancing student engagement: Harnessing "AIED"'s power in hybrid education – A review analysis. *Education Sciences*, 13(7), 632.

Aroyo, L. and Mizoguchi, R. (2003). Authoring support framework for intelligent educational systems. In *Proccedings of AI in Education, (AIED)*. University of Sydney, Sydney, 362–364.

Ateeq, A., Ayyash, M.M., Milhem, M., Alzoraiki, M., Alzaghal, Q.K. (2024). From textbooks to chatbots: The integration of chatgpt in modern university pedagogy. *Journal of Theoretical and Applied Information Technology*, 102(4), 1419–1432.

Bahja, M., Hammad, R., Butt, G. (2020). A user-centric framework for educational chatbots design and development. In *International Conference on Human-Computer Interaction*. Springer, Cham. doi: 10.1007/978-3-030-60117-1_3.

Baskara, F.R. (2023). Chatbots and flipped learning: Enhancing student engagement and learning outcomes through personalised support and collaboration. *IJORER: International Journal of Recent Educational Research*, 4(2), 223–238.

Brewer, R. and Movahedazarhouligh, S. (2018). Successful stories and conflicts: A literature review on the effectiveness of flipped learning in higher education. *Journal of Computer Assisted Learning*, 34(4), 409–416.

Brusilovsky, P. and Peylo, C. (2002). Adaptive and intelligent web-based educational systems. *International Journal of Artificial Intelligence in Education*, 13, 156–169.

Byrne, B.M. (2010). *Structural Equation Modeling with AMOS: Basic Concepts, Applications, and Programming (Multivariate Applications Series)*. Taylor & Francis Group, New York.

Chen, X., Zou, D., Xie, H., Cheng, G. (2021). Twenty years of personalized language learning. *Educational Technology & Society*, 24(1), 205–222.

Colchester, K., Hagras, H., Alghazzawi, D., Aldabbagh, G. (2017). A survey of artificial intelligence techniques employed for adaptive educational systems within e-learning platforms. *Journal of Artificial Intelligence and Soft Computing Research*, 7(1), 47–64.

Dai, Y., Liu, A., Lim, C.P. (2023). Reconceptualizing ChatGPT and generative AI as a student-driven innovation in higher education. *Procedia CIRP*, 119, 84–90. doi: 10.1016/j.procir.2023.05.002.

Dijkstra, T. (1983). Some comments on maximum likelihood and partial least squares methods. *Journal of Econometrics*, 22(1–2), 67–90.

Diwanji, P., Hinkelmann, K., Witschel, H.F. (2018). Enhance classroom preparation for flipped classroom using AI and analytics. In *Proceedings of the 20th International Conference on Enterprise Information Systems (ICEIS 2018)*. SCITEPRESS, Setúbal, 477–483.

Dżega, D. and Pietruszkiewicz, W. (2013). Intelligent decision-making support within the e-learning process. In *Intelligent and Adaptive Educational-Learning Systems: Achievements and Trends*, Pẽna-Ayala, A. (ed.). Springer, Berlin, Heidelberg.

Ernestivita, G., Kumar, V., Anisah, T.N. (2024). Role of gamification in crowdsourcing. In *Marketing and Gamification: Applications, Challenges, and Ethics*, Gupta, S., Nagina, R., Paruthi, M., Gupta, G. (eds). Routledge, Oxford.

Farhi, F., Jeljeli, R., Aburezeq, I., Dweikat, F.F., Al-shami, S.A., Slamene, R. (2023). Analyzing the students' views, concerns, and perceived ethics about chatGPT usage. *Computers and Education: Artificial Intelligence*, 5, 100180. doi: 10.1016/j.caeai.2023.100180.

Ferguson, J.S. (2023). Flipping the (COVID-19) classroom: Redesigning a first-year information literacy program during a pandemic. *Portal: Libraries and the Academy*, 23(1), 145–168.

Fornell, C. and Larcker, D.F. (1981). Evaluating structural equation models with unobservable variables and measurement error. *Journal of Marketing Research*, 18(1), 39–50.

Hair, J.F., Ringle, C.M., Sarstedt, M. (2011). PLS-SEM: Indeed a silver bullet. *Journal of Marketing Theory and Practice*, 19(2), 139–152.

Hair, J.F., Sarstedt, M., Ringle, C.M., Mena, J.A. (2012). An assessment of the use of partial least squares structural equation modeling in marketing research. *Journal of the Academy of Marketing Science*, 40, 414–433.

Kadir, A.Z.A. and Aziz, N.S. (2016). Learning management system of higher education institution. *Indian Journal of Science and Technology*, 9(9), 1–5.

Khlaisang, J. and Teo, T. (2024). An innovation-based virtual flipped learning system in a ubiquitous learning environment the 21st century skills of higher education learners. *Educational Technology & Society*, 27(1), 100–116.

Khlaisang, J., Teo, T., Huang, F. (2021). Acceptance of a flipped smart application for learning: A study among Thai university students. *Interactive Learning Environments*, 29(5), 772–789.

Kumar, V. and Bhardwaj, A. (2020). Role of cloud computing in school education. In *Handbook of Research on Diverse Teaching Strategies for the Technology-Rich Classroom*, Tomei, L.A. and Carbonara, D.D. (eds). IGI Global, Hershey.

Kumar, V. and Lata, M. (eds) (2022). *The Future of E-Commerce*. Nova Science Publishers, New York. doi: 10.52305/KMUB3774.

Kumar, V. and Rewari, M. (eds) (2023). *Pandemics in the Age of Social Media: Information and Misinformation in Developing Nations*. Taylor & Francis, Singapore.

Kumar, J.A. and Silva, P.A. (2020). Work-in-progress: A preliminary study on students' acceptance of chatbots for studio-based learning. *In 2020 IEEE Global Engineering Education Conference (EDUCON)*, New York.

Lata, M. and Kumar, V. (2021). Internet of Energy (IoE) applications for smart cities. In *Internet of Energy for Smart Cities*, 1st edition, Jindal, A., Kumar, N., Aujla, G.S. (eds). CRC Press, Boca Raton.

Lata, M. and Kumar, V. (2022). Security and privacy issues in fog computing environment. *International Journal of Electronic Security and Digital Forensics*, 14(3), 289–307. doi: 10.1504/IJESDF.2022.122588.

Lata, M. and Kumar, V. (2023). Challenges to IoT security: Industry perspective. *Grenze International Journal of Engineering and Technology (GIJET)*, 9(1–2), 61–67.

Lata, M. and Kumar, V. (2024). A framework for security of public cloud environment. *International Journal of Electronic Security and Digital Forensics*, 16(4), 486–502.

Lata, M., Kumar, V., Sharma, V. (2024). Cloud computing applications in online learning. *Grenze International Journal of Engineering & Technology (GIJET)*, 10(2), 408–411.

Li, L., Ma, Z., Fan, L., Lee, S., Yu, H., Hemphill, L. (2023). ChatGPT in education: A discourse analysis of worries and concerns on social media. *arXiv* [Online]. Available at: https://arxiv.org/abs/2305.02201 [Accessed 14 October 2024].

Lin, C.J. and Mubarok, H. (2021). Learning analytics for investigating the mind map-guided AI chatbot approach in an EFL flipped speaking classroom. *Educational Technology & Society*, 24(4), 16–35.

Lo, C.K. (2023). What is the impact of ChatGPT on education? A rapid review of the literature. *Education Sciences*, 13(4), 410.

Luckin, R., Holmes, W., Griffiths, M., Forcier, L.B. (2016). *Intelligence Unleashed: An Argument for AI in Education*. UCL/Pearson, London [Online]. Available at: https://discovery.ucl.ac.uk/id/eprint/1475756/.

McConnell, D. (2005). Examining the dynamics of networked elearning groups and communities. *Studies in Higher Education*, 30(1), 25–42.

Migadadi, M.M. (2009). A knowledge-centered culture as an antecedent of effective knowledge management at information technology centers in the Jordanian universities. *Journal of Systems and Information Technology*, 11(2), 89–116.

Mittal, S. and Kumar, V. (2024). Analyzing the role of technological capabilities and digital marketing on the performance of E-commerce-based SMEs. *Indian Journal of Marketing*, 54(12), 45–60.

Mogavi, R.H., Deng, C., Kim, J.J., Zhou, P., Kwon, Y.D., Metwally, A.H.S., Hui, P. (2024). ChatGPT in education: A blessing or a curse? A qualitative study exploring early adopters' utilization and perceptions. *Computers in Human Behavior: Artificial Humans*, 2(1), 100027.

Mollick, E.R. and Mollick, L. (2023). Using AI to implement effective teaching strategies in classrooms: Five strategies, including prompts. Research Paper, The Wharton School [Online]. Available at: https://papers.ssrn.com/sol3/papers.cfm?abstract_id=4391243 [Accessed 14 October 2024].

Motaghian, H., Hassanzadeh, A., Moghadam, D.K. (2013). Factors affecting university instructors' adoption of web-based learning systems: Case study of Iran. *Computers & Education*, 61, 158–167.

Nanda, P. and Kumar, V. (2024). New generation technologies: Development vs. ethical challenges. *International Journal of Business Information Systems*, 46(3), 411–434.

Oakes, K. (2002). E-learning: LCMS, LMS – They're not just acronyms but powerful systems for learning. *Training & Development*, 56(3), 73–75.

OpenAI (2022). Introducing ChatGPT [Online]. Available at: https://openai.com/blog/chatgpt [Accessed 21 September 2024].

Owoc, M.L., Sawicka, A., Weichbroth, P. (2019). Artificial intelligence technologies in education: Benefits, challenges and strategies of implementation. In *IFIP International Workshop on Artificial Intelligence for Knowledge Management*. Springer, Cham.

Pedro, F., Subosa, M., Rivas, A., Valverde, P. (2019). Artificial intelligence in education: Challenges and opportunities for sustainable development. Report, UNESCO [Online]. Available at: https://repositorio.minedu.gob.pe/handle/20.500.12799/6533 [Accessed 14 October 2024].

Qazi, S., Kadri, M.B., Naveed, M., Khawaja, B.A., Khan, S.Z., Alam, M.M., Su'ud, M.M. (2024). AI-driven learning management systems: Modern developments, challenges and future trends during the age of ChatGPT. *Computers, Materials & Continua*, 80(2), 3289–3314.

Rai, S. and Lata, M. (2024). Futuristic outlook of online learning: The post-pandemic era. In *Technology-mediated Learning During the Pandemic*, Singh, J. and Kumar, V. (eds). Routledge, New Delhi.

Salajan, F.D., Perschbacher, S., Cash, M., Talwar, R., El-Badrawy, W., Mount, G.J. (2009). Learning with webbased interactive objects: An investigation into student perceptions of effectiveness. *Computers & Education*, 53(3), 632–43.

Sharma, D. and Kumar, V. (2017). A framework for collaborative and convenient learning on cloud computing platforms. *International Journal of Web-Based Learning and Teaching Technologies (IJWLTT)*, 12(2), 1–20.

Sharma, S. and Yadav, R. (2022). Chat GPT – A technological remedy or challenge for education system. *Global Journal of Enterprise Information System*, 14(4), 46–51.

Singh, J., Kumar, V., Kumar, D. (2022). Combating the pandemic with ICT-based learning tools and applications: A case of indian higher education platforms. *International Journal of Virtual and Personal Learning Environments (IJVPLE)*, 12(1), 1–21.

Stöhr, C., Ou, A.W., Malmström, H. (2024). Perceptions and usage of AI chatbots among students in higher education across genders, academic levels and fields of study. *Computers and Education: Artificial Intelligence*, 7, 100259. doi: 10.1016/j.caeai.2024.100259.

Suhel, S.F., Shukla, V.K., Vyas, S., Mishra, V.P. (2020). Conversation to automation in banking through chatbot using artificial machine intelligence language. In *2020 8th International Conference on Reliability, Infocom Technologies and Optimization (Trends and Future Directions (ICRITO)*. IEEE, New York.

Tangkittipon, P., Sawatdirat, A., Lakkhanawannakun, P., Noyunsan, C. (2020). Facilitating a flipped classroom using chatbot: A conceptual model. *Engineering Access*, 6(2), 103–107.

Teo, T. and Zhou, M. (2014). Explaining the intention to use technology among university students: A structural equation modeling approach. *Journal of Computing in Higher Education*, 26(2), 124–142.

Wang, Y., Liu, C., Tu, Y. F. (2021). Factors affecting the adoption of AI-based applications in higher education. *Educational Technology & Society*, 24(3), 116–129.

Watson, W.R. and Watson, S.L. (2007). An argument for clarity: What are learning management systems, what are they not, and what should they become? *TechTrends*, 51, 28–34.

Yang, S. (2008). An ontological website models-supported search agent for web services. *Expert Systems with Applications*, 35(4), 2056–2073.

Yeşilyurt, E., Ulaş, A.H., Akan, D. (2016). Teacher self-efficacy, academic self-efficacy, and computer self-efficacy as predictors of attitude toward applying computer-supported education. *Computers in Human Behavior*, 64, 591–601.

Yusuf, B. and Taiye, M.A. (2021). A flipped learning environment: A disruptive approach for traditional classrooms. *International Journal of Education, Psychology and Counseling*, 6(42), 83–93.

Zawacki-Richter, O., Marín, V.I., Bond, M., Gouverneur, F. (2019). Systematic review of research on artificial intelligence applications in higher education: Where are the educators? *International Journal of Educational Technology in Higher Education*, 16(1), 1–27.

8

An Analysis of the Quality of Technology Integration in Learning Management Systems and Its Impact on Teaching Performance

This study investigates the relationships among perceived ease of use (PEU), technology integration quality (TIQ), resource accessibility and academic performance, focusing on the mediating role of user engagement. For 120 university students, structural equation modeling–partial least squares (SEM–PLS) was employed for data analysis. The findings revealed that PEU does not directly improve academic performance, indicating that ease of use alone is inadequate without active student engagement. Rooted in the technology acceptance model (TAM) and self-determination theory (SDT), the results emphasize the significance of intrinsic motivation and intentional participation in achieving academic success. User engagement emerges as a vital mediator between PEU and academic performance. Engagement, which includes behavioral, emotional and cognitive involvement, converts the accessibility of learning management systems (LMS) into tangible academic outcomes, highlighting the necessity of pairing usability with proactive student participation. Moreover, the analysis shows that TIQ does not directly influence academic performance. While high-quality technology is essential, its effectiveness increases when it is combined with structured instructional methods and student-centered engagement. Ultimately, user engagement mediates the relationship between TIQ and academic results, underscoring the need for educational institutions to prioritize student engagement alongside usability and technology quality to enhance educational outcomes.

Chapter written by FAISOL and Diah NURDIWATY.

8.1. Introduction

The incorporation of technology in education has transformed traditional learning environments, creating new avenues for improved teaching and learning experiences (Kumar and Rewari 2023). Central to this evolution are learning management systems (LMS), which serve as digital platforms for organizing course content and assignments and facilitating communication between educators and students (Wang et al. 2020). These systems not only streamline educational workflows but also enhance access to resources, ultimately aiming to increase educational quality and foster interactive learning (Alduaij et al. 2023). However, the success of LMS in enhancing academic performance hinges on several key factors, including the quality of technology integration, perceived ease of use (PEU) and resource accessibility (Sharma and Kumar 2017).

As educational institutions increasingly implement LMS to bolster their teaching practices, it becomes vital to comprehend the specific elements that crucially contribute to their effectiveness (Parker and Chao 2007). Factors such as the quality of technology integration, ease of use and resource availability play a significant role in shaping user experiences and educational outcomes. For example, effective technology integration can create a smoother user experience and enhance system functionality, whereas PEU influences the levels of adoption and engagement among both students and instructors (Olipas and Leona 2022). Additionally, ensuring straightforward access to educational resources is crucial for maximizing the advantages of LMS and facilitating effective learning (Irsyad and Hapsari 2023). Despite the increasing use of LMS, comprehensive research investigating how these factors interact to affect user engagement and academic performance is lacking (Lata and Kumar 2021; Ren et al. 2022). While some studies have examined aspects of LMS usability and user satisfaction, they often treat these components in isolation rather than as interconnected elements within a cohesive system (Aulia and Marsasi 2024). Furthermore, the role of user engagement as a mediator and user technology readiness as a moderator in the context of LMS remains insufficiently explored (Alduaij et al. 2023). Addressing these research gaps is crucial for enhancing our understanding of how LMS can be optimized to improve educational outcomes (Furqon et al. 2023; Lata et al. 2024). This study seeks to fill this void by investigating the effects of technology integration quality (TIQ), PEU, and resource accessibility on user engagement, as well as how user technology readiness moderates these relationships (Nanda and Kumar 2024). By providing a comprehensive perspective on these interactions, the research aims to provide practical insights for the development of more effective LMS platforms and the enhancement of academic performance. The anticipated findings will offer valuable guidance for educational institutions in designing and implementing more effective LMS solutions. By understanding how these variables interplay and impact academic performance, universities can formulate strategies to boost user engagement and learning outcomes. Practically, the study emphasizes the importance of enhancing TIQ, simplifying LMS usage, ensuring adequate resource access and providing necessary support and training to improve user technology readiness. This multifaceted approach can lead to greater engagement and significant advancements in academic performance.

8.2. Literature review and hypothesis

8.2.1. *The impact of PEU on enhancing academic performance*

PEOU, a key component of the technology acceptance model (TAM), plays a crucial role in influencing students' readiness to adopt and effectively utilize educational technologies. According to Huang (2020), when students view a learning system as user friendly, their likelihood of engaging with that system increases, which subsequently contributes to improved academic outcomes. A platform that is easy to navigate minimizes the cognitive load, allowing students to focus more on their learning processes rather than grappling with technical difficulties (Lata and Kumar 2022; Armouti et al. 2023). This notion is further reinforced by findings indicating that systems characterized by high PEU tend to increase user satisfaction levels, which in turn can lead to increased academic performance (Kholilah et al. 2022). In essence, when students feel comfortable using educational technologies, they are more inclined to engage deeply with the content, thereby fostering a more effective learning environment (Kumar and Bhardwaj 2020; Singh et al. 2022). This relationship highlights the importance of designing intuitive and accessible learning platforms to maximize educational success.

8.2.2. *The function of user engagement as a mediating factor*

User engagement serves a vital function in mediating the connection between PEU and academic performance. Grounded in self-determination theory (SDT), it is suggested that students are more inclined to engage with learning platforms when they find the technology to be user friendly, which nurtures their sense of competence and autonomy (Armouti et al. 2023; Lata and Kumar 2023). This heightened engagement leads to increased interaction with educational materials, ultimately contributing to improved academic performance (Al-Adwan et al. 2023). Moreover, research indicates that students who are actively engaged tend to dedicate greater effort to their studies, resulting in more favorable learning outcomes (Barz et al. 2024). This underscores the critical role of user engagement as a mediator in the educational process, illustrating how it can amplify the positive effects of PEU on academic success.

On the basis of this theoretical framework, the following hypotheses can be formulated:

1) *H1*: perceived ease of use has a positive influence on the improvement of academic performance.

2) *H2*: user engagement positively mediates the relationship between PEU and increased academic performance.

8.2.3. *The impact of TIQ on enhancing academic performance*

TIQ pertains to how effectively educational technologies are woven into teaching and learning processes, creating seamless, efficient and supportive learning environments. According to technology integration theory, the purposeful application of digital tools within education is essential for enhancing learning outcomes, improving information accessibility and fostering collaboration among students (Udto and Kusain 2023; Lata and Sharma 2024a). When technology is skillfully integrated into the educational landscape, it significantly boosts academic performance by facilitating personalized learning experiences tailored to individual student needs. This integration also provides access to a diverse array of learning resources, which enriches the educational experience and encourages active engagement with the content being studied (Al-Adwan et al. 2023; Lata and Sharma 2024b). Moreover, effective technology integration resonates with cognitive load theory, which posits that well-designed technological interventions can alleviate extraneous cognitive load (Ernestivita et al. 2024). By minimizing distractions and simplifying complex tasks, technology allows students to concentrate on meaningful learning activities, ultimately leading to improved academic performance (Paas and van Merriënboer 2020). In summary, the quality of technology integration is a crucial determinant of academic success, as it not only enhances the learning experience but also equips students with the tools they need to engage deeply with their studies, thereby fostering better educational outcomes.

8.2.4. *The function of user engagement as a mediating factor*

User engagement, characterized by active participation and interaction with learning activities, serves a vital mediating role in the relationship between TIQ and academic performance. According to SDT, the effective integration of technology within the learning environment fosters a sense of competence and autonomy among students. This heightened sense of self-efficacy enhances intrinsic motivation, prompting students to engage more deeply with the learning materials (Legault 2017). When students are actively engaged, they are more inclined to utilize technological resources effectively, leading to increased interactions with both learning materials and their peers. Such interactions are pivotal, as they create opportunities for collaborative learning and knowledge sharing, ultimately contributing to improved academic outcomes (Tao et al. 2022; Lata and Kumar 2024). This perspective aligns with engagement theory, which posits that learners who are actively engaged in their educational experiences are more likely to achieve favorable academic performance. Meaningful interactions with educational technology not only enrich the learning experience but also deepen the understanding and retention of knowledge (Miliszewska and Horwood 2006). On the basis of this theoretical foundation, the following hypotheses can be proposed:

1) *H3*: TIQ positively influences the enhancement of academic performance.

2) *H4*: user engagement positively mediates the relationship between TIQ and improvements in academic performance.

8.2.5. *The impact of resource access on enhancing academic performance*

Access to resources is a fundamental component of academic success, as it equips students with the essential tools, materials and support necessary for engaging in meaningful learning experiences. These resources encompass a wide range of elements, including technological infrastructure, educational materials such as textbooks and databases, and access to expert guidance or mentorship. resource-based learning theory posits that having access to diverse and high-quality learning resources significantly enhances the educational experience. This access enables students to effectively gather, process and apply information, which is crucial for deep learning and understanding (Ryan et al. 2011; Rai and Lata 2024). As a result, improved access to educational resources correlates with better academic performance, as students are more likely to complete assignments, adequately prepare for exams and engage in comprehensive learning activities. Furthermore, cognitive load theory highlights the importance of resource accessibility in managing cognitive demands. When students have easy access to appropriate resources, cognitive overload is minimized, allowing them to concentrate on higher order thinking tasks rather than expending energy on locating information or grappling with insufficient materials (Sweller 1994; Yadav 2023). This reduction in extraneous cognitive load facilitates deeper engagement with the content, ultimately leading to enhanced academic performance. In summary, increased access to educational resources not only enriches the learning experience but also plays a pivotal role in improving academic outcomes by fostering a more effective and focused learning environment.

8.2.6. *The mediating role of user engagement in academic performance*

User engagement, which refers to the degree of active involvement students have in their learning experiences, is a vital factor influencing academic outcomes. According to engagement and motivation theory, students who participate more actively in learning activities tend to demonstrate higher levels of academic performance. This is attributed to their increased effort, persistence and deeper interaction with educational content (Miliszewska and Horwood 2006). Furthermore, user engagement acts as a mediator in the relationship between access to resources and academic performance. SDT suggests that when students have improved access to learning resources, they are likely to feel a greater sense of autonomy, competence and connection to their academic environment. This sense of empowerment fosters intrinsic motivation, which in turn enhances their engagement with the material (Legault 2017). When students are actively engaged, they are more adept at utilizing available resources effectively, which can lead to improved learning outcomes. In this context, engagement serves as a crucial link that amplifies the positive impact of resource access on academic performance.

On the basis of this theoretical framework, the following hypotheses can be proposed:

1) *H5*: access to resources positively influences improvements in academic performance.

2) *H6*: user engagement positively mediates the relationship between access to resources and increased academic performance.

These hypotheses underscore the importance of resource availability in achieving academic success and highlight the essential role that student engagement plays in maximizing the benefits derived from these resources.

Figure 8.1 illustrates a conceptual framework that delineates the interrelationships among various factors that impact academic performance (Kumar and Lata 2022). The primary components of the model include the following:

1) *Perceived ease of use*: this factor is directly linked to academic performance and exerts an indirect influence through user engagement. The premise is that when users perceive a system as easy to navigate and utilize, it enhances their overall engagement with the platform. This increased engagement, in turn, positively affects their academic outcomes.

2) *User engagement*: serving as a mediating variable, user engagement connects PEU to academic performance. The underlying concept is that higher levels of engagement in utilizing a system or educational platform correlate with improved

academic results. Engaged students are more likely to interact deeply with the learning materials, leading to better comprehension and retention.

3) *Access to resources*: this factor has direct associations with both user engagement and academic performance. When students have easy and sufficient access to educational resources, they are more likely to engage actively with the learning process. This accessibility not only fosters greater engagement but also contributes directly to enhanced academic performance.

4) *Technology integration quality*: this factor is also directly related to both user engagement and academic performance. High-quality integration of technology into the educational experience is expected to facilitate greater user engagement. When technology is effectively integrated, it enhances the learning experience, which can lead to improved academic outcomes.

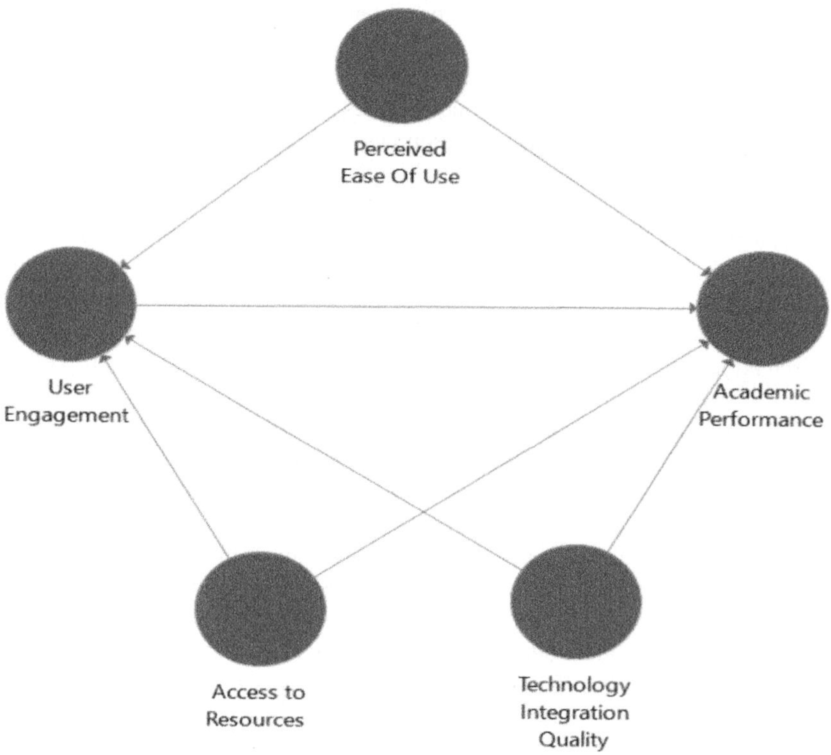

Figure 8.1. *Riset model*

In summary, the conceptual model suggests that PEU, access to resources and TIQ significantly influence user engagement. This engagement, in turn, plays a crucial role in determining academic performance. Additionally, both access to resources and TIQ directly impact academic performance. The model underscores the critical importance of fostering user engagement and ensuring adequate access to resources as essential elements for achieving improved academic outcomes.

8.3. Method

This research utilizes a quantitative approach, specifically using structural equation modeling–partial least squares (SEM–PLS), to examine the relationships among various factors influencing academic performance. SEM–PLS is particularly suitable for this study because of its ability to manage complex models that involve multiple interrelated constructs, making it an excellent choice for exploratory research within the social sciences. The focus of the study includes several key variables: PEU, which assesses how easily users can navigate the LMS; TIQ, which evaluates how effectively the LMS incorporates technological elements to support educational activities; and access to resources, which looks at the availability and ease of obtaining educational materials within the LMS. Additionally, user engagement serves as a mediating variable, reflecting the level of interaction and involvement users have with the LMS and its impact on learning outcomes. The dependent variable, academic performance improvement, measures the enhancement in academic results attributed to the use of the LMS. The sample consists of 120 university students selected through stratified random sampling to ensure a diverse representation across different academic programs and levels. Data are collected through a structured questionnaire distributed electronically via the university's LMS platform, incorporating validated scales for each variable to ensure accuracy and reliability. The analysis begins with descriptive statistics to summarize demographic characteristics and survey responses, followed by the use of Smart PLS to assess the validity of the measurement model through factor loadings, reliability and discriminant validity. Structural equation modeling is then conducted to test the hypothesized relationships between the variables, allowing for a comprehensive evaluation of both direct and indirect effects (Faisol and Sri Aliami 2022; Faisol et al. 2023). To validate the model, metrics such as average variance extracted (AVE) and composite reliability (CR) are reviewed, along with the R^2 values of the endogenous constructs to gauge explanatory power. Bootstrapping techniques are employed to test the significance of path coefficients, ensuring the stability and reliability of the results. Ultimately, this SEM–PLS analysis aims to enhance the understanding of how PEU, TIQ and access to resources influence user engagement and academic performance. Furthermore, the study explores the moderating role of user technology readiness, providing insights into how this readiness impacts the effectiveness of LMS features. The findings are expected to yield practical recommendations for improving LMS design and implementation, thereby fostering greater user engagement and enhancing academic performance.

8.4. Results

This section outlines two models designed to meet the research objectives and validate the hypotheses: the measurement model (outer model) and the structural model (inner model). The measurement model focuses on assessing the reliability and validity of each construct, ensuring that the observed indicators accurately reflect the underlying concepts. In contrast, the structural model investigates the relationships between constructs, offering insights into how variables interact to either support or challenge the proposed hypotheses. A detailed discussion of these analyses follows.

8.4.1. *The measurement model*

The assessment of the measurement model (outer model) focuses on evaluating its validity and reliability. This process includes testing for convergent validity, which is determined by analyzing the loading factor (λ). This factor helps to ascertain whether the indicators accurately represent the latent variables. To satisfy the criteria for convergent validity, an indicator must have an absolute loading factor exceeding 0.6; any indicators that do not meet this requirement are excluded from the model. Furthermore, the outer model is evaluated based on the AVE and CR. The outcomes of these tests for reliability and validity are presented in Table 8.1, while Figure 8.2 illustrates the SEM–PLS processed measurement model.

8.4.2. *Results of convergent validity and reliability*

Table 8.1 displays the results of the analysis regarding the convergent validity and reliability of the various constructs within the research model. Convergent validity, which verifies whether the indicators accurately reflect their respective underlying constructs, is assessed through the loading factor and AVE. An indicator is considered valid if its loading factor exceeds 0.6 and its AVE is greater than 0.5, indicating that the indicators effectively capture the intended construct. In contrast, reliability measures the internal consistency of each construct and is evaluated using Cronbach's alpha (α) and CR. High values for both α (ideally above 0.7) and CR (also preferably above 0.7) indicate that the indicators consistently measure the same underlying concept.

Construct	Convergent validity		Reliability		
	Loading factor	Significance	AVE	α	CR
Academic performance			0.644	0.814	0.878
API1	0.750	***			
API2	0.908	***			
API3	0.784	***			
API4	0.758	***			
Access to resources			0.735	0.879	0.916
AR1	0.890	***			
AR2	0.925	***			
AR3	0.883	***			
AR4	0.714	***			
Perceived ease of use			0.674	0.839	0.892
PEOU1	0.748	***			
PEOU2	0.813	***			
PEOU3	0.878	***			
PEOU4	0.839	***			
Technology integration quality			0.712	0.900	0.925
TIQ1	0.856	***			
TIQ2	0.804	***			
TIQ3	0.832	***			
TIQ4	0.875	***			
TIQ5	0.849	***			
User engagement			0.646	0.889	0.916
UE1	0.718	***			
UE2	deleted				
UE3	0.859	***			
UE4	0.875	***			
UE5	0.798	***			
UE6	0.769	***			

Table 8.1. *Results of convergent validity and reliability. ***p < 0.001; AVE = average variance extracted; α = Cronbach's alpha; CR = composite reliability*

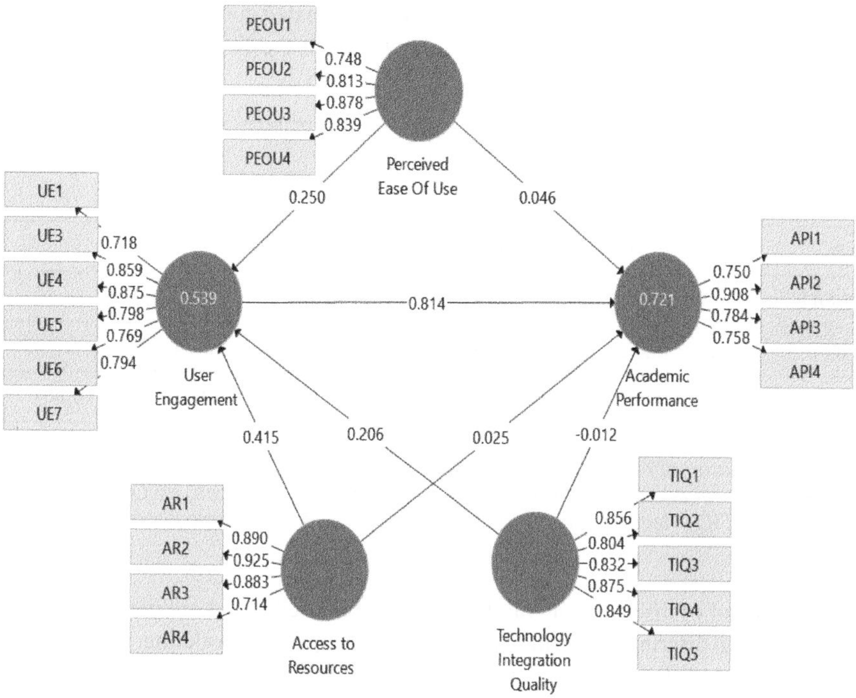

Figure 8.2. *The measurement model. For a color version of this figure, see www.iste.co.uk/kumar/chatbots.zip*

8.4.3. *Discriminant validity*

To assess the discriminant validity of the constructs, both the Fornell–Larcker criterion and cross-loading methods were utilized. Discriminant validity evaluates how distinct a construct is from others in the model, ensuring that each construct encapsulates unique elements of the data. The Fornell–Larcker criterion involves comparing the square root of the AVE for each construct with its correlations to other constructs. For a construct to demonstrate discriminant validity, the square root of its AVE must exceed its highest correlation with any other construct. This indicates that a construct shares more variance with its indicators than with other constructs, thereby affirming that it measures a distinct concept. Cross-loading examines the correlation between each indicator and the constructs, where an indicator should show a higher loading with its own construct to others. Indicators that fulfill this requirement strengthen the model's discriminant validity by confirming their stronger association with their designated constructs. A summary of the discriminant validity values, evaluated using both the Fornell–Larcker criterion and the cross-loading criterion, is presented in Table 8.2.

	AP	AR	PEOU	TIQ	UE
AP	0.803				
AR	0.593	0.857			
PEOU	0.485	0.479	0.821		
TIQ	0.512	0.709	0.400	0.844	
UE	0.802	0.681	0.531	0.600	0.801

Table 8.2. *Summary of discriminant validity values based on the Fornell–Larcker criterion. AP = academic performance, AR = access to resources, PEOU = perceived ease of use, TIQ = technology integration quality, UE = user engagement*

Assessment of discriminant validity using the Fornell–Larcker criterion is crucial for evaluating discriminant validity in structural equation modeling. The diagonal values represent the square roots of the AVE for each construct, whereas the off-diagonal entries reflect the correlations between the constructs. The diagonal values are as follows: academic performance (0.803), access to resources (0.857), PEU (0.821), TIQ (0.844) and user engagement (0.801). To establish discriminant validity, the square root of each construct's AVE must exceed its correlations with other constructs.

In this analysis, academic performance demonstrates valid discriminant validity, as its square root of AVE is greater than its correlations with other constructs. Similarly, access to resources and PEU also exhibit strong discriminant validity, with their square roots surpassing their respective correlations with all other constructs. TIQ maintains its distinctiveness, showing a square root of AVE higher than its correlations, whereas user engagement also demonstrates validity, especially in its significant correlation with academic performance (0.802). The analysis indicates that although significant relationships exist among the constructs – particularly between TIQ and access to resources (0.709) – each construct retains its discriminant validity. Overall, these findings confirm that all the constructs are sufficiently distinct, reinforcing the robustness of the research framework and enhancing the validity of the study's outcomes.

8.4.4. *The structural model*

The subsequent step involves evaluating the structural model (inner model) after the measurement model assessment. This evaluation sheds light on the proposed relationships between constructs by analyzing path coefficients and their corresponding t values, which reflect the strength and significance of these connections. Path coefficients indicate the estimated effect of one construct on another and are essential for determining whether the proposed relationships are consistent with the observed data. The t value serves to assess the statistical significance of each path coefficient, with values exceeding 1.64 (for a one-tailed test at a 5% significance level) suggesting a significant relationship, as noted by (Henseler et al. 2009; Hair et al. 2021). This threshold is critical for identifying which hypotheses are supported, enabling researchers to draw conclusions based on statistical findings. Direct relationships illustrate the immediate impact of one variable on another, whereas indirect relationships highlight mediated effects, providing a more detailed understanding of the interactions within the model. Figure 8.3 presents a visualization of the structural model, showcasing the links between constructs along with their respective path coefficients. This comprehensive representation allows for a more in-depth analysis of the model's predictive capabilities and assists in confirming or refining the theoretical framework.

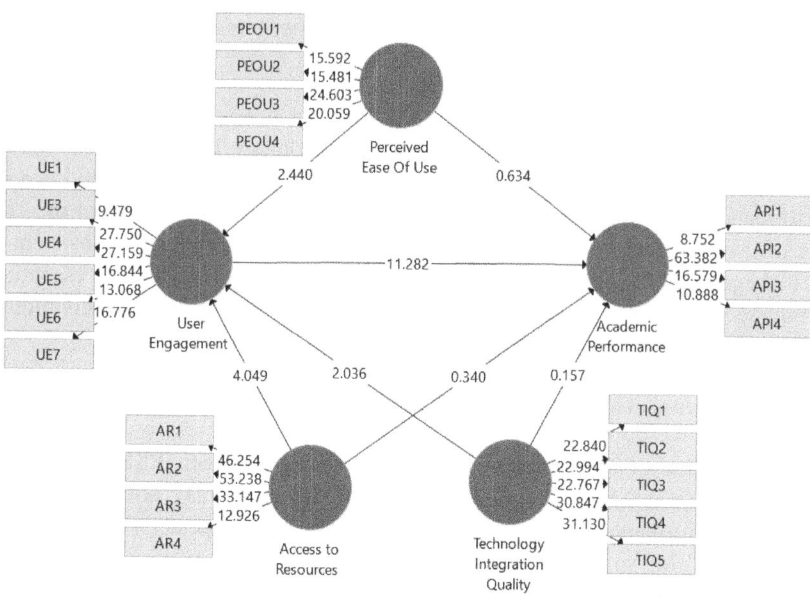

Figure 8.3. *Structural model. For a color version of this figure, see www.iste.co.uk/kumar/chatbots.zip*

Hypothesis results

	Original sample (O)	Sample mean (M)	Standard deviation (STDEV)	T statistics (|O/STDEV|)	*p* values
H1: Perceived ease of use -> academic performance	0.046	0.046	0.072	0.634	0.526
H2: Perceived ease of use -> user engagement -> academic performance	0.203	0.209	0.087	2.350	0.019
H3: Technology integration quality -> academic performance	–0.012	–0.006	0.079	0.157	0.875
H4: Technology integration quality -> user engagement -> academic performance	0.167	0.174	0.086	1.948	0.046
H5: Access to resources -> academic performance	0.025	0.022	0.074	0.340	0.734
H6: Access to resources -> user engagement -> academic performance	0.338	0.327	0.085	3.959	0.000

Table 8.3. *The results of hypothesis testing*

The results of the hypothesis testing reveal that user engagement plays a vital role in converting PEU, TIQ and access to resources into enhanced academic performance. While the direct relationships between these constructs and academic performance did not reach statistical significance, the findings highlight the crucial role of user engagement as a mediating factor. This observation is consistent with SDT (Legault 2017), indicating that active participation by students is essential for achieving academic success. Such engagement fosters intrinsic motivation and facilitates the effective utilization of available resources and technology.

H1: Perceived ease of use (PEU) and improvement in academic performance

The absence of a significant direct relationship between PEU and academic performance ($p = 0.526$) suggests that ease of use alone may not be sufficient to enhance performance without active student engagement. For example, a user-friendly LMS might be accessible to students, yet they may not fully utilize its resources. According to Anaam et al. (2023), while PEU influences the intention to engage with a system, it may not necessarily result in improved learning outcomes without user involvement. This perspective aligns with the unified theory of acceptance and use of technology (UTAUT), which highlights that elements such as social influence and facilitating conditions can enhance performance outcomes when paired with user engagement.

H2: Role of user engagement as a mediator between perceived ease of use and academic performance

The analysis reveals a significant positive mediating effect of user engagement ($p = 0.019$), indicating that active participation by students is essential for translating PEU into tangible academic benefits. When students are engaged, they are more likely to actively participate in discussions and complete assignments through the LMS, effectively leveraging its user-friendly features to enhance their learning outcomes. Research by Huang (2020) supports this notion, highlighting that students who actively engage with educational technologies tend to show improved understanding and retention of the material. Furthermore, findings from Tao et al. (2022) and Kusmawan and Scholar (2024) emphasize that engagement encompasses three critical dimensions: behavioral, emotional and cognitive. Each of these aspects plays a vital role in promoting deeper learning experiences and contributing to overall academic success. In summary, the evidence suggests that user engagement not only mediates the relationship between PEU and academic performance but also enhances the educational experience by fostering an environment conducive to effective learning.

H3: The impact of TIQ on academic performance improvement

The lack of a significant direct relationship between TIQ and academic performance ($p = 0.875$) suggests that simply providing high-quality technology is not enough to enhance academic outcomes. For example, a school may invest in cutting-edge equipment, but without adequate training or well-structured integration strategies, students might struggle to utilize these resources effectively, leading to suboptimal performance. This observation aligns with the research conducted by Jusop et al. (2024), which highlights that the quality of technology can positively influence learning outcomes, but only when it is accompanied by effective pedagogical practices. Their findings emphasize that merely having advanced technology does not automatically translate into academic success; instead, it is the thoughtful integration of technology into the learning process that fosters meaningful educational benefits. In summary, while technology quality is important, its impact on academic performance is significantly enhanced when it is combined with supportive teaching methods and structured application strategies. This underscores the necessity for educational institutions to focus not only on acquiring high-quality technology but also on developing comprehensive training and integration plans that empower students to fully leverage these tools for their academic growth.

H4: Role of user engagement as a mediator between TIQ and academic performance

The analysis indicates a significant mediating effect of user engagement ($p = 0.046$), highlighting that when students actively participate in their learning, high-quality technology can lead to improved academic performance. A pertinent example of this is the flipped classroom model, where students utilize technology for learning before class, allowing them to prepare for interactive activities. This approach not only enhances their understanding of the material but also increases their overall performance during class (Jusop et al. 2024). Furthermore, this finding is reinforced by Legault's SDT (Legault 2017), which emphasizes that student engagement, driven by intrinsic motivation, plays a crucial role in enhancing academic outcomes. When technology is integrated effectively within this framework, it creates an environment where students are motivated to engage deeply with the content. In conclusion, the evidence suggests that user engagement acts as a vital bridge between TIQ and academic performance, demonstrating that the benefits of high-quality technology are maximized when students are actively involved in their learning process. Educational strategies that foster such engagement can significantly enhance the effectiveness of technological tools in achieving better academic results.

H5: The influence of access to resources on academic performance improvement

The analysis reveals a non-significant direct relationship between access to resources and academic performance ($p = 0.734$), indicating that merely having access to resources is insufficient to enhance academic outcomes without active user engagement. For instance, a library may offer an extensive collection of online journals, but if students are not provided guidance on how to utilize these resources effectively, their academic performance may not improve. Research conducted by Spica (2023) supports this notion, emphasizing that access to resources must be complemented by active user engagement to achieve meaningful learning outcomes. Engagement plays a critical role in motivating students to make use of available resources, thereby enhancing their understanding and retention of information. In summary, while access to resources is important, its impact on academic performance is significantly amplified when students are actively engaged in the learning process. Educational institutions should focus not only on providing resources but also on implementing strategies that encourage student participation and guidance in utilizing these resources effectively.

H6: The mediating role of user engagement in the relationship between access to resources and academic performance

The analysis indicates a significant mediating effect of user engagement ($p = 0.000$), suggesting that access to educational resources can positively influence academic performance when students are actively engaged in their learning. For example, in a research-oriented course, students might frequently utilize library resources to enhance their assignments, particularly when these tasks are designed to be engaging and provide constructive feedback. In support of this perspective, research conducted by Çali et al. (2024) emphasized that students who are actively engaged in their learning processes tend to use available resources more effectively. This increased utilization not only facilitates deeper understanding but also contributes to improved academic outcomes. In summary, the evidence underscores the importance of user engagement as a crucial mediator in the relationship between access to resources and academic performance. Educational strategies that foster student engagement can significantly enhance the effectiveness of resource access, ultimately leading to better academic results.

8.5. Discussion

8.5.1. *PEU and academic performance*

The analysis indicates the lack of a significant direct relationship between PEU and academic performance ($p = 0.526$). This finding underscores a critical insight: simply having technology that is easy to use does not automatically lead to improved academic outcomes unless students are actively engaged in their learning. Even if learners find an LMS user friendly, this does not guarantee substantial educational benefits unless they are motivated to interact meaningfully with the content. This perspective aligns with the UTAUT proposed by Rençber (2020), which emphasizes that factors such as social influence, facilitating conditions and particularly behavioral intention are vital for the meaningful impact of technology on performance. According to UTAUT, while PEU can make a platform more approachable, significant improvements in performance often necessitate structured interaction and intentional engagement with technology.

In support of this viewpoint, research by Anaam et al. (2023) indicates that although ease of use enhances user satisfaction and the intention to utilize technology, it does not inherently lead to better academic results. Their findings highlight the importance of intentional engagement as a crucial link between ease of use and performance, especially in the context of LMS platforms in higher education. This aligns with the TAM articulated by Ma and Liu (2011), which suggests that PEU primarily influences attitudes toward technology use rather than guaranteeing performance improvements on its own. While ease of use is essential for fostering technology acceptance, it does not automatically drive academic success without meaningful engagement or motivating factors. Contrasting evidence, however, exists in the literature. For example, Kholilah et al. (2022) identified PEU as a significant predictor of performance among university students, particularly when technology was perceived as enjoyable or when faculty actively encouraged the use of digital resources. These findings imply that while PEU can have a direct impact on performance, this effect is often context dependent and may hinge on the motivational environment. Additionally, Huang (2020) demonstrated that ease of use positively influenced learning outcomes, but only when students exhibited high self-regulation and motivation to explore the technology further. This suggests that PEU may exert a direct influence in contexts where students possess strong intrinsic motivation or external incentives to engage.

The findings of this study further reinforce the principles of SDT proposed by Evans et al. (2024), which posits that intrinsic motivation is essential for active and effective learning. According to SDT, students are more likely to engage deeply with their learning and enhance their performance when they perceive educational activities as meaningful and autonomous. Thus, PEU alone may be insufficient if students do not view educational tasks as valuable or fulfilling. This implies that ease of use must be complemented by motivating factors to achieve better academic outcomes. To elucidate why PEU did not directly enhance academic performance in this study, constructivist learning theory (Mishra 2023) offers valuable insights. This theory posits that learning occurs through active participation and exploration rather than passive consumption of information. Even if a technology platform is user friendly, students may struggle to construct meaningful knowledge unless they are actively engaged. Consequently, while PEU may reduce initial barriers to accessing technology, it does not inherently promote the deeper cognitive processing required for academic improvement. This highlights the need to pair user-friendly technology with instructional strategies or incentives that encourage students to engage critically and actively with educational resources. In conclusion, while ease of use is an important factor in promoting technology adoption, it is not sufficient on its own to enhance academic performance without active student engagement. This finding suggests that educational institutions should prioritize not only the usability of LMS platforms but also the creation of learning environments that foster and facilitate engagement. By making technology an integral part of an interactive learning experience, rather than merely an accessible tool, institutions can better support academic success. This approach is corroborated by previous research (Tao et al. 2022; Çali et al. 2024), which emphasizes the necessity of combining usability with engagement strategies to unlock the full potential of educational technologies.

8.5.2. User engagement as a mediator between PEU and academic performance

The significant positive mediation effect ($p = 0.019$) indicates that user engagement plays a crucial role in transforming PEU into meaningful academic outcomes. This finding emphasizes that while a user-friendly LMS may encourage initial usage, active engagement ultimately leads to improved learning and academic performance. When students actively interact with the LMS – through participating in discussions, completing assignments or exploring additional resources – they are more likely to take full advantage of its accessibility, resulting in enhanced comprehension and retention of material. This observation aligns with the TAM proposed by McCord (2006), which highlights that although ease of use influences initial user acceptance, sustained benefits are realized only through active engagement with the technology. In support of this perspective, Tao et al. (2022) and Çali et al. (2024) define engagement as comprising behavioral, emotional and cognitive dimensions, all of which are essential for fostering deeper learning. Behavioral engagement pertains to participation in learning activities, emotional engagement relates to interest and positive attitudes, and cognitive engagement involves deep and reflective thinking. This comprehensive model of engagement elucidates why students who are actively engaged tend to perform better academically – they are not merely present but also invest effort, focus and emotion in their learning process, thereby increasing their likelihood of academic success.

Consequently, when students find an LMS easy to use and engage with it meaningfully, they leverage both the platform's usability and the depth of engagement necessary for achieving academic excellence. Moreover, Çali et al. (2024) reported that students who were engaged while using online learning platforms achieved higher performance outcomes, as their engagement facilitated effective utilization of the system's resources. Similarly, Hatahet et al. (2021) asserted that engagement is a reliable predictor of student success, particularly in technology-enhanced learning environments, because it promotes active learning and sustained motivation. These findings suggest that when user engagement mediates the relationship between PEU and academic performance, students are more likely to experience educational benefits, highlighting that a user-friendly design alone is insufficient for promoting academic success in the absence of student-driven engagement. However, contrasting studies provide additional nuance to this relationship. For instance, Nuryakin et al. (2023) discovered that PEU could directly influence academic performance in scenarios where course design incentivized student participation through graded interactions with the LMS. This implies that under structured conditions, ease of use alone may have a direct effect on performance outcomes, particularly when students perceive tangible rewards for their engagement. Additionally, Wilson et al. (2021) found that PEU had a direct effect on performance in contexts where students exhibited high intrinsic motivation, suggesting that the influence of PEU on performance may vary based on motivational factors and instructional design. From a theoretical standpoint, SDT, as articulated by Ryan and Deci (2022), underscores the importance of intrinsic motivation in mediating the relationship between technology use and performance.

According to SDT, students are more engaged when they experience autonomy, competence and relatedness – elements that can be fostered by an LMS that is both accessible and conducive to active participation. Constructivist learning theory Chuang (2021) further reinforces this mediated relationship by emphasizing that active engagement in learning activities is essential for meaningful knowledge construction. An LMS, even if easy to navigate, requires students to engage deeply with the content for effective learning to occur. Thus, engagement is not merely an added advantage; it is a vital process that connects usability with academic outcomes, enabling students to participate in reflective and constructive learning activities that enhance their comprehension and academic performance. In conclusion, the positive mediation effect identified in this study underscores that while ease of use is foundational for initial technology acceptance, active engagement is crucial for translating this usability into tangible academic benefits. The findings advocate educational institutions to prioritize strategies that foster engagement, enhancing students' motivation and interaction with LMS platforms, as these elements are key to unlocking the full academic potential of educational technology. This perspective aligns with various theories and empirical studies, reinforcing the indispensable role of engagement in linking ease of use with academic success.

8.5.3. *Relationship between TIQ and academic performance improvement*

The absence of a significant direct relationship between TIQ and academic performance ($p = 0.875$) suggests that even well-designed, high-quality technology does not inherently lead to improved learning outcomes unless accompanied by structured guidance and active instructional support. This finding indicates that while high-quality educational technology is essential for providing learning tools, it may not enhance academic results if students lack clear instructional direction or effective engagement strategies. For instance, in educational environments where schools invest in advanced tools but fail to provide teacher training or systematic implementation plans, the technology may be underutilized or misaligned with learning objectives, thereby limiting its impact on academic success.

Al-Adwan et al. (2023) support this finding by arguing that effective technology integration involves more than just having high-quality tools; it requires thoughtful pedagogical practices for their implementation. Their study revealed that teachers who adapted technology to align with curriculum goals and student needs achieved greater educational benefits than those who used technology without such alignment. This suggests that successful technology integration transcends the tools themselves; it necessitates that instructors create structured learning contexts and clear instructional goals, thereby facilitating student engagement with technology in ways that foster deep learning and knowledge construction. Moreover, Venkatesh and Davis (2000) found that technological tools alone are insufficient for improving academic performance without strong alignment with educational goals and curricular content.

Their research emphasizes that for technology to positively affect student learning, it must be embedded within a supportive instructional framework that helps students understand how to use these tools effectively for specific learning purposes. For example, in classrooms where teachers relied on technology primarily for administrative tasks, students experienced minimal academic benefits compared with those in classrooms where technology was utilized to promote interactive learning and critical thinking. Conversely, some studies suggest that high-quality technology can independently improve learning outcomes, particularly in settings where students demonstrate high levels of self-regulation or technological competence. Muñoz-Carril et al. (2021) reported that self-motivated students proficient in digital literacy could effectively leverage advanced technological resources, achieving high academic performance even without explicit teacher guidance. Similarly, Alduaij et al. (2023) argue that high-quality technology can enhance outcomes when it is intuitive and includes self-guided learning resources. These findings imply that under certain conditions – such as when students are highly autonomous or when the technology is exceptionally user-friendly, TIQ may exert a more direct influence on performance.

From a theoretical perspective, constructivist learning theory (Prakash Chand 2023) supports the notion that meaningful learning necessitates active student engagement rather than mere access to high-quality technology (Mittal and Kumar 2024). Within this framework, students construct knowledge through experience and reflection, processes that rely on structured interactions with content instead of passive exposure. This aligns with the idea that TIQ must be coupled with interactive instructional methods to yield measurable academic outcomes. Similarly, social constructivism posits that learning occurs within social contexts (Mishra 2023); thus, technology integrated without opportunities for guided interaction, collaboration or teacher facilitation may not fully support student learning and performance.

Additionally, SDT (Ryan and Deci 2022) highlights the importance of autonomy, competence and relatedness in student motivation and academic success. SDT suggests that the quality of technology, if not paired with strategies that foster student autonomy and a sense of purpose, may fail to encourage meaningful engagement with academic content. This aligns with the findings of the current study, indicating that TIQ alone lacks the motivational component necessary to positively impact performance, reinforcing the need for tools to be implemented in ways that promote student engagement and active participation in learning.

In summary, the results of this study indicate that high-quality technology alone does not guarantee improved academic performance. Instead, effective outcomes require the integration of TIQ within pedagogically sound, student-centered learning environments. While high-quality technology provides an important foundation, its academic potential is realized only when combined with structured guidance and instructional strategies that align with curriculum goals and encourage active student participation. This conclusion is supported by a range of research (Koi-Akrofi et al. 2023; Förster 2024) and theories of constructivist and self-determined learning, emphasizing the necessity of not only providing state-of-the-art tools but also ensuring their purposeful and guided application in educational settings.

8.5.4. *The role of user engagement in mediating TIQ and academic performance*

The significant mediating effect of user engagement ($p = 0.046$) on the relationship between TIQ and academic performance highlights the crucial role that active engagement plays in transforming technology quality into academic benefits. This finding indicates that while high-quality technology serves as a valuable resource, its full potential is realized only when students actively participate and engage with the technology in meaningful ways. For example, in a flipped classroom model (Uluçınar Sağır and Sakar 2017), students utilize technology at home for preclass learning, which prepares them to engage actively in class discussions and activities. This preparation not only enhances their understanding but also fosters deeper engagement with the material, ultimately leading to improved academic performance. Legault's SDT (Legault 2017; Ryan and Deci 2022) provides a valuable framework for interpreting these results, emphasizing that engagement driven by intrinsic motivation is essential for achieving positive learning outcomes. According to SDT, students are more likely to engage meaningfully with learning materials when they experience autonomy, competence and relatedness – elements that can be supported by high-quality technology when integrated purposefully. For example, in environments where students have control over their learning pace and activities – such as interactive platforms that facilitate self-paced exploration – academic performance tends to improve as students become more invested in their learning process. Supporting studies reinforce the mediating role of engagement. Kusmawan and Scholar (2024) identified that engagement encompasses behavioral, emotional and cognitive components, each of which is vital for facilitating learning. In the context of high-quality technology, these dimensions of engagement enable students to concentrate, emotionally invest and critically process content, thereby enhancing their academic performance. This is further supported by research from Alhamad et al. (2024), which found that technology-supported learning environments that actively engage students lead to better retention and understanding of complex information compared to those that merely provide access to information.

Moreover, constructivist learning theory supports the notion that engagement is critical for effective learning through technology. Constructivist theory, as proposed by Prakash Chand (2023), posits that students actively construct knowledge through interactions with materials and their environment. In line with this theory, technology that encourages exploration, interaction and application of learning (such as simulations or collaborative platforms) can promote deeper learning and better performance outcomes. Additionally, cognitive load theory (Evans et al. 2024) sheds light on the role of engagement in the learning process. This theory suggests that high-quality technology can reduce the cognitive load and enhance learning by providing structured and interactive content. However, if students are not actively engaged, they may fail to utilize these features effectively, potentially leading to superficial learning.

Overall, these findings align with a substantial body of research emphasizing the importance of engagement in leveraging technology quality for academic success. Therefore, instructors and educational institutions should focus not only on providing high-quality technological resources but also on fostering engagement through interactive, student-centered learning environments. By integrating technology with methods that enhance student motivation and active participation, the impact on academic performance can be maximized.

8.5.5. *Access to resources and improvement in academic performance*

The absence of a significant relationship between access to resources and academic performance (p = 0.734) indicates that merely having access to resources does not lead to improved academic outcomes without active student engagement. For example, a library that offers a vast array of online journals may not enhance students' performance unless they engage with these resources purposefully and strategically. This finding underscores the importance of student engagement as a critical factor for resources to be effectively utilized in the learning process. Research conducted by Ayongo and Obande (2024) supports this notion, revealing that students who participate in guided research projects, where resources are assigned and integrated into the learning process, demonstrate significantly better comprehension and retention of information. This suggests that structured engagement with resources can facilitate deeper learning and understanding. Additionally, SDT (Ryan and Deci 2022) emphasizes that engagement fosters a sense of autonomy and competence among students. When students feel empowered to use resources to achieve their learning goals, they are more likely to invest time and effort in their studies. Conversely, some studies, such as those by Ajayi et al. (2020), argue that access to resources can benefit highly motivated and self-regulated learners. These students may effectively utilize available resources even in the absence of structured engagement. This perspective highlights the variability in how different students interact with resources based on their motivation and self-management skills.

Furthermore, constructivist learning theory, as articulated by Chuang (2021) and Mishra (2023), supports the idea that interactive engagement with resources is essential for knowledge construction. According to this theory, students learn best when they actively engage with materials and collaborate with peers. On the other hand, cognitive load theory (Evans et al. 2024) suggests that while access to resources is beneficial, guidance is necessary to prevent students from becoming overwhelmed by the information available to them. Without proper direction, students may struggle to process and integrate new knowledge effectively.

In conclusion, the findings indicate that engagement is crucial for students to fully realize the benefits of the resources available to them. Educational institutions should prioritize the development of engagement strategies, such as guided assignments, collaborative projects and interactive learning experiences. By fostering an environment that encourages active participation, institutions can help students utilize resources more effectively, ultimately leading to improved academic outcomes.

8.5.6. *User engagement as a mediator between access to resources and academic performance*

The mediation effect of user engagement in the relationship between access to resources and academic performance is substantial, as indicated by a significant p value of 0.000. This suggests that while access to resources is beneficial, its impact on academic performance largely hinges on the extent to which students actively engage with these resources. For instance, in research-based courses, students who consistently utilize library resources within a structured framework, such as through guided assignments or tutorials, tend to achieve better academic outcomes. This aligns with the *engagement theory* proposed by Kearsley and Shneiderman (1998), which argues that active engagement enhances learning. Engaged students are more likely to make effective use of available resources, leading them to achieve their academic goals more efficiently. Further supporting this view is SDT by Ryan and

Deci (2022), which suggests that engagement cultivates autonomy, competence and relatedness. These factors, in turn, motivate students to use resources in a focused and purposeful manner. In the absence of engagement, however, access to resources may fail to stimulate the intrinsic motivation required for effective use, resulting in underutilization of those resources. Nevertheless, Dong et al. (2020) argue that students with high motivation may still benefit from resource access alone without needing additional engagement. Their study highlights that while engagement is generally beneficial, certain students who possess strong self-regulation and intrinsic motivation might be able to achieve academic success even with minimal guidance. Additionally, *constructivist learning theory* (McLeod 2023) emphasizes the importance of active interaction with resources in constructing meaningful knowledge. On the other hand, *cognitive load theory* (Evans et al. 2024) cautions that an overload of resources, when not coupled with adequate engagement, can overwhelm students, potentially hindering their learning outcomes.

In conclusion, these findings underscore the importance of institutions implementing strategies to foster student engagement. Approaches such as structured assignments, collaborative projects and guided resource use can help students fully leverage available resources, thereby maximizing their academic performance. By prioritizing engagement, educational institutions can increase the effectiveness of resource access and support better academic outcomes for all students.

8.6. References

Ajayi, T., Amosun, P.A., Ige, O.A. (2020). Impact of online resources on pre-service teachers' academic performance in social studies concepts. *Universal Journal of Educational Research*, 8(11B), 5716–5721. doi: 10.13189/ujer.2020.082205.

Al-Adwan, A.S., Li, N., Al-Adwan, A., Abbasi, G.A., Albelbisi, N.A., Habibi, A. (2023). Extending the technology acceptance model (TAM) to predict university students' intentions to use metaverse-based learning platforms. *Education and Information Technologies*, 28(11), 15381–15413. doi: 10.1007/s10639-023-11816-3.

Alduaij, M.Y., Alterkait, M.A., Almutarie, A. (2023). Employing the technology acceptance model to explore moodle's online learning system and its effect on perceived usefulness and ease of use. *International Journal of Business and Management*, 18(5), 154. doi: 10.5539/ijbm.v18n5p154.

Alhamad, A., Makhluf Abuketaba, A.A., Salem Baadhem, A.M. (2024). The mediator role of student engagement in the relationship between charismatic leadership and student learning performance. *International Research Journal on Advanced Science Hub*, 6(4), 52–62. doi: 10.47392/irjash.2024.010.

Anaam, E.A., Haw, S.C., Palanichamy, N., Ali, A., Azni, S. (2023). Analysis of perceived usefulness and perceived ease of use in relation to employee performance. *International Journal of Membrane Science and Technology*, 10(2), 1607–1616. doi: 10.15379/ijmst.v10i2.1836.

Armouti, M., Alhajhassan, S., Alsamara, K. (2023). An adapted Technology Acceptance Model (TAM 5) framework to enhance user acceptance and experience. *Eurasia Proceedings of Science, Technology, Engineering and Mathematics*, 26, 190–201. doi: 10.55549/epstem.1409471.

Aulia, N.S. and Marsasi, E.G. (2024). The role of perceived usefulness, perceived ease of use, and task technology fit to increase perceived impact on learning. *Sentralisasi*, 13(1), 163–181. doi: 10.33506/sl.v13i1.3031.

Ayongo, G. and Obande, B.O. (2024). Influence of access and utilization of electronic information resources on academic performance of postgraduate students in universities in Benue State, Nigeria. *SSRN Electronic Journal*, 1–21. doi: 10.2139/ssrn.4756560.

Barz, N., Benick, M., Dörrenbächer, L., Franziska, U. (2024). Students' acceptance of e-learning: Extending the technology acceptance model with self-regulated learning and affinity for technology. *Discover Education*. doi: 10.1007/s44217-024-00195-7.

Çali, M., Lazimi, L., Ippoliti, B.M.L. (2024). Relationship between student engagement and academic performance. *International Journal of Evaluation and Research in Education*, 13(4), 2210–2217. doi: 10.11591/ijere.v13i4.28710.

Chuang, S. (2021). The applications of constructivist learning theory and social learning theory on adult continuous development. *Performance Improvement*, 60(3), 6–14. doi: 10.1002/pfi.21963.

Dong, A., Jong, M.S.Y., King, R.B. (2020). How does prior knowledge influence learning engagement? The mediating roles of cognitive load and help-seeking. *Frontiers in Psychology*, 11(October), 1–10. doi: 10.3389/fpsyg.2020.591203.

Ernestivita, G., Kumar, V., Anisah, T.N. (2024). Role of gamification in crowdsourcing. In *Marketing and Gamification: Applications, Challenges, and Ethics*, Gupta, S., Nagina, R., Paruthi, M., Gupta, G. (eds). Routledge, Oxford.

Evans, P., Vansteenkiste, M., Parker, P., Kingsford-Smith, A., Zhou, S. (2024). Cognitive load theory and its relationships with motivation: A self-determination theory perspective. *Educational Psychology Review*, 36(1), 1–25. doi: 10.1007/s10648-023-09841-2.

Faisol and Sri Aliami, M.A. (2022). Pathway of building SMEs performance in cluster through innovation capability. *Economics Development Analysis Journal*, 11(2), 140–152. doi: 10.15294/edaj.v11i2.46442.

Faisol, Kumar, V., Aliami, S. (2023). Mediating role of inter-firm linkages and innovation capability towards the sustainability of SMEs in Indonesia. *International Journal of Technology, Policy and Management*, 23(4), 387–409. doi: 10.1504/IJTPM.2023.133918.

Förster, K. (2024). Extending the technology acceptance model and empirically testing the conceptualized consumer goods acceptance model. *Heliyon*, 10(6). doi: 10.1016/j.heliyon.2024.e27823.

Furqon, M., Sinaga, P., Liliasari, L., Riza, L.S. (2023). The impact of learning management system (LMS) usage on students. *TEM Journal*, *12*(2), 1082–1089. doi: 10.18421/TEM122-54.

Hair, J.F., Hult, T.M., Ringle, C.M., Sarstedt, M., Danks, N.P., Ray, S. (2021). Partial least squares structural equation modeling with R. *Practical Assessment, Research and Evaluation*, 21(1), 155–172.

Hatahet, T., Mohamed, A.A.R., Malekigorji, M., Kerry, E.K. (2021). Remote learning in transnational education: Relationship between virtual learning engagement and student academic performance in BSc pharmaceutical biotechnology. *Pharmacy*, 10(1), 4. doi: 10.3390/pharmacy10010004.

Henseler, J., Ringle, C.M., Sinkovics, R.R. (2009). The use of partial least squares path modeling in international marketing. *Advances in International Marketing*, 20(2009), 277–319. doi: 10.1108/S1474-7979(2009)0000020014.

Huang, C.H. (2020). The influence of self-efficacy, perceived usefulness, perceived ease of use, and cognitive load on students' learning motivation, learning attitude, and learning satisfaction in blended learning methods. In *Proceedings of the 2020 3rd International Conference on Education Technology Management (ICETM'20)*. ACM, New York, 29–35. doi: 10.1145/3446590.3446595.

Irsyad, M. and Hapsari, R.D.V. (2023). Pengaruh perceived usefulness, perceived ease of use, perceived security, Dan Social Influence Terhadap Continuance Intention. *Jurnal Manajemen Pemasaran Dan Perilaku Konsumen*, *2*(4), 932–943. doi: 10.21776/jmppk.2023.02.4.08.

Jusop, M., Abdullah, N., Shaharuddin, S., Mohd Fadhil, N.F. (2024). Exploring the impact of digital technology integration on undergraduate accounting performance: An evaluation and analysis. *International Journal of Academic Research in Progressive Education and Development*, 13(3), 3158–3167. doi: 10.6007/ijarped/v13-i3/22767.

Kearsley, G. and Shneiderman, B. (1998). Engagement theory: A framework for technology-based teaching and learning. *Educational Technology*, 38(5), 20–23 [Online]. Available at: http://www.scopus.com/inward/record.url?eid=2-s2.0-37849033883&partnerID=40&md5=f0e60f66fac03c430a9d28f0c36df73f.

Kholilah, K., Kawulur, H.R., Subekti, I. (2022). Perceived usefulness, perceived ease of use, facilitating condition, social influence, and personal innovativeness of accounting students cloud computing adoption. *Organum: Jurnal Saintifik Manajemen Dan Akuntansi*, 5(2), 141–151. doi: 10.35138/organum.v5i2.257.

Koi-Akrofi, G.Y., Aboagye-Darko, D., Nyame, J., Gaisie, E., Danquah, I.O. (2023). Students' acceptance of learning management systems at the peak of Covid-19 pandemic by employing a modified technology acceptance model. *Indian Journal of Science and Technology*, 16(14), 1069–1081. doi: 10.17485/ijst/v16i14.2451.

Kumar, V. and Bhardwaj, A. (2020). Role of cloud computing in school education. In *Handbook of Research on Diverse Teaching Strategies for the Technology-Rich Classroom*, Tomei, L.A. and Carbonara, D.D. (eds). IGI Global, Hershey.

Kumar, V., and Lata, M. (eds) (2022). *The Future of E-Commerce.* Nova Science Publishers, New York. doi: 10.52305/KMUB3774.

Kumar, V. and Rewari, M. (eds) (2023). *Pandemics in the Age of Social Media: Information and Misinformation in Developing Nations.* Taylor & Francis, Singapore.

Kusmawan, U. and Scholar, G. (2024). Self-esteem, student engagement, and academic performance in Universitas Terbuka, Indonesia. *Preprints*. doi: 10.20944/preprints20240 9.1372.v1.

Lata, M. and Kumar, V. (2021). Smart energy management in green cities. In *Handbook of Green Engineering Technologies for Sustainable Smart Cities*, Saravanan, K. and Sakthinathan, G. (eds). CRC Press, Boca Raton, FL.

Lata, M. and Kumar, V. (2022). Security and privacy issues in fog computing environment. *International Journal of Electronic Security and Digital Forensics*, 14(3), 289–307. doi: 10.1504/IJESDF.2022.122588.

Lata, M. and Kumar, V. (2023). Challenges to IoT security: Industry perspective. *Grenze International Journal of Engineering and Technology (GIJET)*, 9(1&2), 61–67.

Lata, M. and Kumar, V. (2024). A framework for security of public cloud environment. *International Journal of Electronic Security and Digital Forensics*, 16(4), 486-502.

Lata, M. and Sharma, V. (2024a). Cloud computing based blended learning: Quality assurance challenges. In *2024 International Conference on Communication, Computer Sciences and Engineering (IC3SE)*. IEEE, New York.

Lata, M. and Sharma, V. (2024b). Smart city environment management: Challenges and opportunities. *Grenze International Journal of Engineering & Technology (GIJET)*, 10(2), 2159–2166.

Lata, M., Kumar, V., Sharma, V. (2024). Cloud computing applications in online learning. *Grenze International Journal of Engineering & Technology (GIJET)*, 10(2), 408–411.

Legault, L. (2017). Self-determination theory. In *Encyclopedia of Personality and Individual Differences*, Zeigler-Hill, V. and Shackelford, T. (eds). Springer, Berlin. doi: 10.1007/978-3-319-28099-8.

Ma, Q. and Liu, L. (2011). The technology acceptance model. In *Advanced Topics in End User Computing, Volume 4*, Mahmood, M.A. (ed.). IGI Global, Hershey. doi: 10.4018/9781591404743.ch006.ch000.

McCord, M. (2006). Technology acceptance model. In *Handbook of Research on Electronic Surveys and Measurements*, Reynolds, R.A., Woods, R., Baker, J.D. (eds). IGI Global, Hershey. doi: 10.4018/978-1-59140-792-8.ch038.

McLeod, S. (2023). Constructivism learning theory & philosophy of education. *SimplyPsychology* [Online]. Available at: https://www.simplypsychology.org/constructivism.html#Constructivism-Philosophy.

Miliszewska, I. and Horwood, J. (2006). Engagement theory. *ACM SIGCSE Bulletin*, 38(1), 158–162. doi: 10.1145/1124706.1121392.

Mishra, N.R. (2023). Constructivist approach to learning: An analysis of pedagogical models of social constructivist learning theory. *Journal of Research and Development*, 6(01), 22–29. doi: 10.3126/jrdn.v6i01.55227.

Mittal, S. and Kumar, V. (2024). Analyzing the role of technological capabilities and digital marketing on the performance of E-commerce-based SMEs. *Indian Journal of Marketing*, 54(12), 45–60.

Muñoz-Carril, P.C., Hernández-Sellés, N., Fuentes-Abeledo, E.J., González-Sanmamed, M. (2021). Factors influencing students' perceived impact of learning and satisfaction in computer supported collaborative learning. *Computers and Education*, 174(February). doi: 10.1016/j.compedu.2021.104310.

Nanda, P. and Kumar, V. (2024). New generation technologies: Development vs. ethical challenges. *International Journal of Business Information Systems*, 46(3), 411–434.

Nuryakin, N., Rakotoarizaka, N.L.P., Musa, H.G. (2023). The effect of perceived usefulness and perceived easy to use on student satisfaction: The mediating role of attitude to use online learning. *Asia Pacific Management and Business Application*, 011(03), 323–336. doi: 10.21776/ub.apmba.2023.011.03.5.

Olipas, C.N.P. and Leona, R.F. (2022). The perceived usefulness, perceived ease of use, behaviour towards, and intention to use mobile compilers in learning computer programming. *Path of Science*, 8(8), 2006–2014. doi: 10.22178/pos.84-7.

Paas, F. and van Merriënboer, J.J.G. (2020). Cognitive-load theory: Methods to manage working memory load in the learning of complex tasks. *Current Directions in Psychological Science*, 29(4), 394–398. doi: 10.1177/0963721420922183.

Parker, R.K. and Chao, T.J. (2007). Wiki as a teaching tool. *Interdisciplinary Journal of E-Skills and Lifelong Learning*, 3, 057–072. doi: 10.28945/386.

Prakash Chand, S. (2023). Constructivism in education: Exploring the contributions of Piaget, Vygotsky, and Bruner. *International Journal of Science and Research (IJSR)*, 12(7), 274–278. doi: 10.21275/sr23630021800.

Rai, S. and Lata, M. (2024). Futuristic outlook of online learning: The post-pandemic era. In *Technology-mediated Learning During the Pandemic*, Singh, J. and Kumar, V. (eds). Routledge, Delhi.

Ren, L., Yang, F., Gu, C., Sun, J., Liu, Y. (2022). A study of factors influencing Chinese college students' intention of using metaverse technology for basketball learning: Extending the technology acceptance model. *Frontiers in Psychology*, 13(December). doi: 10.3389/fpsyg.2022.1049972.

Rençber, H. (2020). United theory of acceptance and use of technology. *Consumer Behavior Models*, 181–192. doi: 10.1007/978-3-030-10576-1_300692.

Ryan, R.M. and Deci, E.L. (2022). Self-determination theory. In *The Wiley Encyclopedia of Personality and Individual Differences, Models and Theories*, Maggino, F. (ed.), Springer, Berlin.

Ryan, M., Wells, J., Freeman, A., Hallam, G. (2011). Resource-based learning strategies: Implications for students and institutions. *Research in Learning Technology*, 4(1). doi: 10.3402/rlt.v4i1.9957.

Sharma, D. and Kumar, V. (2017). A framework for collaborative and convenient learning on cloud computing platforms. *International Journal of Web-Based Learning and Teaching Technologies (IJWLTT)*, 12(2), 1–20.

Singh, J., Kumar, V., Kumar, D. (2022). Combating the pandemic with ICT-based learning tools and applications: A case of indian higher education platforms. *International Journal of Virtual and Personal Learning Environments (IJVPLE)*, 12(1), 1–21.

Spica, E. (2023). Inclusive access: A multi-institutional study of academic outcomes from a statewide community college automatic billing e-textbook pilot. *Community College Journal of Research and Practice*, 47(3), 197–216. doi: 10.1080/10668926.2021.1990161.

Sweller, J. (1994). Cognitive load theory, learning difficulty, and instructional design. *Learning and Instruction*, 4(4), 295–312. doi: 10.1016/0959-4752(94)90003-5.

Tao, X., Shannon-Honson, A., Delaney, P., Li, L., Dann, C., Li, Y., Xie, H. (2022). Data analytics on online student engagement data for academic performance modeling. *IEEE Access*, 10(August), 103176–103186. doi: 10.1109/ACCESS.2022.3208953.

Udto, K.T. and Kusain, Z.S. (2023). Integration of technology in the classroom instruction in relation to academic performance. *International Journal of Information Technology and Computer Engineering*, 33, 1–5. doi: 10.55529/ijitc.33.1.5.

Uluçınar Sağır, Ş. and Sakar, D. (2017). Flipped classroom model in education. *International Journal of Social Sciences and Education Research*, 3(5S), 1904–1916. doi: 10.24289/ijsser.348068.

Venkatesh, V. and Davis, F.D. (2000). Theoretical extension of the technology acceptance model: Four longitudinal field studies. *Management Science*, 46(2), 186–204. doi: 10.1287/mnsc.46.2.186.11926.

Wang, X., Tan, S.C., Li, L. (2020). Measuring university students' technostress in technology-enhanced learning: Scale development and validation. *Australasian Journal of Educational Technology*, 36(4), 96–112. doi: 10.14742/ajet.5329.

Wilson, N., Keni, K., Tan, P.H.P. (2021). The role of perceived usefulness and perceived ease-of-use toward satisfaction and trust which influence computer consumers' loyalty in China. *Gadjah Mada International Journal of Business*, 23(3), 262–294. doi: 10.22146/gamaijb.32106.

Yadav, V.K. (2023). An introduction to cognitive load theory. *Cognitive Load: A Learning-Teaching Perspective*, Ghosh, R., Dey, K.N., Adi, M.T. (eds). ABS Books, Delhi.

9

The 4IR Paradox: Navigating Autonomy and Regulation in Higher Education

Universities in the 21st century, particularly the age of the Fourth Industrial Revolution (4IR), confront the challenges of disruptive technologies for development and adaptation. This chapter explores institutional freedom, innovation and change with the need for oversight of quality, ethical standards and data protection. This research examines the process' 4IR technologies, including artificial intelligence (AI) and data analytics. It also covers AI-powered education: speaking of the effects of algorithms on the autonomy of instruction, teaching pedagogy and student experience at the faculty level; and additionally, emerging technologies: students face ethical issues related to blockchain, virtual reality (VR) and augmented reality (AR) technologies. This chapter scrutinizes successful universities to identify the following: (1) autonomy-based university strategies to encourage responsible innovation within existing regulations; (2) appropriate regulation-based strategies to incentivize innovation and corporate responsibility; and (3) integrated approaches – working with HEIs, legislators and regulators to create flexible contexts that connect independence and responsibility. Suggested actions are as follows: (1) universities: build strong ethical compliance and internal controls; (2) policymakers: enact adaptive, risk-sensitive and technology-neutral legislation; and (3) timely engage with regulators. It is imperative for academic institutions to effectively negotiate to leverage the 4IR technologies to build up resilience and augment societal engagement within the terrain of higher learning.

9.1. Introduction

The 4IR presents new technical novelties that have altered social relations and sectors of the economy (Nanda and Kumar 2024). An exception to this trend is higher education institutions (HEIs), which play a pivotal role in civilized nations, and HEIs contribute significantly to academic and sociopolitical growth (Kumar and Rewari 2023). In particular, this disruption has contributed to forcing HEIs to adopt

Chapter written by Linda PAUL and Ravinder RENA.

technologies such as AI, Big Data, blockchain, VR and AR, among others, in the new environment according to Rahman et al. (2024). Depending on the particularity of their implementation across learning contexts, these tools can revolutionize instructional approaches, tailor learning and increase administrative efficiency (Kumar and Bhardwaj 2020). However, their implementation turns universities into a dilemma because they have to locate the balance between institutional governance and regulations. On the other hand, legislative frameworks ensure that ethical norms, data protection and accountability are accorded their due respect, and legislative frameworks also entail the level of flexibility that enables the autonomy needed for experimentation and innovation. This research demonstrates how the analyzed universities coordinate autonomy and regulation to offer sustainable dimensions of the 4IR in higher education institutions.

There have been expressions of the spirit of revolution from scholars on the technological exposure of the contemporary literature of the 4IR. AI-integrated platforms can create more conducive learning environments and more focused training on learners' needs, leading to enhanced performance for students (Rahman et al. 2024). Bhardwaj and Kumar (2024) noted that data analytics enable timely interventions that improve students' performance and hence retention and success rates. Programs in the form of VR and AR can improve the level of interactivity and students' understanding of lessons (Gleason 2018). Nevertheless, the adoption of such technologies entails severe challenges. While the adoption of AI in a learning environment may bring useful traits into the classroom, reliance on data collection tends to prompt some critical issues regarding permission and data privacy (Holmes et al. 2022). Furthermore, the ethical implications of applying VR and AR, including equity and accessibility needs, require further analysis (Kaplan and Haenle 2021; Fernandez and Wagner 2022).

The tensions between institutional autonomy and regulation clearly emerged as universities tried to innovate in a regulated setting. Universities have hitherto cherished their autonomy because it enables discretion over research, the curriculum and the type of technology to be adopted. Autonomous schools are free to change their programmes to meet the vocation and fast-evolving needs of both the market and learners (Saito 2022; Rahman et al. 2024). However, this comes with its disadvantages, which include unethical practices that are encouraged, such as inadequate handling of data security, for example, the absence of equal provisions for technology resources (Altbach and Hanstedt 2018; Rahman et al. 2024). From their side, the regulations provide the needed safeguards that would ensure that development in education does not compromise privacy or ethics. This aspect, however, implies that complex and stringent legislation may limit the ability of universities to create and implement innovative solutions in the constantly progressing technology world (Kim and Park 2020). The lack of comprehensive works that assess how universities maintain independence and accountability in the application of 4IR technology is a major research gap. Some analyses have been carried out on the efficiencies and problems that characterize the given technologies and their impact on institutions and society (Mittal and Kumar 2024). This chapter aims to fill that gap by examining how HEIs can effectively address this dilemma of balancing creativity for learning with compliance with legal requirements that protect base values and student interests (Lata and Sharma 2024a).

Thus, the purpose of this research is to establish how HEIs balance autonomy and regulation when responding to emerging 4IR technologies. To mediate these opposing claims, this research seeks to identify strategies that successful universities apply. Specifically, this research aims to determine how the independence of universities is used to foster experimentation and innovation while adhering to the legal perimeters necessary to maintain morality and protect individuals' data privacy. Intellectual development and societal advancement are not exceptions to this trend. AI, Big Data, blockchain, VR and augmented reality (AR) are disruptive technologies that HEIs are forced to incorporate into their curricula in this new environment (Rahman et al. 2024). These tools have the potential to transform instructional strategies, customize learning and increase administrative effectiveness. However, their implementation places universities in a difficult position, as they must strike a balance between institutional autonomy and the regulatory framework (Lata and Kumar 2024). While legislative frameworks guarantee that ethical norms, data protection and accountability are maintained, autonomy encourages the flexibility required for experimentation and innovation (Singh et al. 2022). This study presents sustainable options for responsible innovation in higher education by examining how universities manage the conflict between autonomy and regulation in the context of the 4IR.

The revolutionary potential of 4IR technologies in education has been extensively discussed in the literature. Platforms with AI capabilities can design adaptive learning environments that customize training to meet the needs of specific students, greatly improving learning results and student engagement (Rahman et al. 2024). According to Bhardwaj and Kumar (2024), data analytics offer valuable insights into student performance, facilitating early interventions that can increase retention and success rates. Students' engagement and comprehension can be enhanced by immersing them in interactive environments through VR and AR (AlGerafi et al. 2023). However, despite these advantages, the use of these technologies presents serious issues. The application of AI in the classroom and increasing dependence on data gathering have raised important concerns about permission and data protection (Holmes et al. 2022). Additionally, the ethical ramifications of utilizing immersive technologies such as VR and AR necessitate rigorous evaluation, especially with respect to equity and accessibility (Kaplan and Haenle 2021; Fernandez and Wagner 2022).

Higher education institutions have traditionally valued autonomy because it allows them to be flexible in their research, curriculum design and adoption of new technology. Institutions that have autonomy can modify their programmes to accommodate the quickly changing demands of both the labor market and students (Sharma and Kumar 2017; Saito 2022). Unrestrained autonomy, however, may result in unethical behavior, such as a failure to adequately address data security or provide equal access to technology resources (Altbach and Hanstedt 2018; Rahman et al. 2024). Regulatory frameworks, on the other hand, offer the necessary protection to guarantee that advances in education do not jeopardize confidentiality or moral principles. Overly stringent regulations, however, may hinder universities' capacity to innovate and adapt quickly to the rapidly evolving technology environment (Kim and Park 2020; Lata et al. 2024). The deficiency of thorough studies that examine how universities strike a balance between autonomy and regulation when they implement 4IR technology is the main gap in the current body of research. The advantages and difficulties of certain technologies have been the subject of several studies, but few studies have examined the wider ramifications of this balance for institutional growth and societal effect (Rahman et al. 2024). This study attempts to close that gap by examining how HEIs can successfully manage this conundrum, encouraging creativity while guaranteeing adherence to legal frameworks that safeguard moral principles and the interests of students.

This study's main goal is to determine how HEIs handle the inherent conflict between regulation and autonomy when implementing 4IR technologies. To reconcile these conflicting needs, this study aims to pinpoint the tactics used by prosperous universities. Specifically, the study investigates how universities use their independence to promote experimentation and innovation while simultaneously abiding by the legal obligations required to uphold moral principles and data privacy. Additionally, it assesses how framework regulations promote the use of appropriate technology in higher learning institutions, especially the 4IR technologies, including AI and Big Data, VR and AR. This chapter discusses various successful cases to offer information that may be important to current regulatory bodies, academic institutions and politicians.

The following is a breakdown of how this chapter is structured. The relevance of the study is stated, the research problem is described and the objectives of the investigation are defined. The literature review subsequently provides a critical synthesis of the literature on the chosen topics of the 4IR, autonomy and regulation in higher education as well as the opportunities and challenges of new technologies (Lata and Kumar 2023). The section on research gap and aim outlines the goals of the study and highlights the gaps in the existing body of knowledge. In the methodology section of the study, the research techniques applied and case studies of academic institutions addressing the 4IR dilemma are explained. The major findings from these cases are included together with guidelines concerning how this study envisages that a balance between autonomy and control can be achieved in higher learning institutions. In the course of the discussion of the implications of the findings for academic institutions and policymakers, this chapter underlines the need for the flexibility of rules.

The conclusion offers suggestions to academic institutions, authorities and prospective scholars, in addition to restating the major findings of the study. In essence, the 4IR age presents a major issue for higher education institutions: keeping pace with the demands for the creation of innovation while at the same time conserving the principles and codes of ethics and keeping legal policies in mind (Kumar and Lata 2022). To understand how HEIs can innovate when the interests of their students matter, there is a need to understand the balance between autonomy and regulation, an aspect that will remain pertinent to understanding the relationships between universities and new technology. By doing so, this work provides universities with guidelines on how to proceed with the process of implementing 4IR technology by borrowing from the strategies adopted by successful institutions.

9.2. Literature review

Education, especially higher learning, has transformed paradigms because of the 4IR, which has incorporated teaching, learning and other related processes and new technologies, such as blockchain, VR, AI, AR and data analytics (Ernestivita et al. 2024). The integration of new technologies is redesigning the management of universities and how they deliver educational services, which has benefits as well as vices (Rena 2024). The use of these technologies for enhancing learning outcomes, the ethical issues related to the use of these technologies and the issues of the rights of institutions against monitoring agencies, are discussed in this study. This literature review ensures an understanding of the 4IR dilemma in higher education by examining these major themes and analyzing prior research. To comprehend how 4IR technologies and higher education interact, it is essential to grasp a few fundamental ideas: 4IR is a fusion of digital, physical and biological systems brought about by exponential advancements in technological frontiers, including AI, robotics, the Internet of Things (IoT) and Big Data (Schwab 2016). 4IR in higher education therefore refers to the application of these technologies in research and learning as well as institutional processes.

Scholars have paid increasing attention to applying 4IR technologies in higher education in the past few years, especially from some pioneers in the field. Schwab (2016) is one of the most prominent theorists in the 4IR, and he noted that technologies such as AI, VR and Big Data are reconfiguring industries, including the education sector, and forcing organisations to reframe instructional/didactic as well as administrative-governance paradigms (Rai and Lata 2024). These technologies have the potential to provide individualized learning, increase operational efficiency and strengthen research, according to Schwab (2016).

Supporting views: scholars that support Schwab's perspective

Chaka (2022), Bhardwaj and Kumar (2024), and Kaplan and Haenle (2021), all of whom agree with Schwab's ideas, stress that 4IR technologies may foster change. Chaka (2022) discusses ethical implications for learning and the importance of developing digital literacy frameworks for reforms for education. This makes sense since Bhardwaj and Kumar (2024) also pointed out the potential for Big Data analytics to greatly revolutionize decision-making related to academic management, such as the use of predictive analytics to assess students' withdrawal risk. Kaplan and Haenle (2021) pay much attention to data privacy; the authors argue that as 4IR technologies create new possibilities, they create the need to safeguard students' data from misuse.

Diverging views: variations in the theme

Some scholars whose works resonate in a general way but at the same time better outline the perspective that Schwab focuses on include Altbach and Hanstedt (2018), Kim and Park (2020), and Scott (2020). To this end, Altbach and Hanstedt (2018) claim that institutional autonomy is critical in promoting innovations and that universities need to try out new, emerging technologies. On the other hand, Kim and Park (2020) proposed moderation, with the assertion that failure to maintain accountability may result in ethical violation or poor implementation. Scott (2020) is concerned with governance, and for radical innovation, he maintains that adaptable regulatory systems must enable responsible innovation.

Opposing views: this viewpoint has been under attack from critics of unfettered technological integration

Holmes et al. (2022) and Lahoz-Bengoechea and Bell (2022) revealed that the adoption of 4IR technologies should not be unchecked. According to Holmes et al. (2022), the use of AI systems amplifies unfairness resulting from inherent algorithmic prejudice, leading to increased questions on the ethics of appropriateness. Refuting the positive claims of Technology Enhanced Teaching (TET), Lahoz-Bengoechea and Bell (2022) showed that it can compromise academic freedom because technology diminishes the faculty's bargaining power in curriculum and assessment.

Resulting dilemma

These differing perspectives create a dilemma: in what ways should higher education institutions be able to attain their purpose of innovative independence while also receiving regulatory control to monitor unethical practices and enforce the rule of law and equality? This question forms the core of this study: in what ways is self-governance in the diffusion of 4IR technologies both a weakness and a strength of higher education institutions?

9.2.1. *Conceptual framework*

To answer this question, this study provides insights from other scholars and builds a conceptual framework. Prominent works used as part of this framework include Rogers (2003), Braun and Clarke (2006), and Yin (2018). Braun and Clarke's (2006) thematic analysis methodology is useful in analyzing patterns of institutional practices, and Yin's (2018) case study methodology is useful when comparing various forms of institutional context.

9.2.2. *Emerging concepts*

From the literature, several key concepts emerge:

– Institutional autonomy: the autonomy and ability of universities to self-administer and determine the pace at which they embrace certain technologies (Altbach and Hanstedt 2018).

– Regulatory oversight: regulations, guidelines and protocols of good practice toward professionalism, personal integrity and protection of data in technology incorporation (Kim and Park 2020).

– Ethical challenges: concerns include privacy, fairness of AI systems and access to technology (Kaplan and Haenle 2021; Holmes et al. 2022).

– Collaboration: it includes cooperation among universities, the business world and policy-making institutions in developing EU networks of adaptive governance (Scott 2020).

– Societal contribution: some of the conventional areas of the 4IR technologies and their effects on workforce readiness and overall societal enhancement can be found by Chaka (2022).

9.2.3. *Introducing relations between conceptions*

The concepts are interconnected:

– Autonomy and oversight: there is therefore the issue of flexibility in the management of universities against the backdrop of meeting setup requirements such as compliance with regulations.

– Ethical challenges and collaboration: the management of ethical issues must involve both internal members in institutions and other parties from outside of the institutions.

– Societal contribution: making use of technologies properly can help the readiness state of the workforce and the furthering of societal advancement, revealing the purpose of effective and correct innovation.

In the following literature, there is enough background information to build a framework that will facilitate the analysis of 4IR technology adoption in higher education. However, current research still lacks insights into how institutions manage the dilemma of autonomy and control of cultural and regulatory differences (Lata and Kumar 2021). This chapter serves to fill such gaps by presenting a conceptual review of the relevant literature and developing an integrative framework for conceptual review, on the one hand, and analyzing actual institutional practices, on the other hand.

9.2.4. *Critical evaluation*

While the literature provides a detailed and comprehensive account of all of the potential benefits associated with 4IR technologies, there is often inadequate analysis regarding how educational institutions can leverage technologies responsibly and meet their moral and legal commitments. Unfortunately, there is relatively limited reference to the implications of IT for the broader social, ethical and policy spheres; instead, most of the literature focuses more on the actual configuration of IT adoption. For all the promise that AI and data analytics hold for personalizing, for example, education, far less consideration is given to how universities might minimize the risks of algorithmic bias or safeguard the rights of student data beyond what the law mandates (Lahoz-Bengoechea and Bell 2022; Baidya et al. 2024).

Additionally, instead of analyzing how institutional autonomy and regulatory supervision may coexist, the literature often presents them as mutually exclusive phenomena. Future research is needed on cooperative models when academic institutions, regulators, and legislators work on creating hybrid regulatory frameworks for innovation that ensure compliance with moral values (Kim and Park 2020). Thus, more practical outcomes from such a shift in focus would be in the interest of universities that seek to appropriately adopt 4IR technologies. The literature then notes the contrast existing in access to 4IR technologies, noting that the results are skewed to institutes with less funding or nationally developed nations. As impressive as VR and AI technologies may be, these technologies are of no use to students who have no access to technology or Internet connections. Access to technology is a current issue that requires further study because its neglect threatens to exacerbate existing inequalities in learning (AlGerafi et al. 2023; Sharma et al. 2024).

9.3. Methodology

The introduction of 4IR technologies universally requires universities and colleges to negotiate more autonomy and regulatory control. This section includes a discussion of the research methods of the study, population and sample selection, data collection instruments and implementation of the study. Owing to its core focus on undertaking qualitative research practices for deeper analyses, the methodology is designed to ensure maximum understanding of the institutional practices and policies regarding the deployment of 4IR technology. By applying case study research and multiple sources of data, this study explores how different HEIs manage tensions between innovation morality and the rule of law.

Research design

Since organisational structure and processes entail many intricate activities, the form of research employed in the study is the qualitative case study method (Yin 2018). The key findings are obtained through a case study analysis of HEIs' internal decision-making process on the adoption of 4IR technologies as well as their strategies toward regulatory compliance. This architecture provides overall information about how institutions can be autonomous and regulated and, at the same time, provides space to look at the accomplishments and challenges of HEIs. For this reason, the study seeks to understand how and why particular technology innovations are adopted in certain institutional settings as opposed to quantifying adoption levels, that is, the use of case studies. With this method, the instructor can provide procedural, political, and even problematic understandings of institutions. In the words of Creswell and Poth (2018), this method provides a richer understanding of the practices and policies of an institution and the problems that would not be described as vividly in quantitative terms.

9.3.1. *Study population and sampling*

The study will therefore target both public and private universities from across the world that are implementing 4IR technologies such as AI, Big Data analytics, blockchain and VR. The choice includes institutions of different sizes, teaching and research focuses, and belonging to a private or public sector. Convenience sampling was used in the selection of the secondary data sources that concerned institutions that had embraced the 4IR technologies. The sampling was intended to incorporate different types of institutions, both public and private universities, and different governance and regulation contexts around the world. For the above reasons, examining how different HEIs resolve the clash between innovation and regulation becomes possible. The study examined data from 12 higher education institutions across three regions: North America, Europe, and Asia, on average, had four institutions each. It was possible to choose only a few institutions, and these institutions were chosen to cover a range of regulatory and innovation environments.

9.3.2. *Data analyzed using NVivo*

The sources of data for this study comprised organizational documents such as institutional reports, strategic plans, academic and other published works, and official policies accessible to the public. Data analysis for thematic analysis was performed via NVivo software because it provides a tool for coding and categorizing data to allow the researcher to distinguish patterns and insights regarding the implementation of 4IR technologies in the offering of higher education.

Results and themes

The analysis identified five main themes:

– this chapter focuses on the use of autonomy as a means of encouraging innovation;

– the other challenge that comes from regulatory barriers;

– thus, there is a need to adopt suitable governance frameworks for adopting technological innovations;

– interests of universities, regulators and industry;

– implications on society of the implementation of 4IR technologies.

Amount of data

A total of 50 institutional reports, 30 academic articles and 15 policy documents were included in the final dataset, which contained approximately 500,000 analyzed words. This approach also made it possible to research and document, in a broader and more balanced way, how HEIs manage the tension between innovation and regulation using secondary data that are freely and publicly accessible. In general, institutions of higher learning around the world are grappling with the swift adoption of 4IR technologies, which forms the basis for this research. A sample of universities has been selected from different regions of the world – North America, Europe and Asia – providing a broad spectrum of regulatory environments and levels of technology integration. A slightly versatile sampling of different HEIs provides a broader understanding of how international regulatory systems influence technology applications and how organisations can be innovative and compliant with these regulations.

9.4. Findings

In this study, conclusions were derived from peer-reviewed articles, institutional reports, academic publications, strategic plans, and publicly available policy document analyses to elucidate how HEIs navigate the tension between regulatory surveillance and independence in regard to 4IR technology implementation. The research questions directly applicable to this study were as follows: how do institutions pursue autonomy for innovation, and in doing so, what regulatory challenges do they face? Some of the tactics employed by institutions as they try to balance autonomy and regulation are the central research questions applicable in this study. The main findings are presented in this part of the study question and are compared with those of prior studies. The findings obtained in this study are subsequently discussed concerning their implications for HEIs in the 4IR era, followed by an establishment of the differences between the findings and those of the literature.

9.4.1. *In what ways do academic institutions utilize their autonomy to leverage new innovative 4IR technologies?*

Another main finding of the study is that HEIs possessing higher powers of institutional autonomy are likely to adopt 4IR technologies faster and more innovatively. The use of AI, Big Data analytics and VR testing was more exhaustive in institutions whose decision-making processes were relatively unfettered, especially private and research-oriented universities. Leveraging their autonomy, these universities formed specialized divisions, idea hubs and associations with technological companies to integrate efficient technologies in their research, teaching, and administrative processes.

For example, to apply machine learning models in functional problems such as boosting arraying decisions and learning analytics in universities, several universities have set up AI labs where scholars and learners work together.

This finding provides additional support for the thesis that the relative advantage of Rogers' (2003) Diffusion of Innovations theory is that an imperative incentive to adopt innovations in the shape of new technologies is also evidenced by the fact that institutions that applied blockchain for credential verification systems identified efficiency and transparency in the management of student records. These findings align with previous findings on the importance of institutional autonomy in fostering innovation. Altbach and Hanstedt (2018) further noted that autonomy allows institutional change to occur more quickly in response to technological change, resulting in modifications to the curricula that fit the students' desires and market conditions. The study did find, however, that several technologies adopted at the department level without a unified strategic intention may stem from strategic autonomy but lack proper governance structures. As many studies focus on the benefits of autonomy while neglecting the challenges that stem from the lack of a coordinated system of governance, this finding hints at a gap in the literature.

– *Interpretation*: the findings of this study imply that greater autonomy is needed to advance innovation in higher education and thus the 4IR technologies. To ensure that technology adoption is logical and consistent with the goals of the institution, there must be an adequate degree of self-organization and bureaucratic rules. It stresses how necessary it is for independent institutions to develop a framework for innovation while ensuring strategic congruency.

9.4.2. *What are the main regulatory challenges about the adoption of 4IR technologies by HEI?*

By analyzing the impact of using 4IR technologies in HEIs, this study revealed that there are several legal challenges that universities face, including legal requirements on data privacy and concerns about IP, AI and algorithmic bias. The survey also revealed that universities located in areas with stringent rules that pertain to data usage, especially in research such as the United States, together with countries that are in the European Union and that have brought about the GDPR standards for the usage of data, were slow to adapt to the use of data technologies such as Big Data analytics and AI compared with those in areas with no (or less) regulation. Laws related to data privacy were mentioned by respondents as a significant challenge in addressing the improved use of learning analytics, which is powered by AI. Education institutions were concerned with functions such as the ethical use, capture, and storage of student data, even though the aforementioned technologies could help enhance student success and learning. Chaka (2022) opined that data privacy is one of the more critical concerns associated with the use of technology in teaching/learning, and the findings of this study are consistent with the literature.

Intellectual property (IP) and innovation were again major issues. Some faculty members at several universities stated that managing technology license policies that regulate dealings with outside tech firms to develop VR simulations or other AI instructional tools, was difficult. Such affiliations often require complex agreements to enable businesses to utilize IP while ensuring that the university has rights over the generated discoveries. Whereas data privacy and ethical considerations are often the main focus of the literature on regulatory difficulties, the complexity of IP issues in university–industry partnerships is sometimes lost (Kaplan and Haenle 2021). The findings demonstrate that despite the necessity of implementing strict legal requirements formerly to achieve ethical principles and people's privacy preservation, they can become a barrier to implementing 4IR technologies. These rules must be addressed by HEIs, often at the cost of innovation, limiting the effectiveness of a successful and creative process. Furthermore, the emerging significance of IP issues suggests that colleges should develop more specific principles and terms of reference for interaction with their business counterparts. Two possible approaches are as follows: regulatory agencies should consider how they can create flexible frameworks to support innovation while maintaining essential forms of protection.

9.4.3. *When it comes to conflict between regulation and autonomy, which strategies do universities use?*

The report (Saito 2022) identified several ways through which HEIs manage to balance the degree of decision-making autonomy with regulatory requirements. The elimination of bureaucratic constraints for idea generation was another good strategy; the formation of committees or task groups whose purview is to govern innovation was another effective strategy. These task forces were responsible for ensuring that new technology conformed to regulations and, at the same time, promoted technological advances. They were often composed of administrators, professors, lawyers and judges. For example, one of the universities in the study set up a digital ethics committee that was fully engaged with academics monitoring and evaluating new AI projects for ethical concerns and guaranteeing that any AI teaching resources that were being developed were entirely legal and adhered to institutional guidelines. Another strategy observed was cooperation with industry partners and outside regulatory agencies. Several policies focused on innovation, and these were shaped better by efficient universities, which engaged with regulators and industry associations. This finding supports Kim and Park's (2020) assertion that the growth of flexible and supportive policies involves collaboration among regulators, lawmakers and scholars.

A survey conducted in this study revealed that several universities employed gradualist approaches to experiment with 4IR technologies in pilot initiatives across the campus. This strategy lowered risk, as any ethical or compliance issues could be solved beforehand so that institutions could experiment with evolving technologies. This systematic approach to innovation was distinguished as a best practice for achieving the right balance in terms of addressing the necessary compliance requirements and the need for independence. As noted in the findings, for the decentralized centralization framework to work, organized governance mechanisms coupled with collaborative engagements with outside stakeholders hold the key. Corporate institutions can minimize risk and be innovative and responsible by setting up novel task forces and committees. If academic institutions invest in internal systems to maintain this balance, they are better placed to effectively and ethically apply 4IR technologies.

9.4.4. *What virtuous and/or vicious circles does the 4IR paradox create for higher education institutions to transform society?*

On the basis of these findings, the universities that meet the Osburn paradox, through adequately addressing the degree of decentralization for the benefit of centralization, positioned themselves to enhance the growth of society by producing graduates who can meet the needs of the 4IR job market. The increased adoption and use of AI, Big Data and VR in the learning environment increased student interest and improved performance among learners in business, engineering and health-related professions. Before engaging in clinical experiences, the simple and complex motor skills of individuals can be developed through the completion of mock activities, as revealed by one university that adopted VR in training medical students. Apart from churning out qualified graduates, these universities are contributing to research and solving problems that are faced in real society via 4IR technology, such as developing AI for a health promotion crusade.

The study did, however, find that universities that experienced regulatory challenges or lacked properly synchronized governance strategies were less prepared to capitalize on the benefits of the 4IR technology. The ability of these institutions to produce graduates ready to fit the demand of the 4IR economy was, however, affected by these innovation gaps. This study supports the literature by arguing that innovation in education is important for addressing the needs of the labor market in the future (Saito 2022).

Interpretation: universities that have an appropriate balance of freedom and control are in a better position to make positive contributions to the enhancement of society. Hence, these educational institutions should be able to teach students to prepare them for challenges in the workplace in the modern world through the use of 4IR technology, which must be morally and legally acceptable. Thus, in the context of the 4IR and HEIs' capacity to remain valuable in the future, the relevant institutional approaches that would facilitate both innovation and compliance need to be supported (Lata and Sharma 2024b).

Since HEIs are adopting 4IR technologies in their operations, the study conclusions provide a clear understanding of how they overcome the paradox between autonomy and regulation. Innovation can only occur within strong governance mechanisms to ensure that institutional objectives and legal appropriateness are followed. However, universities with more autonomy are better placed to foster innovation. These important areas regulated by authorities that must be addressed through internal institution-solving and cooperation with regulators are data protection, IP and ethics. Finally, universities that effectively establish the right combination of autonomy and control mechanisms are in a position to train their graduates for the fourth industrial revolutionary workforce, which contributes positively to the development of society.

9.5. Conclusion

Moreover, this study sought to examine how HEIs balance the compliance and innovation of 4IR technologies, which include blockchain, Big Data, AI, VR and AR. The primary purpose was to determine how organisations foster innovation within the context of their autonomy in line with legal requirements that ensure ethical conduct, privacy, and accountability. On the basis of an assessment of several case studies and interviews with other key players in HEIs, such as managers and the hurried students themselves, exactly how HEIs navigate and how they can help shape society in the 4IR environment are well understood in this study. This 4IR has the potential to dramatically change the governance, research, and teaching functions of universities. That being said, there are also a tremendous number of problems with these technologies, not the least of which are those of privacy, morality, and law. Resolving the 4IR paradox, namely, the tension between the norms embodied in legal regulation that can guarantee ethics and ensure accountability, on the one hand, and the freedom required for universities to be innovative, on the other hand, was the purpose of this research. Since HEIs are now more often under pressure to make students ready for a future dominated by technology, they need to understand this paradox. A significantly larger workforce capable of contributing to the growing 4IR demands and contributing to society through research and public service is expected to be produced by universities that have been able to find the right balance between innovation and compliance.

Key findings recap: the study arrived at numerous important conclusions that assist us in comprehending how HEIs manage the 4IR issue. One of the main implications of this study is that institutional autonomy is crucial for the development of innovation. Those institutions that have enhanced organisational freedom, especially private and research universities, can adopt the 4IR technologies at ease and experiment with various uses in many university activities. For example, some of the study's institutions created centralized AI centers, implemented blockchain-based credentials and incorporated VR into their learning environments. By putting these technologies into practice in their independence in administrators' processes and curricula, those institutions established how 4IR technologies may enhance learning and operation.

While autonomy leads to creativity, the study also established that CG systems are vital for the coordination of adoption as well as their strategic integration.

When several departments of an organization embrace the use of technology, the process may not be harmonized, which may sometimes lead to waste and missed opportunities when several departments embrace the use of technology. The findings of this study are that autonomy is vital, but so is the existence of robust governance structures that guide the innovation process. Writing about autonomy, Altbach and Hanstedt (2018) noted that, in line with the literature, it allows organisations to respond swiftly to technological changes. This study goes further by revealing the risks of fragmentation where governance is absent, a point often lost in prior research.

The study also identified several regulatory challenges that HEIs encounter as they seek to adopt 4IR technology. The top challenges include issues related to the ownership of IP, ethical standards and data protection. According to the survey, institutions in regions that are rigid with laws such as the GDPR of the European Union claim lower levels of competence in Big Data analytics and AI. This was a large turnoff since universities were compelled to adhere to high standards of protecting data and ensuring that any data collected from students were protected and used only in a moral way. University systems that partnered with outside technology vendors also had to make decisions concerning the IP in addition to the data. Concerns expressed by the administrators and the faculty were with respect to the handling of the IPR while engaging corporations in the digital space, and particularly concerning ensuring that institutions were not relinquishing control of creation resulting from these collaborations.

These findings are a result of close agreement with past research concerning data privacy, which is well known to contribute to hindering the use of digital technology in the classroom (Chaka 2022). As this study adds to the topic, the complexities of IP management in university–industry partnerships, which are sometimes overshadowed by discussions about regulatory issues, are discussed here.

Ways of regulating and unleashing system freedoms: this study identified several effective strategies that higher education institutions employed while addressing the dilemma of subordination and control. The development of committees and task forces dedicated to regulating innovation governance was among the most effective recommendations. These committees, which included teachers, legal professionals and administrators, played a large role in ensuring that the emerging technology complied with the legal aspect and simultaneously fostered creativity. This is why one university has set up the Digital Ethics Committee to oversee the usage of AI instruments and ensure that the tools have been developed and deployed as per existing norms.

Incremental adoption was the second effective strategy used by the firm. Even some colleges that are in support of 4IR technologies realized that they would use the technologies selectively in some parts of the college before extending the change over the whole college. This approach allowed them to test the technologies on a larger scale before incurring large costs and making any ethical or legal adjustments that they had to work on mildly. Furthermore, to be successful, innovation must be accomplished with industry partners as well as external regulators. Campus-based universities that engaged in policy debates and with regulators were in a better position to shape the types of regulations that would spur innovation. In the same manner, relations with tech companies provided academic institutions with cutting-edge technologies and know-how, but relations involved issues of IP and morality in the bargain. Kim and Park (2020) attributed these strategies to earlier publications in the literature on the importance of institutional structures and collaboration in managing the adoption of new technologies. However, by providing examples of how tactics could be applied by colleges, such as using a formed task team and developing pilot programs, this study contributes to the knowledge base.

ROPs' Social Contribution Consequences: lastly, this chapter examined how HEIs' capacity to maintain the balance of power between autonomy and regulation impacts their ability to contribute to social development. Schools that successfully found this balance were more effective in preparing their pupils for the newly emerging workforce of the 4IR. AI and VR technology integration into teaching-learning processes in the UK improved learners' involvement and enhanced learning outcomes; disciplines such as medical, business and engineering benefited the most from the integration and conflict between regulatory oversight and autonomy. The primary goal was to comprehend how organisations promote innovation within the parameters of their independence while abiding by legal frameworks that guarantee moral behavior, data protection and responsibility. Through the analysis of several case studies and interviews with important stakeholders, the chapter presents a thorough understanding of how HEIs strike a balance between innovation and compliance, ultimately offering insights into how they might support societal growth in the 4IR era.

Reiterating the research's main goals and significance: university administration, research, and instruction could undergo a significant transformation owing to the disruptive technologies brought about by the 4IR. However, there are also many issues with these technologies, especially in regard to data protection, ethics and legal compliance. Exploring the 4IR paradox – the conflict between the regulatory frameworks that protect ethical norms and provide accountability and the autonomy that universities require to innovate – was the main goal of this study. Since HEIs are increasingly being challenged to prepare students for a future driven by technology, they must comprehend this contradiction. More graduates with the skills required in the 4IR workforce and the ability to make significant contributions to society through research and public services are likely to come from universities that can successfully strike a balance between innovation and regulation.

Contribution of the study: in this study, several important findings concerning how HEIs manage the 4IR dilemma are provided as follows. First, it provides evidence for the hypothesis that posits that innovativeness demands levels of institutional independence that are nevertheless insufficient on their own, instead needing effective governance. The literature now in publication, which often focuses solely on the benefits of autonomy while neglecting the risks of fragmentation, is enriched by this finding. Moreover, the research reveals the legal challenges that higher education institutions face, namely, data protection and IP rights, and defines the recommendations for universities as to how these challenges may be mitigated via governance and collaboration. This addition is worthwhile because it specifies certain things that are sometimes left undefined in the literature, including, for instance, the complexity of university–industry relations. To realize its potential to play a key role in transforming society, the study, therefore, concludes by focusing on the need to achieve an appropriate balance between autonomy and control. More ready for the 4IR generation workforce preparedness and the use of research and inventions toward solving emergent social challenges are institutions that balance these two.

In summary, this chapter shows that for the effective implementation of 4IR technologies in higher learning, institutional autonomy and regulatory supervision cannot be overemphasized. To ensure that innovation thrives and that employees, contractors and clients are ethical and meet the law, universities must strike a delicate success between the two forces. HEIs can also realize 4IR technologies in the same manner as external actors can and achieve autonomous governance in conjunction with a structured system. It will also assist in the construction of society more generally and in the education of graduates in the future. Educational institutions that are also seeking to navigate the complex landscape of technological development and diffusion will find these insights invaluable as the 4IR progresses and continues to reshape education and society.

9.6. References

AlGerafi, M.A.M., Zhou, Y., Oubibi, M., Wijaya, T.T. (2023). Unlocking the potential: A comprehensive evaluation of augmented reality and virtual reality in education. *Electronics*, 12(18), 3953. doi: 10.3390/electronics12183953.

Altbach, P.G. and Hanstedt, P. (2018). *Global Perspectives on Higher Education: Issues and Trends*. Routledge, New York.

Baidya, R., Lal, R., Rena, R. (2024). Digital competency assessment and data-driven performance management for start ups. In *Data-Driven Modelling and Predictive Analytics in Business and Finance: Concepts, Designs, Technologies, and Applications*, Khang, A., Gujrati, R., Uygun, H., Tailor, R.K., Gaur, S. (eds). CRC Press, Boca Raton.

Bhardwaj, A. and Kumar, V. (2024). Challenges in online collaboration to augment Industry 4.0. *International Journal of Technology, Policy and Management*, 24(1), 71–92. doi: 10.1504/IJTPM.2024.135977.

Braun, V. and Clarke, V. (2006). Using thematic analysis in psychology. *Qualitative Research in Psychology*, 3(2), 77–101.

Chaka, C. (2022). Digital ethics in the 4IR: Implications for higher education. *Educational Research and Reviews*.

Creswell, J.W. and Poth, C.N. (2018). *Qualitative Inquiry and Research Design: Choosing among Five Approaches*. Sage, London.

Ernestivita, G., Kumar, V., Anisah, T.N. (2024). Role of gamification in crowdsourcing. In *Marketing and Gamification: Applications, Challenges, and Ethics*, Gupta, S., Nagina, R., Paruthi, M., Gupta, G. (eds). Routledge, New York.

Fernandez, M. and Wagner, D. (2022). Virtual reality in higher education: Ethics and accessibility. *International Journal of Education Technology*.

Gleason, N.W. (ed.) (2018). *Higher Education in the Era of the Fourth Industrial Revolution*. Palgrave Macmillan, Springer, Singapore.

Holmes, W., Porayska-Pomsta, K., Holstein, K., Sutherland, E., Baker, T., Shum, S.B., Santos, O.C., Rodrigo, M.T., Cukurova, M., Bittencourt, I.I. et al. (2022). Ethics of AI in education: Towards a community-wide framework. *International Journal of Artificial Intelligence in Education*, 32(3), 504–526.

Kaplan, M. and Haenle, R. (2021). Data privacy in higher education: Challenges and best practices. *Higher Education Policy*.

Kim, H. and Park, J. (2020). Regulatory challenges in higher education: Balancing innovation and oversight. *Journal of Education Policy*.

Kumar, V. and Bhardwaj, A. (2020). Role of cloud computing in school education. In *Handbook of Research on Diverse Teaching Strategies for the Technology-Rich Classroom*, Tomei, L.A. and Carbonara, D.D. (eds). IGI Global, Hershey, 98–108.

Kumar, V., and Lata, M. (eds) (2022). *The Future of E-Commerce*. Nova Science Publishers, New York. doi: 10.52305/KMUB3774.

Kumar, V. and Rewari, M. (eds) (2023). *Pandemics in the Age of Social Media: Information and Misinformation in Developing Nations*. Taylor & Francis, Boca Raton.

Lahoz-Bengoechea, M. and Bell, C. (2022). AI bias in higher education. *Journal of Technology and Society*.

Lata, M. and Kumar, V. (2021). Internet of Energy (IoE) applications for smart cities. In *Handbook of Internet of Energy for Smart Cities*, 1st edition, Jindal, A., Kumar, N., Aujla, G.S. (eds). CRC Press, Boca Raton.

Lata, M. and Kumar, V. (2023). Challenges to IoT security: Industry perspective. *Grenze International Journal of Engineering and Technology (GIJET)*, 9(1–2), 61–67.

Lata, M. and Kumar, V. (2024). A framework for security of public cloud environment. *International Journal of Electronic Security and Digital Forensics*, 16(4), 486–502.

Lata, M. and Sharma, V. (2024a). Cloud computing based blended learning: Quality assurance challenges. In *2024 International Conference on Communication, Computer Sciences and Engineering (IC3SE)*. IEEE, New York, 1731–1736.

Lata, M. and Sharma, V. (2024b). Smart city environment management: Challenges and opportunities. *Grenze International Journal of Engineering & Technology (GIJET)*, 10(2), 2159–2166.

Lata, M., Kumar, V., Sharma, V. (2024). Cloud computing applications in online learning. *Grenze International Journal of Engineering & Technology (GIJET)*, 10(2), 408–411.

Mittal, S. and Kumar, V. (2024). Analyzing the role of technological capabilities and digital marketing on the performance of E-commerce-based SMEs. *Indian Journal of Marketing*, 54(12), 45–60.

Nanda, P. and Kumar, V. (2024). New generation technologies: Development vs. ethical challenges. *International Journal of Business Information Systems*, 46(3), 411–434.

Rahman, Z.T. Lal, R., Rena, R. (2024). Challenges of communication with gen-Z in the era of AI-interceded digital economy: A critical study. In *Artificial Intelligence -Oriented Competency Framework for Talent Management in the Digital Economy: Models, Technologies, Applications, and Implementation,* Khang, A. (ed.). Routledge, London.

Rai, S. and Lata, M. (2024). Futuristic outlook of online learning: The post-pandemic era. In *Technology-mediated Learning During the Pandemic*, Singh, J. and Kumar, V. (eds). Routledge, New Delhi, 173–187.

Rena, R. (2024). Blockchain technology and its importance for the growth and prosperity of Indian small and medium-sized enterprises. *Indian Journal of Commerce and Management Studies*, 15(2), 01–09 [Online]. Available at: https://www.ijcms.in/index.php/ijcms/article/view/666/563.

Rogers, E.M. (2003). *Diffusion of Innovations*, 5th edition. Free Press, New York.

Saito, H. (2022). Higher education for pluriversal diplomacy: Landing the 4IR on habitable earth. In *Global Initiatives and Higher Education in the Fourth Industrial Revolution*, Oliver, E. (ed.). UJ Press, Johannesburg, 195–214.

Schwab, K. (2016). *The Fourth Industrial Revolution.* World Economic Forum, Geneva.

Scott, C. (2020). Managing and regulating commitments to equality, diversity, and inclusion in higher education. *Irish Educational Studies*, 39(2), 175–191.

Sharma, D. and Kumar, V. (2017). A framework for collaborative and convenient learning on cloud computing platforms. *International Journal of Web-Based Learning and Teaching Technologies (IJWLTT)*, 12(2), 1–20.

Sharma, K., Rahman, Z.T., Rena, R (2024), The ChatGPT: Its influence on the jobs market: An analytical study. In *Data-Driven Modelling and Predictive Analytics in Business and Finance: Concepts, Designs, Technologies, and Applications*, Khang, A., Gujrati, R., Uygun, H., Tailor, R.K., Gaur, S.S. (eds). Routledge/Taylor and Francis Group, London.

Singh, J., Kumar, V., Kumar, D. (2022). Combating the pandemic with ICT-based learning tools and applications: A case of Indian higher education platforms. *International Journal of Virtual and Personal Learning Environments (IJVPLE)*, 12(1), 1–21.

Yin, R.K. (2018). *Case Study Research and Applications: Design and Methods.* SAGE Publications, Thousand Oaks.

10

AI-Driven Chatbots: Enhancing Educational Experiences Through Data Analytics

With the ubiquity of chatbots across different industries, a large volume of data is generated from interactions with users. This chapter describes how to extract insights from the data so that action items can be derived to improve the user experience and operational efficiency. First, the variety of data that the chatbots collect are highlighted: conversation logs, sentiment metrics, user behavior patterns and feedback. This chapter explores some of the approaches of data analytics that are used to make sense of data. Basic statistical approaches are presented in concert with more sophisticated approaches, such as natural language processing (NLP) and machine learning algorithms. We describe how NLP can be utilized to determine user sentiment and intention and how machine learning can predict future user needs and improve chatbot responses given the history of interactions. Practical examples are given, which explain how these analytical methodologies can be applied in reality. We look at how insights gained from chatbot data could help drive strategic decision-making, optimize performance in chatbots, and drive user engagement. In addition, the chapter addresses some challenges in terms of data privacy, which are related to the integration of chatbot data with already available data in systems. We review some of the best practices that will help ensure seamless integration of chatbot analytics within larger business analytics frameworks. This chapter aims to equip a reader with tools and knowledge that will help transform these data into valuable insights, providing a step-by-step guide on how to analyze chatbot interaction data. These kinds of insights not only drive better decision-making but also result in greater user satisfaction and smoother operations for the business.

Chapter written by Jyoti ARORA, Charnpreet KAUR, Puneet KAUR, Anupam MITTAL and Manju LATA.

10.1. Introduction

In the early 1960s, the utilization of chatbots began with question-answering tasks. However, in recent years, this approach has become more popular because of the massive use of mobile and chat apps and some conversational interfaces. Chatbots are much more involved in various ways, such as interactions with students and personal assistance. ELIZA is the well-known name of the first chatbot developed by Prof. Joseph Weizenbaum of MIT (Massachusetts Institute of Technology) in the 1960s. In the 20th century, China introduced the chatbot "WeChat", which is considered the advance chatbot (Shrager 2024).

The rapid proliferation of chatbots across diverse industries has changed the way companies communicate with their customers (Nanda and Kumar 2024). These AI-driven tools have become indispensable from dealing with real-time assistance and handling customer queries to improving overall user engagement (Ajiga et al. 2024). As companies continue to deploy chatbots in their operations, large volumes of data emanate from those conversations – a treasure trove that offers substantive improvements in user experience and operational efficiency when analyzed effectively. The data type holds the key to unlocking the potential of chatbot interaction data. Indeed, conversation logs, sentiment metrics, user behavioral patterns and feedback are just a few data points amassed through chatbots. Each of these types of data serves a different purpose in providing insight into user needs, preferences and pain points (Mittal and Kumar 2024). Classifying and analyzing these types of data will be crucially important in mining actionable insights to be used in strategic decision-making for the improvement of chatbot performance. The simplest form of data derived from a chatbot would manifest in the form of conversation logs.

These keep a tab on the user's interaction with the chatbot, whether it is just the flow, questions put up by the user, or responses generated from the chatbot itself. On the basis of these logs, one could easily compile lists of common questions asked, frequent issues and also if the responses worked out by the chatbot are correct or not (Lata and Kumar 2022). These logs are the foundation for improving chatbot algorithms to improve the user experience (Dobbala et al. 2024). However, in addition to conversation logs, sentiment metrics are important for understanding the emotional tone of conversations that users have. Sentiment analysis, which uses NLP techniques, can judge whether a user is expressing a positive, negative or neutral feeling. These data are key to understanding how a user rates the chatbot and where improvements should be made to provide a positive experience. User behavior patterns paint much more detailed pictures of how users can interact with chatbots. When businesses track metrics such as interaction length, the number of user inputs and what paths users take through a conversation, they can find trends and behaviors in those metrics that might suggest user intent (Chakrabarti and Luger 2015). For example, repeated interactions on the same topic may signal that an issue remains unresolved, whereas a high drop-off rate could mean that there is either an issue with the interface or the logic of the chatbot. User feedback is solicited and unsolicited direct feedback on the performance of a chatbot.

10.2. Literature review

Shrager (2024) noted that the first chatbot was more than just the achievement of technology but represented the basis for much deeper conceptions. In its originally envisaged form, it was intended to be extremely simple, just a conversation simulator to test the human response to machines. Reflective consideration of ELIZA, then, reveals how contemporary chatbots begin with something that looks like very simple rule-based systems and builds complex AI models (Lata and Kumar 2021). Ajiga et al. (2024) discuss AI-driven predictive analytics in retail, especially emerging trends that exploit AI chatbots for customer engagement. They provide feedback on how AI tools, with features of chatbots, have become an imperative driver to push customer experience through personalization and data-driven insights, enabling businesses to foresee consumer behavior and hence sell better. Dobbala and Lingolu (2024) provide an outline of how conversational AI and chatbots can be utilized to increase a user's interaction on websites. A core feature suggested by the research is real-time response, collaboration with other digital platforms, and how conversations with chatbots can be analyzed to uncover actionable insights. Chakrabarti and Luger (2015) explore the architecture, algorithms and evaluation metrics used in customer service chatterbots. Their work remains a critical reference point in understanding the technicalities that underpin modern AI-driven chatbots. Hsu and Lin (2023) discuss the revolutionary impact that conversational AI has on the user experience.

This chapter discusses both the technological innovations and practical applications of bots in various industries, from customer service to healthcare, and highlights how AI models are replacing traditional interaction models (Lata and Sharma 2024a). The authors introduce the creation of a conversational data analyst chatbot with some of the newest AI technologies, such as Lang Chain and OpenAI. The chapter elucidates how businesses utilize chatbots as media for delivering insight through natural language queries, thereby making it easy to interact with data (Rittman 2023). In fact, Gartner's magic quadrant report provides a more profound analysis of leading conversational AI platforms (Lata and Kumar 2022). Their report is very rich and detailed, which explains the enterprise-level chatbot technology landscape and the performance metrics of leaders in the industry (Gartner 2022). Anupriya and

Gupta (2022) emphasize how data-driven AI chatbots are changing the face of e-commerce experience, but discuss the dual role of the chatbot – a customer assistant as well as a generator of actionable data for businesses – work concentrating mostly on the critical importance of data as part of a chain in the chatbot interaction. Wen et al. (2023) introduced contextual analytics for chatbot conversations, particularly toward enriching the NLP models for extracting useful insight from user interactions. The text discusses the requirements and challenges involved in the extraction of better contextual understanding by enhanced chatbots. Ahmad and Khan (2023) discuss how AI can be applied to enable customer service. Their research explores ways that AI can deploy these algorithms to streamline the process of customer support while improving its efficiency and satisfaction via real-time data (Kumar and Lata 2022). Silva and Canedo (2022) view user-centric chatbots on the basis of continuous feedback loops that improve interactions over time. They are dependent on insights derived from data related to the feedback of the user to improve the performance and relevance of the chatbots iteratively.

Khalid et al. (2023) discuss the use of AI-based chatbots for real-time data analytics and decision-making support in healthcare applications. The chapter discusses the integration of chatbots in healthcare systems where patient data are monitored to assist medical professionals in making decisions. Xu et al. (2023) focus on how NLP-based chatbot data analysis has improved customer satisfaction. This chapter discusses the integration of advanced language models for more natural interactions with chatbots to extract insights from conversation data. Wu and Chen (2022) use multimodal data for chatbot personalization in an e-learning scenario. Research has shown that by integrating different data sources, personalized learning can be made possible using chatbots (Singh et al. 2022). Dey and Bhaumik (2022) discuss the greater user experience in the retail sector through AI-enabled chatbots. This chapter pinpoints the role of data analytics in driving efficiency within chatbots, mainly the improvement of customer service as well as the operational process. Liu et al. (2025) focus on smart chatbots in their proposed framework that combines analytics and human interaction data. In general, researchers have approached the gap between automated services and personalized customer experience by analyzing the interaction data of chatbots. Kelly et al. (2022) highlighted how AI-powered chatbots are revolutionizing user behavior and personalization across various sectors (Ernestivita et al. 2024). According to the paper, machine learning models dramatically affect how chatbot conversations take place with preferences that correspond to those of individual users. Tang and Zhao (2023) noted that real-time analytics could be applied in conversational AI to better enhance customer engagement through machine learning techniques. This research is important for understanding how chatbots can respond more quickly by adapting to information in real time.

Author(s) and year	Key findings
Shrager (2024)	Revisits the development of ELIZA and its unintended role as the first chatbot. Highlights the evolution of chatbot technology from rule-based systems to AI-driven models.
Ajiga et al. (2024)	Explores how AI chatbots improve customer engagement and drive sales through data-driven personalization in retail.
Dobbala and Lingolu (2024)	Discusses how chatbots enhance user experience with real-time responses and data integration, offering personalized interactions.
Chakrabarti and Luger (2015)	A foundational study on chatbot architecture and algorithms, providing insights into metrics used to evaluate chatbot performance.
Hsu and Lin (2023)	Highlights how AI bots are transforming customer interactions in various industries, improving personalization and satisfaction.
Rittman (2023)	Introduces the design of a chatbot for data analysis using NLP technologies, allowing natural language queries for data insights.
Gartner (2022)	Provides an industry-wide evaluation of top conversational AI platforms, focusing on scalability, features and enterprise applicability.
Anupriya and Gupta (2022)	Explores the role of data analytics in improving the performance of chatbots and enhancing user experience in the e-commerce domain.
Wen et al. (2023)	Focuses on enhancing chatbot contextual understanding through NLP, improving response relevance in user interactions.
Ahmad and Khan (2023)	Examines AI chatbots in customer support, highlighting their role in improving service efficiency and response time.
Silva and Canedo (2022)	Investigates how feedback loops and user data insights are used to continuously improve chatbot performance.
Khalid et al. (2023); Lata et al. (2024)	Discusses the application of AI chatbots in healthcare, particularly for real-time patient data analytics and decision-making support.
Xu et al. (2023)	Reviews how NLP models can be utilized to analyze chatbot conversations and improve customer satisfaction through personalized responses.
Wu and Chen (2022); Lata and Sharma (2024b)	Analyzes how combining various data types (e.g. text and video) in chatbots can enhance personalized learning experiences in e-learning environments.
Dey and Bhaumik (2022)	Examines how data analytics enhance the retail experience by making chatbots more interactive and customer focused.
Liu et al., (2025); Lata and Kumar (2024)	Proposes a framework for integrating analytics and user data to improve chatbot intelligence and personalized responses.
Kelly et al. (2022)	Explores how AI chatbots can use data analytics to personalize customer experiences by predicting user behavior.
Tang and Zhao (2023)	Discusses the role of real-time analytics and machine learning in improving chatbot engagement by providing more accurate and relevant responses.

Table 10.1. *Literature review summary*

10.3. Understanding chatbot interactions: data collection

The interactions with a chatbot are dramatically improved due to advancements in artificial intelligence, NLP and machine learning to improve their application. Early systems such as ELIZA were rule-based, which confined them to very limited ways of response capability and were essentially created more for the appearance of humanity rather than having a real understanding. These systems lay the springboard for modern chatbots, with advanced NLP algorithms that can recognize the context, tone and intent of any message in real time. Most complex tasks, whether as a customer care assistant or medical triage, can be performed with the help of chatbots, which also increase engagement by making responses immediate and personal. Such AI technologies have allowed the shift from providing predefined answers to more sophisticated conversations, which are typically more natural and dynamic. A better understanding of the interaction between the user and the chatbot will improve the user experience and optimize the design of a chatbot. Chatbots, therefore, tap into sources of data such as past interactions, behavioral analytics and customer profiles to yield proper answers and suggestions. They use feedback loops from which they continually fine-tune their responses to make the systems more adaptive over time (Lata and Kumar 2021). This ability to learn from previous conversations and feedback from users, along with the ability to process multimodal inputs of text, voice, images, etc., has opened the possibility for chatbots beyond text-based communication to virtual assistant applications and e-commerce and healthcare, which have also utilized conversational agents. In such settings, chatbots attend to the queries of the users but can also actively interact with the customers to enhance customer satisfaction and operational efficiency. However, with conversational analytics, performance improvement becomes another critical factor in chatbots. Such systems can identify common pain points on the basis of interaction data, such as by optimizing response times and becoming ready to anticipate user needs (Lata and Kumar 2022). This has resulted in smart chatbots equipped with predictive insights that solve customer problems even before a customer articulates their problems. For example, for customer service, analytics-driven chatbots could theoretically sense frustration in user inputs and transfer the conversation directly to human agents with zero interruption when needed. This enables the increasing ability to combine machine learning with real-time data analytics, which is changing chatbot interaction from a simple query-handling tool to more dynamic platforms that not only provide personalized experiences but also predict outcomes on the basis of the behavior of users, making them a critical component of digital transformation in industry.

Gathering data from a chatbot interaction is an important process through which organizations enhance the user experience, improve performance and obtain actionable insights from the conversation. With the increasing use of chatbots in customer service, e-commerce and other applications, the need to understand how to obtain better gathering and analyzing interaction data has increased. Such sources of these data include user inputs, bot responses, contextual information and even non-verbal cues such as sentiment or emotional tone. This information, when captured, can help determine trends, user preference behavior, and pain points, which may eventually contribute to better service delivery and resultant customer satisfaction. Methods for collecting data from chatbots differ in the platform and technology used. Usually, data collection is facilitated by logging mechanisms inherent to the chatbot software. Every interaction is recorded through logs, providing a comprehensive record of conversations. Chatbots can also take metadata – who the user is, what time it was, the length of their session, and what kind of device they are on – on top of direct text inputs. This provides additional texture to the dataset, allowing for a much more nuanced analysis of the way that different variables can affect user interaction. Further advanced systems can even integrate with external APIs to further enrich what one is able to do with the collection of data, resulting in a greater well-rounded understanding of user behavior across different channels (Rai and Lata 2024). Through the collection of data on interactions with a chatbot, analysis may be performed, ranging from simple statistical analysis to advanced algorithms involving machine learning. NLP enables the extraction of insights from textual data. Using the users' language, organizations can identify common questions and topics of interest and even determine the emotional state of users during interactions. Recurrent problems or areas of concern can also be highlighted through the analysis of NLP to improve chatbot responses and, generally, service strategies. Sentiment analysis may, in addition, be used to evaluate user satisfaction levels. By using data-driven changes, businesses can improve their experience.

Data collection for a business through interactive chatbots is always challenging in regard to basic issues: protecting the privacy and safety of users. Because organizations gather sensitive information from conversations, they must also comply with regulations on data protection, such as the GDPR (General Data Protection Regulation) or CCPA (California Community Privacy Act). The ability to have strong frameworks for data governance related to user consent, storage and access to or deletion of personal data serves as a critical requirement. Transparency in how the data are used is very important not only in building user trust but also in meeting legal requirements. As organizations collect critical information about people's actions, data privacy issues continue to be prominent in preventing ethics in such data gathering practices.

Collecting data from text-based conversations with chatbots

In terms of the performance of the chatbot and business-level strategies in general, data collection through interaction with a chatbot determines not only the performance of the chatbot but also business-level strategies. Information from interaction data modifies the way products are developed, with approaches undertaken in terms of marketing and customer relationships. This may be the number of inquiries a customer makes, to which an organization can position its product or develop targeted marketing strategies. Indeed, the feedback from the user following their interaction with a chatbot would remain an excellent source of feedback for business organizations to continuously iterate about their services. In such a context, the information gathered through chatbot interaction might become strategic assets and facilitate organizations' shift toward more committed customers and efficient practices.

Data collection method	Description	Data type	Sources	Purpose
User interactions	Capturing text, voice or click-based inputs from users during conversations with the chatbot.	Text data, voice, recordings	Chat logs, voice interaction logs	Analyze user behavior and preferences, enhance response accuracy based on actual queries.
User feedback	Collecting user ratings and comments regarding their experiences with the chatbot.	Structured feedback Unstructured feedback	Post-interaction surveys, ratings and reviews	Identify areas for improvement. Measure user satisfaction and engagement levels.
Analytics data	Tracking various metrics such as session duration, drop-off rates and interaction frequency.	Quantitative data	Analytics tools Dashboard reports	Assess chatbot, performance. Optimize engagement strategies based on user interaction patterns.
Demographic information	Gathering information about users such as age, gender, location and device type for analysis.	Structured data	User profiles Registration forms	Understand user demographics, tailor interactions based on user segments.
Integration with CRM systems	Linking chatbot data with customer relationship management systems to gather holistic user data.	Mixed data types (text, metrics)	CRM databases Third-party integrations	Enhance customer support. Provide personalized experiences based on comprehensive user data.

Table 10.2. *Data collection methods from chatbot interactions, including key aspects such as data type, sources and purposes*

10.4. Gaining insights from chatbot data

The collected data can be analyzed using analytics techniques by systematically reviewing them for patterns and trends. They can, for example, know which topics are being discussed most frequently, how long, on average, the interaction lasts and what kind of intent users use the most. This type of insight can help companies better understand what their customers need so that they can design and tailor their chatbots to such needs.

Insight area	Description	Key metrics	Actionable insights
Identifying trends and patterns	Analyzing chatbot interactions to uncover common user inquiries and behaviors over time.	– Frequency of queries – Peak usage times Common issues reported	– Improve knowledge base for frequently asked questions. – Optimize chatbot availability during peak hours.
User segmentation	Classifying users based on demographics, behavior and preferences to tailor interactions and services.	– User demographics – Interaction frequency – Conversion rates	– Personalize responses based on user profiles. – Target specific user groups with tailored marketing strategies.
Feedback analysis	Evaluating user feedback and ratings to enhance chatbot performance and user satisfaction.	– User satisfaction scores – Feedback comments – Response accuracy rates	– Identify areas for improvement based on negative feedback. – Implement changes to enhance user experience.
Engagement levels	Measuring how users interact with the chatbot, including conversation length and follow-up questions.	– Average session duration – Number of interactions per session – Drop-off rates	– Increase engagement by offering more interactive features. – Revise scripts to keep conversations flowing.
Predictive analytics	Utilizing historical data to forecast future interactions and user needs, enhancing proactive support.	– Predictive models – Anticipated user needs – Trends in user behavior	– Adjust resource, allocation based on predicted demand. – Prepare responses for anticipated queries to improve efficiency.

Table 10.3. *The insights gained from chatbot data focus on key aspects such as trends, user segmentation, and feedback analysis*

This would further be possible through the use of a machine learning algorithm, which makes it possible to conduct a more elaborate analysis of the interactions of a chatbot so that an organization can predict user behavior and, in turn, optimize the responses. By analyzing historical data, enterprises can develop models that predict which inquiries from users could be raised on the basis of previously encountered interactions. The ability of prediction will not only improve the satisfaction of the users by providing relevant and timely responses but also reduce the workload of a human agent. In this context, organizations can efficiently use their resources in more complex queries, making overall customer support operations more efficient.

Finally, understanding insights into chatbot data contributes to the continuity of improvement cycles. Organizations may offer feedback loops in which insights derived from data analysis inform iterative changes to the design and content of a chatbot. This enables companies to be agile and react to the real-time needs of users, as well as being reflected through their offerings. To illustrate where data analysis would indicate a sudden spurt in inquiries involving a particular feature of a product, an organization can immediately update its knowledge base in the chatbot to include more detailed information about that feature. This responsiveness not only creates a fantastic user experience but also fosters loyalty to, as well as trust in, the brand.

10.5. Identifying trends, patterns and user segmentation

Identification of trends and patterns in the interactions that occur with a chatbot equips an organization with actionable insights into how strategic decisions are immediately affected. The systematic analysis of conversation logs enables businesses to identify patterns of recurrence, common questions asked by users and what pain points happen most often. For example, if more users are complaining about the payment process, then this insight could be used to revisit the checkout experience to make it friendly to the end-users. A form of volume over time is a sense of seasonality that may be helpful for organizations when they notice peak periods and may orient their marketing campaigns toward that. Additionally, using tools for sentiment analysis on interactions with user emotions can analyze the sentiment of user emotions. The conversation can be analyzed as positive, negative or neutral to identify the topics that require improvement. For example, when there is a surge in conversations regarding negative sentiment about a certain feature or service, businesses can easily identify and address those problems. Organizations could take proactive measures to prevent customer complaints from becoming worse and improve the customer experience and retention. Data trend visualizations through dashboards and reports can be used to help stakeholders better understand the performance of chatbots. Such data visualization allows decision-makers to analyze complex information at one glance and respond appropriately to emerging problems or opportunities quickly. Regular reports on trend analysis provided to stakeholders cultivate a culture of data-driven decisions within the organization. When such insights are integrated into strategic planning, companies can ensure that their chatbots remain relevant, effective and much more aligned with changing customer expectations.

The segmentation of users during engagement with chatbots provides an easy method for extracting useful meaning and optimizing engagement. User grouping can be arranged along different criteria, such as demographics, behavior, or purchase history, to help organizations create experiences that are personalized enough to resonate better with each group. For example, a retail chatbot can separate new customers seeking information about the product from regular customers wanting recommendations. This focused approach increases the satisfaction levels of the users because customers feel that they have been understood and valued. Another important aspect is that user segmentation aids in establishing the various needs and preferences of different groups. Interaction data analytics further enable organizations to establish patterns that represent specific issues or interests for various user segments. For example, youths tend to focus on the speed and efficiency attached to responses, especially in returns, but more mature customers may be more interested in elaborative answers. The small variations become known to organizations, and, they thus tailor their interactions so that the chatbot represents the appropriate discussion for a particular segment. The marketing and sales strategies also need to be improved with segmentation. For example, when user groups have some specific buying behaviors or interests, marketing campaigns can be tailored directly to those segments. Thus, if a company finds that a particular group of users often inquiries about eco-friendly products, it can customize promotions or content around that to promote its sustainable offerings. This niche approach not only increases the chances of conversion but also cements brand loyalty because of a visible dedication to fulfilling user needs.

10.6. Challenges and best practices

The greatest challenge that organizations face while rolling out and sustaining the use of chatbots is obtaining the NLP algorithms to interpret user queries and return relevant answers. However, in simple terms, because the ability of NLP is limited, it can lead to misunderstandings or misinterpretations and user frustrations. For example, slang, idioms, and unclear phrases can pose challenges for the chatbot, hence resulting in incorrect or unrelated information. This may lower the users' satisfaction levels and reduce trust in the effectiveness of the chatbot, thus contributing to a general effect on the overall customer experience. Another challenge is the control of the great array of user queries with the need for continuous learning. This means that the users may ask a number of questions ranging from fairly ordinary to just one-of-a-kind, unique questions depending upon individual situations. A good chatbot therefore needs to adapt itself well to common inquiries as well as rare ones. This requires consistent updating of its knowledge base and machine learning techniques that enable it to learn from the interactions that take place with users. Failure to update the chatbot regularly will result in stale responses, which decreases the practicality of the bot with time and forces users to find more convenient ways to answer their questions elsewhere. Security and privacy issues are also considerable problems related to interactions where chatbots exist. As chatbots strive to collect and process personal data while trying to deliver personalized experiences, there is a great need for organizations to ensure that they observe data protection policies, such as the GDPR or HIPAA. This risks sensitive information being compromised by data breaches or weak security measures. Organizations need to invest in strong security policies, ensure that the chatbots developed are secure and do not compromise user data. The lack of this could result in legal issues, reputation loss and a loss of trust by users.

Challenge	Description	Best practice	Implementation
Data privacy concerns	Users may be hesitant to share personal information with chatbots, fearing misuse of their data.	Implement robust privacy policies	Develop clear privacy policies that outline data usage and ensure compliance with regulations such as GDPR. Clearly communicate these policies to users.
Integration with existing systems	Chatbots need to be integrated with various backend systems (CRM, databases), which can be technically challenging and time consuming.	Plan for seamless integration	Conduct a thorough analysis of existing systems before implementation and utilize APIs or middleware solutions to facilitate integration.
Handling complex queries	Chatbots may struggle to address complex or nuanced user queries, leading to frustration.	Implement hybrid models	Combine rule-based and AI-driven approaches to ensure that chatbots can handle a wider range of queries effectively.
User experience and engagement	Poorly designed chatbots can lead to a subpar user experience, resulting in disengagement.	Focus on user-centered design	Regularly conduct user testing and gather feedback to refine chatbot interactions, ensuring a smooth and engaging user experience.
Continuous learning and improvement	Chatbots may not evolve with changing user needs and preferences, leading to outdated responses and functionalities.	Establish feedback loops	Implement systems for ongoing data collection and analysis to inform updates. Use analytics to identify areas for improvement and iterate on the chatbot's capabilities regularly.

Table 10.4. *The challenges and best practices related to chatbot analytics*

These best practices would therefore ensure the successful negotiation of challenges that come with the interactions experienced during chats. First, organizations need to invest in the advanced capabilities of NLP, thus enhancing the ability of chatbots to understand and interpret user queries effectively. The application of machine learning algorithms would lead to a much better understanding of contextual information and user intent, which would lead to a more relevant and accurate response. Moreover, the inclusion of user feedback mechanisms will reveal every possible enhancement and create an opportunity for organisations to continuously enhance their chatbot capabilities. Another significant mechanism is the regular updating of the knowledge base about the chatbot. Organizations, therefore, need to arrange routine reviews and refresh the content and responses provided by the chatbot, taking into consideration that all of these processes incorporate new information, product upgrades, and emerging trends. Similarly, historical interaction data can be utilized for training chatbots such that past mistakes are learned from and performance improves progressively over time. This may be rendered possible via a culture of continuous improvement so that the chatbots implemented by the business do not become outdated but remain appropriate as needs evolve. The second-best practice includes a hybrid approach in which the functionality of the chatbot includes the element of human oversight. While this makes the chatbot very efficient at processing routine questions, complex scenarios would always emerge that required human intervention. The process is set up to ensure smooth handoffs from the chatbot to human agents when needed. This enhances the experience of the user in that complex issues are addressed as soon as possible but allows the chatbot, through interaction, to learn how to refine its responses in subsequent interactions. The final requirement for organizations will be educating the users about its capability and limitation. In some manner, they can provide clear guidance to them on how to interact with the chatbot. Realistic expectations are also achievable for these organizations, for instance, an introduction from the organization at the beginning of a chatbot interaction stating purpose and scope. This kind of proactive approach may enable users to know what to expect and, therefore, create a more positive and productive interaction with increased trust toward the chatbot.

10.7. Future trends and conclusions in chatbot analytics

The analytics landscape for chatbots is rapidly changing in the wake of breakthroughs in AI, machine learning and NLP. Among the several trends that will characterize the future landscape of chatbot analytics is the integration of more sophisticated algorithms with AI, which are intended to increase the ability of the chatbot to understand and process complex user interactions in a way that will deliver more relevant and context-aware responses. The more advanced that AI models become, the better at analyzing users' sentiment and emotions chatbots will be, which means that there will be a deeper understanding of user intent and satisfaction. This can further lead to profound interactions and improved customer engagement, which may provide a gateway to more intelligent and responsive chatbot systems.

The second trend is multimodal interaction usage, which is experiencing increasing adoption within chatbots. Although traditional chatbots rely on strictly text-based user interactions, they can combine text, voice images and even videos for future chatbots to offer richer user experiences. This means that users interact with new generations of chatbots in more natural ways, using their preferred mode of communication. Furthermore, multimodal capabilities enable analytics for chatbots to be developed in a manner in which they can track and process interaction data in various formats.

Trend	Description	Impact
Increased personalization	Enhanced algorithms will enable chatbots to offer more personalized experiences by analyzing user data and preferences.	Users will experience more relevant interactions, relevant interactions leading to higher satisfaction and engagement rates.
Integration of multimodal interfaces	Future chatbots will support multiple communication modes, such as voice, text and visual elements, creating richer interactions.	This will cater to diverse user preferences, making chatbots more accessible and effective across different platforms.
AI-driven predictive analytics	Leveraging machine learning, chatbots will anticipate user needs and provide proactive assistance based on behavioral patterns.	This predictive capability will enhance user experience by addressing queries before they arise, reducing friction in user interactions.
Real-time sentiment analysis	Advanced natural language processing techniques will allow chatbots to gauge user sentiment during interactions.	Understanding user emotions will enable more empathetic responses improving customer satisfaction and loyalty.
Enhanced data privacy and security measures	As data privacy concerns grow, chatbots will adopt stricter protocols to protect user information while complying with regulations.	This focus on security will build trust with users, fostering long-term relationships and encouraging more extensive data sharing.

Table 10.5. *Summarizing future trends in chatbot analytics*

In this general approach, this makes it easier to understand the user's preferences and behaviors better, as organizations are better placed to optimize strategies for their respective chatbots. Conversational analytics is an emergent trend in chatbot analytics. The approach is based on the analysis of the information created during conversations, deriving actionable insights from it and identifying trends. Advanced analytics can reveal patterns in queries, preferences and pain points; organizations can further refine their chatbot offerings. Even real-time monitoring can be enabled through conversational analytics where immediate amendments and improvements are made on the basis of user feedback. As this trend continues to grow, businesses increasingly depend on data-driven insights to improve their chatbot strategies and thus deliver more satisfying customer experiences. One of the most likely future trends in chatbot analytics is compliance with regulations such as the GDPR and CCPA. This number is likely to increase, considering the increasing demand for data privacy and security. Organizations must learn how to use robust data governance practices to handle user data ethically and securely. Data anonymization techniques, user consent for data collection and revealing transparency in data use will all be included. With a focus on information security and privacy for data, businesses will be able to gain the trust of users to open themselves up in chatting with chatbots and provide valuable information that will be helpful in making the analytics process better. The last trend in representing the future of chatbot analytics is the realization of the concept of self-learning chatbots. As technology advances in machine learning, it will eventually pave the way to the possibility that chatbots will be able to learn through interactions and improve their response and capability on a day-to-day basis without the need for interventions from human beings. This method of self-learning enables chatbots to learn and adjust according to user requirements and preferences that keep changing over time; this makes them more adaptable, thereby becoming increasingly effective in their performance. Organizations experience lower maintenance costs coupled with improved performance in chats, which ultimately impacts customer satisfaction and loyalty levels. As chatbot analytics move in this direction, from manual updates and monitoring to automated systems, intelligent systems that can actively optimize user interactions dynamically will revolutionize the whole landscape.

In summary, the development of analytics for chatbots is the actual revolution in how organizations talk to their users. Improving in areas such as artificial intelligence, machine learning and NLP sets the impetus for this movement. Therefore, with better chatbots, we will see much more intelligent personalization and increased user satisfaction with how they interact with them. The channels of multimedia communication will be better leveraged to create organic engagement between the users and the bot. Analyzing user conversations through conversational analytics will build upon them over time, thereby allowing organizations to continue improving on the functionalities of the chatbot. Data security and confidentiality will also inform the practice of analytics in the future, as organizations strive to handle the data of their users ethically and win them to adopt more interactive and conversational interfaces with chatbots. Therefore, this will revolutionize the last mile of change by supporting autonomous learning and adaptation, which increases the amount of decreased required oversight of humans and ensures that chatbots do not become obsolete in fulfilling the needs of the users. These trends illustrate how a data-driven approach is crucial for leveraging the best chatbot strategy for increasing customer interactions, making operations more efficient and driving business success at the hub of digital technologies.

10.8. References

Ahmad, T. and Khan, F. (2023). *Utilizing AI for Enhanced Customer Support through Chatbots*. IEEE, New York.

Ajiga, D.I., Ndubuisi, N.L., Asuzu, O.F., Owolabi, O.R., Tubokirifuruar, T.S., Adeleye, R.A. (2024). AI-driven predictive analytics in retail: A review of emerging trends and customer engagement strategies. *International Journal of Management & Entrepreneurship Research*, 6(2), 307–321.

Anupriya, K. and Gupta, R. (2022). Leveraging data-driven AI chatbots for user experience in e-commerce. *IJSAT-International Journal on Science and Technology*, 16(2).

Chakrabarti, C. and Luger, G.F. (2015). Artificial conversations for customer service chatter bots: Architecture, algorithms, and evaluation metrics. *Expert Systems with Applications*, 42(20), 6878–6897.

Dey, D. and Bhaumik, D. (2022). Inter-relational model for understanding chatbot acceptance across retail sectors. arXiv. doi: 10.48550/ arXiv.2207.01596.

Dobbala, M.K. and Lingolu, M.S.S. (2024). Conversational AI and chatbots: Enhancing user experience on websites. *American Journal of Computer Science and Technology*, 13(3), 62–70.

Ernestivita, G., Kumar, V., Anisah, T.N. (2024). Role of gamification in crowdsourcing. In *Marketing and Gamification: Applications, Challenges, and Ethics*, Gupta, S., Nagina, R., Paruthi, M., Gupta, G. (eds). Routledge, New York.

Gartner (2022). Magic quadrant for enterprise conversational AI platforms 2022. *CX Today* [Online]. Available at: https://www.cxtoday.com/customer-data-platform/gartner-magic-quadrant-for-enterprise-conversational-ai-platforms-2022/.

Hsu, C.L. and Lin, J.C.C. (2023). Understanding the user satisfaction and loyalty of customer service chatbots. *Journal of Retailing and Consumer Services*, 71, 103211. doi: 10.1016/j.jretconser.2022.103211.

Kelly, S., Kaye, S.A., Oviedo-Trespalacios, O. (2022). A multi-industry analysis of the future use of AI Chatbots. *Human Behavior and Emerging Technologies*, 2022(1), 2552099. doi: 10.1155/2022/2552099.

Khalid, N., Qayyum, A., Bilal, M., Al-Fuqaha, A., Qadir, J. (2023). Privacy-preserving artificial intelligence in healthcare: Techniques and applications. *Computers in Biology and Medicine*, 158, 106848. doi: 10.1016/j.compbiomed.2023.106848.

Kumar, V. and Lata, M. (eds). (2022). *The Future of E-Commerce*. Nova Science Publishers, New York. doi: 10.52305/KMUB3774.

Lata, M. and Kumar, V. (2021). Smart energy management in green cities. In *Handbook of Green Engineering Technologies for Sustainable Smart Cities*, Saravanan, K. and Sakthinathan, G. (eds). CRC Press, Boca Raton, FL.

Lata, M. and Kumar, V. (2022). Fog computing infrastructure for smart city applications. In *Recent Advancements in ICT Infrastructure and Applications*, Chaturvedi, M., Patel, P., Yadav, R. (eds). Springer, Singapore.

Lata, M. and Kumar, V. (2024). A framework for security of public cloud environment. *International Journal of Electronic Security and Digital Forensics*, 16(4), 486–502.

Lata, M. and Sharma, V. (2024a). Cloud computing based blended learning: Quality assurance challenges. In *2024 International Conference on Communication, Computer Sciences and Engineering (IC3SE)*. IEEE, New York.

Lata, M. and Sharma, V. (2024b). Smart city environment management: Challenges and opportunities. *Grenze International Journal of Engineering & Technology (GIJET)*, 10(2), 2159–2166.

Lata, M., Kumar, V., Sharma, V. (2024). Cloud computing applications in online learning. *Grenze International Journal of Engineering & Technology (GIJET)*, 10(2), 408–411.

Liu, J., Wang, X., Zhang, J. (2025). Investigating elderly individuals' acceptance of Artificial Intelligence (AI)-powered companion robots: The influence of individual characteristics. *Behavioral Sciences*, 15(5), 697.

Mittal, S. and Kumar, V. (2024). Analyzing the role of technological capabilities and digital marketing on the performance of E-commerce-based SMEs. *Indian Journal of Marketing*, 54(12), 45–60.

Nanda, P. and Kumar, V. (2024). New generation technologies: development vs. ethical challenges. *International Journal of Business Information Systems*, 46(3), 411–434.

Rai, S. and Lata, M. (2024). Futuristic outlook of online learning: The post-pandemic era. In *Technology-mediated Learning During the Pandemic*, Singh, J. and Kumar, V. (eds). Routledge, Singapore.

Rittman, M. (2023). *Creating a Conversational Data Analyst Chatbot Using LangChain, OpenAI, Google BigQuery and Google Cloud Functions*. Routledge, Delhi.

Shrager, J. (2024). ELIZA reinterpreted: The world's first chatbot was not intended as a chatbot at all. *arXiv*. doi: 10.48550/arXiv.2406.17650.

Silva, G.R.S. and Canedo, E.D. (2022). Towards user-centric guidelines for chatbot conversational design. *International Journal of Human–Computer Interaction*, 40(2), 98–120. doi: 10.1080/10447318.2022.2118244.

Singh, J., Kumar, V., Kumar, D. (2022). Combating the pandemic with ICT-based learning tools and applications: A case of Indian higher education platforms. *International Journal of Virtual and Personal Learning Environments (IJVPLE)*, 12(1), 1–21.

Tang, H. and Zhao, Y. (2023). *Real-Time Analytics in Conversational AI: Enhancing Customer Engagement with Machine Learning*. Springer, Singapore.

Wen, J., Liu, H., Wang, Y. (2023). *Contextual Analytics for Chatbot Conversations: Enhancing Insights from NLP Models*. Elsevier.

Wu, L. and Chen, Z. (2022). *Exploring Multimodal Data for Chatbot Personalization in E- Learning*. Elsevier.

Xu, Y., Zhang, J., Chi, R., Deng, G. (2023). Enhancing customer satisfaction with chatbots: The influence of anthropomorphic communication styles and anthropomorphised roles. *Nankai Business Review International*, 14(2), 249–271. doi: 10.1108/NBRI-06-2021-0041.

11

A Chatbot-integrated Deep Learning Approach for Rice Leaf Disease Detection in the Mekong Delta Region of Vietnam

Rice is one of the most important fields for food security in the Mekong Delta region of Vietnam. However, climate change, frequent flooding and other environmental factors have exacerbated the spread and severity of rice diseases. Safeguarding rice production has become a critical priority, necessitating innovative and accessible solutions in disease detection and management to sustain both the agricultural economy and food security. This chapter introduces an innovative solution to rice disease management through a chatbot-integrated rice leaf disease detection system specifically designed for the agricultural needs of the Mekong Delta. The proposed system comprises two primary components, a rice leaf disease detection model and an interactive chatbot, both of which work together to provide actionable insights to farmers. With a smartphone, farmers can capture images of rice leaves in the field, which are then analyzed by the system to detect common rice diseases. Upon diagnosis, the chatbot enables farmers to interact via text or voice to gain additional insights into treatment options, preventive strategies, disease forecasts and potential impacts on yield.

11.1. Introduction

The Mekong Delta region is a cornerstone of rice cultivation and export, sustaining both Vietnam's economy and Southeast Asia's food security. Accounting for more than 90% of Vietnam's rice exports, this area supports millions of livelihoods and supplies a staple food on a global scale. However, the region's rice fields face intensifying environmental challenges that threaten their productivity and stability. Owing to its erratic weather patterns, rising temperatures and frequent flooding, climate change has exacerbated the spread and severity of rice diseases.

Chapter written by Huu-Hoa NGUYEN, Van-Kiet VO and Thai-Nghe NGUYEN.

These environmental shifts create favorable conditions for disease outbreaks, complicating traditional disease management approaches and jeopardizing crop yields. In this context, safeguarding rice production has become a critical priority, necessitating innovative, accessible solutions in disease detection and management to sustain both the agricultural economy and food security.

To address these pressing challenges, an integrated support system that provides farmers with accurate, timely and practical guidance on rice disease identification, prevention and treatment is essential. The rapid adoption of mobile technology among rural and agricultural communities, especially in Vietnam, offers a unique avenue for delivering such support directly to farmers in the field. A majority of farmers in the Mekong Delta now own smartphones, which they use not only for communication but also increasingly for managing their agricultural activities. This digital shift presents an opportunity to develop an artificial intelligence (AI)-powered system that combines real-time data with expert knowledge, providing essential disease management resources directly to farmers' fingertips.

The ongoing digital transformation and the Fourth Industrial Revolution are reshaping agriculture, bridging knowledge gaps and delivering expert support to even the most remote farming areas (Nanda and Kumar 2024). In rice agriculture, a smartphone-based system capable of detecting rice leaf diseases would enable farmers to respond swiftly and accurately to disease outbreaks. Such a system, which allows farmers to capture images of affected rice plants and receive immediate diagnostic feedback, could transform crop management practices, minimizing time and resource expenditure in accessing critical agricultural guidance (Gopi et al. 2023).

This chapter introduces an innovative solution to rice disease management through a chatbot-integrated rice leaf disease detection system specifically designed for the agricultural needs of the Mekong Delta. The proposed system comprises two primary components: a rice leaf disease detection model and an interactive chatbot, both of which work together to provide actionable insights to farmers. With a smartphone, farmers can capture images of rice leaves in the field, which are then analyzed by the system to detect common rice diseases, including brown spot, leaf blast, bacterial leaf blight, yellow leaf and healthy leaf diseases. Upon diagnosis, the chatbot enables farmers to interact via text or voice to gain additional insights into treatment options, preventive strategies, disease forecasts and potential impacts on yield.

The disease detection component employs advanced deep learning techniques to identify rice diseases accurately and efficiently automatically. By training on extensive datasets, the model can recognize a range of diseases from field images, facilitating rapid diagnosis and response. The chatbot, on the other hand, serves as a virtual agricultural assistant, offering expert-verified, contextually relevant advice to help farmers make informed decisions quickly (Mittal and Kumar 2024). Powered by sophisticated natural language processing (NLP), the chatbot interprets various farmer queries, providing tailored, actionable information that extends beyond diagnosis to include comprehensive disease management strategies. Drawing on an extensive database of agricultural knowledge, the chatbot ensures precise and timely support for farmers, helping them protect and optimize their crops effectively.

Pilot implementation of this system in selected areas of the Mekong Delta has yielded positive feedback from farmers. As a digitally integrated tool, the proposed system aligns with Vietnam's broader goals for agricultural digital transformation, offering a scalable, resilient solution for farmers across the region. This integration of AI and mobile technology represents a promising step toward strengthening agricultural resilience and productivity, especially in the face of climate change and disease pressures.

The remainder of this chapter is structured as follows: section 11.2 presents a review of related work, summarizing recent advancements in AI-driven disease detection in agriculture. Section 11.3 describes the system architecture of the proposed solution, outlining the interconnections between its components. Section 11.4 focuses on the rice leaf disease detection component, detailing the methodologies and deep learning techniques employed. Section 11.5 explores the chatbot component, explaining its design, NLP capabilities and user interaction model. Section 11.6 provides an in-depth experimental analysis of system performance. Finally, section 11.7 concludes the chapter with perspectives on future improvements and broader implications for digital transformation in agriculture.

11.2. Related work

The significant decline in global rice yields, estimated at 37% annually, can be attributed to various rice plant diseases. Despite this pressing issue, few comprehensive applications exist that can accurately diagnose and manage these diseases. This gap is largely due to limited awareness and expertise in disease identification and control among farmers. Integrating AI into agriculture, however, is transforming disease diagnosis and treatment recommendations, providing farmers with more effective, data-driven tools for crop management. This section reviews recent advancements in deep learning applications for rice disease diagnosis, focusing on methodologies, model performance and existing limitations in the state-of-the-art literature.

A notable study by Kiratiratanapruk et al. (2020) developed a chatbot system on the LINE platform to assist rice farmers in disease identification. The system, which is based on a deep neural network with the YOLOv3 model, diagnoses rice diseases from field images with impressive 95.6% accuracy within 2–3 s, making it highly practical for real-time field diagnostics. However, its accuracy relies heavily on image quality and is limited to a small range of specific diseases, highlighting a common challenge of dependency on high-quality visual data and limited disease coverage in agricultural AI tools.

Similarly, Bhardwaj et al. (2021) applied the InceptionV3 deep learning model to classify four common rice leaf diseases, achieving 97.4% accuracy on a dataset of 2,500 images. While this high accuracy is promising, the limited scope of diseases restricts its practical application in diverse agricultural conditions. Expanding the disease range could increase its utility as a broader diagnostic tool for farmers who encounter various crop diseases.

Other research initiatives underscore AI's potential for sustainable agriculture. Bhardwaj et al. (2021) demonstrated the utility of machine learning in identifying crop diseases across agricultural environments. The E-Crop Doctor application developed by Jain et al. (2022) offers mobile-based disease diagnosis and management recommendations, aiming to make AI tools accessible to farmers. While promising, these systems face challenges related to data quality, adaptability to environmental variations and versatility across different crop types, underscoring the need for solutions that can address a broad spectrum of agricultural contexts.

In another study, Bari et al. (2021) employed the Faster R-CNN algorithm to classify rice diseases, such as blast, brown spot and Hispa, achieving a high accuracy of 99.25%. Trained on a dataset combining self-collected images and Kaggle data, this study created the Rice Leaf Disease Dataset (RLDD), incorporating both online and field data. While successful, the focus was limited to a few specific rice diseases, leaving room for further exploration of broader disease classifications.

Expanding on similar objectives, Pandian et al. (2022) developed a ResNet19 model optimized with evolutionary search techniques, achieving a classification accuracy of 99.58% by training on a large-scale dataset with extensive data augmentation. Despite its high performance, the model's computational intensity and resource demands remain obstacles to real-world deployment, particularly in resource-limited agricultural settings.

Studies on non-rice crops also offer insights into the potential transferability of deep learning models across agricultural domains. For example, Roy and Bhaduri (2021) created a model for early apple disease detection, achieving high accuracy (91.2% mAP) and speed (56.9 FPS). This model's efficiency in complex orchard conditions suggests that similar approaches could benefit rice disease models, enhancing adaptability under variable field environments.

Anari (2022) explored a hybrid approach with model engineering (ME) learning, integrating deep transfer learning, support vector machines (SVMs) and radial basis function networks to improve disease recognition. Although focused on fruit leaf diseases, this multimodel approach holds promise for treating rice diseases, which often require various feature extraction and classification methods.

In a study focused on rice diseases, Deng et al. (2021) trained multiple submodels on a large dataset of 33,026 images, encompassing six rice disease types, demonstrating the potential of extensive datasets for improving model accuracy. Zhou et al. (2023) employed a fusion of Fuzzy C-Means clustering and Faster R-CNN, achieving high accuracy rates for diseases such as rice blast and bacterial blight, underscoring the efficacy of clustering techniques combined with deep learning for rice disease classification (Rai and Lata 2024).

Other studies, such as those by Sethy et al. (2020) and Ramesh and Vydeki (2020), have applied optimized algorithms and the Faster R-CNN model for specific rice diseases, achieving accuracies exceeding 90%. While effective, these models are often constrained by environmental variations and dataset limitations, suggesting room for further enhancement to ensure consistent field applicability.

SVMs have also been utilized as simpler alternatives for rice disease classification, as demonstrated by Prajapati et al. (2017). While SVMs require less computational power than CNNs, their classification accuracy is generally lower, indicating that SVMs may serve better as complementary tools than standalone solutions in high-stakes diagnostics.

Recent studies have focused on handcrafted feature engineering to improve classification accuracy. Velusamy et al. (2023) employed segmentation and augmentation to refine data, resulting in a 3.1% accuracy improvement. Aggarwal et al. (2023) utilized watershed and graph cut segmentation, achieving 94% accuracy in classifying diseases such as leaf blight and rice blast, although without severity-based differentiation. To address this gap, our study integrates severity classification to provide a more nuanced assessment.

Our research builds on these findings by introducing an integrated system that combines rice leaf disease detection using advanced deep learning models and an NLP-based chatbot. These two components complement each other, creating a comprehensive solution for rice disease diagnosis and management (Kumar et al. 2023; Kumar and Lata 2022). The deep learning model enhances accuracy through advanced techniques such as transfer learning and deep feature extraction, whereas the chatbot component ensures accessible, real-time support for farmers. This integrated approach provides reliable disease identification and management guidance, promoting effective and sustainable agricultural practices.

11.3. System architecture

This section outlines the architecture of the proposed system, which is designed to empower farmers with tools for early detection, diagnosis, and treatment guidance for rice diseases. Each component of the architecture plays a crucial role in delivering accurate, timely and user-friendly disease insights directly to farmers' smartphones. Figure 11.1 illustrates the flow and interaction between the components, from initial image capture to the delivery of actionable information through chatbot responses. The main components of this system are detailed below.

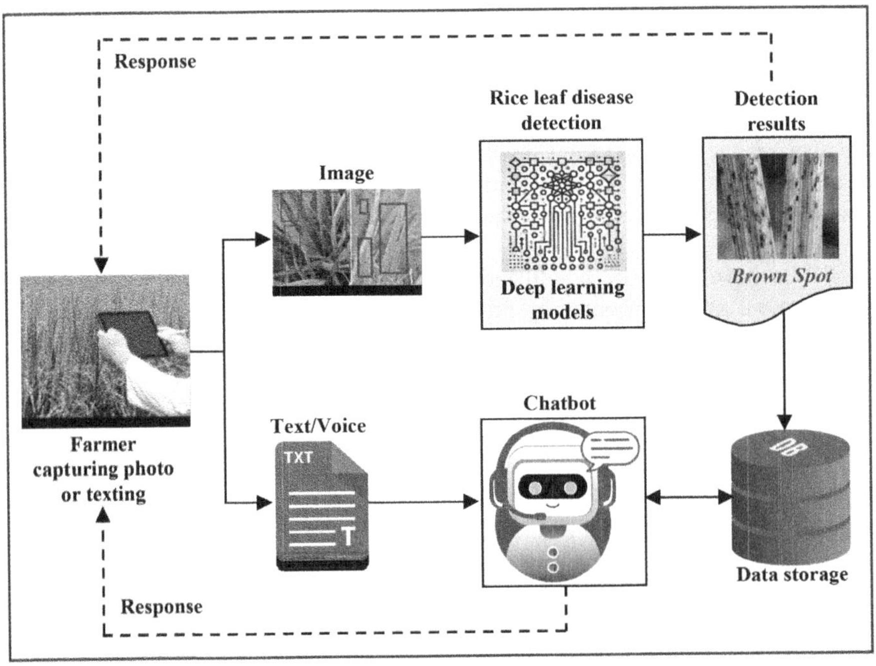

Figure 11.1. *Proposed system architecture. For a color version of this figure, see www.iste.co.uk/kumar/chatbots.zip*

Farmers' interaction: this component is the entry point of the system, where farmers interact via their smartphones. Farmers can capture a photo of a rice leaf in the field or submit a textual query about rice leaf diseases. Smartphones act as conduits, sending images to the rice leaf disease detection component or forwarding text queries to the chatbot component. This mobile-based approach leverages the accessibility of affordable smartphones among farmers in Vietnam and similar regions, enabling field use without specialized equipment. Farmers can choose image or text inputs depending on their immediate needs.

Rice leaf disease detection: upon receiving an image, this component preprocesses it through resizing, noise reduction and normalization to improve quality and enhance prediction accuracy. The processed image is then analyzed by a deep learning model, which is specifically chosen for agricultural image classification. The selected models – ResNet50, EfficientNetB7, VGG19 and InceptionV3 – are widely recognized for their efficiency and reliability in image processing. The model that achieves the highest accuracy is deployed in the live system, providing real-time diagnostic feedback to farmers.

Chatbot: developed using the Rasa API, this component serves as an interactive support tool, enabling farmers to ask questions related to disease prevention, treatment, etc. Rasa's open-source nature, customizability and NLP capabilities allow for precise intent recognition and seamless integration with backend data. The chatbot supports both text and voice inputs, making it accessible to users with varying literacy levels. Responses are based on a knowledge base containing expert information and real-world data, ensuring reliable and context-specific guidance for farmers.

Data storage: this central repository stores images of both diseased and healthy rice leaves, along with corresponding labels, which may be system-generated or verified by farmers. Data storage supports the continuous improvement of deep learning models, as confirmed diagnoses are used for model retraining, maintaining system accuracy over time. Additionally, the stored data enrich the chatbot component, enabling it to offer responses based on historical data and disease trends.

11.4. Rice leaf disease detection component

The rice leaf disease detection component is designed to automatically identify common diseases in rice leaves using advanced deep learning techniques. This section outlines the processes of data collection, preprocessing and model configuration.

11.4.1. *Data collection*

Data collection is a foundational step in building an effective deep learning model. To create a robust dataset, we gathered images from two primary sources:

publicly available datasets and field-specific images from the Mekong Delta. This dual approach enhances the model's ability to generalize across various disease patterns.

Kaggle and Internet data: the first source of data includes images collected from Kaggle and other Internet repositories, contributing a total of 6,034 images. Benchmark datasets from Kaggle are frequently used in machine learning research because of their high quality and standardized labeling. These data were further supplemented with images from various online sources, enhancing the dataset's diversity. As shown in Figure 11.2, this combined dataset covers five distinct classes: leaf blight, brown spot, leaf blast, yellow leaf and healthy leaf. Figure 11.3 provides a visual representation of diseased and healthy leaf samples, showcasing typical symptoms for each class.

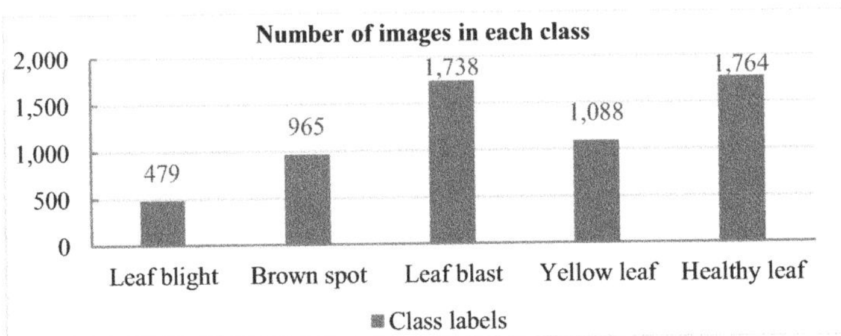

Figure 11.2. *Image data gathered from Kaggle and the Internet*

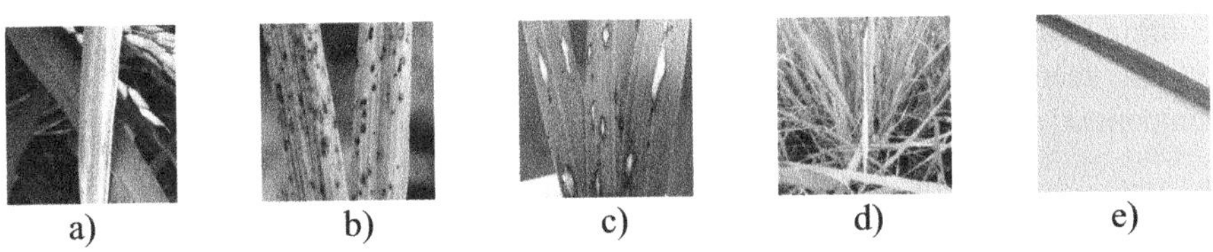

Figure 11.3. *Visualization of diseased and healthy leaves: (a) leaf blight; (b) brown spot; (c) leaf blast; (d) yellow leaf; (e) healthy leaf. For a color version of this figure, see www.iste.co.uk/kumar/chatbots.zip*

Field data from the Mekong Delta: to fine-tune the model for practical deployment in Vietnam, we collected images directly from rice fields in the Mekong Delta during the summer–autumn crop seasons of 2023 and 2024. Our team visited three provinces – Bac Lieu, Can Tho and Tien Giang – to capture real-life examples of rice leaf diseases. This effort yielded 1,253 labeled images, each validated by agricultural experts. Figure 11.4 illustrates the class distribution of these field-collected images, further enriching the dataset with locally relevant disease patterns.

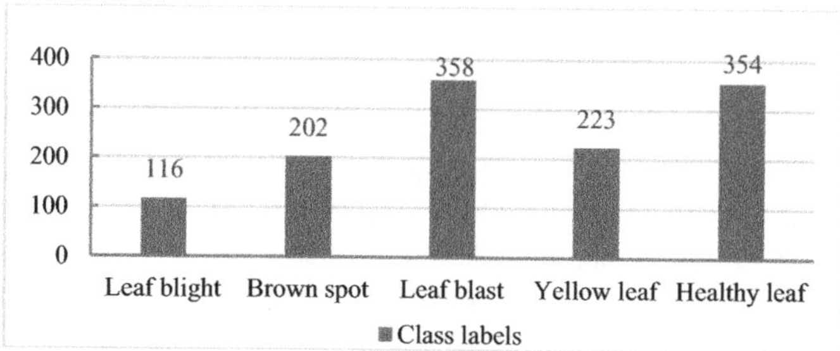

Figure 11.4. *Image data collected from the Mekong Delta*

By integrating these two sources, we compiled a comprehensive dataset of 7,287 images, capturing a wide spectrum of disease symptoms. Figure 11.5 displays the final distribution of images across classes. This consolidated dataset forms the foundation for training the deep learning models.

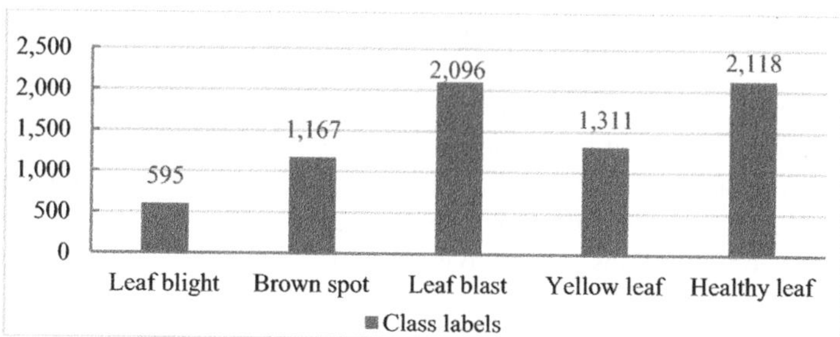

Figure 11.5. *Combined image data from Kaggle, the Internet and the Mekong Delta*

11.4.2. *Data preprocessing*

Data preprocessing is essential for enhancing dataset quality and ensuring that the model can be effectively generalized. Each preprocessing step contributes to creating a high-quality dataset that supports robust model training.

– *Noise and blur removal*: due to the diverse data sources, some images contained noise, blurring or low-quality pixels that could interfere with accurate feature extraction. Filtering techniques were applied to remove these artifacts, thereby improving the overall image quality within the dataset.

– *Data augmentation*: to increase dataset diversity and strengthen model robustness, we applied data augmentation techniques using the Keras ImageDataGenerator library. Transformations such as rescaling, shearing, zooming and random horizontal flipping were used to create variations in each image. This approach enables the model to learn from a broader range of examples, which is especially valuable for detecting disease features under different field conditions.

– *Class imbalance handling*: as illustrated in Figure 11.5, some disease classes were underrepresented compared with the healthy leaf class. Class imbalance can lead the model to favor majority classes, reducing its accuracy in identifying minority classes. To address this, we employed oversampling techniques, increasing the number of images in minority classes to match the majority class size. This approach, combined with data augmentation, allowed the model to learn features across all classes more effectively, enhancing the overall classification performance.

– *Dataset splitting*: for effective training and evaluation, the dataset was divided into training (70%) and testing (30%) subsets using stratified sampling to ensure proportional representation of each class in both subsets. This stratified approach maintains consistency in class distribution across training and evaluation phases.

11.4.3. *Deep learning model configurations*

As mentioned above, four prominent deep learning architectures – ResNet50, EfficientNetB7, VGG19 and InceptionV3 – were selected based on their strengths in image detection tasks. Each model was configured and fine-tuned to meet the specific challenges of detecting rice leaf diseases. The following subsections summarize the configurations applied to each model.

ResNet50 model

The ResNet50 model, known for its residual connections, was adapted for our task using transfer learning on pretrained ImageNet weights. We removed the final fully connected layer to add custom layers, as shown in Figure 11.6.

After the feature extraction layers were frozen, additional layers were introduced: batch normalization for stability, a dense layer with 256 ReLU-activated units and a dropout layer (rate 0.3) to reduce overfitting. The output layer used softmax activation for multiclass classification. The model was compiled with the Adam optimizer and categorical crossentropy loss, with EarlyStopping applied to prevent overfitting.

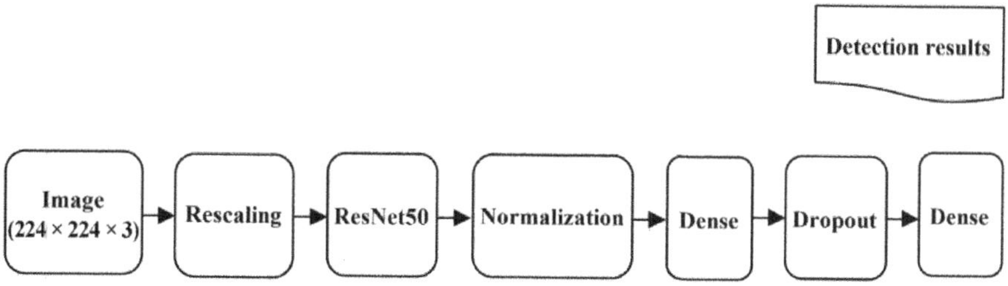

Figure 11.6. *Customized configuration of ResNet50*

EfficientNetB7 model

EfficientNetB7, known for its compound scaling method, was modified by removing the default classification head and adding custom layers, as shown in Figure 11.7. The input images were resized to 224 × 224 pixels, and a GlobalAveragePooling2D layer was added to reduce overfitting while retaining essential features. A dense layer with 128 ReLU-activated units and a dropout layer (rate 0.25) followed, with a final softmax layer for classification. The model was constructed with the Adam optimizer (learning rate 0.00001) and categorical crossentropy loss, with EarlyStopping for training control.

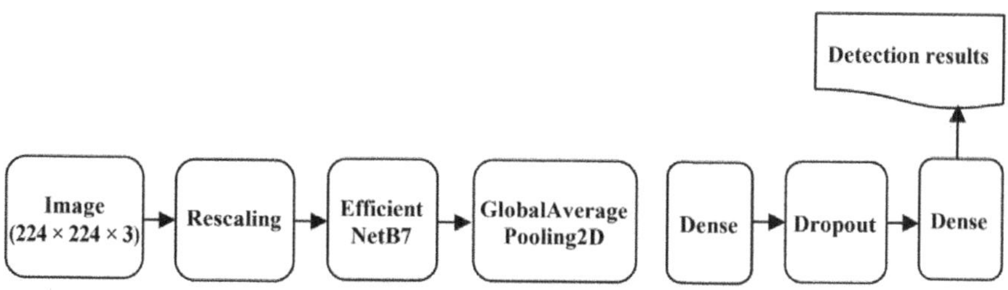

Figure 11.7. *Customized configuration of EfficientNetB7*

VGG19 model

The VGG19 model, which is appreciated for its simplicity and effectiveness in image classification, was customized by removing the final fully connected layers and retaining only the pretrained convolutional base, as depicted in Figure 11.8. A flatten layer converts feature maps into a 1D vector, followed by a dense layer with 512 ReLU-activated units and a dropout layer (with a rate of 0.5) to mitigate overfitting. The model was compiled with the RMSprop optimizer and categorical crossentropy loss. Data augmentation techniques were employed using Keras' ImageDataGenerator to further improve robustness.

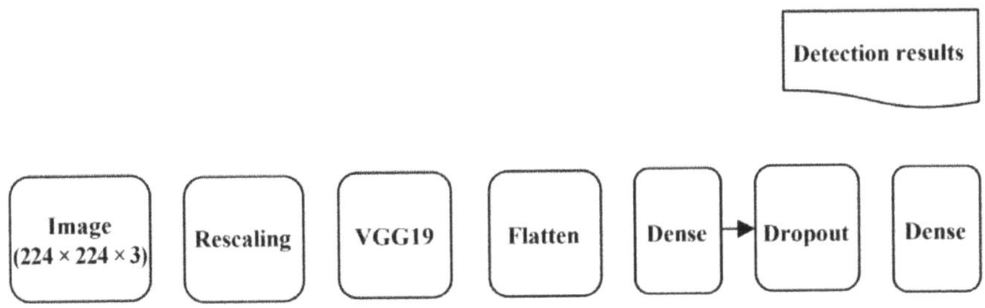

Figure 11.8. *Customized configuration of VGG19*

InceptionV3 model

The modules of InceptionV3 allow it to capture multiscale features that are useful for varying disease textures. For customization, the default classification head was removed, retaining only the convolutional layers, with further modifications similar to those shown in Figure 11.8. A flattened layer converted features into a 1D vector, followed by two softmax-activated dense layers for classification across five categories. The model was compiled with the Adam optimizer and categorical crossentropy loss, leveraging its ability to handle the intricate disease patterns found in rice leaves.

11.5. Chatbot component

The chatbot component is designed to provide farmers with instant access to information on rice leaf diseases and their treatments. This section covers data collection and preprocessing for chatbot training, the configuration of the Rasa framework and key architectural decisions to ensure high-quality user interaction.

11.5.1. *Data collection and preprocessing*

An effective chatbot requires a robust dataset of question–answer pairs that reflect real-world inquiries about rice leaf diseases. To build this dataset, we collected information from two main sources, ensuring that the chatbot could respond accurately and comprehensively to various farmer queries.

The primary data sources included the official portals of the Vietnam Ministry of Agriculture and Rural Development and several agricultural forums where farmers actively discuss crop health and disease management. The Ministry's portals provide reliable, expert-verified information on agricultural practices, including rice disease identification, prevention and treatment. This source established the foundational knowledge for the chatbot, enabling it to deliver scientifically accurate advice. Figure 11.9 illustrates an example of data sourced from these official portals.

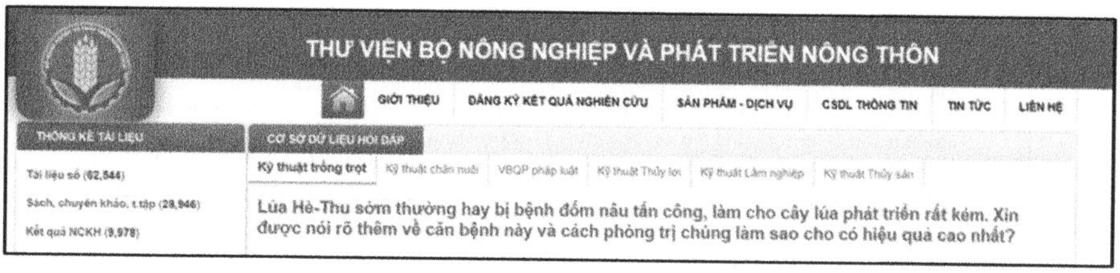

Figure 11.9. *Data from Vietnam Ministry of Agriculture and Rural Development Portals. The green text reads "Early summer-autumn rice is often attacked by brown spot disease, causing poor growth. Please explain more about this disease and how to prevent and treat it most effectively?". For a color version of this figure, see www.iste.co.uk/kumar/chatbots.zip*

In addition to these formal resources, data from agricultural forums have contributed with valuable and practical insights. These forums capture the everyday language and specific concerns of farmers, equipping the chatbot with context-sensitive knowledge relevant to real-world challenges. By incorporating data from these community-driven sources, the chatbot is able to respond in a conversational and accessible manner that resonates with its primary users. Figure 11.10 provides a snapshot of the data collected from these forums.

Once collected, the data underwent preprocessing to ensure clarity, consistency, and relevance. This included steps such as removing punctuation and special characters, expanding abbreviations and normalizing language. Special characters (e.g. @, # and $) were removed, and common abbreviations or "teencode" were replaced with full words, standardizing the language. Additional formatting adjustments ensured uniformity across the dataset. These preprocessing steps enhanced data quality, improving the chatbot's NLP capabilities and enabling it to interpret questions with greater accuracy (Lata et al. 2024).

After preprocessing, the final question-answer dataset included entries for 11 distinct rice disease types, enabling the chatbot to handle a broad range of disease-related queries. Figure 11.11 shows a breakdown of the number of question–answer pairs for each disease type, illustrating the extensive data used to train the chatbot. This comprehensive dataset enables the chatbot to provide information on various aspects of rice disease management, from diagnosis to treatment and prevention.

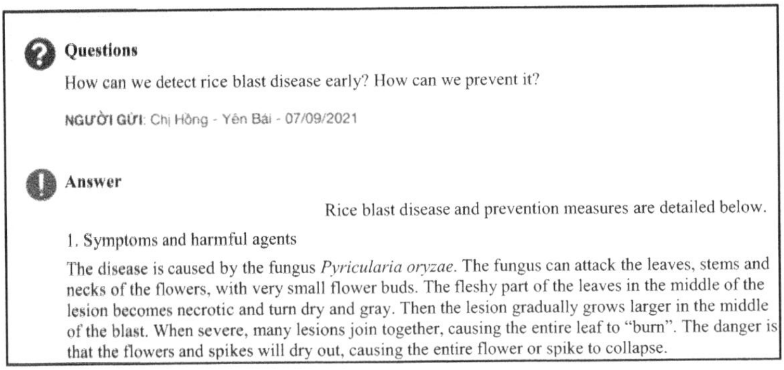

Questions

How can we detect rice blast disease early? How can we prevent it?

NGƯỜI GỬI: Chị Hồng - Yên Bái - 07/09/2021

Answer

Rice blast disease and prevention measures are detailed below.

1. Symptoms and harmful agents

The disease is caused by the fungus *Pyricularia oryzae*. The fungus can attack the leaves, stems and necks of the flowers, with very small flower buds. The fleshy part of the leaves in the middle of the lesion becomes necrotic and turn dry and gray. Then the lesion gradually grows larger in the middle of the blast. When severe, many lesions join together, causing the entire leaf to "burn". The danger is that the flowers and spikes will dry out, causing the entire flower or spike to collapse.

Figure 11.10. *Data from agricultural forums*

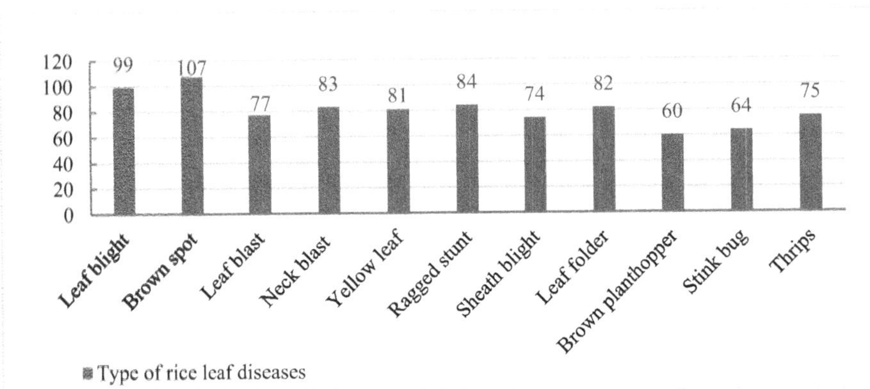

Figure 11.11. *Number of question–answer pairs for rice leaf diseases*

11.5.2. *Rasa framework*

The Rasa framework was chosen for chatbot development because of its flexibility, open-source nature and strong NLP capabilities, making it ideal for creating scalable and customizable conversational AI. Rasa's architecture comprises two main components: Rasa NLU (natural language understanding) for interpreting user input, identifying intents and extracting entities, and Rasa Core for managing conversational flow. For example, if a farmer asks, "how can I treat brown spot on my rice leaves?", the NLU identifies "treat" as the intent and "brown spot" as the entity, enabling the chatbot to deliver relevant treatment advice.

A custom pipeline was configured for Vietnamese language processing, including specialized tokenization, to accommodate the unique structure of

Vietnamese text. The chatbot was also trained to recognize synonyms and variations in farmers' vocabulary, enhancing its ability to understand diverse expressions related to rice diseases. The dialogue flow is designed to provide contextual responses based on intent classification and entity extraction, allowing the chatbot to handle follow-up questions seamlessly. For example, if a farmer initially asks about disease symptoms and then inquires about treatments, the chatbot maintains context without restarting the conversation.

Rasa's open-source environment also supports integration with external databases, enabling the chatbot to access up-to-date information on emerging disease trends and treatment recommendations. The system's scalability is facilitated by Docker and Kubernetes, which allow for flexible deployment on cloud platforms or local servers, ensuring that the chatbot can manage multiple simultaneous queries from farmers across different regions.

11.6. Experimental analysis

11.6.1. *Computational environment and evaluation metrics*

The experimental analysis was conducted on Google Colab Pro using an L4 GPU with 32 GB of GDDR6 memory, optimized for high-performance machine learning tasks. This setup enabled faster training and efficient handling of large datasets, making it ideal for deep learning tasks such as rice leaf disease detection. Colab Pro's integration with essential libraries, such as TensorFlow and Keras, streamlined the setup, allowing researchers to focus on model tuning and experimentation. It also offered easy model saving and loading through Google Drive, facilitating seamless experimentation across sessions (Lata and Kumar 2024).

To evaluate model performance, the following key metrics were used: accuracy, F1 score, precision and recall. These metrics provided a balanced assessment of each model's classification capabilities, enabling researchers to identify the best-performing architecture for real-world deployment (Lata and Sharma 2024a). High precision indicates reliable disease identification, whereas high recall ensures comprehensive disease detection coverage, making these metrics essential for selecting an effective model (Lata and Sharma 2024b).

11.6.2. *Deep learning model performance*

This section evaluates the performance of each deep learning model, highlighting key insights from the experimental analysis.

ResNet50 performance

ResNet50 demonstrated strong generalizability, with training and test accuracies of 0.844 and 0.836, respectively, as illustrated in Figures 11.12(a) and 11.2(b). The close alignment between the training and test metrics suggests effective learning without overfitting. The model's loss trajectory stabilized at 0.335 for training and 0.389 for testing, further confirming stable learning progression. Figure 11.13 provides a summary of ResNet50's classification metrics, with a test F1 score of 0.819, precision of 0.852, and recall of 0.821. This balance across metrics highlights ResNet50's reliable performance in identifying true disease instances without excessive false positives, a crucial factor for practical disease diagnosis.

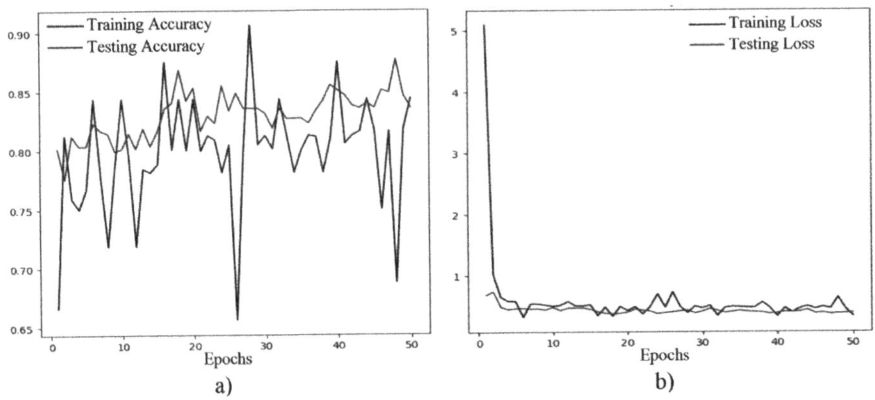

Figure 11.12. *ResNet50 performance: (a) accuracy; (b) loss. For a color version of this figure, see www.iste.co.uk/kumar/chatbots.zip*

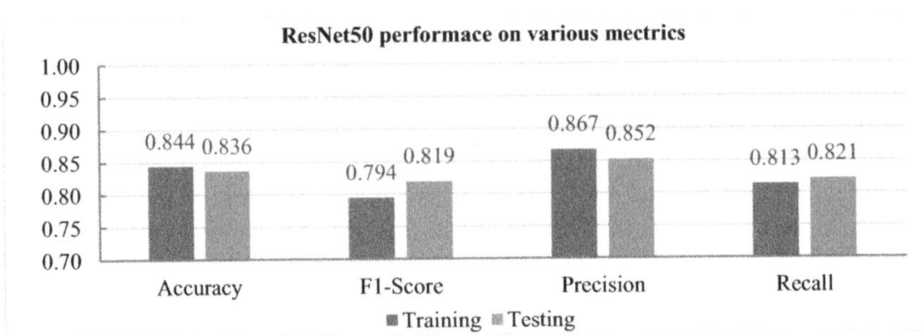

Figure 11.13. *ResNet50 performance on various metrics. For a color version of this figure, see www.iste.co.uk/kumar/chatbots.zip*

EfficientNetB7 performance

EfficientNetB7 reached a high training accuracy of 0.969 but a lower test accuracy of 0.875, as shown in Figures 11.14(a) and 11.14(b). This gap indicates a slight overfitting tendency, as the model performed well on the training data but was less consistent on the test set. Early stopping at epoch 55 helped limit overfitting, but the discrepancy between the training and test loss values (0.174 vs. 0.442) suggests that further regularization may improve generalization. According to Figure 11.15, EfficientNetB7 achieved a high precision of 0.879 on the test set, reflecting strong identification accuracy for diseased leaves, whereas a recall of 0.864 indicates comprehensive coverage of actual disease cases. Although EffectiveNetB7 is efficient and accurate, this overfitting trend suggests a need for tuning if applied in real-world deployment.

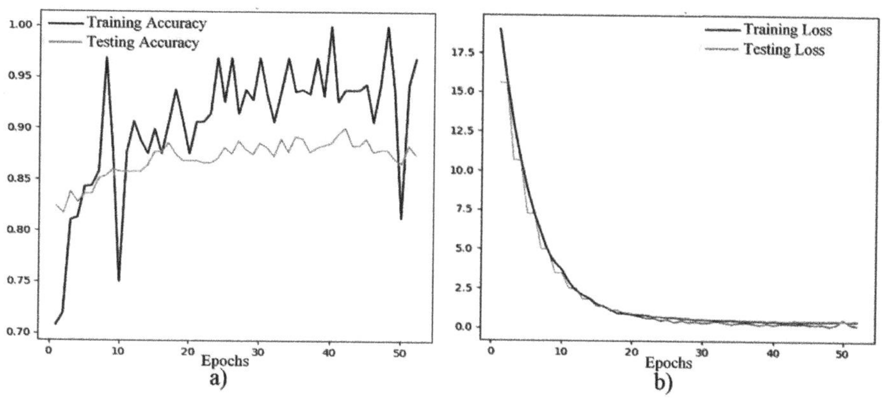

Figure 11.14. *EfficientNetB7 performance: (a) accuracy; (b) loss. For a color version of this figure, see www.iste.co.uk/kumar/chatbots.zip*

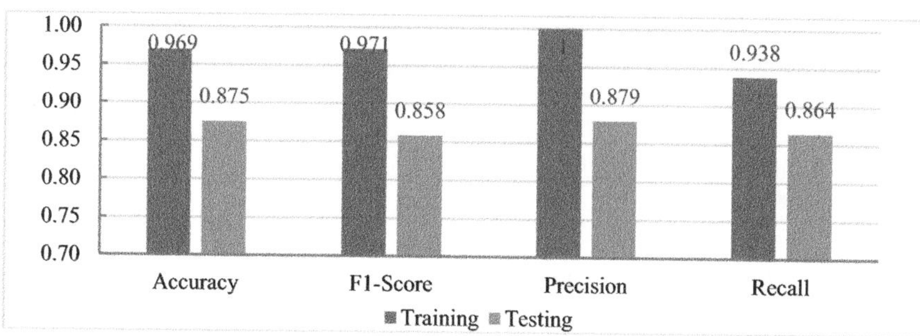

Figure 11.15. *EfficientNetB7 performance on various metrics. For a color version of this figure, see www.iste.co.uk/kumar/chatbots.zip*

VGG19 performance

VGG19 showed robust generalization with a test accuracy of 0.853, which was slightly higher than its training accuracy of 0.811, as depicted in Figures 11.16(a) and 11.16(b). This stable performance across datasets, combined with early stopping at epoch 13, allowed the model to avoid overfitting while maintaining accuracy. The loss metrics further support this, with a test loss (0.422) lower than the training loss (0.470), indicating that the model adapted well to unseen data. Figure 11.17 highlights VGG19's high test F1 score (0.838), precision (0.866), and recall (0.834), demonstrating an effective balance between precision and recall. This balance is essential for accurate disease identification, ensuring both the reduction of false positives and comprehensive disease detection, which makes VGG19 a strong candidate for deployment.

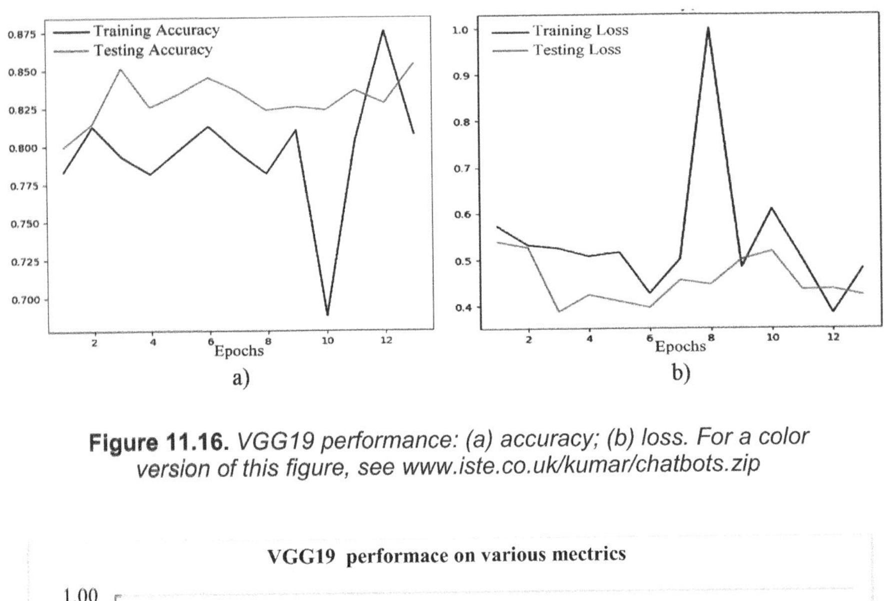

Figure 11.16. *VGG19 performance: (a) accuracy; (b) loss. For a color version of this figure, see www.iste.co.uk/kumar/chatbots.zip*

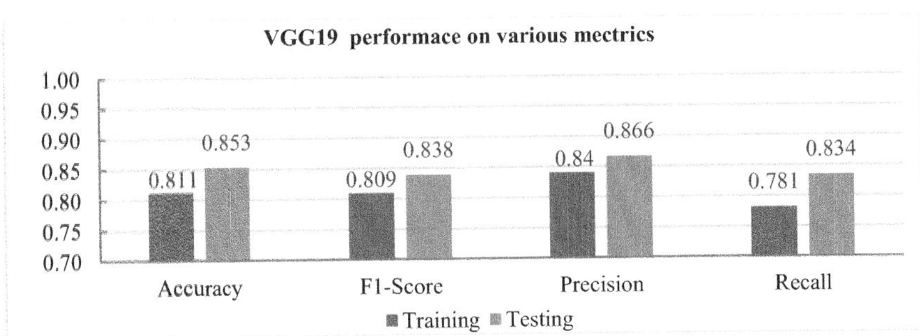

Figure 11.17. *VGG19 performance on various metrics. For a color version of this figure, see www.iste.co.uk/kumar/chatbots.zip*

InceptionV3 performance

InceptionV3 displayed a notable gap between the training and test metrics, reaching a training accuracy of 0.791 but a lower test accuracy of 0.750, as shown in Figures 11.18(a) and 11.18(b). This discrepancy, along with increasing test loss (0.741 compared with training loss at 0.649), indicates overfitting, where the model learned training-specific patterns that did not generalize well to new data. As Figure 11.19 illustrates, the test precision and recall decreased to 0.774 and 0.730, respectively, indicating reduced effectiveness in accurately identifying diseased leaves in a practical setting. InceptionV3's multiscale inception modules enabled detailed feature extraction but struggled with stability on unseen data, suggesting the need for tuning or additional regularization.

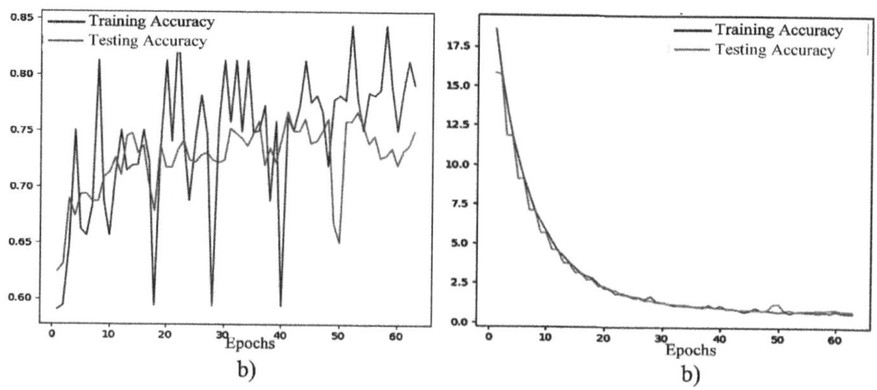

Figure 11.18. *InceptionV3 performance: (a) accuracy; (b) loss. For a color version of this figure, see www.iste.co.uk/kumar/chatbots.zip*

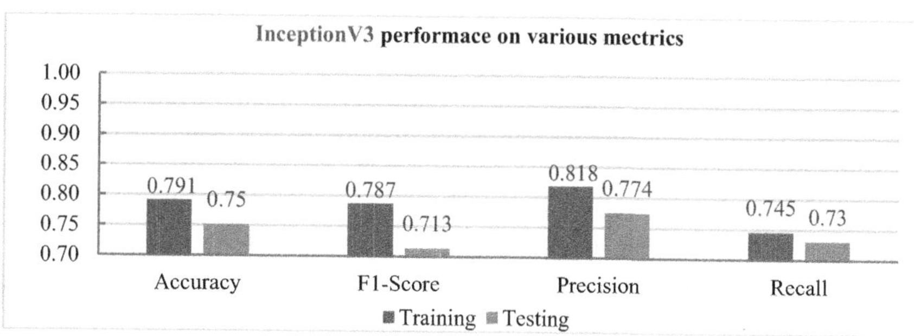

Figure 11.19. *InceptionV3 performance on various metrics. For a color version of this figure, see www.iste.co.uk/kumar/chatbots.zip*

Discussion and model selection

The comparative analysis of ResNet50, EfficientNetB7, VGG19 and InceptionV3 underscores each model's strengths and limitations for rice leaf disease detection. ResNet50 performed well across metrics, achieving a test accuracy of 0.836 and an F1 score of 0.819. However, it required more epochs to stabilize, indicating higher computational demands. EfficientNetB7 showed the highest training accuracy (0.969) but tended to overfit, as indicated by a lower test accuracy of 0.875 and significant test loss. InceptionV3 exhibited the largest discrepancy between training and test performance, suggesting challenges in generalizing to unseen data.

VGG19 emerged as the most balanced model, achieving a test accuracy of 0.853 and an F1 score of 0.838. As shown in Figures 11.16 and 11.17, VGG19 maintained consistent performance across the training and test datasets, with high precision (0.866) and recall (0.834) on the test set. The model's simpler architecture enabled effective learning of essential disease features without overfitting, making it adaptable to various datasets in real-world settings. This balance in metrics makes VGG19 the most suitable model for deployment in rice leaf disease detection.

On the basis of these findings, VGG19 was selected for implementation. Its stable performance across metrics ensures reliable and accurate disease detection, providing farmers with timely and trustworthy diagnostic information (Labadze et al. 2023). This robustness across different datasets reinforces the effectiveness of VGG19 in practical agricultural applications, supporting the goal of the proposed system.

11.6.3. *Chatbot creation*

Chatbot model

The development of the chatbot model followed a structured workflow to ensure accurate and context-sensitive responses for diagnosing rice leaf diseases. Figure 11.20 illustrates this workflow, which consists of the following key stages: building intent, defining sample responses, establishing conversation flow and rules, configuring the Rasa environment and training the NLU model.

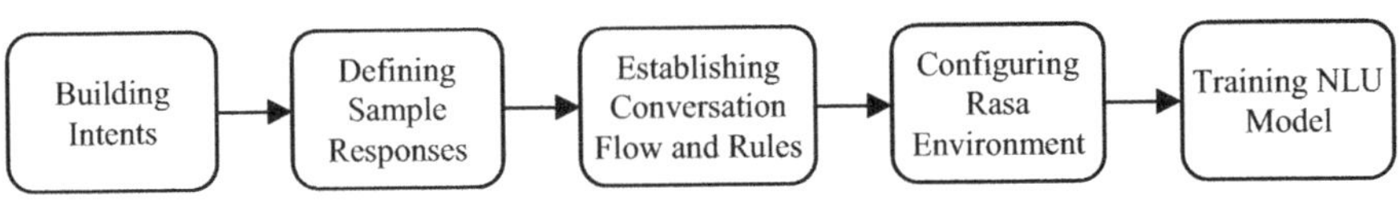

Figure 11.20. *Workflow for building chatbots*

The stages below detail each component of the workflow, emphasizing the unique considerations for developing a diagnostic chatbot for agricultural use.

– *Building intents*: this initial stage involved defining intents to represent the purpose behind various user queries, such as asking about symptoms, treatment methods, or prevention strategies (Lata and Kumar 2023). Each intent groups related questions, enabling the chatbot to accurately recognize user needs. For example, the intent “ask about bacterial leaf blight” could include questions such as “what are the symptoms of bacterial leaf blight?” and “how can I treat this disease?”. By categorizing questions, the chatbot improves its ability to understand and respond appropriately to diverse user inputs.

– *Defining sample responses for intents*: each intent is linked to sample responses that provide clear, accurate information. These responses are designed to be user friendly, including concise text, images, or links to further resources when necessary. This approach ensures that users receive comprehensive, easy-to-understand information, reinforcing the chatbot’s role as a reliable source of agricultural knowledge. The responses are continuously tested and refined to maintain consistency and accuracy.

– *Establishing conversation flow and rules*: effective conversation flow and rules manage the interaction between the user and the chatbot. Scenarios define sequential steps on the basis of identified intents and entities (e.g. disease name), allowing the chatbot to follow a logical response pattern. Rules ensure consistent interaction by guiding the chatbot to request missing information or provide additional support when needed. For example, if a user asks about treatment, but does not specify the disease, the chatbot will prompt clarification to provide a more accurate answer.

– *Custom component setup and workflow design*: tailored components were implemented for Vietnamese language processing to meet the specific requirements of diagnosing rice leaf diseases. Using the VietnameseTokenizer (from the Underthesea library), the chatbot effectively segments Vietnamese text, whereas the LanguageModelFeaturizer applies the multilingual LaBSE BERT model to capture contextual meanings, enhancing intent recognition accuracy. Figure 11.21 illustrates the training process for the Rasa chatbot model, integrating these customized components.

The chatbot employs additional NLP components to support accurate intent classification in Vietnamese, including the RegexFeaturizer and LexicalSyntactic-Featurizer for syntactic patterns and the CountVectorsFeaturizer for word frequency analysis. The DIETClassifier model, trained over 100 epochs, handles both intent classification and entity recognition, which are essential for precise responses. EntitySynonymMapper standardizes recognized entities, whereas ResponseSelector chooses the most appropriate response based on intent. A FallbackClassifier manages uncertain cases, prompting the chatbot to seek clarification or offer additional support.

```
pipeline:
  - name: custom.VietnameseTokenizer
  - name: LanguageModelFeaturizer
    model_name: "bert"
    model_weights: "rasa/LaBSE"
    cache-dir: null
  - name: RegexFeaturizer
  - name: LexicalSyntacticFeaturizer
  - name: CountVectorsFeaturizer
  - name: CountVectorsFeaturizer
    analyzer: char_wb
    min_ngram: 1
    max_ngram: 4
  - name: DIETClassifier
    epochs: 100
    constrain_similarities: true
  - name: EntitySynonymMapper
  - name: ResponseSelector
    epochs: 100
    constrain_similarities: true
  - name: FallbackClassifier
    threshold: 0.3
    ambiguity_threshold: 0.1
```

Figure 11.21. *Chatbot training process*

This structured approach has resulted in a robust, adaptable chatbot capable of accurately diagnosing rice leaf diseases and providing detailed guidance based on user queries (Lata and Kumar 2022). The integration of custom NLP components and language-specific adjustments in the Rasa framework ensures that the chatbot delivers meaningful, actionable information, supporting farmers in effectively managing rice diseases.

Chatbot model performance evaluation

The Rasa chatbot model was evaluated to assess its accuracy in classifying intents and identifying relevant entities, which is crucial for delivering precise diagnostic information to farmers. Performance was measured through cross-validation on an 80:20 train–test split, capturing metrics such as accuracy, F1 score and precision for both training and test datasets to provide a comprehensive view of the model's capabilities.

On the training set, the model exhibited high performance, achieving an accuracy of 0.997 with a standard deviation of 0.001, which indicates consistent learning across epochs. This near-perfect training accuracy, along with the F1 score and precision both reaching 0.997, highlights the model's effectiveness in correctly classifying intents and recognizing entities from labeled data, as shown in Figure 11.22.

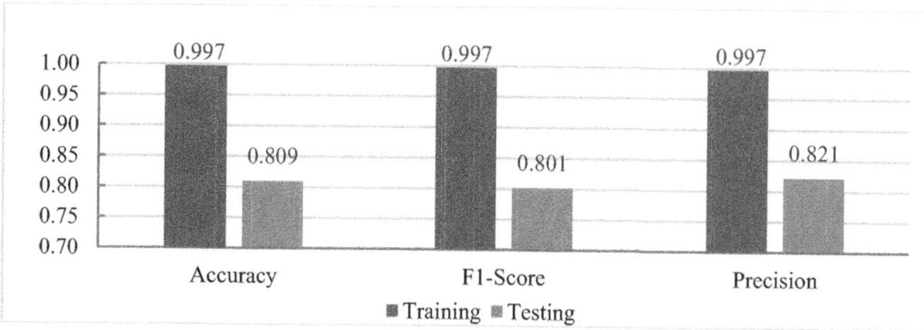

Figure 11.22. *Chatbot performance on various metrics. For a color version of this figure, see www.iste.co.uk/kumar/chatbots.zip*

In contrast, the test set performance saw a noticeable decline, with accuracy dropping to 0.809 and a standard deviation of 0.022. While a reduction in test accuracy is expected due to the challenge of generalizing to new data, this gap suggests potential for further model fine-tuning. The test set F1 score and precision were slightly lower, at 0.801 and 0.821, respectively, reflecting a modest decrease in the chatbot's balance between precision and recall. This decline indicates that while the model effectively classifies intents and entities, it may occasionally struggle with less common intents, impacting accuracy in edge cases.

In summary, the chatbot model demonstrated strong performance on the training set, achieving high accuracy, precision and F1 score, showing its capability to learn effectively from labeled data. On the test set, the model maintained reasonable accuracy and precision, although the lower F1 score suggests that improvements in generalization could be beneficial. Future enhancements could include fine-tuning with additional data, optimizing entity recognition thresholds, or employing advanced regularization methods (Lata and Kumar 2022). Overall, the chatbot provides a solid foundation for diagnosing rice leaf diseases and addressing farmer queries, with room for further refinement to enhance real-world reliability.

User interface building

To ensure accessibility and user-friendliness for the rice leaf disease diagnostic system, Flutter 3.19.5 was chosen as the primary framework for developing the chatbot application. Flutter's cross-platform compatibility enabled a seamless interface on both iOS and Android, ensuring that farmers, regardless of device type, can access the system conveniently. This approach promotes accessibility, especially in rural and agricultural settings.

Flutter's widget-based architecture facilitated rapid prototyping and customization, allowing for a responsive design tailored to user needs. Key features include image upload for disease detection, a chatbot for queries and organized response sections displaying diagnostic results and treatment recommendations. The UI emphasizes simplicity and clarity, acknowledging that many users may have limited digital experience. Figure 11.23 shows snapshots of the interface, highlighting its clean and accessible design.

To connect the Flutter application with the backend models, Flask 3.0.0 was used to develop APIs, enabling efficient communication between the frontend and both the disease detection and chatbot components. Flask handles tasks such as image uploads, diagnostic result retrieval, and user input processing for the chatbot. This backend setup supports real-time responses, a critical feature for farmers requiring timely guidance in the field (Bock et al. 2022).

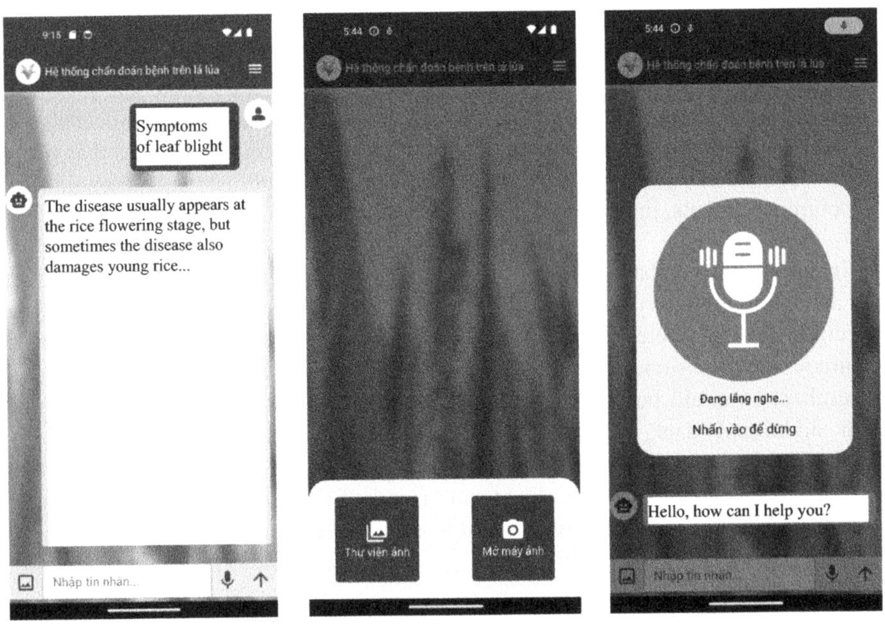

Figure 11.23. *Snapshot of the user interface: rice leaf disease diagnosis system. For a color version of this figure, see www.iste.co.uk/kumar/chatbots.zip*

The Rasa API (version 3.9) was integrated into the backend to manage NLP and conversation flow within the chatbot. Rasa's NLP capabilities allow the chatbot to interpret queries on symptoms, treatments and preventive measures accurately. With machine learning-based intent classification and entity recognition, the Rasa API ensures that responses are contextually relevant, providing farmers with AI-driven support directly within the app.

The integration of Flutter, Flask and Rasa resulted in a comprehensive and responsive system for diagnosing rice leaf diseases. By combining a user-friendly mobile interface with robust backend and advanced conversational AI, the application provides an intuitive, accessible tool for farmers, streamlining the process of disease diagnosis, information retrieval and treatment guidance within a single platform.

11.7. Conclusion and perspectives

This chapter has presented a comprehensive solution for rice leaf disease detection and management, specifically designed to address the critical agricultural needs of the Mekong Delta. By combining deep learning techniques for image-based disease identification with an AI-powered chatbot system, this approach provides farmers with timely, reliable and practical guidance accessible directly from their smartphones. This innovative system presents a promising tool to help farmers address the mounting challenges posed by climate change, environmental pressures and the increasing prevalence of crop diseases.

The rice leaf disease detection component applies advanced deep learning architectures – namely, ResNet50, EfficientNetB7, VGG19 and InceptionV3 – to diagnose common rice diseases with high accuracy and resilience. Experimental analysis has demonstrated the superior generalization and balanced performance of the VGG19 model across diverse disease categories, establishing it as the preferred model for deployment in real-world applications (Labadze et al. 2023). This deep learning-based detection system meets the need for rapid, reliable and user-friendly diagnostic tools, empowering farmers to respond swiftly to disease outbreaks and effectively manage crop health.

The chatbot component further enhances this support, offering an interactive platform where farmers can query the system about disease treatment, prevention and other agricultural practices. Developed using the Rasa framework and customized to accommodate Vietnamese language nuances, the chatbot provides expert-verified, contextually relevant advice to support informed decision-making.

By including both text- and voice-based interaction, the chatbot ensures accessibility for users across varying literacy levels, thereby broadening its reach and utility in rural communities.

In the future, several perspectives offer promising pathways to strengthen and expand the impact of this rice disease diagnostic and management system. First, enhancing the system's diagnostic accuracy can be achieved by enriching the dataset with images that represent diverse field conditions, crop growth stages and varying disease severity levels. A more diverse dataset will provide the model with a richer basis for identifying disease patterns and adapting to unique symptoms. Additionally, incorporating advanced deep learning techniques such as transformer models or attention-based networks could further improve the model's ability to recognize subtler disease indicators, expanding its diagnostic capacity across a broader range of conditions.

Another important direction involves integrating severity-based classification within the disease detection model. Currently, the system identifies whether a disease is present, but adding an assessment of its intensity would enable farmers to understand the level of threat posed by the disease. This development would guide farmers in prioritizing their treatment actions based on the severity of infection, allowing for more efficient resource allocation and effective disease management strategies that consider disease progression over time.

Moreover, real-time data integration and predictive analytics represent a significant opportunity to make the system more dynamic and proactive. Incorporating real-time environmental data, such as temperature, humidity and precipitation, could enrich the diagnostic process by supporting predictive disease risk modeling.

By analyzing these environmental factors with machine learning algorithms, the system could offer insights into potential disease outbreaks before they occur, allowing farmers to take preventive actions. This predictive capability would add a proactive dimension to the system, helping farmers stay ahead of disease threats and implement timely interventions to protect their crops.

These perspectives provide a practical path for enhancing and expanding this diagnostic system, in line with Vietnam's goals for digital transformation in agriculture. By improving diagnostic accuracy, adding severity assessments and incorporating predictive analytics, this system can offer valuable support to rice farmers, aiding sustainable crop production and helping to manage environmental challenges effectively.

11.8. References

Aggarwal, M., Khullar, V., Goyal, N. (2023). Exploring classification of rice leaf diseases using machine learning and deep learning. In *Proceedings of the 2023 3rd International Conference on Innovative Practices in Technology and Management, ICIPTM 2023*. IEEE, New York. doi: 10.1109/ICIPTM57143.2023.10117854.

Anari, S.M. (2022). A hybrid model for leaf diseases classification based on the modified deep transfer learning and ensemble approach for agricultural AIoT-based monitoring. *Computational Intelligence and Neuroscience*, 2022(18), 1–15. doi: 10.1155/2022/6504616.

Bari, B.S., Islam, M.N., Rashid, M., Hasan, M.J., Razman, M.A.M., Musa, R.M., Nasir, A.F.A., Majeed, A.P.P.A. (2021). A real-time approach of diagnosing rice leaf disease using deep learning-based faster R-CNN framework. *PeerJ Computer Science*, 7, e432. doi: 10.7717/PEERJ-CS.432/SUPP-1.

Bhardwaj, T., Deshpande, P., Murke, T., Deshpande, S., Deshpande, K. (2021). Farmer-assistive chatbot in Indian context using learning techniques. In *Security Issues and Privacy Threats in Smart Ubiquitous Computing*, Mahalle, P.N., Shinde, G.R., Dey, N., Hassanien, A.E. (eds). Springer, Singapore. doi: 10.1007/978-981-33-4996-4_16.

Bock, C.H., Chiang, K.S., Del Ponte, E.M. (2022). Plant disease severity estimated visually: A century of research, best practices, and opportunities for improving methods and practices to maximize accuracy. *Tropical Plant Pathology*, 47(1), 25–42. doi: 10.1007/S40858-021-00439-Z/TABLES/3.

Deng, R., Tao, M., Xing, H., Yang, X., Liu, C., Liao, K., Qi, L. (2021). Automatic diagnosis of rice diseases using deep learning. *Frontiers in Plant Science*, 12, 701038. doi: 10.3389/FPLS.2021.701038.

Gopi, S.C. and Kondaveeti, H.K. (2023). Transfer learning for rice leaf disease detection. In *Proceedings of the 3rd International Conference on Artificial Intelligence and Smart Energy (ICAIS 2023)*. IEEE, New York. doi: 10.1109/ICAIS56108.2023.10073711.

Jain, S., Sahni, R., Khargonkar, T., Gupta, H., Verma, O.P., Sharma, T.K., Bhardwaj, T., Agarwal, S., Kim, H. (2022). Automatic rice disease detection and assistance framework using deep learning and a chatbot. *Electronics*, 11(14), 2110. doi: 10.3390/electronics111 42110.

Kiratiratanapruk, K., Temniranrat, P., Kitvimonrat, A., Sinthupinyo, W., Patarapuwadol, S. (2020). Using deep learning techniques to detect rice diseases from images of rice fields. In *Trends in Artificial Intelligence Theory and Applications. Artificial Intelligence Practices*, Fujita, H., Fournier-Viger, P., Ali, M., Sasaki, J. (eds). Springer, Cham. doi: 10.1007/978-3-030-55789-8_20.

Kumar, V.S. and Lata, M. (eds) (2022). *The Future of E-Commerce*. Nova Science Publishers, New York. doi: 10.52305/KMUB3774.

Kumar, V.S., Jaganathan, M., Viswanathan, A., Umamaheswari, M., Vignesh, J. (2023). Rice leaf disease detection based on bidirectional feature attention pyramid network with YOLO v5 model. *Environmental Research Communications*, 5(6), 065014. doi: 10.1088/2515-7620/ACDECE.

Labadze, L., Grigolia, M., Machaidze, L. (2023). Role of AI chatbots in education: Systematic literature review. *International Journal of Educational Technology in Higher Education*, 20, 56.

Lata, M. and Kumar, V. (2022). Security and privacy issues in fog computing environment. *International Journal of Electronic Security and Digital Forensics*, 14(3), 289–307. doi: 10.1504/IJESDF.2022.122588.

Lata, M. and Kumar, V. (2024). A framework for security of public cloud environment. *International Journal of Electronic Security and Digital Forensics*, 16(4), 486–502.

Lata, M. and Sharma, V. (2024a). Cloud computing based blended learning: Quality assurance challenges. In *2024 International Conference on Communication, Computer Sciences and Engineering (IC3SE)*. IEEE, New York.

Lata, M. and Sharma, V. (2024b). Smart city environment management: Challenges and opportunities. *Grenze International Journal of Engineering & Technology (GIJET)*, 10(2), 2159–2166.

Lata, M., Kumar, V., Sharma, V. (2024). Cloud computing applications in online learning. *Grenze International Journal of Engineering & Technology (GIJET)*, 10(2), 408–411.

Mittal, S. and Kumar, V. (2024). Analyzing the role of technological capabilities and digital marketing on the performance of E-commerce-based SMEs. *Indian Journal of Marketing*, 54(12), 45–60.

Nanda, P. and Kumar, V. (2024). New generation technologies: Development vs. ethical challenges. *International Journal of Business Information Systems*, 46(3), 411–434.

Pandian, J., Kanchanadevi, K., Rajalakshmi, N.R., Arulkumaran, G. (2022). An improved deep residual convolutional neural network for plant leaf disease detection. *Computational Intelligence and Neuroscience*, 2022(2). doi: 10.1155/2022/5102290.

Prajapati, H.B., Shah, J.P., Dabhi, V.K. (2017). Detection and classification of rice plant diseases. *Intelligent Decision Technologies*, 11(3), 357–373. doi: 10.3233/IDT-170301.

Rai, S. and Lata, M. (2024). Futuristic outlook of online learning: The post-pandemic era. In *Technology-mediated Learning During the Pandemic*, Singh, J. and Kumar, V. (eds). Routledge, Delhi.

Ramesh, S. and Vydeki, D. (2020). Recognition and classification of paddy leaf diseases using optimized deep neural network with Jaya algorithm. *Information Processing in Agriculture*, 7(2), 249–260. doi: 10.1016/J.INPA.2019.09.002.

Roy, A. M. and Bhaduri, J. (2021). A deep learning enabled multi-class plant disease detection model based on computer vision. *AI*, 2(3), 413–428. doi: 10.3390/AI2030026.

Sethy, P.K., Barpanda, N.K., Rath, A.K., Behera, S.K. (2020). Deep feature based rice leaf disease identification using support vector machine. *Computers and Electronics in Agriculture*, 175, 105527. doi: 10.1016/J.COMPAG.2020.105527.

Velusamy, D., Mounika, A., Ragulraj, D., Vigneshwaran, K. (2023). Automatic disease classification of paddy leaf images using deep learning algorithms. In *4th International Conference on Signal Processing and Communication (ICSPC 2023)*. IEEE, New York. doi: 10.1109/ICSPC57692.2023.10125872.

Zhou, C., Zhong, Y., Zhou, S., Song, J., Xiang, W. (2023). Rice leaf disease identification by residual-distilled transformer. *Engineering Applications of Artificial Intelligence*, 121, 106020. doi: 10.1016/J.ENGAPPAI.2023.106020.

12

Opportunities, Limitations and Challenges of EDA Playground and ChatGPT Regarding Verification: A Case Study on Testbench Failures

If ChatGPT was an unexpected innovation for others, it was a goal achieved for professionals in the area of hardware and software development. It took a long time until this goal was achieved. Part of this goal was achieved by utilizing improvements in the verification and testing process, which allowed for optimizing the steps between the project and the hardware. As a result, year after year, over the last three decades, the capacity for data storage and processing has advanced to the point where we can use ChatGPT today. This chapter presents how traditional tools migrated to the web and expanded their teaching, enabling students and professionals to access advanced technologies. By doing so, EDA Playground was able to expand access to verification tools and techniques worldwide. With ChatGPT, doubts and possible failures can be translated into steps that can be compiled. Thus, the union of these tools allowed this study to project challenges and opportunities for future generative artificial intelligence tools.

12.1. Introduction

The development of the hardware production process has allowed software to improve. What were once ideas of a possible future are now accessible solutions on mobile devices. Artificial intelligence (AI) has finally left scientific articles behind and entered the real world. This was only possible owing to advances in the hardware production process, supported by new testing solutions, which have reduced the time between coding and manufacturing a chip. On the other hand, the demand for solutions has grown faster than the training of professionals to meet this

---

Chapter written by Joel Gonçalves DE OLIVEIRA and Marcio Eduardo KREUTZ.

demand (Nanda and Kumar 2024). Could AI contribute to hardware development, thus helping to reduce the shortage of skilled or unskilled labor? This study considers whether AI can correct testbench errors with the same accuracy as a person or whether its expertise is limited to code generation. Over the past three decades, verification models and methods have changed in line with coding and synthesis techniques and the development of simulation (EDA 2024) and synthesis tools (Kumar and Lata 2022). The universal verification methodology (UVM 2015) has been widely applicable, as it allows the integration of tests developed in multiple programming languages. These languages include C, C++, SystemC, Verilog, SystemVerilog (Accellera 2015), VHDL, Python, Assembly and E. While this verification methodology (Accellera 2015) is free, its use depends on the tool. The best tools cost thousands or millions of dollars. Many researchers have suffered a reduction in investment during the pandemic, so research related to vaccine development advanced, and the pandemic was controlled. The EDA Playground (EDA 2024) proved a great opportunity in this context. It allowed the user to generate simulations via a browser without requiring minimum computer configurations, enabling remote work via smartphones or tablets. This work aims to highlight the advantages and challenges related to developing research and solutions involving functional verification and the development of AI. Both are dependent on each other. On the one hand, for AI to continue to grow, new chips need to be developed, which require functional verification. Thus, this study presents the limitations found in developing solutions that aim to disseminate knowledge and the practice of verification.

12.2. Testbench and software testing

This new era of technology can be divided into three challenges: the first is associated with the capacity to produce, the second is the capacity to deliver quickly and the third is the quality of what is produced. With this, AI is growing as an option to support this new era of technological development (Mittal and Kumar 2024). However, for this to occur, it is necessary to test and improve the capacity and speed with which tests are generated and simulated and their results analyzed. For this reason, verification represents an excellent challenge for what we have available in terms of AI tools. To better understand this challenge, let us look at the following example: a temperature sensor. Sensors are present in various products and areas (Lata and Kumar 2023). The temperature of natural foods, such as fish, or environments, such as refrigerators, should be controlled. Therefore, each sensor needs to be trained for its function. The problem is that temperature sensors are not made with a single purpose in mind, which would increase production costs. In times of economic expansion, the production chain must be efficient and capable of producing more with less time and less design and production. Therefore, sensors are designed to work in environments with temperatures below zero and up to

125°C. In this way, they can be inserted into air conditioning units, refrigerators and freezers. However, this example hides a challenge: how to test it to work in these environments without them existing in the design phase. This is where test benches come in. The verification team is responsible for creating tests that simulate all (or almost all) possible functionalities that allow the sensor to be used in various ways (Lata and Kumar 2022).

Targeted tests are tests in which we know exactly what to expect regarding performance. Random tests are tests in which we want to discover possibilities, whether they are valid or not. Targeted tests stimulate all inputs, seeking to compare the output with the expected results. If any result differs from expected, something needs to be adjusted. Failures can be due to data being lost along the way during transmission (Lata and Kumar 2022). They can also be lost upon arrival when, for example, a certain step is suppressed or corrupted. Sometimes, when transmitting quickly, there is no way to wait for the data, or when it takes too long to communicate, it can generate successive retransmissions, creating a looping condition. Therefore, the greater the diversity of a device is, the greater the need to test it, which implies simulation time and specific tools (Lata and Kumar 2024). This is where a problem and an opportunity arise. The problem is the shortage of professionals who know the testing routine and a possible area in which AI can contribute. AI can provide both the testing routine and the ability to test all possible testing conditions, which creates a problem for development, since several of these conditions may not be valid.

Another point is that even with tests, without simulating them in groups of features, failures may never be discovered, but failures appear when possible conditions are combined. It is necessary to recognize failure patterns from imperfect representations. Data can be transmitted in bursts or one at a time. If the information transmitted is not essential, losses are accepted. This procedure for recognizing failure patterns can also be trained via AI (Lata and Sharma 2024). The idea is that at some point in the future, AI will be able to acknowledge failure patterns, indicating solutions or avoiding these patterns. It would need to be coupled with the tools, which is impossible. There are some prohibitive factors for this, such as the fact that most simulation tools are from companies external to the projects; they simulate tests only without knowing the codes and projects. Another problem associated with this is that the companies that manufacture these devices are not the same, that is, there is a company making simulation software, a company developing projects and simulating in this software and a third company manufacturing these projects (Lata et al. 2024).

This example covers the problems and challenges. On the one hand, creating a testbench requires technical knowledge about the device being designed and the programming language used in these projects. This project must be compiled to avoid typing, programming logic and functional errors. This requires a compiler; inserting AI into this process would allow it to learn from mistakes seen and indicate, even in the coding phase, sections that may impact the project, reducing debugging time. However, this does not eliminate the need for simulation. With each new simulation, it is necessary to maintain the known functions and remove the errors discovered, thereby generating a history of code and project improvements, which could also be accomplished via AI (Rai and Lata 2024). Verification involves steps ranging from RTL to netlist and SDF, with parameters affected by delays in the best-case and worst-case scenarios. In this context, UVM has emerged as a methodology capable of uniting several programming languages in a single environment, allowing people with knowledge of object-oriented programming languages to also work on hardware verification. This is a way to attract more people to this area, which requires a workforce. Although this represents an opportunity, it is still necessary to understand how UVM works. This creates an opportunity for AI, which can be trained to be an expert in UVM, providing support and optimized code solutions. This would reduce the time spent connecting tests and creating or simulating them.

Many tools promise to automate the creation of test benches, but we have generic models that need to be edited. This editing requires practical and theoretical knowledge about the area, which reduces the number of people able to work in the area. One solution for this is the EDA Playground, which allows simple examples to be simulated within the platform for free and enables simple projects to be created, edited, and shared, which could also be accomplished via AI. This allows both students and companies to have access to verification techniques.

The EDA Playground is an open web platform that provides access to a database of examples and languages, with versions ranging from older models to recent standards. It allows practice on any device connected to the Internet. Its great advantage is that it will enable the creation of real-time test benches that simulate and generate waveforms. On the other hand, with the emergence of ChatGPT, programming has ceased to be a problem and has become part of the automatic development of AI solutions. This case study presents the opportunities, limitations, and challenges of EDA Playground and ChatGPT regarding verification.

12.3. The case of EDA Playground

In digital circuit designs, reuse is fundamental, whether of the code or the verification environment. In this way, there is no limit to language integration. A VHDL project must be integrated with Verilog, which needs to work with a SystemC instance; both are verified with System Verilog. Using UVM (Accellera 2015) for complex environments, we can see the effectiveness in designing the environment and the complexity that needs to be assembled for all functions to work within the specifications of the methodology. Thus, a challenge arises: to unite different languages in the same project, guaranteeing all functionality during the integration process. Reuse is fundamental because several microelectronic projects need to be verified. Working with microcontrollers, NoC, Soc and FPGAs is common. However, updating operating systems and some tools has proven to be a problem, as we will see. UVM is a methodology for building class-based verification environments in System Verilog. It leverages object-oriented programming techniques to aid in code reuse. This can be done by using an existing VIP (Verification Intellectual Property) and replacing subcomponents, changing the sequence of transactions it generates, or extending its behavior without changing the source code and without the original author of the VIP having to anticipate their changes, other than following good coding guidelines. This is achieved using object-oriented programming. Each of these three object types is instantiated by calling a factory method, allowing the code it created to be reused. Consistently using the UVM factory in this way is one key to exploiting object-oriented programming in UVM.

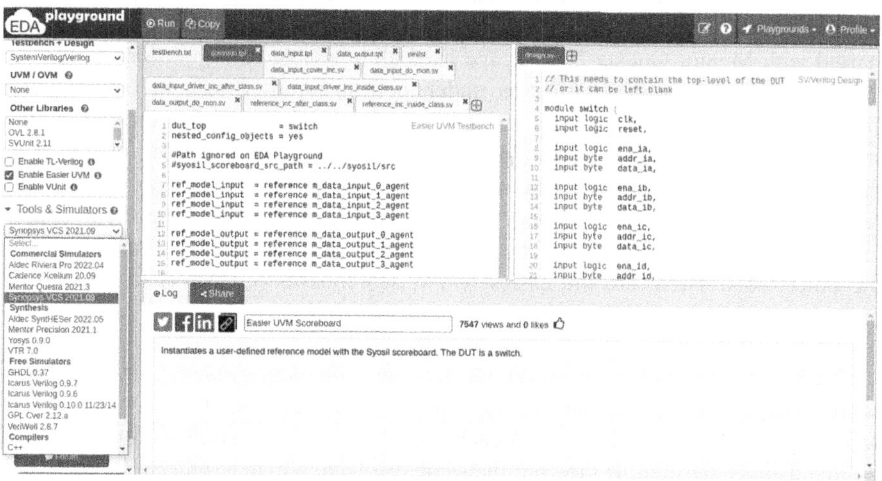

Figure 12.1. *Operation of the EDA Playground online tool for simulating a verification environment in the UVM. Simulation image extracted from the EDA Playground tool (EDA 2024)*

EDA Playground (EDA 2024) is an online tool that allows students with an institutional email to register and use it. Professional use is also possible. It runs on a server and can be used on any device connected to the Internet. Online solutions have gained ground, mainly because of the pandemic and mandatory remote learning. In addition, it is possible to choose which version of the UVM library to use in the tests and the version and distribution of the simulation tool (Li et al. 2016). In other words, it allows training in testing capacity and the quality of testing tools simultaneously, comparing results between the different tools available on the platform. Figure 12.1 shows the tools studied and the available resources, at least some of them. The login field is in the upper right corner. Next to the tool log is the option to run or copy. On the right, we see the window representing the hardware model in the center of the UVM environment (Dietl et al. 2012). At the bottom, there is space for the execution log. This is located on the left side, according to the required configuration.

Another advantage of this tool is that it provides examples, from the simplest, such as a hello word, to the most complex. The complexity is associated with the resources used, not a gigantic code. In this way, we can practice and learn a little about verification strategies and testing levels. This tool allows us to choose which simulator the example will run on. Four well-known commercial tools are included: Aldec Riviera Pro, Cadence Xcelium, Siemens Questa and Synopsys VCS. Since it is based on UVM, any example could be simulated using all of the listed tools, which should not interfere with the results. This is the advantage of using a universal methodology (Ramesh and Gadkari 2011). The first of the four available options started with Mentor Questa 2021.3. We used all available configurations to choose the easiest configuration. Easiest is understood as intuitive use; in common, all simulation tools present solution icons that are very similar; what changes is the strategy for compiling and organizing data, which can make a simulation slower or faster. We chose to analyze examples of tests available in the tool itself, thus reproducing conditions that the tool was designed to support. Among the available tests, two were compatible with this work proposal, being simulated and reused in the other tools. These are the easiest UVM scoreboards (Qamar et al. 2020) and parameterized interfaces.

These two examples are essential for the following reasons: first, when a scoreboard is chosen, the data testing model, which can be stacked, where each written dataset is copied into it and each read dataset is compared with the stack of written data, is selected. If they are the same, we have a match; otherwise, there is a mismatch. There can be several reasons behind a data mismatch, as already mentioned. Second, when choosing to parameterize an interface, it is assumed that it can be used in several projects by altering the sizes of its inputs and outputs. This is a clear example of code reuse compatible with the example used in the previous section. The UVM scoreboard is used as a basis for data checking; in our study on Precision Time Protocol (PTP) in 5G in Brazil (de Oliveira and Kreutz 2024), it is essential to use this UVM resource. We also consider the coverage achieved. However, it is common for the tool to present flaws, such as the one we see in Figure 12.2.

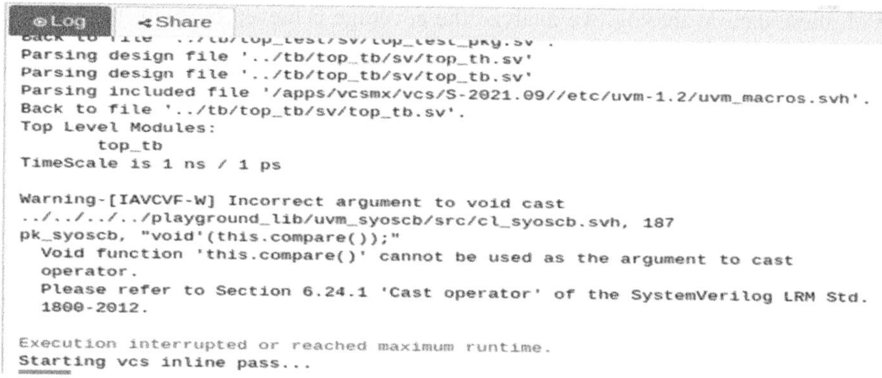

Figure 12.2. *A slowdown crash in the EDA Playground tool (EDA 2024)*

The example shown in the figure above is a classic verification problem, a test that ends due to excess time, that is, it was not able to process everything that was planned because some step was omitted in the simulation, which generated an excess condition, leading the test to a long simulation, but without results – a loop of useless data. This type of problem can occur due to an error in test planning or when steps need to be completed; for some reason, these steps were performed at different times than planned. In simulations at the logic gate level, the data path may be optimized, making the simulation faster than supported by the tested protocol or very slow, generating excesses caused by the following steps, which are not executed. This failure is known as a timeout. With this failure, it was impossible to observe the behavior of the environment, which forced us to redo the simulation. This allowed us to simulate actual conditions for developing hardware projects. Note that the "this.compare()" function (Dietl et al. 2012; Accellera 2015) cannot be used as an argument. It is one of the many UVM functions that EDA Playground (EDA 2024) does not compile. In the second attempt, using Mentor Questa 2021.3, we obtain the behavior shown in Figure 4.3. A test scenario was built without using "this" or impossible "void" in the UVM, and we encountered build failures there.

When using coverage in tests, some indicators show how much of the code was stimulated by the tests. For example, a low coverage of 10% of the code indicates that 90% of the structure of possible uses was not stimulated. With parameterizable interfaces, this can be a serious problem. For example, the stimuli must also grow as the data storage capacity increases.

Figure 12.3 shows how the tool should simulate the test environment in UVM because we have a UVM_TOP, four instances of data_input_coverage and another four instances of data_output_coverage. We can see the compile-time options used.

With these data in the log, we analyze the coverage achieved by each instance, as shown in Figure 12.4.

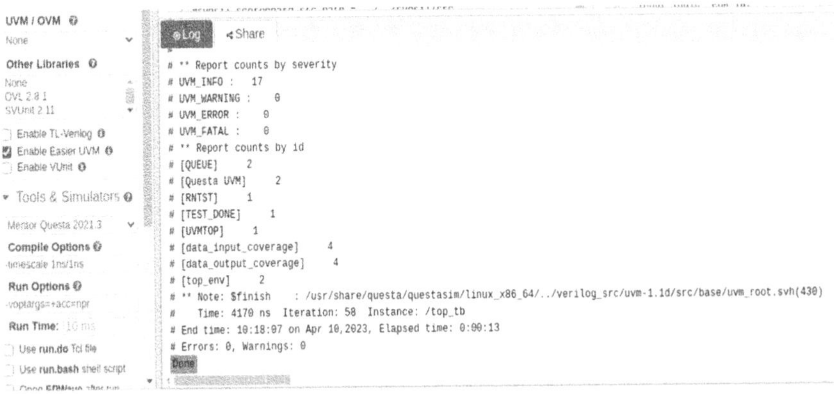

Figure 12.3. *A successfully completed simulation using Mentor (Siemens) Questa 2021.3 in the EDA Playground (EDA 2024)*

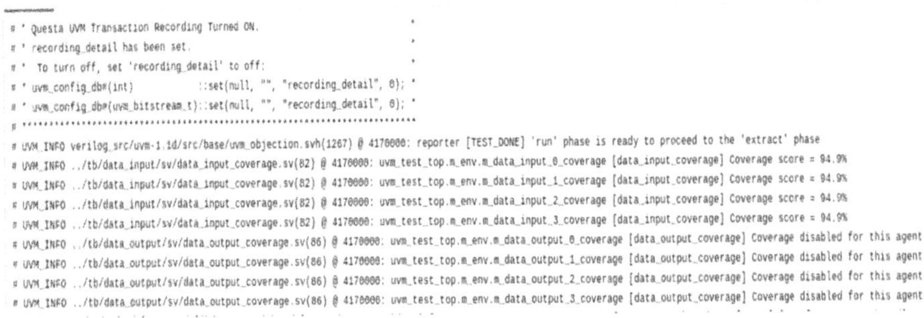

Figure 12.4. *The coverage achieved by testing using Mentor Questa as a simulation tool. EDA Playground tool (EDA 2024)*

With the Mentor Questa tool, the coverage rate for all instances is 94%, as shown in Figure 12.4, indicating that something was not stimulated, possibly a transition from zero to one or vice versa. In such cases, there are two possible solutions. The first is to analyze whether stimulation is necessary since a scenario may occur in which the signal remains at a defined value. For this purpose, excluding this condition from the coverage analysis is possible. The second possibility is to randomly stimulate that which was not stimulated to achieve 100% coverage. A routine for writing the analyzed case should be established to evaluate the best course of action. Since this example uses UVM, which is known for code reuse, the same code is expected to work in all tools available on the platform.

The same coverage rate is expected to be found. Otherwise, it is necessary to analyze what differs between them, for example, if there is correct instantiation since the same code is instantiated four times, and it may be necessary to configure differently in each tool during the simulation routine, that is, in the script that calls the tool.

We reproduced the same test with the available tools to evaluate the behavior of the EDA Playground when changing the tool choice. Figure 12.5 shows the log of the same test but with the Synopsys VCS 2021.09 tool. As we can see below, differences were found in the coverage and disabling of agents. The coverage rate decreased to 52.7%, revealing inconsistency.

If this problem were in a chip manufacturing project, it would result in production delays, as all of the tests would have to be redone. Rework is not cheap, so it must be studied, and we move onto the third available configuration.

```
UVM_INFO /apps/vcsmx/vcs/S-2021.09//etc/uvm-1.2/base/uvm_objection.svh(1276) @ 4130000: reporter [TEST_DONE] 'run' phase is ready to proceed to the 'extract' phase
UVM_INFO ../tb/data_input/sv/data_input_coverage.sv(82) @ 4130000: uvm_test_top.m_env.m_data_input_0_coverage [data_input_coverage] Coverage score = 52.7%
UVM_INFO ../tb/data_input/sv/data_input_coverage.sv(82) @ 4130000: uvm_test_top.m_env.m_data_input_1_coverage [data_input_coverage] Coverage score = 52.3%
UVM_INFO ../tb/data_input/sv/data_input_coverage.sv(82) @ 4130000: uvm_test_top.m_env.m_data_input_2_coverage [data_input_coverage] Coverage score = 52.0%
UVM_INFO ../tb/data_input/sv/data_input_coverage.sv(82) @ 4130000: uvm_test_top.m_env.m_data_input_3_coverage [data_input_coverage] Coverage score = 55.1%
UVM_INFO ../tb/data_output/sv/data_output_coverage.sv(86) @ 4130000: uvm_test_top.m_env.m_data_output_0_coverage [data_output_coverage] Coverage disabled for this agent
UVM_INFO ../tb/data_output/sv/data_output_coverage.sv(86) @ 4130000: uvm_test_top.m_env.m_data_output_1_coverage [data_output_coverage] Coverage disabled for this agent
UVM_INFO ../tb/data_output/sv/data_output_coverage.sv(86) @ 4130000: uvm_test_top.m_env.m_data_output_2_coverage [data_output_coverage] Coverage disabled for this agent
UVM_INFO ../tb/data_output/sv/data_output_coverage.sv(86) @ 4130000: uvm_test_top.m_env.m_data_output_3_coverage [data_output_coverage] Coverage disabled for this agent
UVM_INFO ../../../../playground_lib/uvm_syoscb/src/cl_syoscb_queue.svh(118) @ 4130000: uvm_test_top.m_env.m_reference_scoreboard.DUT [QUEUE] [m_reference_scoreboard]: Statistics
Inserts: 400, Macthed: 400, Orphans: 0
UVM_INFO ../../../../playground_lib/uvm_syoscb/src/cl_syoscb_queue.svh(118) @ 4130000: uvm_test_top.m_env.m_reference_scoreboard.REF [QUEUE] [m_reference_scoreboard]: Statistics
Inserts: 400, Macthed: 400, Orphans: 0
UVM_INFO /apps/vcsmx/vcs/S-2021.09//etc/uvm-1.2/base/uvm_report_catcher.svh(705) @ 4130000: reporter [UVM/REPORT/CATCHER]
--- UVM Report catcher Summary ---
```

Figure 12.5. *A figure showing that the agents were disabled and that the coverage rate was reduced to almost half, using Synopsys as a simulation tool. EDA Playground tool (EDA 2024)*

```
SDI2 Transaction Recording API Version 20.09-s003
xmsim: *N,COVNSM: (File: ../tb/data_input/sv/data_input_coverage.sv, Line: 69):(Time: 90 NS + 0) Sampling of covergroup type "data_input_coverage::m_cov" (../tb/data_input/sv/data_input_
UVM_INFO /xcelium20.09/tools/methodology/UVM/CDNS-1.2/sv/src/base/uvm_objection.svh(1271) @ 4130000: reporter [TEST_DONE] 'run' phase is ready to proceed to the 'extract' phase
UVM_INFO ../tb/data_input/sv/data_input_coverage.sv(82) @ 4130000: uvm_test_top.m_env.m_data_input_0_coverage [data_input_coverage] Coverage score = 0.0%
UVM_INFO ../tb/data_input/sv/data_input_coverage.sv(82) @ 4130000: uvm_test_top.m_env.m_data_input_1_coverage [data_input_coverage] Coverage score = 0.0%
UVM_INFO ../tb/data_input/sv/data_input_coverage.sv(82) @ 4130000: uvm_test_top.m_env.m_data_input_2_coverage [data_input_coverage] Coverage score = 0.0%
UVM_INFO ../tb/data_input/sv/data_input_coverage.sv(82) @ 4130000: uvm_test_top.m_env.m_data_input_3_coverage [data_input_coverage] Coverage score = 0.0%
UVM_INFO ../tb/data_output/sv/data_output_coverage.sv(86) @ 4130000: uvm_test_top.m_env.m_data_output_0_coverage [data_output_coverage] Coverage disabled for this agent
UVM_INFO ../tb/data_output/sv/data_output_coverage.sv(86) @ 4130000: uvm_test_top.m_env.m_data_output_1_coverage [data_output_coverage] Coverage disabled for this agent
UVM_INFO ../tb/data_output/sv/data_output_coverage.sv(86) @ 4130000: uvm_test_top.m_env.m_data_output_2_coverage [data_output_coverage] Coverage disabled for this agent
UVM_INFO ../tb/data_output/sv/data_output_coverage.sv(86) @ 4130000: uvm_test_top.m_env.m_data_output_3_coverage [data_output_coverage] Coverage disabled for this agent
UVM_INFO ../../../../playground_lib/uvm_syoscb/src/cl_syoscb_queue.svh(118) @ 4130000: uvm_test_top.m_env.m_reference_scoreboard.DUT [QUEUE] [m_reference_scoreboard]: Statistics for queu
Inserts: 400, Macthed: 400, Orphans: 0
UVM_INFO ../../../../playground_lib/uvm_syoscb/src/cl_syoscb_queue.svh(118) @ 4130000: uvm_test_top.m_env.m_reference_scoreboard.REF [QUEUE] [m_reference_scoreboard]: Statistics for queu
Inserts: 400, Macthed: 400, Orphans: 0
UVM_INFO /xcelium20.09/tools/methodology/UVM/CDNS-1.2/sv/src/base/uvm_report_catcher.svh(705) @ 4130000: reporter [UVM/REPORT/CATCHER]
--- UVM Report catcher Summary ---
```

Figure 12.6. *Simulation with the Cadence Xcelium 20.09 too. EDA Playground tool (EDA 2024)*

The third usage option, Cadence Xcelium 20.09, is shown in Figure 12.6. This Cadence log shows the same agents disabled in the Synopsys simulation. Changing the simulation choice configuration is not a reason to change the code coverage, as the tests are the same, and what has changed is the way it can be seen.

The coverage achieved by Cadence Xcelium 20.09 for the test example is 0.00%. This result made us doubt the test first. Afterward, we concluded that it could have been a failure due to the Internet connection. Finally, we studied the case, analyzed the entire log file generated, and the diagnosis was unique; the EDA Playground has severe flaws in its construction. A good result was no longer expected with the fourth configuration, and even so, it was surprising that Aldec still needed to be used to compile the test. Figure 12.7 shows the simulation log using Aldec.

```
eval $cmd
# ALOG: Pass 1. Scanning modules hierarchy.
# ALOG: Info: VCP2113 Module \$root found in current working library.
# ALOG: Info: VCP2124 Package uvm_pkg found in library uvm_1800_2_2017.
# ALOG: Info: VCP2113 Module switch found in current working library.
# ALOG: Pass 2. Processing instantiations.
# ALOG: Pass 3. Processing behavioral statements.
# ALOG: Error: VCP5183 /home/runner/generated_tb/tb/data_input/sv/data_input_seq_lib.sv : (55, 24): Undeclared identifier: starting_phase.
# ALOG: Warning: VCP2814 /home/runner/generated_tb/tb/data_input/sv/data_input_seq_lib.sv : (54, 20): Function get_starting_phase should return a value.
# ALOG: Error: VCP5183 /home/runner/generated_tb/tb/data_input/sv/data_input_seq_lib.sv : (60, 18): Undeclared identifier: starting_phase.
# ALOG: Error: VCP5183 /home/runner/generated_tb/tb/data_output/sv/data_output_seq_lib.sv : (55, 24): Undeclared identifier: starting_phase.
# ALOG: Warning: VCP2814 /home/runner/generated_tb/tb/data_output/sv/data_output_seq_lib.sv : (54, 20): Function get_starting_phase should return a value.
# ALOG: Error: VCP5183 /home/runner/generated_tb/tb/data_output/sv/data_output_seq_lib.sv : (60, 18): Undeclared identifier: starting_phase.
# ALOG: Warning: VCP7862 /playground_lib/uvm_syoscb/src/cl_syoscb.svh : (187, 23): Casting to void of a function returning void is redundant.
# ALOG: Error: VCP5183 /home/runner/generated_tb/tb/top/sv/top_seq_lib.sv : (164, 24): Undeclared identifier: starting_phase.
# ALOG: Warning: VCP2814 /home/runner/generated_tb/tb/top/sv/top_seq_lib.sv : (163, 20): Function get_starting_phase should return a value.
# ALOG: Error: VCP5183 /home/runner/generated_tb/tb/top/sv/top_seq_lib.sv : (169, 18): Undeclared identifier: starting_phase.
# ALOG: Compile failure 6 Errors 4 Warnings  Analysis time: 6[s].
# SCRIPTER: Error: ../sim/compile_riviera.do : (35, 1): Script execution terminated due to error(s).
Done
```

Figure 12.7. *Simulation with the Aldec Riviera Pro 2022.04. EDA Playground tool (EDA 2024)*

The simulation with the Aldec Riviera Pro 2022.04, by name and release date, was expected to be more efficient than competitors, and agile. However, we noticed severe flaws, compatibility with a test version tool and an inability to simulate the example. With this test and the result of the logs of each of the four tools, we decided to conduct a second test to analyze whether it is a standard EDA Playground behavior or an exception. This first analysis indicates that the EDA Playground does not recognize data structures in the form of stacks typically used in the scoreboard. The parameterization of interfaces is a simple and fundamental resource when developing versioned projects, that is, aimed at high performance and low consumption. It has a reused base and improvements to each project model. We note here that it is impossible to keep the interfaces parameterizable, simulating with the EDA Playground. Figure 12.8 shows our first simulation log using Mentor Questa, as in the previous example.

Despite the stimuli, the coverage in this simulation, shown in Figure 12.8, is 0.00%. This is equivalent to saying that there was no simulation, which is not true because the log was generated, and if there were failures in the port connection, an error would be displayed, aborting the test. What did not happen? So what would justify such a lack of coverage? One hypothesis would be that the coverage bits differ from those receiving the stimuli, which is false. We forced a stimulus, and still, coverage did not go up.

```
# UVM_INFO design.sv(19) @ 70000: reporter [] mydut data_8 = 03
# UVM_INFO verilog_src/uvm-1.1d/src/base/uvm_objection.svh(1267) @ 90000: reporter [TEST_DONE] 'run' phase is ready to proceed to the 'extract' phase
# UVM_INFO ../tb/clkndata_4/sv/clkndata_4_coverage.sv(82) @ 90000: uvm_test_top.m_env.m_clkndata_4_coverage [clkndata_4_coverage] Coverage score = 0.0%
# UVM_INFO ../tb/clkndata_8/sv/clkndata_8_coverage.sv(82) @ 90000: uvm_test_top.m_env.m_clkndata_8_coverage [clkndata_8_coverage] Coverage score = 0.0%
#
# --- UVM Report Summary ---
#
# ** Report counts by severity
# UVM_INFO :   17
# UVM_WARNING :    3
# UVM_ERROR :    0
# UVM_FATAL :    0
# ** Report counts by id
# []     8
# [Questa UVM]     2
# [RNTST]     1
# [TEST_DONE]     1
# [TPRGED]     1
# [UVMTOP]     1
# [clkndata_4_agent]     1
# [clkndata_4_coverage]     1
# [clkndata_8_agent]     1
# [clkndata_8_coverage]     1
# [top_env]     2
# ** Note: $finish    : /usr/share/questa/questasim/linux_x86_64/../verilog_src/uvm-1.1d/src/base/uvm_root.svh(430)
#    Time: 90 ns  Iteration: 63  Instance: /top_tb
# End time: 15:19:33 on Apr 10,2023, Elapsed time: 0:00:14
# Errors: 0, Warnings: 0
Done
```

Figure 12.8. *UVM environment for parameterizable interfaces. EDA Playground tool (EDA 2024)*

```
#   data_tx
#   my_clkndata_4_seq
#   my_clkndata_8_seq
#   questa_uvm_recorder
#   top_default_seq
#   top_env
#   top_test
# (*) Types with no associated type name will be printed as <unknown>
#
####
#
# ***********************************************************************
# * Questa UVM Transaction Recording Turned ON.                         *
# * recording_detail has been set.                                      *
# *  To turn off, set 'recording_detail' to off:                        *
# * uvm_config_db#(int)              ::set(null, "", "recording_detail", 0); *
# * uvm_config_db#(uvm_bitstream_t)::set(null, "", "recording_detail", 0); *
# ***********************************************************************
# UVM_INFO design.sv(15) @ 10000: reporter [] mydut data_4 = 0
# UVM_INFO design.sv(19) @ 10000: reporter [] mydut data_8 = 00
# UVM_INFO design.sv(15) @ 30000: reporter [] mydut data_4 = 1
# UVM_INFO design.sv(19) @ 30000: reporter [] mydut data_8 = 01
# UVM_INFO design.sv(15) @ 50000: reporter [] mydut data_4 = 2
# UVM_INFO design.sv(19) @ 50000: reporter [] mydut data_8 = 02
# UVM_INFO design.sv(15) @ 70000: reporter [] mydut data_4 = 3
# UVM_INFO design.sv(19) @ 70000: reporter [] mydut data_8 = 03
# UVM_INFO verilog_src/uvm-1.1d/src/base/uvm_objection.svh(1267) @ 90000: reporter [TEST_DONE] 'run' phase is ready to proceed to the 'extract' phase
# UVM_INFO ../tb/clkndata_4/sv/clkndata_4_coverage.sv(82) @ 90000: uvm_test_top.m_env.m_clkndata_4_coverage [clkndata_4_coverage] Coverage score = 0.0%
# UVM_INFO ../tb/clkndata_8/sv/clkndata_8_coverage.sv(82) @ 90000: uvm_test_top.m_env.m_clkndata_8_coverage [clkndata_8_coverage] Coverage score = 0.0%
```

Figure 12.9. *A figure showing too little stimulation using Mentor Questa 2021.3. EDA Playground tool (EDA 2024)*

It would be necessary to include more stimuli in this test, and this was only done after the other available tools were analyzed. Figure 12.10 shows the simulation with Synopsys; we present the exact number of stimuli, UVM_INFO and UVM_WARNING.

```
UVM_INFO ../dut/design.sv(19) @ 10000: reporter [] mydut data_8 = 00
UVM_INFO ../dut/design.sv(15) @ 10000: reporter [] mydut data_4 = 0
UVM_INFO ../dut/design.sv(19) @ 30000: reporter [] mydut data_8 = 01
UVM_INFO ../dut/design.sv(15) @ 30000: reporter [] mydut data_4 = 1
UVM_INFO ../dut/design.sv(19) @ 50000: reporter [] mydut data_8 = 02
UVM_INFO ../dut/design.sv(15) @ 50000: reporter [] mydut data_4 = 2
UVM_INFO ../dut/design.sv(19) @ 70000: reporter [] mydut data_8 = 03
UVM_INFO ../dut/design.sv(15) @ 70000: reporter [] mydut data_4 = 3
UVM_INFO /apps/vcsmx/vcs/S-2021.09//etc/uvm-1.2/base/uvm_objection.svh(1276) @ 90000: reporter [TEST_DONE] 'run' phase is ready to proceed to the 'extract' phase
UVM_INFO ../tb/clkndata_4/sv/clkndata_4_coverage.sv(82) @ 90000: uvm_test_top.m_env.m_clkndata_4_coverage [clkndata_4_coverage] Coverage score = 0.0%
UVM_INFO ../tb/clkndata_8/sv/clkndata_8_coverage.sv(82) @ 90000: uvm_test_top.m_env.m_clkndata_8_coverage [clkndata_8_coverage] Coverage score = 0.0%
UVM_INFO /apps/vcsmx/vcs/S-2021.09//etc/uvm-1.2/base/uvm_report_server.svh(904) @ 90000: reporter [UVM/REPORT/SERVER]
--- UVM Report Summary ---

** Report counts by severity
UVM_INFO :    17
UVM_WARNING :     3
UVM_ERROR :     0
UVM_FATAL :     0
** Report counts by id
[]     8
[RNTST]     1
[TEST_DONE]     1
[TPRGED]     1
[UVM/FACTORY/PRINT]     1
[UVM/RELNOTES]     1
[UVMTOP]     1
[clkndata_4_agent]     1
[clkndata_4_coverage]     1
```

Figure 12.10. *Simulation with the Synopsys VCS 2021.09 tool. EDA Playground tool (EDA 2024)*

With the result of the simulation log shown in Figure 12.10, we have the first coherence of effects associated with low stimulus and low coverage. In both cases, we can see the same number of stimuli, only 8, generating the same rate of 0.00%. This is an acceptable result, but it is not correct; this tool needs to know basic UVM functionalities. Figure 12.11 shows the simulation log with Cadence Xcelium 20.09.

```
UVM_INFO ../dut/design.sv(15) @ 50000: reporter [] mydut data_4 = 2
UVM_INFO ../dut/design.sv(19) @ 70000: reporter [] mydut data_8 = 03
UVM_INFO ../dut/design.sv(15) @ 70000: reporter [] mydut data_4 = 3
UVM_INFO /xcelium20.09/tools/methodology/UVM/CDNS-1.2/sv/src/base/uvm_objection.svh(1271) @ 90000: reporter [TEST_DONE] 'run' phase is ready to proceed to the 'extract' phase
UVM_INFO ../tb/clkndata_4/sv/clkndata_4_coverage.sv(82) @ 90000: uvm_test_top.m_env.m_clkndata_4_coverage [clkndata_4_coverage] Coverage score = 0.0%
UVM_INFO ../tb/clkndata_8/sv/clkndata_8_coverage.sv(82) @ 90000: uvm_test_top.m_env.m_clkndata_8_coverage [clkndata_8_coverage] Coverage score = 0.0%
UVM_INFO /xcelium20.09/tools/methodology/UVM/CDNS-1.2/sv/src/base/uvm_report_catcher.svh(705) @ 90000: reporter [UVM/REPORT/CATCHER]
--- UVM Report catcher Summary ---


Number of demoted UVM_FATAL reports  :    0
Number of demoted UVM_ERROR reports  :    0
Number of demoted UVM_WARNING reports:    0
Number of caught UVM_FATAL reports   :    0
Number of caught UVM_ERROR reports   :    0
Number of caught UVM_WARNING reports :    6

UVM_INFO /xcelium20.09/tools/methodology/UVM/CDNS-1.2/sv/src/base/uvm_report_server.svh(847) @ 90000: reporter [UVM/REPORT/SERVER]
--- UVM Report Summary ---

** Report counts by severity
UVM_INFO :    18
UVM_WARNING :     3
UVM_ERROR :     0
UVM_FATAL :     0
** Report counts by id
[]     8
[RNTST]     1
[TEST_DONE]     1
```

Figure 12.11. *Simulation performed with Cadence Xcelium 20.09. EDA Playground tool (EDA 2024)*

Similar behavior is observed thus far, in this test, in the Cadence, Mentor, and Synopsys tools, which motivates us to expect the same behavior from Aldec.

Even though Cadence's tool accounted for one more UVM_INFO than its competitors, the behavior remained similar; however, as shown in Figure 12.12, Aldec did not obtain the same result.

```
append cmd " +incdir+../tb/" $tb_name "/sv"
# alog -uvm  +incdir+../tb/include  ../tb/include/common_pkg.sv +incdir+../tb/clkndata_4/sv ../tb/clkndata_4/sv/clkndata_4_pkg.sv ../tb/clkndata_4/sv/clkndata_4_if.sv +incdir+../tb/clkndata_8/
append cmd " ../tb/" $tb_name "/sv/" $tb_name "_pkg.sv"
# alog -uvm  +incdir+../tb/include  ../tb/include/common_pkg.sv +incdir+../tb/clkndata_4/sv ../tb/clkndata_4/sv/clkndata_4_pkg.sv ../tb/clkndata_4/sv/clkndata_4_if.sv +incdir+../tb/clkndata_8/
append cmd " ../tb/" $tb_name "_test/sv/" $tb_name "_test_pkg.sv"
# alog -uvm  +incdir+../tb/include  ../tb/include/common_pkg.sv +incdir+../tb/clkndata_4/sv ../tb/clkndata_4/sv/clkndata_4_pkg.sv ../tb/clkndata_4/sv/clkndata_4_if.sv +incdir+../tb/clkndata_8/
append cmd " ../tb/" $tb_name "_tb/sv/" $tb_name "_th.sv"
# alog -uvm  +incdir+../tb/include  ../tb/include/common_pkg.sv +incdir+../tb/clkndata_4/sv ../tb/clkndata_4/sv/clkndata_4_pkg.sv ../tb/clkndata_4/sv/clkndata_4_if.sv +incdir+../tb/clkndata_8/
append cmd " ../tb/" $tb_name "_tb/sv/" $tb_name "_tb.sv"
# alog -uvm  +incdir+../tb/include  ../tb/include/common_pkg.sv +incdir+../tb/clkndata_4/sv ../tb/clkndata_4/sv/clkndata_4_pkg.sv ../tb/clkndata_4/sv/clkndata_4_if.sv +incdir+../tb/clkndata_8/
eval $cmd
# ALOG: Pass 1. Scanning modules hierarchy.
# ALOG: Info: VCP2113 Module \$root found in current working library.
# ALOG: Info: VCP2124 Package uvm_pkg found in library uvm_1800_2_2017.
# ALOG: Info: VCP2113 Module mydut found in current working library.
# ALOG: Pass 2. Processing instantiations.
# ALOG: Pass 3. Processing behavioral statements.
# ALOG: Error: VCP5103 /home/runner/generated_tb/tb/clkndata_4/sv/clkndata_4_seq_lib.sv : (55, 24): Undeclared identifier: starting_phase.
# ALOG: Warning: VCP2814 /home/runner/generated_tb/tb/clkndata_4/sv/clkndata_4_seq_lib.sv : (54, 20): Function get_starting_phase should return a value.
# ALOG: Error: VCP5103 /home/runner/generated_tb/tb/clkndata_4/sv/clkndata_4_seq_lib.sv : (60, 18): Undeclared identifier: starting_phase.
# ALOG: Error: VCP5103 /home/runner/generated_tb/tb/clkndata_8/sv/clkndata_8_seq_lib.sv : (55, 24): Undeclared identifier: starting_phase.
# ALOG: Warning: VCP2814 /home/runner/generated_tb/tb/clkndata_8/sv/clkndata_8_seq_lib.sv : (54, 20): Function get_starting_phase should return a value.
# ALOG: Error: VCP5103 /home/runner/generated_tb/tb/clkndata_8/sv/clkndata_8_seq_lib.sv : (60, 18): Undeclared identifier: starting_phase.
# ALOG: Warning: VCP7862 /playground_lib/uvm_syoscb/src/cl_syoscb.svh : (187, 23): Casting to void of a function returning void is redundant.
# ALOG: Error: VCP5103 /home/runner/generated_tb/tb/top/sv/top_seq_lib.sv : (98, 24): Undeclared identifier: starting_phase.
# ALOG: Warning: VCP2814 /home/runner/generated_tb/tb/top/sv/top_seq_lib.sv : (97, 20): Function get_starting_phase should return a value.
# ALOG: Error: VCP5103 /home/runner/generated_tb/tb/top/sv/top_seq_lib.sv : (103, 18): Undeclared identifier: starting_phase.
# ALOG: Compile failure 6 Errors 4 Warnings  Analysis time: 5[s].
# SCRIPTER: Error: ../sim/compile_riviera.do : (38, 1): Script execution terminated due to error(s).
```

Figure 12.12. *Aldec Riviera Pro 2022.04 tool simulation for the same test. EDA Playground tool (EDA 2024)*

As with the scoreboard tests, Aldec Riviera Pro failed to compile without errors; the environment cannot be compared with the other tools. Scoreboard failures should be analyzed as a learning opportunity, as they indicate real problems, even if the different behavior between the tools suggests that it is a compilation error in the platform. These errors do not diminish the potential effect and scope of the initiative proposed by EDA Playground.

Therefore, this experiment showed that access to verification techniques and methods has diversified but faces barriers, including compilation limitations. Since it is an area with few companies operating, the data and codes developed in it are expected to be protected. This makes it difficult for students and professionals who want to enter the area to access it. EDA Playground proved to be a tool capable of disseminating this knowledge, but it has limitations. The problems found in the examples of parameterizable interfaces and the scoreboard indicate much to be done. At this point, generative AI can be crucial for expanding professionals in the area, whether in research or in companies.

12.4. Using ChatGPT

When the online tool is used, errors are encountered that reproduce the same results in each attempt to produce a chip, which is terrific from a learning perspective. On the other hand, when you realize that the results become worse as you change the simulation tool to run the same example, it means that something is wrong with the execution. This indicates two possible problems: first, the code, which may indeed be a flaw in the code, and second, the simulation environment. When considering code errors, since it is a code available on the Internet when ChatGPT (OpenAI 2024) is used, it is expected to indicate possible points of failure in the code and potential solutions for this failure. ChatGPT works like an oracle, where questions are entered, and comments, suggestions and possible solutions are presented. In this case, an error message of a code would be displayed. Programming codes can be entered into ChatGPT with the symbol ###. This symbol indicates that everything after it is an algorithm or part of a code. The error message from the simulation log is chosen to analyze what type of response would be provided by ChatGPT, as shown below.

Input Logfile: xmsim: *N,COVNSM: (File: ../tb/data_input/sv/data_input_coverage.sv, Line: 69):(Time: 90 NS + 0) Sampling of covergroup type "data_input_coverage::m_cov" (../tb/data_input/sv/data_input_coverage.sv:30), referred in the statement is not enabled. As a result, coverage methods get_coverage(), get_inst_coverage(), get_hitcount(), and get_inst_hitcount() will return 0 coverage.

Chatgpt response to log file error:

The sampling of covergroup type "data_input_coverage::m_cov" is not enabled in your simulation configuration. As a result, the coverage methods such as get_coverage(), get_inst_coverage(), get_hitcount(), and get_inst_hitcount() will return 0 coverage. You should enable the sampling of the cover group to generate accurate coverage data.

Input: How can I fix that?

Chatgpt response: to enable the sampling of the cover group in your simulation configuration and generate accurate coverage data, follow these steps:

1) Check the configuration file or script where the simulation is defined. Look for any parameters or flags related to coverage sampling or enablement.

2) Ensure that the covergroup "data_input_coverage::m_cov" is instantiated and configured properly in your testbench code.

3) If specific coverage options or commands exist in a simulation tool or testbench, ensure that they are set correctly to enable coverage collection for the cover group.

4) Verify that the sampling event for the cover group is triggered at the appropriate points in your design to capture the desired coverage metrics.

5) Rerun your simulation after making any necessary changes to enable the sampling of the cover group. Check if the coverage methods now return the expected coverage values.

By following these steps, we can enable the sampling of the cover group and obtain accurate coverage data in your simulation. ChatGPT can understand the error message and provide a solution to the error. As you know, the steps indicated could not resolve the issue. New interventions are needed. This is one of many examples (a failed example would be a parameterized interface) of failure in the EDA Playground. In all of the tests carried out, ChatGPT was able to recognize the error, but its solution did not solve the problem in any of them. In other words, regarding the UVM tests for RTL verification, ChatGPT proved efficient in indicating what the error means but could not present an efficient solution for any of the six tests.

This study suggests that AI is on its way to transforming coding, potentially resulting in the end of human coding in the coming years. However, this panorama will require more research time for RTL verification until efficient AI is developed.

The primary barrier behind this difficulty is that verification is still an area of extensive private development, and ChatGPT can develop solutions on the basis of open, published and accessible data. This is one of the reasons why it can recognize errors but cannot identify solutions. It will be necessary to expand the access base, which means having access to confidential information. On the one hand, it comes up against ethical and professional issues; on the other hand, it requires data processing. We train AI to list solutions for the recognized errors that present efficient results.

Version 4 of ChatGPT has limited support for interpretation, which prevents a test from being performed. Shortly thereafter, the results of the logs are compared, and the failures that may have occurred are presented to justify the difference in behavior presented for the same example with different tools within the EDA Playground. This automated procedure for analyzing simulation logs is not yet possible because such logs do not have maximum character limits, such as the tool; therefore, the greater the number of instances in the test is, the larger the log will be, and the variation can be millions of lines of code. In this case, ChatGPT does not yet support this type of analysis, not even the paid version. However, assuming that there was no character limit, the comparison of the four generated logs could have been made, representing 117 pages of logs together.

These logs were analyzed separately and then as a group; the standard timestamps were studied to assess where each of them failed so that it was possible to understand the reasons behind the errors. It was impossible to find a single solution; perhaps ChatGPT could find such a solution, but its character limitation makes this impossible. It is necessary to understand that this character limitation is needed because both the data are processed. The number of users grows daily, requiring active servers to save and more processing resources, which are limited, even if they are expanded daily; this is an open question waiting for quantum computing.

12.5. Comparative analysis

Access to simulation tools is expensive, which makes it difficult for small businesses to emerge in the area without some investment, whether from the government or private sources. In this context, the EDA Playground has proven to be an unparalleled solution. It allows any user with a Gmail account to connect to the platform; simple registration is required for other emails. In the case of Gmail, all you need to do is authorize the connection and start using it. This work focused on showing the options for using simulators compatible with UVM, but the tool goes beyond that. This niche was chosen because of the widespread business use of this methodology. Another positive point is that the most prominent and widely used simulation tools are available on this platform. Another positive aspect is the division into modules of the examples available for simulation. This allows any user to understand how the platform and UVM work. This helps to break down a barrier to knowledge distribution, which is one of the major bottlenecks in training professionals for verification. Traditionally, access to UVM education and training is provided to graduates and professionals with experience in some areas who have found a job opportunity. This is increasingly difficult because of the diversity of areas of activity. However, without these professionals, the entire technology production chain runs the risk of being paralyzed, which would result in a collapse of the global economy, which is digital.

On the other hand, ChatGPT does not allow any simulation, but it can generate answers to any question entered, even if some of them are general answers. The best way to obtain good results with ChatGPT is to create a new dialog and ask specific questions related to the previous question. In this way, it can present contextualized answers as if it were being trained to answer that type of question. At the time of this research, there were five positive points about this technology and five challenges. The positive points are as follows: (1) it allows for the summarization of problems, which helps find a solution or customize one; (2) it displays answers in steps, which can be as detailed as possible. This indicates which steps need detail, and more details will be displayed; (3) there are common problems, such as those presented in the previous section, for which ChatGPT can suggest solutions on the basis of statistics of occurrence probabilities, which optimizes the solution process; (4) it suggests optimizations in the code; (5) it can be used to search for known and available solutions, which optimize the process of documenting failure cases.

Among the challenges, we have the following: of the examples used in this research, the one that uses the parameterized interface proved to be easier to solve and optimize with the help of ChatGPT. In this case, the tool indicated multiple ways to parameterize the signals. The use of solutions is optional, but the diversity of possibilities tends to be expanded, which can generate answers that do not apply to the problem. Problems related to tools depend on the cataloging of the responsible company. This means that the problem may be solved by updating the tool. In this case, ChatGPT can find the solution. Nevertheless, in cases where there is no public documentation of the problem, its suggestions are limited to indicating direct contact with the support of the company responsible for the tool. In this case, these companies are expected to present their AI solution, capable of solving problems with tool versions, which would allow them to compare all of the improvements consolidated over time and avoid failures in their updates, in addition to allowing a filter of doubts to be made, preventing the support team from having to be responsible for multiple services and optimizing the support process for doubts and solutions.

With respect to data verification, where data are written, stacked and read, compared with what was written, ChatGPT has proven to be a great support tool, showing where failures can occur and what the most common types are. Considering that it is an expanding technology, it is an open question whether, at some point, it will be able to produce verification tests and functional simulation, which would represent an industrial revolution. The major problem behind this challenge is the companies; creating a version of ChatGPT specifically for this would require opening all of the source code used in the tools and cell characterization libraries. At the same time that these companies are seeing expansion in the market, opening this version of AI could mean the end of their monopoly. When this happens, AI could produce hardware, representing the end of control over technology and opening up the critical possibility of self-management, which is unsafe.

With this study, the versioning of AI tools is projected for the near future, with chats developed to be trained for specific areas, such as verification. Ideally, this first chat version could be within the EDA Playground, which would represent a complete learning environment, allowing at the same time to train people and professionals in methodologies such as UVM and train ChatGPT to understand the entire process and how to improve test performance. This combination of technical content, tools and calculations of possibilities represents the ideal environment for creating a new way of producing technology. This challenge will be especially crucial for the commercialization of quantum computers.

Two technologies have opened up many possibilities. The first is by bringing to the web the teaching and practice of a sensitive and indispensable area, such as developing and testing hardware projects. This possibility of action makes the EDA Playground a milestone in the accessibility of teaching cutting-edge technologies. On the other hand, ChatGPT emerged as a complete environment for developing optimized solutions. This production was exclusively textual in its first versions, but now it produces videos from texts, images and codes. It is expected that in five years, ChatGPT will allow us to understand all of the stages of hardware project verification testing, and in up to ten years, this will allow the creation of purely automated chips. The main challenge behind this is how to ensure control and ethics in the development of these devices.

Another challenge is processing long texts, such as simulation logs, which, unlike books and scientific articles, cannot be counted by pages or the number of characters. This is because errors can be found at different points in the simulation with each new compilation. Thus, for the first time, the log may have 10,000 characters, and after reviewing the code and removing all errors, the complete version of this simulation may have, for example, one million lines. This is if the test is not finished within the maximum time limit, which would indicate a loop, that is when the same message is printed until the memory of the computer where the simulation is being processed is exhausted or the maximum simulation time that was established for that test, which can vary from minutes to more than a day, depending on the complexity of the test, is exhausted. This is also an open question, whether, for example, ChatGPT will be able to solve this type of problem before quantum computing, or whether AI will only achieve this type of processing with quantum computing.

12.6. Conclusion

Creating tests is not a simple task because it requires knowledge of programming languages, whether the language is geared toward hardware or software development, making professional functional hardware verification scarce. The challenge is attracting professionals with experience in a programming language, among those mentioned in this research, with those specific to verification, such as System C and System Verilog. In this context, the EDA Playground has proven to be an essential tool by providing an open environment, available via connection to the user's email, and from there, providing access to an environment with integrated tools and practical examples, which use theoretical definitions of models used by the semiconductor industry. These advantages make the EDA Playground an essential online learning tool for academics and professionals seeking to expand their knowledge of testing techniques and methodologies, such as UVM. Owing to the complexity of combining many languages and tools in a single environment, this tool has several limitations. On the other hand, ChatGPT applies theories discussed in AI, which have long been awaited. This wait was due to hardware limitations. For ChatGPT to become a reality, both the manufacturing process and the hardware had to advance in terms of information processing and storage capacity, as well as in the time taken to manufacture the product and the associated costs. Part of this was due to advances in testing and synthesis tools, which optimize the process between the coding and marketing of chips. This study presented the difficulty in accessing information about verification and testing and how the EDA Playground contributed to expanding access to this information by allowing anyone with an active email address to use tools that the semiconductor industry uses. By combining the two solutions, we open the debate on challenges and opportunities since it cannot be said that the flaws found in one or both technologies are a problem. They represent a stage of innovation that sets precedents for new solutions. It is expected that the entire chip production project will soon be automated. However, there are barriers to prevent this from happening. On the one hand, ethics are needed to prevent chips developed in this way from being trusted, not only from the point of view of safety of use but also from the point of view of data protection security and the ability to control these data.

12.7. References

Accellera (2015). Universal Verification Methodology (UVM) 1.2 User's Guide [Online]. Available at: https://www.accellera.org/downloads/standards/uvm. [Accessed 26 July 2024].

Dietl, D.S., Michael, E.D., Mote, N., Walker, B., Cooper, S., Pavlik, T., Popović, Z. (2012). Verification games: Making verification fun. In *FTfJP'12*, Beijing. doi: 10.1145/2318202.2318210.

EDA (2024). Playground homepage [Online]. Available at: https://www.edaplayground.com/x/5KbL [Accessed 26 June 2024].

Kumar, V. and Lata, M. (eds) (2022). *The Future of E-Commerce*. Nova Science Publishers, New York. doi: 10.52305/KMUB3774.

Lata, M. and Kumar, V. (2022). Fog computing infrastructure for smart city applications. In *Recent Advancements in ICT Infrastructure and Applications*, Chaturvedi, M., Patel, P. Yadav, R. (eds). Springer, Singapore.

Lata, M. and Kumar, V. (2023). Challenges to IoT security: Industry perspective. *Grenze International Journal of Engineering and Technology (GIJET)*, 9(1–2), 61–67.

Lata, M. and Kumar, V. (2024). A framework for security of public cloud environment. *International Journal of Electronic Security and Digital Forensics*, 16(4), 486–502.

Lata, M. and Sharma, V. (2024). Smart city environment management: Challenges and opportunities. *Grenze International Journal of Engineering & Technology (GIJET)*, 10(2), 2159–2166.

Lata, M., Kumar, V., Sharma, V. (2024). Cloud computing applications in online learning. *Grenze International Journal of Engineering & Technology (GIJET)*, 10(2), 408–411.

Li, B., Vendome, C., Linares-Vásquez, M., Poshyvanyk, D., Kraft, N.A. (2016). Automatically documenting unit test cases. In *2016 IEEE International Conference on Software Testing, Verification and Validation*, Chicago, 341–352. doi: 10.1109/ICST.2016.30.

Mittal, S. and Kumar, V. (2024). Analyzing the role of technological capabilities and digital marketing on the performance of E-commerce-based SMEs. *Indian Journal of Marketing*, 54(12), 45–60.

Nanda, P. and Kumar, V. (2024). New generation technologies: Development vs. ethical challenges. *International Journal of Business Information Systems*, 46(3), 411–434.

de Oliveira, J.G. and Kreutz, M.E. (2024). The blind spots of two-factor authentication tools. In *Proceedings of the Third International Conference on Innovations in Computing Research (ICR'24)*. Springer, Cham [Online]. Available at: https://link.springer.com/chapter/10.1007/978-3-031-65522-7_50.

OpenAI (2024). ChatGPT 4 [Online]. Available at: https://chatbotapp.ai/landing?utm_source=GoogleAds&utm_medium=cpc&utm_campaign=%7Bcampaign%7D&utm_id=21162266110&utm_term=159251680286&utm_content=695620902927&gad_source=1&gbraid=0AAAAA9X0Rz3g7nVh2RMRSHQjzcr1sYN5v&gclid=Cj0KCQiA9667BhDoARIsANnamQYCGJcWXR74nQRQ8MA-svzMpyEEU02ZNQtNQ13N-32yXA1qzBVNEmcaAuBOEALw_wcB [Accessed 23 December 2024].

Qamar, S., Butt, W.S., Anwar, M.W., Azam, F. Khan, M.Q. (2020). A comprehensive investigation of universal verification methodology (UVM) standard for design verification. In *ICSCA 2020*, Langkawi, 18–21 February. doi: 10.1145/3384544.3384547.

Rai, S. and Lata, M. (2024). Futuristic outlook of online learning: The post-pandemic era. In *Technology-mediated Learning During the Pandemic*, Singh, J. and Kumar, V. (eds). Routledge, New Delhi.

Ramesh, S. and Gadkari, A. (2011). Rigorous model-based design & verification flow for in-vehicle software. In *DAC'11*, San Diego, CA, 5–10 June. doi: 10.1145/2024724.20247.

UVM (Universal Verification Methodology) (2015). 1.2 User's Guide [Online]. Available at: https://www.accellera.org/images/downloads/standards/uvm/uvm_users_guide_1.2.pdf.

List of Authors

Andika ANDIKA
Janabadra University
Yogyakarta
Indonesia

Tiara Nur ANISAH
Janabadra University
Yogyakarta
Indonesia

Jyoti ARORA
Chandigarh University
Mohali
Punjab
India

Amitabh BHARGAVA
Amity University
Greater Noida Campus
India

Subhajit BHATTACHARYA
XIM University
Bhubaneswar
India

Sailaja BOHARA
Amity University
Greater Noida Campus
India

Shilpi CHAKRAVARTY
Manipal University
Jaipur
India

Arunava DALAL
Praxis Business School
Kolkata
India

FAISOL
Universitas Nusantara PGRI Kediri
Indonesia

Thomas FOTIADIS
University of Cyprus
Aglantzia
Cyprus

Iti GAUR
Manipal University
Jaipur
India

Gaurav GUPTA
Amity University
Greater Noida Campus
India

Mahesh Chandra JOSHI
Manipal University
Jaipur
India

Charnpreet KAUR
Chandigarh University
Mohali
India

Puneet KAUR
Chandigarh University
Mohali
India

Marcio Eduardo KREUTZ
UFRN
Natal-RN
Brazil

Vikas KUMAR
Central University of Haryana
Mahendergarh
India

Manju LATA
Chandigarh University
Mohali
India

Vy Ngoc LE HO
Dong Nai Technology University
Bien Hoa City
Vietnam

Ikbal MAULANA
National Research and Innovation
Agency (BRIN)
Jakarta
Indonesia

Christos METTOURIS
University of Cyprus
Aglantzia
Cyprus

Anupam MITTAL
Chandigarh University
Mohali
India

Huu-Hoa NGUYEN
Can Tho University
Vietnam

Thai-Nghe NGUYEN
Can Tho University
Vietnam

Diah NURDIWATY
Universitas Nusantara PGRI Kediri
Indonesia

Joel Gonçalves DE OLIVEIRA
UFRN
Natal-RN
Brazil

George Angelos PAPADOPOULOS
University of Cyprus
Aglantzia
Cyprus

Mandakini PARUTHI
IBS Hyderabad, IFHE
(Deemed-to-be University)
Telangana
India

Linda PAUL
Durban University of Technology
ML Sultan Campus
South Africa

Sandhya RAI
Bennett University
Greater Noida
India

Sonam RANI
Amity University
Greater Noida Campus
India

Ravinder RENA
Durban University of Technology
ML Sultan Campus
South Africa

Ioanna THEOPHILOU
University of Cyprus
Aglantzia
Cyprus

Evangelia VANEZI
University of Cyprus
Aglantzia
Cyprus

Van-Kiet VO
Can Tho University
Vietnam

Tuan Hung VU
Southern Institute of Social Sciences
Ho Chi Minh City
Vietnam

Index

A, B

C, D

E, F

G, H

I

L, M

N, O

Other titles from

iSTE

in

Computer Engineering

2025

CHIKH Azeddine
Systemic Approach to Categorizing and Modeling Requirements

2024

CHAKRABORTY Rajdeep, GHOSH Anupam, KUMAR MANDAL Jyotsna, CHOUDHURY Tanupriya, CHATTERJEE Prasenjit
Smart Edge Computing: An Operation Research Perspective (International Perspectives in Decision Analytics and Operations Research Set – Volume 2)

HOMÈS Bernard
Fundamentals of Software Testing (2nd edition, revised and updated)

JERBI Abdessalem
Discrete-Event Simulation: Concepts and Production in Arena

PRADHAN Devasis, KUMAR SAHU Prasanna, MYO TUN Hla, CHATTERJEE Prasenjit
Artificial and Cognitive Computing for Sustainable Healthcare Systems in Smart Cities
(International Perspectives in Decision Analytics and Operations Research Set – Volume 3)

2023

CHOUDHURY Tanupriya, KHANNA Abhirup, CHATTERJEE Prasenjit, UM Jung-Sup, BHATTACHARYA Abhishek
Blockchain Applications in Healthcare: Innovations and Practices
(International Perspectives in Decision Analytics and Operations Research Set – Volume 1)

PAI G A Vijayalakshmi
A Textbook of Data Structures and Algorithms 1: Mastering Linear Data Structures
A Textbook of Data Structures and Algorithms 2: Mastering Nonlinear Data Structures
A Textbook of Data Structures and Algorithms 3: Mastering Advanced Data Structures and Algorithm Design Strategies

2022

HOMÈS Bernard
Advanced Testing of Systems-of-Systems 1: Theoretical Aspects
Advanced Testing of Systems-of-Systems 2: Practical Aspects

MEHTA Shikha, TIWARI Sanju, SIARRY Patrick, JABBAR M.A.
Tools, Languages, Methodologies for Representing Semantics on the Web of Things

SIDHOM Sahbi, KADDOUR Amira
Systems and Uses of Digital Sciences for Knowledge Organization
(Digital Tools and Uses Set – Volume 9)

ZAIDOUN Ameur Salem
Computer Science Security: Concepts and Tools

2021

DELHAYE Jean-Loïc
Inside the World of Computing: Technologies, Uses, Challenges

HARDIN Thérèse, JAUME Mathieu, PESSAUX François,
VIGUIÉ DONZEAU-GOUGE Véronique
Concepts and Semantics of Programming Languages 1: A Semantical Approach with OCaml and Python
Concepts and Semantics of Programming Languages 2: Modular and Object-oriented Constructs with OCaml, Python, C++, Ada and Java

MKADMI Abderrazak
Archives in The Digital Age: Preservation and the Right to be Forgotten (Digital Tools and Uses Set – Volume 8)

TOKLU Yusuf Cengiz, BEKDAŞ Gebrail, NIGDELI Sinan Melih
Metaheuristics for Structural Design and Analysis (Optimization Heuristics Set – Volume 3)

2020

DARCHE Philippe
Microprocessor 1: Prolegomenes – Calculation and Storage Functions – Models of Computation and Computer Architecture
Microprocessor 2: Core Concepts – Communication in a Digital System
Microprocessor 3: Core Concepts – Hardware Aspects
Microprocessor 4: Core Concepts – Software Aspects
Microprocessor 5: Software and Hardware Aspects of Development, Debugging and Testing – The Microcomputer

DUVAUT Patrick, DALLOZ Xavier, MENGA David, KOEHL François,
CHRIQUI Vidal, BRILL Joerg
Internet of Augmented Me, I.AM: Empowering Innovation for a New Sustainable Future

LAFFLY Dominique
TORUS 1 – Toward an Open Resource Using Services: Cloud Computing for Environmental Data
TORUS 2 – Toward an Open Resource Using Services: Cloud Computing for Environmental Data
TORUS 3 – Toward an Open Resource Using Services: Cloud Computing for Environmental Data

LAURENT Anne, LAURENT Dominique, MADERA Cédrine
Data Lakes
(Databases and Big Data Set – Volume 2)

OULHADJ Hamouche, DAACHI Boubaker, MENASRI Riad
Metaheuristics for Robotics
(Optimization Heuristics Set – Volume 2)

SADIQUI Ali
Computer Network Security

VENTRE Daniel
Artificial Intelligence, Cybersecurity and Cyber Defense

2019

BESBES Walid, DHOUIB Diala, WASSAN Niaz, MARREKCHI Emna
Solving Transport Problems: Towards Green Logistics

CLERC Maurice
Iterative Optimizers: Difficulty Measures and Benchmarks

GHLALA Riadh
Analytic SQL in SQL Server 2014/2016

TOUNSI Wiem
Cyber-Vigilance and Digital Trust: Cyber Security in the Era of Cloud Computing and IoT

2018

ANDRO Mathieu
Digital Libraries and Crowdsourcing
(Digital Tools and Uses Set – Volume 5)

ARNALDI Bruno, GUITTON Pascal, MOREAU Guillaume
Virtual Reality and Augmented Reality: Myths and Realities

CARDON Alain
Beyond Artificial Intelligence: From Human Consciousness to Artificial Consciousness

HOMAYOUNI S. Mahdi, FONTES Dalila B.M.M.
Metaheuristics for Maritime Operations
(Optimization Heuristics Set – Volume 1)

JEANSOULIN Robert
JavaScript and Open Data

PIVERT Olivier
NoSQL Data Models: Trends and Challenges
(Databases and Big Data Set – Volume 1)

SEDKAOUI Soraya
Data Analytics and Big Data

SALEH Imad, AMMI Mehdi, SZONIECKY Samuel
Challenges of the Internet of Things: Technology, Use, Ethics
(Digital Tools and Uses Set – Volume 7)

SZONIECKY Samuel
Ecosystems Knowledge: Modeling and Analysis Method for Information and Communication
(Digital Tools and Uses Set – Volume 6)

2017

BENMAMMAR Badr
Concurrent, Real-Time and Distributed Programming in Java: Threads, RTSJ and RMI

BOUHAÏ Nasreddine, SALEH Imad
Internet of Things: Evolutions and Innovations
(Digital Tools and Uses Set – Volume 4)

HÉLIODORE Frédéric, NAKIB Amir, ISMAIL Boussaad, OUCHRAA Salma, SCHMITT Laurent
Metaheuristics for Intelligent Electrical Networks
(Metaheuristics Set – Volume 10)

MA Haiping, SIMON Dan
Evolutionary Computation with Biogeography-based Optimization
(Metaheuristics Set – Volume 8)

PÉTROWSKI Alain, BEN-HAMIDA Sana
Evolutionary Algorithms
(Metaheuristics Set – Volume 9)

PAI G A Vijayalakshmi
Metaheuristics for Portfolio Optimization: An Introduction using MATLAB®
(Metaheuristics Set – Volume 11)

REYES-GARCIA Everardo
The Image-Interface: Graphical Supports for Visual Information
(Digital Tools and Uses Set – Volume 3)

REYES-GARCIA Everardo, BOUHAÏ Nasreddine
Designing Interactive Hypermedia Systems
(Digital Tools and Uses Set – Volume 2)

SZONIECKY Samuel, BOUHAÏ Nasreddine
Collective Intelligence and Digital Archives: Towards Knowledge Ecosystems
(Digital Tools and Uses Set – Volume 1)

2016

BLUM Christian, FESTA Paola
Metaheuristics for String Problems in Bio-informatics
(Metaheuristics Set – Volume 6)

DEROUSSI Laurent
Metaheuristics for Logistics
(Metaheuristics Set – Volume 4)

DHAENENS Clarisse, JOURDAN Laetitia
Metaheuristics for Big Data
(Metaheuristics Set – Volume 5)

LABADIE Nacima, PRINS Christian, PRODHON Caroline
Metaheuristics for Vehicle Routing Problems
(Metaheuristics Set – Volume 3)

LEROY Laure
Eyestrain Reduction in Stereoscopy

LUTTON Evelyne, PERROT Nathalie, TONDA Alberto
Evolutionary Algorithms for Food Science and Technology
(Metaheuristics Set – Volume 7)

MAGOULÈS Frédéric, ZHAO Hai-Xiang
Data Mining and Machine Learning in Building Energy Analysis

RIGO Michel
Advanced Graph Theory and Combinatorics

ZELM Martin, DOUMEINGTS Guy, MENDONÇA Joao Pedro
Enterprise Interoperability: in the Digitized and Networked Factory of the Future

2015

BARBIER Franck, RECOUSSINE Jean-Luc
COBOL Software Modernization: From Principles to Implementation with the BLU AGE® Method

CHEN Ken
Performance Evaluation by Simulation and Analysis with Applications to Computer Networks

CLERC Maurice
Guided Randomness in Optimization
(Metaheuristics Set – Volume 1)

DURAND Nicolas, GIANAZZA David, GOTTELAND Jean-Baptiste, ALLIOT Jean-Marc
Metaheuristics for Air Traffic Management
(Metaheuristics Set – Volume 2)

MAGOULÈS Frédéric, ROUX François-Xavier, HOUZEAUX Guillaume
Parallel Scientific Computing

MUNEESAWANG Paisarn, YAMMEN Suchart
Visual Inspection Technology in the Hard Disk Drive Industry

2014

BOULANGER Jean-Louis
Formal Methods Applied to Industrial Complex Systems
Formal Methods Applied to Complex Systems: Implementation of the B Method

EXPOSITO Ernesto, DIOP Codé
Smart SOA Platforms in Cloud Computing Architectures

GARDI Frédéric, BENOIST Thierry, DARLAY Julien, ESTELLON Bertrand, MEGEL Romain
Mathematical Programming Solver based on Local Search

KRICHEN Saoussen, CHAOUACHI Jouhaina
Graph-related Optimization and Decision Support Systems

LARRIEU Nicolas, VARET Antoine
Rapid Prototyping of Software for Avionics Systems: Model-oriented Approaches for Complex Systems Certification

LAURAS Matthieu, ZELM Martin, ARCHIMÈDE Bernard, BÉNABEN Frédérick, DOUMEINGTS Guy
Enterprise Interoperability: Interoperability for Agility, Resilience and Plasticity of Collaborations

OUSSALAH Mourad Chabane
Software Architecture 1
Software Architecture 2

QUESNEL Flavien
Scheduling of Large-scale Virtualized Infrastructures: Toward Cooperative Management

RIGO Michel
Formal Languages, Automata and Numeration Systems 1: Introduction to Combinatorics on Words
Formal Languages, Automata and Numeration Systems 2: Applications to Recognizability and Decidability

SAINT-DIZIER Patrick
Musical Rhetoric: Foundations and Annotation Schemes

TOUATI Sid, DUPONT DE DINECHIN Benoit
Advanced Backend Code Optimization

2013

ANDRÉ Etienne, SOULAT Romain
The Inverse Method: Parametric Verification of Real-time Embedded Systems

BOULANGER Jean-Louis
Safety Management for Software-based Equipment

DELAHAYE Daniel, PUECHMOREL Stéphane
Modeling and Optimization of Air Traffic

FRANCOPOULO Gil
LMF — Lexical Markup Framework

GHEDIRA Khaled
Constraint Satisfaction Problems: CSP Formalisms and Techniques

GOVAERT Gérard, NADIF Mohamed
Co-Clustering: Models, Algorithms and Applications

LANDRAGIN Frédérick
Man–Machine Dialogue: Design and Challenges

LUCAS Laurent, LOSCOS Céline, REMION Yannick
3D Video: Models, From Capture to Diffusion

ROCHANGE Christine, UHRIG Sascha, SAINRAT Pascal
Time-Predictable Architectures

WAHBI Mohamed
Algorithms and Ordering Heuristics for Distributed Constraint Satisfaction Problems

ZELM Martin, VAN SINDEREN Marten, FERRAIRA PIRES Luis, DOUMEINGTS Guy
Enterprise Interoperability: Research and Applications in the Service-oriented Ecosystem

2012

ARBOLEDA Hugo, ROYER Jean-Claude
Model-Driven and Software Product Line Engineering

BLANCHET Gérard, DUPOUY Bertrand
Computer Architecture

BOULANGER Jean-Louis
Industrial Use of Formal Methods: Formal Verification
Formal Methods: Industrial Use from Model to the Code

CALVARY Gaëlle, DELOT Thierry, SÈDES Florence, TIGLI Jean-Yves
Computer Science and Ambient Intelligence

MAHOUT Vincent
Assembly Language Programming: ARM Cortex-M3 2.0: Organization, Innovation and Territory

MARLET Renaud
Program Specialization

SOTO Maria, SEVAUX Marc, ROSSI André, LAURENT Johann
Memory Allocation Problems in Embedded Systems: Optimization Methods

2011

BICHOT Charles-Edmond, SIARRY Patrick
Graph Partitioning

BOULANGER Jean-Louis
Static Analysis of Software: The Abstract Interpretation

CAFERRA Ricardo
Logic for Computer Science and Artificial Intelligence

KORDON Fabrice, HADDAD Serge, PAUTET Laurent, PETRUCCI Laure
Distributed Systems: Design and Algorithms
Models and Analysis in Distributed Systems

LORCA Xavier
Tree-based Graph Partitioning Constraint

RIDHA MAHJOUB A.
Progress in Combinatorial Optimization: ISCO2010

TRUCHET Charlotte, ASSAYAG Gerard
Constraint Programming in Music

VICAT-BLANC Pascale, GOGLIN Brice, GUILLIER Romaric,
SOUDAN Sébastien
Computing Networks: From Cluster to Cloud Computing

2010

AUBRUN Christophe, SIMON Daniel, SONG Ye-Qiong
Co-design Approaches for Dependable Networked Control Systems

AUDIBERT Pierre
Mathematics for Informatics and Computer Science

BABAU Jean-Philippe, BLAY-FORNARINO Mireille, CHAMPEAU Joël,
ROBERT Sylvain, SABETTA Antonino
Model Driven Engineering for Distributed Real-Time Systems: MARTE modeling, model transformations and their usages

BOULANGER Jean-Louis
Safety of Computer Architectures

SIGAUD Olivier, BUFFET Olivier
Markov Decision Processes in Artificial Intelligence

MONMARCHÉ Nicolas, GUINAND Frédérick, SIARRY Patrick
Artificial Ants

SOLNON Christine
Ant Colony Optimization and Constraint Programming

2009

FOURNIER Jean-Claude
Graph Theory and Applications: with exercises and problems

GUÉDON Jeanpierre
The Mojette Transform: theory and applications

JARD Claude, ROUX Olivier H.
Communicating Embedded Systems: Software and Design

LECOUTRE Christophe
Constraint Networks: Techniques and Algorithms

2008

BANÂTRE Michel, MARRON Pedro Jose, OLLERO Anibal, WOLITZ Adam
Cooperating Embedded Systems and Wireless Sensor Networks

MERZ Stephan, NAVET Nicolas
Modeling and Verification of Real-time Systems: Formalisms and Software Tools

PASCHOS Vangelis Th
Combinatorial Optimization and Theoretical Computer Science: Interfaces and Perspectives

WALDNER Jean-Baptiste
Nanocomputers and Swarm Intelligence

2007

BENHAMOU Frédéric, JUSSIEN Narendra, O'SULLIVAN Barry
Trends in Constraint Programming

JUSSIEN Narendra
A to Z of Sudoku

2006

BABAU Jean-Philippe, CHAMPEAU Joël, GÉRARD Sébastien
From MDD Concepts to Experiments and Illustrations – DRES 2006

HABRIAS Henri, FRAPPIER Marc
Software Specification Methods: An Overview Using a Case Study

MURAT Cécile, PASCHOS Vangelis Th
Probabilistic Combinatorial Optimization on Graphs

PANETTO Hervé, BOUDJLIDA Nacer
Interoperability for Enterprise Software and Applications: Proceedings of the Workshops and the Doctorial Symposium of the Second IFAC/IFIP I-ESA International Conference: EI2N, WSI, IS-TSPQ 2006

2005

GÉRARD Sébastien, BABAU Jean-Philippe, CHAMPEAU Joël
Model Driven Engineering for Distributed Real Time Embedded Systems

PANETTO Hervé
Interoperability of Enterprise Software and Applications: Workshops of the INTEROP-ESA 2005 International Conference (EI2N, WSI, ISIDI and IEHENA 2005)

Printed and bound by CPI Group (UK) Ltd, Croydon, CR0 4YY

13/09/2026

14961011-0003